Windows Forensic Analysis Toolkit

Windows Forensic Analysis Toolkit

Advanced Analysis
Techniques for Windows 8

Fourth Edition

Harlan Carvey

AMSTERDAM • BOSTON • HEIDELBERG • LONDON
NEW YORK • OXFORD • PARIS • SAN DIEGO
SAN FRANCISCO • SINGAPORE • SYDNEY • TOKYO

Syngress is an imprint of Elsevier

SYNGRESS.

Acquiring Editor: *Chris Katsaropoulos*
Editorial Project Manager: *Benjamin Rearick*
Project Manager: *Malathi Samayan*
Designer: *Maria Ines Cruz*

Syngress is an imprint of Elsevier
225 Wyman Street, Waltham, MA 02451, USA

First edition 2009
Second edition 2010
Third edition 2012
Fourth edition 2014

Notices
Knowledge and best practice in this field are constantly changing. As new research and experience broaden our
understanding, changes in research methods or professional practices may become necessary. Practitioners and
researchers must always rely on their own experience and knowledge in evaluating and using any information or
methods described herein. In using such information or methods, they should be mindful of their own safety and
the safety of others, including parties for whom they have a professional responsibility.

To the fullest extent of the law, neither the Publisher nor the authors, contributors, or editors assume any liability
for any injury and/or damage to persons or property as a matter of products liability, negligence or otherwise, or
from any use or operation of any methods, products, instructions, or ideas contained in the material herein.

Library of Congress Cataloging-in-Publication Data

Carvey, Harlan A.
  Windows forensic analysis toolkit : advanced analysis techniques for Windows 8 / Harlan Carvey. --
Fourth edition.
    pages cm
  Revised edition of the author's Windows forensic analysis toolkit : advanced analysis techniques
for Windows 7, 3rd ed.
  Includes bibliographical references and index.
  ISBN 978-0-12-417157-2 (paperback)
1. Computer crimes--Investigation--United States--Methodology. 2. Microsoft Windows (Computer file)--
Security measures. 3. Computer networks--Security measures. 4. Internet--Security measures.
5. Computer security. I. Title.
  HV8079.C65C3726 2014
  363.25'968--dc23

                                                                                        2014003508

British Library Cataloguing-in-Publication Data
A catalogue record for this book is available from the British Library

ISBN: 978-0-12-417157-2

Transferred to Digital Printing in 2014

For information on all Syngress publications,
visit our website at www.syngress.com.

  Working together
to grow libraries in
developing countries

www.elsevier.com • www.bookaid.org

To Terri and Kylie; you are my light and my foundation.

Contents

Preface

I am not an expert. I have never claimed to be an expert at anything, least of all when it comes to incident response and digital forensic analysis of Windows systems. I am simply someone who has found a deep, abiding interest in my chosen field of employment, and a bit of passion to make things more efficient for myself and develop a deeper understanding. I enjoy delving into and extending my analysis process, as well as exploring new ways to approach problems in the fields of digital forensic analysis and incident response. It was more than 16 years ago that I decided to focus on Windows systems specifically, in large part because no one else in the team I worked with at the time did so; we had folks who focused on routers and firewalls, as well as those who focused on Linux. However, almost no effort, beyond enabling configuration settings in the vulnerability scanner we used, was put toward really understanding Windows systems. As I moved from vulnerability assessments into incident response and digital forensic analysis, understanding what was happening "under the hood" on Windows systems, understanding what actions could create or modify certain artifacts, became a paramount interest. Even so, I am not an expert.

When I sat down to update the material for this edition, I wanted to not only include new information that I'd found or developed since the third edition was published, but I also wanted to try to include as much information as possible regarding Windows 8 and 8.1. With Windows 8.1 becoming available while I was updating the book, the inevitable questions were being asked, and invariably it won't be long before we start seeing the systems appear on analyst's workbenches. As such, I've tried to provide as much information as I could with respect to newer versions of Windows (i.e., 8 and 8.1), either by writing it directly into the book or linking to the sources of information on the Internet, when attempting to summarize it would simply not do the content justice. Keep in mind, however, that new information is being discovered and developed all the time, and at some point, I needed to stop writing and submit the book for final review and publishing. I'm sure that even more information will become available during the time between when the book goes to the printer, and when it actually comes out on the shelves at bookstores.

As I've said in previous editions, there are some things that are simply not covered in this edition. There are some topics, such as Windows memory collection and analysis that are best addressed by those who are much better versed in and capable of presenting the topic than I; I have used available tools for collecting memory dumps, and I have used Volatility to analyze memory dumps, including converting a hibernation file into a raw format and then using it to find a malicious process. However, that does not necessarily make me an authority on using Volatility during even a moderate range of analysis. Many times, I've relied on assistance from others regarding how to get started or even just maintain forward momentum. That being said, I wanted to focus on topics with which I was much more familiar. For example, in this book, I also discuss malware detection within an acquired image, but I do not discuss the in-depth analysis of any malware found using this process, as this topic has been much more thoroughly addressed in other books.

Intended Audience

This book is intended for anyone with an interest in developing a greater understanding of digital forensic analysis, specifically of Windows systems. This includes digital forensic analysts, incident responders, students, law enforcement officers, and researchers, or just anyone who's interested in digital forensic analysis of Windows 7 systems. Even system administrators and hobbyists will get something useful from this book. I've tried to point out how the information in this book can be used by both forensic analysts and incident responders alike.

In reading this book, you'll notice that there are several tools described throughout that were written in the Perl scripting language. Don't worry, you don't need to be a Perl expert (after all, neither am I) to use these scripts; not only are the scripts very simple to use but in most cases, they are accompanied by Windows executables, "compiled" using Perl2Exe (found online at http://www.indigostar.com/perl2exe.php). While some programming capability would be beneficial if you want to develop your own RegRipper plugins, several folks with little to no Perl programming skill have written working plugins for that particular tool. Others have rewritten tools like RegRipper in other languages, because again, it's not about *the tool* you use to solve the problem, it's about solving the problem.

Organization of This Book

This book consists of nine chapters following this preface. Those are:

Chapter 1 Analysis Concepts

This chapter addresses the core investigative and analysis concepts that I've found to be so critical to what we do, yet somehow glaringly absent from many books and discussions. As professionals within the digital forensic analysis community, there are a number of concepts that are central to what we do, and while (at this time) there isn't a centralized authority to mandate and manage this sort of information, I've found these concepts to be absolutely critical to the work I've been doing. Further, whether presenting at a conference or discussing analysis with someone one-on-one, I see "the light come on" when talking about these concepts. These concepts are vitally important because we cannot simply load an acquired image into a forensic analysis application and start pushing buttons; this really gets us nowhere. What do we do when something doesn't work or gives us output that we didn't expect? How do we handle or address that? Do we move on to another tool, documenting what we're doing? I hope so—too many times, I've seen or heard of analysts who've accepted whatever the tool or application has provided, neglecting to conduct any critical thought, and moved on to their findings. Operating systems and targets may change, but the core concepts remain the same, and it's imperative that analysts understand and employ these concepts in their analysis.

Chapter 2 Incident Preparation

In this chapter, we discuss the need for immediate response once an incident has been identified. Often, an organization is notified by another entity (e.g., bank, law enforcement agency) that they've been compromised, and an external third party consulting firm that provides incident response services is immediately contacted. Once contracting issues have been addressed, consultants are sent on-site, and once they arrive, they need to gather further information regarding what was identified, as well as the "lay of the land" with respect to the network infrastructure. All of this takes additional time, during which information that could prove to be very critical to addressing the inevitable questions faced by the potentially compromised organization is fading and expiring (this says nothing about sensitive data that may continue to flow from the infrastructure). Processes complete, deleted files get overwritten and new Volume Shadow Copies are created as old ones are deleted. Windows systems are surprisingly active even when supposedly sitting idle; therefore, it is paramount that response activities begin immediately, not whenever someone from outside the organization, who isn't familiar with the infrastructure, can arrive on-site.

Chapter 3 Volume Shadow Copies

The existence of Volume Shadow Copies (VSCs) is relatively well known within the digital forensics community, but means by which analysts can exploit their forensic value is still not something that's discussed at great length, particularly when it comes to accessing and processing data within VSCs in a timely manner, without purchasing additional software. As much of the digital forensic analysis that I've been engaged in occurs using images acquired from systems, this chapter addresses how analysts can access the wealth of information available in VSCs without having to interact with the live system, and without having to purchase expensive solutions.

Chapter 4 File Analysis

This chapter addresses not only the analysis of some of the usual files available on Windows systems but also files and data structures that are new to Windows 7 (or Vista) and have been identified and better understood through research and testing. Some files available on Windows 7 systems have changed formats, while others are simply new, and both need to be understood by analysts. For example, Jump Lists are new to Windows 7 systems, and some of them use the compound document binary format (popular in MS Office documents prior to version 2007 of the office suite), in conjunction with the SHLLINK format most often seen in Windows shortcut files. As such, Jump Lists can contain considerable information (including metadata) that can be very valuable during an investigation.

Chapter 5 Registry Analysis

This chapter addresses some of the information provided through other sources, most notably *Windows Registry Forensics*, and takes that information a step further, particularly with respect to Windows 7 systems. Rather than reiterating the information available in other sources, this chapter uses that information as a foundation and presents additional information specific to the Windows 7 Registry.

Chapter 6 Malware Detection

Oddly enough, this chapter does not contain the word "analysis" in the title, because we're not going to be discussing either static or dynamic malware analysis. Instead, we're going to discuss a specific type of analysis that is becoming very prominent within the digital forensic community; that is, given an image acquired from a Windows system, how can we go about detecting the presence of malware within that image? Professionally, I've received quite a number of images with the goal being to determine if there was malware on the system. Sometimes, such a request is accompanied by little additional information, such as the name of a specific malware variant, or specific information or artifacts that can be used to help identify the malware. Given that malware authors seem to be extremely adept at keeping their code hidden from commercial antivirus scanning applications, analysts need other tools (preferably a process) in their kits for detecting malware within an acquired image.

Chapter 7 Timeline Analysis

The idea of timeline analysis has been around for over 14 years. Over time, we've seen how a considerable amount of time stamped information is maintained by the Windows operating systems, and all of this can potentially be extremely valuable to our analysis. Also, much of this time stamped information is contained in artifacts that persist even after applications and malware have been removed from the system, and can be revealed through timeline analysis. In addition, incorporating multiple data sources of time stamped data into a timeline will provide considerably more value to an examination. This chapter walks the reader through the process for creating a timeline, so that that process can be understood to the point where reasoned decisions can be made with respect to the tools used and the data incorporated into the timeline.

Chapter 8 Correlating Artifacts

Over the years, as I've presented at conferences, written blog posts, and talked with other analysts, a topic that keeps coming up is that analysts very often want to see how other analysts have accomplished tasks; in short, what everyone seems to want to hear about are "case studies" or "war stories" from the front lines. What I've attempted to do in this chapter is harken back to the second edition and share some aspect of the analysis process I've used during various examinations. No two analysis engagements are ever the same, and I tend to carry forward things I've learned from past engagements, in an effort to make the next one just a bit more efficient and comprehensive. My hope is that something I've shared will be useful to you.

Chapter 9 Reporting

In this chapter, my intention was to present the reporting process that I've found to be useful. In my experience in the technical information security industry, I've seen the reporting is the most difficult, and perhaps the most important, task. After all, regardless of the type of work that you're doing, such as digital forensic analysis or penetration testing, if you can't communicate your findings to your customer in a manner that they can understand and use the information, what have you really accomplished? What I wanted to do with this chapter is share what I've learned over my professional career, including my time in the military, in hopes that the lessons I've learned can be useful to others. Please keep in mind as you're reading this chapter that it's based solely on my own experiences; if you're looking for something specifically to address a very narrow niche, you most likely won't find it there. However, my hope is that the information is useful to others.

DVD Contents

There is no DVD that accompanies this book; instead, you'll be able to find a link the code that I've written and described in this book online at the Books page for the WindowsIR blog, found online at http://windowsir.blogspot.com/p/books. Just find the entry for this edition and follow the appropriate link to download an archive of the tools.

Acknowledgments

I begin this section of the book by thanking God for His many blessings, without which this book would not be possible. He has blessed me with a wonderful, loving, supportive family, as well as what might best be described as a curiosity and love for digital forensic analysis and digging deeper in that analysis, as well as sharing what I've seen and learned with others. I try to thank Him daily, although I find myself thinking that it's not nearly enough because a man's achievements are not his alone. In my heart, I know that being able to and being provided the environment to write books like this is a gift and a blessing in so many ways. My hope is that this effort benefits many more than just those who purchase and use the books.

I'd like to thank my true love and the light of my life, Terri, and my stepdaughter, Kylie. Both of these wonderful ladies have put up with my antics yet again (intently staring off into space, scribbling in the air, and of course, there are my terribly excellent imitations taken from some of the movies we've seen), and I thank you both yet again as much for your patience as for being there for me when I needed to get away from the keyboard and decompress. It can't be easy to have a nerd like me in your life, but I do thank you both for the opportunity to "put pen to paper" and get all of this stuff out of my head.

I'd like to thank Brett Shavers, my tech editor, for putting in the time to review what I've written. Admittedly, I did not start from scratch; this edition builds on the foundation of writing that was already available in the previous edition, but there were some things that needed to be added, as well as new information in two chapters. It would not have been possible to get this edition through the publisher's process without Brett's time, effort, and patience.

I'd also like to thank Corey Harrell for taking the time out of his busy schedule to take a look at the outline for what I wanted to do with edition, and to provide thoughtful and insightful feedback. Thanks for all you do for the community, Corey. Semper Fi, Marine!

I want to be sure to thank everyone who contributed to the DFIR community in some way, through providing open source or commercial tools, blogging, and even just asking questions. There are a number of you who've done research and shared your findings with others, written blog posts or papers, and presented some very interesting topics at conferences. I thank you for your efforts and for sharing with the community.

I'm sure at this point I've missed some folks, so please accept my sincerest apologies and "thank you" if I engaged with you or read something you wrote, and came away with something that became the seed of an idea that ended up in this book.

Finally, I'd like to thank the Syngress staff for their patience throughout this process. I'm sure it can't be easy if your job is publishing books, but for those writing the books, authoring is not their primary job, and sometimes not their primary focus. Your efforts in herding cats down a beach is what puts books on shelves.

About the Author

Harlan Carvey has been involved in information security since 1989, with an introduction to the topic during his initial military training. He served as Communications Officer in the United States Marine Corps, earning a Master's Degree prior to leaving military service in 1997. Harlan's background in commercial information security work includes vulnerability assessments, penetration testing, as well as incident response and digital forensics analysis, which he has performed in order to assist companies and organizations in a variety of verticals, including financial, health care, and others. Harlan is an accomplished public speaker and has presented at a number of conferences. He has had books published in Korean, Chinese, and French. Harlan is a Senior InfoSec Researcher for Dell SecureWorks, which is headquartered in Atlanta, GA. He resides in Northern Virginia with his family.

About the Technical Editor

Brett Shavers is a former law enforcement officer of a municipal police department and has been an investigator assigned to state and federal task forces. Besides working many specialty positions, he was the first digital forensics examiner at his police department, attended over 1000 hours of digital forensic training courses across the country, collected more than a few certifications along the way, and set up his department's first digital forensics lab in a small, cluttered storage closet.

He has been an adjunct instructor at the University of Washington's Digital Forensics Program, an expert witness and digital forensics consultant, a prolific speaker at conferences, a blogger on digital forensics, and is an honorary member of the Computer Technology Investigators Network. He has worked cases ranging from child pornography investigations as a law enforcement investigator to a wide range of civil litigation cases as a digital forensics expert consultant.

He is also a Former Corporal of Marines.

Analysis Concepts

CHAPTER OUTLINE

INFORMATION IN THIS CHAPTER

- Analysis Concepts
- Setting Up An Analysis System

INTRODUCTION

If you've had your eye on the news media, or perhaps more appropriately the online lists and forums over the past couple of years, there are a couple of facts or "truths" that will be glaringly obvious to you. First, computers and computing devices are more ubiquitous in our lives. Not only do most of us have computer systems, such as desktops at work and school, laptops at home and on the go, but we also have "smart phones," tablet computing devices, and even smart global positioning systems (GPSs) built into our cars. We're inundated with marketing ploys every day, being told that we have to get the latest-and-greatest device, and be connected not just to WiFi, but also to the ever-present "4G" (whatever that means …) cellular networks. If we don't have a phone-type device available, we can easily open up our laptop or turn on our tablet device and instantly reach to others using instant messaging, email, Twitter, or Skype applications.

The second truth is that as computers become more and more parts of our lives, so does crime involving those devices in some manner. Whether it's "cyberbullying" or "cyberstalking," identity theft, the "advanced persistent threat (APT)," or intrusions and data breaches that result in some form of data theft, a good number of real-world physical crimes are now being committed through the use of computers, and as such, get renamed by prepending "cyber" to the description of the crime. As we began to move a lot of the things that we did in the real world to the online world (i.e., banking, shopping, filing taxes), we became targets for cybercrime. Organizations become targets (and subsequently, victims) of online crime, simply because they have something someone wants, be it data or computing power. What makes this activity even more insidious and apparently "sophisticated" is that we don't recognize it for what it is, because conceptually, the online world is simply so foreign to us. If someone shatters a storefront window to steal a television set, there's a loud noise, possibly an alarm, broken glass, and someone fleeing with their stolen booty. Cybercrime doesn't "look like" this; often, something isn't stolen and then absent, so much as it's copied, and then used for malicious purposes. The data (credit card numbers, personally identifiable information, etc.) still exists in its original location, but is now also in the possession of someone who intends to sell it to others. Other times, the crime does result in something that is stolen and is removed from our ownership, but we may not recognize that immediately, because we're talking about 1s and 0s in the "ether" of cyberspace, not a car that should be sitting in your driveway, in plain view.

These malicious activities also appear to be increasing in sophistication. In many cases, the fact that a crime has occurred is not evident until someone notices a significant decrease in an account balance, which indicates that the perpetrator has already gained access to systems, gathered the data needed, accessed that bank account, and left with the funds. The actual incidents are not detected until days after (in some cases, weeks or even months) they've occurred. In other instances, the malicious activity continues and even escalates after we become aware of it, because we're unable to transition our mindset from the real world (lock the doors and windows, post a guard at the door, etc.) to the online world, and effectively address the issue.

Clearly, no one person, and no organization, is immune. The early part of 2011 saw a number of high-visibility computer security incidents splashed across the pages (both web and print) of the media. The federal arm of the computer consulting firm HBGary suffered an embarrassing exposure of internal, sensitive data, and equally devastating was the manner in which it was retrieved. RSA, owned by EMC and the provider of secure authentication mechanisms, reported that they'd been compromised. On April 6, Kelly Jackson Higgins published a story (titled "Law

Firms Under Siege") at DarkReading.com that revealed that law firms were becoming a more prevalent target of APT actor groups. The examples continue on through 2012 and into 2013, but the point is that there's no one specific type of attack, or victim that gets targeted. The end of 2012 saw some banks and other organizations falling victim to massive distributed denial of service attacks, and the spring of 2013 saw a specific group in China, and even specific individuals, identified as being responsible for long-term and long-standing data theft attacks on US companies. Shortly thereafter, a group in India was identified as being responsible for other attacks, predominantly against targets in Pakistan. Anyone can be a target.

In order to address this situation, we need to have responders and analysts who are at least as equally educated, knowledgeable, and collaborating as those committing these online crimes. Being able to develop suitable detection and deterrence mechanisms depends on understanding how these online criminals operate, how they get in, what they're after, and how they exfiltrate what they've found from the infrastructure. As such, analysts need to understand how to go about determining which systems have been accessed, and which are used as primary jump points that the intruders use to return at will. They also need to understand how to do so without tipping their hand and revealing that they are actively monitoring the intruders, or inadvertently destroying data in the process. These goals are best achieved by having knowledgeable groups of responders working together, and sharing information across arbitrary boundaries.

In this book, we're going to focus on the analysis of Windows computer systems, laptops, desktops, servers, because they are so pervasive. This is not to exclude other devices and operating systems; to the contrary, we're narrowing our focus to fit the topic that we're covering into a manageable volume. Our focus throughout this book will be primarily on the Windows 7 operating system, and much of the book, after Chapter 2, will be tailored specifically to the analysis of forensic images acquired from those systems. I will be including information regarding Windows 8 artifacts, where appropriate, throughout the book. While there are some notable differences between Windows 7 and Windows 8, the simple fact is that there are also some similarities, so I will attempt to highlight those in addition to pointing out some of what is different. However, at this writing, analysts should be more concerned with what is available in Windows 7, as understanding data structures and developing skills in addressing the available data will be very beneficial when analyzing a Windows 8 system.

In this chapter, we're going to start our journey by discussing and understanding the core concepts that set the foundation for our analysis. It is vitally important that responders and analysts understand these concepts, as it is these core concepts that shape what we do and how we approach a problem or an incident. Developing an understanding of the fundamentals allows us to create a foundation upon which to build, allowing analysts to be able to address new issues effectively, rather than responding to these challenges by using the "that's what we've always done" methodology, which may be unviable.

Analysis concepts

Very often when talking to analysts, especially those who are new to the field, I find that there are some concepts that shape not only your thought processes but also your investigative processes and how we look at and approach the various problems and issues that we encounter. For new analysts, without a great deal of actual experience to fall back on, these fundamental analysis concepts make up for that lack of experience and allow them to overcome the day-to-day challenges that they face.

Consider how you may have learned to acquire images of hard drives. Many of us started out our process of learning by first removing the hard drive from the computer system, and hooking it up to a write-blocker. We learned about write-blockers that allowed us to acquire an image of a hard drive to another hard drive, as well as those that we could hook up to a laptop and use acquisition software to acquire an image to an external USB hard drive. However, the act of removing the hard drive from the computer system isn't the extent of the foundational knowledge; it's the documentation that we developed and maintained during this process that was so critical. What did we do, how did we do it, and how do we know that we'd done it correctly? Did we document what we'd done to the point where someone else could follow the same process and achieve the same results, making our process repeatable? It's this aspect that's critically important, because what happens when we encounter an ecommerce server that needs to be acquired but cannot be taken offline for any reason? Or what happens when the running server doesn't actually have any hard drives, but is instead a boot-from-SAN server? Or if the running laptop uses whole disk encryption so that the entire contents of the hard drive are encrypted when the system is shut down? As not every situation is going to be the same or fit neatly into a nice little training package, understanding the foundational concepts of what you hope to achieve through image acquisition is far more important than memorizing the mechanics of how to connect source and target hard drives to a write-blocker and perform an acquisition. This is just one example of why core foundational concepts are so critically important.

Windows versions

I've been told by some individuals that there are three basic computer operating systems that exist: Windows, Linux, and Mac OS X. That's it, end of story. I have to say that when I hear this I'm something a bit more than shocked. This sort of attitude tells me that someone views all versions of Windows as being the same, and that kind of thinking can be extremely detrimental to even the simplest examination. This is due to the fact that there are significant differences between the versions of Windows, particularly from the perspective of a forensic analyst. In fact, there are some fairly significant differences between in Windows when service packs, or even just patches, are installed. In some ways, there are significant differences between Windows XP with no service packs installed and XP SP1, SP2, etc.

The differences between Windows versions go beyond just what we see in the graphical user interface (GUI). Some of the changes that occur between versions of Windows affect entire technologies. For example, the Task Scheduler version 1.0 that shipped with Windows XP was pretty straightforward. The scheduled task (.job) files have a binary format, and the results of the tasks running are recorded in the Task Scheduler log file (i.e., SchedLgU.txt). With Vista and Task Scheduler version 2.0, there are significant differences; while the Task Scheduler log file remains the same, the .job files are XML format files. In addition (and this will be discussed in greater detail later in the book), not only do Vista and Windows 7 systems ship with many default scheduled tasks, but information about the tasks (including a hash of the .job file itself) is recorded in the Registry.

On Windows XP and 2003 systems, the Event Log (.evt) files follow a binary format that is well documented at the Microsoft web site. In fact, the structures and format of the .evt files and their embedded records are so well documented that open-source tools for parsing these files are relatively easy to write. Beginning with Vista, the Event Log service was rewritten and the Windows Event Log (.evtx) framework was implemented, and only a high-level description of the binary XML format of the logs themselves is available at the Microsoft site. In addition, there are two types of Windows Event Logs implemented; one group is the Window Logs and includes the Application, System, Security, Setup, and ForwardedEvent logs. The other group is the Application and Services logs, which record specific events from applications and other components on the system. While there are many default Application and Services logs that are installed as part of a Windows 2008 and Windows 7, for example, these logs may also vary depending on the installed applications and services. In short, the move from Windows XP/2003 to Vista brought a completely new logging format and structure, requiring new tools and techniques for accessing the logged events.

From a purely binary perspective, there is no difference among the Registry hive files of the various versions of Windows, from Windows 2000 all the way through to Windows 7. In some cases, there are no differences in what information is maintained in the Registry; for the most part, information about Windows services, as well as the contents of the *USBStor* key, is similar between the two versions of Windows. However, there are significant differences between the two versions of Windows with respect to the information that is recorded regarding USB devices, access to wireless access points, and a number of other areas. Another example of a difference in what's recorded in the Registry is that with Windows XP, searches that a user performed through the Explorer shell (i.e., Start→Search) were recorded in the *ACMru* key. With Vista, information about searches was moved to a file, and with Windows 7, user searches are now recorded in the *WordWheelQuery* key.

Other differences in Windows versions are perhaps unintentional. In December 2010, there was a question posted to an online forum asking about the purpose of the Microsoft\ESENT\Process Registry key within the Software hive on a Windows XP system. During the ensuing exchange, various respondents included references to Google searches that indicated that there were some versions of malware that modified the contents of that key. For example, one reference at the ThreatExpert.com site indicated that a Trojan associated with online games modified this key when installed. Ultimately, with the assistance of Troy Larson (senior forensic investigator at Microsoft), it was determined that the key should only exist on Windows XP systems, as Windows XP shipped with a debug or "checked build" of esent.dll. This indicated that the dynamic link library (DLL) had been compiled to generate additional information for debugging purposes, and then had not been recompiled for "production" delivery, and the debug version of the DLL was shipped with the operating system installation. In checking the Software hives on several available test systems, as well as within acquired images of Vista, Windows 2003/2008, and Windows 7 systems I had access to, I didn't find any indication that the key existed on other than Windows XP systems.

Some differences between versions of the Windows operating system can be subtle, while others can be covert and not visible to the casual user or administrator. However, the fact remains that, as a forensic analyst, what you look for (based on your examination goals) and what you see, and how you access and interpret it will be impacted significantly by the version of Windows that you're examining. Troy Larson has been putting considerable effort toward highlighting many of the new technologies within Windows 7 and identifying possible sources of forensic artifacts, and discussing these areas in presentations. There are a number of other presentations available (via searching) online that discuss similar findings, indicating that there are those, in the forensic community as well as within academia, who feel that it's important to identify as many of the new potential sources of forensic artifacts or "evidence" as possible.

Documenting all of the differences between the various versions of Windows would simply be a never-ending task. Throughout the rest of this book, as different topics are discussed, I will attempt to point out the differences between the Windows versions, where this is pertinent to the understanding of the topic. The point, however, is to understand that "Windows" is not simply "Windows," and the version of Windows (XP, Windows 7, 32- or 64-bit, etc.) will have a significant impact on the tools used or the investigative approach used.

Analysis principles

Many times when discussing forensic analysis with other folks, particularly new analysts, it seems that when someone gets into this business, the primary focus of their training (and therefore, their investigative approach) is on tools. So when they're given an image to analyze, these analysts sit down and the first thought is to open up the commercial forensic analysis application that they're familiar with or were trained on. However, if you were to take that application away, where would they be? What would they be left with, and what would they be able to do? I ask this, because I have heard analysts state, "I need < insert app name > " when given an examination.

Many of the principles and concepts discussed throughout the rest of this chapter will likely be familiar to many analysts. You may have seen them in my blog, or you may have heard another analyst or responder discuss them in a presentation at a conference. Chris Pogue's *Sniper Forensics* presentations cover many of these ideas; Chris and I worked at IBM together and spent time discussing many of these concepts. I'm presenting the principles again here because they're important, and I really feel that analysts need to understand them, or at least have a familiarity with them.

Goals

The goals of our analysis are perhaps the most important aspect of what we do. Without having goals for our analysis, we'd likely end up spending weeks or months combing through a few images, finding all manner of potentially "bad stuff." But to what end? Analysts and consultants in the private sector most often work under the auspices of a contract that specifies a set number of hours. The same is true for law enforcement examiners, although any limits or constraints are often more of a resource issue than from a contract. Cases are often prioritized by how serious the crime was, or the odds of identifying and successfully prosecuting a suspect; therefore, some cases may not receive a great deal of attention due to being low on the priority list.

When handed a drive image, the first question that should come to every analyst's mind is, "What question am I trying to answer?" Locate and identify malware? Locate indications of access to (or attempts to access) specific files? Locate indications of attempts to hide activity? Determine if a user accessed specific web sites or remote computer systems? Without having some kind of concise, achievable goal for analysis, a small stack of hard drives (or images acquired from them) can easily engage an analyst for a significant (perhaps inordinate) amount of time, but to what end? At the end of, say, two weeks of dedicated analysis, what is the final result? What does the report look like, if a report can be written at all? What are the analyst's findings and conclusions? Without a destination, how do you know when you get there?

As such, "find all bad stuff" is NOT a goal of forensic analysis. I know of an analyst who acquired an image of a desktop hard drive and was told to "find all bad stuff." Accepting that as a goal, the analyst returned to their lab and began analysis, and found quite a bit of "bad stuff." However, it turned out that the employee whose system had been imaged was tasked with "hacking" activities in order to protect the company web site; once that context was added to the examination, it was clear that all of the work that had been done had simply found the tools that the employee used in his job.

Developing goals for an examination can be pretty straightforward. When I was in the military, I had a company commander who told me that if I couldn't sum up an issue in a couple of bullet statements on a 3 × 5 card, I didn't know enough about that issue. At the time, I didn't think that I had a very good idea of what he was talking about, but over time, I learned the wisdom of what he'd said. Let's say that you're tasked with examining an image of a system; do you know why that system was acquired in the first place? What was the event that occurred that caused someone to acquire an image of that system? Did a pop-up appear on the desktop reporting a virus? Was some sort of network traffic observed emanating from or going to the system that triggered an intrusion detection system alert, or caught a security operations center analyst's attention? Were there some unusual firewall logs or domain name service requests that indicated a possible issue with the system? If this is what happened, then the goals of the examination go from "find bad stuff" to something a bit more specific and achievable, such as "determine if malware was present on the system that could have caused or resulted in the observed event/traffic."

The goals of an examination can be important for other reasons, as well. Back in 2000, I was working as the network security engineer at a now-defunct (and nonexistent) telecommunications company. At one point, the security manager was considering having some forensic analysis performed, and we'd heard that another group within the company had worked with a particular vendor that provided forensic analysis services. When we asked some of the members of this group about the vendor, we were told that they didn't do a very thorough analysis of one drive in particular, as they had missed a hidden DOS partition. That was it … no mention of the reason the vendor had been hired or what the goal of the analysis was, just this one negative comment. When we spoke to the vendor, he was prepared for our questions, and brought a copy of the contract that specified the goal of the analysis, which was to determine if the system had the SubSeven Trojan installed. There was nothing in the contract that specified the need to determine if there were any other partitions, particularly hidden ones, although the analyst did see the partition and noted it. The issue of the hidden DOS partition was a distraction, and aside from that, the vendor had fulfilled the terms and conditions of the contract; they'd met the goals of the examination that they'd been given. Regardless of any personal or professional issues that the company employee may have had, the forensic analyst for the vendor had remained focused on the goals of the analysis.

Another important aspect of your goals is that they can often help you scope and better define an incident. For example, in data breach investigations, the primary question that needs to be answered is, "what data, if any, left the infrastructure?" Various state notification laws, or mandates set forth by regulatory bodies, may come into play, and may result in significant costs and negative press exposure for the organization. Most incident responders know that in order to definitively answer this question, you need full packet traffic captures from the time when the data actually left the systems and the infrastructure. However, understanding what data may have left the infrastructure and been exposed helps responders scope the incident. This leads responders to those systems that may be involved in the incident, including where the data may have been stored (i.e., database server) or may have been processed (i.e., back office payment processor server, user's workstation). During one particular response engagement, we found that an intruder had gained access to the infrastructure for a healthcare organization, but was searching for terms such as "banking" and "password." The IT staff had already identified the locations of sensitive information, such as patient data, as well as credit card data (some processing of credit cards occurred within the organization). As such, we were able to demonstrate that the intruder had accessed neither the systems where the sensitive data was located, nor the sensitive data itself.

Tools versus processes

When it comes to analysis, too many times we seem to focus on tools, rather than the process. This is a trap that new analysts often fall into, as their initial introduction and training is often focused on developing familiarity with one or two tools (such as a commercial forensic analysis application) in order to get them up and running as quickly as possible. However, even more experienced analysts can find themselves focusing on a specific tool or application, rather than the overall process used for analysis.

Consider the implementation of the Volume Shadow Copy Service (VSS) in Windows systems beginning with Vista (VSS had actually been implemented in Windows XP, but in a somewhat limited manner) and continuing into Windows 7. Long after this technology was implemented (Vista was released in November, 2006), most commercial forensic analysis applications had not provided a means for easily accessing Volume Shadow Copies (VSCs, discussed in detail in Chapter 3) within acquired images. For example, ProDiscover, from Technology Pathways, did not allow easy access to VSCs until the spring of 2011. However, as will be described in detail in Chapter 3, there are a number of methods for accessing VSCs within an acquired image that do not require that the analyst purchase a commercial product. The point is that by focusing on specific tools ("my tool can't do that, so I can't answer that question"), analysts often lose sight of the process and what's really required to meet their goals ("what tool or method is most appropriate for obtaining the data I need?"). By understanding what it is you hope to achieve, as well as the technology you're faced with, you can understand the overall process you need to follow in order to achieve your goals. After all, if all you have is a hammer, every problem becomes a nail.

The tool validation myth-odology

Speaking of tools, many times during a conference presentation or a training course, I will mention several tools that can be used to parse a particular data structure, such as the NTFS Master File Table (MFT). Sometimes I will also mention a Perl script that I wrote to parse MFT records, and those attending the presentation will invariably ask for a copy of the script. When I ask why they want a copy of the script, which is most often just a very alpha version of the script that simply parses the available data, their response is most often, "so I can validate the output of other tools."

Tools provide a layer of abstraction over the data that we have available, allowing us to interact with that data and often parsing the data into a format that allows us to understand it a bit better. This is often helpful and even necessary, as accessing an acquired image with nothing more than a hex editor is simply not an analysis methodology that lends itself well to providing timely answers. As such we use tools to provide that layer of abstraction, converting 1s and 0s into something a little more meaningful to us. If we have or suspect that we have an issue with a tool, should we be validating the output of that tool with another tool, perhaps one that we have little experience with?

The usual methodology employed by most analysts is to validate that a particular tool is providing correct output by running another tool, and then comparing the output from both tools. Is this methodology correct or sufficient, simply because it's common? In using this methodology, what are we really demonstrating, about the tools, the data, and more importantly, our own ability to analyze data?

When running either tool, other questions come up? Who wrote the tools? Was it a developer simply writing a tool, or was it written by an analyst who has need of the data? How does the tool parse the data; does it use the application programming interface (API) provided by Microsoft, or does it parse the data on binary level? How is either tool validated if both tools use the same method for parsing the data, and they're both incorrect? Or, to add to the confusion, what if they're both incorrect, but in different ways, with different output?

My point is simply that analysts need to understand the underlying data structures that the tools are parsing so that they can determine the validity of the output they produce. I've used this information myself a number of times. For example, I had scanned an acquired image for potential credit card numbers (CCNs) as part of our analysis process for Payment Card Industry (PCI) forensic audits, and found several potential CCNs "in" the Software and NTUSER.DAT hives. As I have an understanding of the various data structures that make up Registry hive files (key nodes, value nodes, etc.), I was quickly able to determine that the CCNs were not actually stored in the Registry, but were instead part of previously unallocated sectors that comprised the free space of the logical hive file itself. This determination had a significant impact on the outcome of the analysis, which in turn impacted not only decisions made by the compromised firm, but also fines levied against them in response to the data breach. Something similar occurred in the spring of 2013, when a friend asked me about search hits found within a Windows 7 Jump List file; understanding the format of the file and the underlying data structures allowed us to determine that the search hit was not part of the logical contents of the Jump List file, but was instead part of the physical content of the file that had not yet been allocated to the compound file binary file format.

Both of these determinations had a significant impact on their respective examinations. As such, the usual "methodology" becomes more of a "myth-odology," as one analyst after another passes down the "wisdom" of using one tool to validate the output of another tool, while never determining how either tool does what it does nor understanding the underlying data structures.

Windows systems contain a wide variety of data structures within their files, and Microsoft provides clear definitions and descriptions of many of these data structures. For example, the Windows 2000, XP, and 2003 Event Log data structures (header, records, etc.) are detailed at the Microsoft web site (found online at http://msdn.microsoft.com/en-us/library/windows/desktop/aa363659(v=vs.85).aspx), and information about other structures can be found there, as well. The definitions of some data structures, such as those commonly referred to as "shellbags," are not provided by Microsoft, and are instead developed through repeated testing and analysis, and posted online. Not all data structures are available, but many are, and as such, we can then use this information in order to validate the tools that we use.

Locard's exchange principle

This is an analysis concept that has been addressed and discussed in a number of resources; I'm including it here because no discussion of analysis concepts would be complete without it. In short, Locard was a French scientist who postulated that when two objects came into contact, material was from each was transferred to the other. We see this mentioned quite often in TV crime shows, like *CSI*, when analyst Nick Stokes declares, "…possible transfer."

Okay, so how does this principle apply to digital forensic analysis, you ask? That is an excellent question. In short, any interaction between two entities (one being the computer operating system) results in the transfer or creation of data. For example, when a user logs into a system, even when auditing of logins is not enabled, artifacts of the login, as well as the user's activities, are created. When a user interacts with the system, there are traces of this activity, whether the user logs in locally or accesses the system remotely. Whenever a program runs within the operating system, there is a "transfer" or creation of data of some kind. The data or artifacts may vary in how persistent they are (and is an example of the "order of volatility"), but they will be created. Many of these artifacts will exist only for a very short time, and some may persist until the system is rebooted. Other artifacts will persist well after the system is shutdown and rebooted. But the thing to remember is that artifacts will be created.

Avoiding speculation

Whether working as an incident responder or as a digital forensics analyst, we need to be sure that we don't fall into the trap of filling in gaps in our information with guesses, and answering questions through speculation. This is also an issue (perhaps even more so) for IT staff attempting to scope or deal with a computer security incident, but doing so without the benefit of the training and experience of skilled incident responders. The fact is that many times, we simply don't know what we don't know, and fill in the gaps in our information with speculation rather than facts. This most often results with incorrect information being provided to decision makers higher up the corporate ladder.

One of the things I used to hear a lot that really made me cringe was when an analyst would say, "…if I had been the hacker, I would have done this" or "…I would have done it this way." I'm not entirely sure I see how that applies during an examination, other than to provide some possible avenues of investigation that can (and should be, possibly even before the statement is made) quickly be run down.

More often than not, these speculative statements develop into avenues of reason and pseudo-fact, and can lead the incident response completely offtrack.

Don't get me wrong; during incident response or even forensic analysis, brainstorming can be good, and a valuable tool; throwing out ideas to be discussed, run down, or refuted can be an excellent exercise. Questions such as "…what if…" and "…why did you…" can lead to some pretty interesting findings. Where this goes wrong is when assumptions are made and used to move the examination forward, without those assumptions being verified, and facts are not used (rather than the assumptions) to fill in gaps in the analysis. This is something that we all have to be careful of, as it happens to all of us at one time or another; we'll make an assumption about how an artifact is created or modified without performing any research or verification, and our analysis will progress based on that assumption, however incorrectly. Unchecked, this can lead us down the road of incorrect findings and conclusions, or worse, lead us down a rabbit hole of confusion. We have to remember that as analysts, we're not doing our work in a vacuum; rather, we are providing our expertise so that others can then make critical decisions based on the information that we provide them. Speculating as to the course of events during an examination or incident can lead to the classic "garbage in, garbage out" situation, and end up with someone making an important business decision based on that bad information. I have seen attorneys move forward thinking that they had a solid case, when their expert provided them with a single, "definitive" piece of information that placed an individual behind the keyboard of the computer at a specific time. However, that case unraveled when the speculation and assumption were peeled away like the layers of an onion.

One way to avoid using assumptions to replace facts is to correlate multiple facts in order to support your findings. This concept is discussed in greater detail in Chapter 7 of this book, when we dig into the specifics of timeline creation and analysis; however, the basic idea is to look at your analysis and determine where your analysis and reasoning is based on a single artifact or finding, and then attempt to locate additional artifacts that support (or refute) your conclusions. An example of this might be an application file that you found on a system; you think that this application (remote access program, etc.) may be critical to the incident, but you find that the file appears to have been created on the system several years prior to the actual incident; in fact, the creation date of the file appears to correspond with other files copied over from the installation media. So, with this finding, what do you do? Do you accept the creation date as legitimate and simply rule the application out from being associated with the incident? I would hope not; file system creation dates are trivial to modify. Or, do you attempt to determine whether the creation date was modified to disguise the file's presence on the system?

There are a number of artifacts that you could use to quickly validate the creation date finding, such as additional attributes from the file's entry in the MFT (discussed in greater detail in Chapter 4). With respect to launching the application, is there a Prefetch file, or any indication in the user's Registry hive that they launched the application? Are there any other artifacts that can be directly associated with the application having been executed? Some tools, such as the Cain & Abel password collection and cracking tool, produce a series of output files when run. These artifacts of execution may be used to better determine when a file or an application had been added to a system; why would it have been added to the system in 2008 but not executed until 2011? How likely would that be? It would be far more likely that the application had been added to the system in relative close proximity to the first execution of the application, particularly during a compromise or breach.

The key concept to understand here is that filling in gaps in information with speculation can be very misleading, and ultimately detrimental to an organization attempting to respond to an incident. Whenever possible, seek out multiple supporting artifacts, particularly if those artifacts are found in network or firewall logs, or on other systems not associated with the system being examined. Regardless of whether a cluster of artifacts are all found within or external to the system being examined, a knowledgeable analyst will be able to correlate them quickly and efficiently, as they understand not only the system being examined, but also their analysis goals.

Direct and indirect artifacts

Generally, there are two types of artifacts that you can expect to find when performing an examination: direct and indirect artifacts. Some analysts might not make a clear distinction between the two, but when I've been looking for something new or undefined (i.e., the request is to "find the malware" or "find the bad stuff"), it helps to look to where the indirect artifacts tend to collect to see if there are any indications of anything new.

A direct artifact is something that is the direct result of an incident, such as a malware infection or an intrusion. These are usually things like files that are added or copied to a system, and any modifications made by the intrusion or compromise, such as Windows services or other Registry keys and values being created on the system. Other direct artifacts include files produced as a result of the infection or addition of malware, such as key stroke captures or the output of native commands (i.e., ipconfig, "net start").

When I was working data breach examinations, I ran across a set of malicious programs that constituted a "memory scraper"; that is, one program would collect the contents of virtual memory for any of eight specifically named processes, and then another would comb through the memory dump for track data (the stuff in that magnetic stripe on the back of your credit card). The program that looked for the track data was a Perl script that had been "compiled" with Perl2Exe (found on the web at http://www.indigostar.com/perl2exe.php) so that the script could be run as a standalone executable, and not require that Perl be installed on the compromised system. Besides the program files themselves, the direct artifacts for this incident included the Windows service that was created when the files were installed (along with the associated Registry keys) and the files created every time the malware was run (i.e., the memory dump file, the archive of extracted track data, and the DLLs extracted from the "compiled" Perl script as a result of the use of Perl2Exe).

An indirect artifact is something that is the result of the ecosystem or environment in which the incident occurs and is not a direct result of the incident. Sounds kind of fancy, I know, but the simple fact is that there's a lot that occurs on Windows systems when a program or a process is launched, regardless of whether it's for a legitimate application or for malware or malicious activity of some kind. Some of these things that go on, we never see—they just happen in the background. For example, if you use Microsoft's Process Monitor (the use of which will be demonstrated later in this book) and look at what Registry keys are accessed when any program is started, you'll begin to notice that there's one (the "Image File Execution Options" key) that is read whenever you launch a program. This is not what the malware does; it's what the operating system does when a program is launched.

NOTE

Consequential Artifacts

After writing this chapter of the third edition, I wondered if I'd made any sense to folks. Do I assume that because there were no comments or questions, that what I discussed regarding direct versus indirect artifacts was accepted? Or was this an indication that I was completely off-base? Then, in April 2013, Gary Colomb of Cylance published a blog article, titled "Uncommon Event Log Analysis for Incident Response and Forensic Investigations" (found online at http://cylance.com/techblog/Uncommon-Event-Log-Analysis-for-Incident-Response-and-Forensic-Investigations.shtml), which discusses "artifacts created after a compromise, but not directly related to the malware itself." Gary's post shows me that this is a valid line of reasoning, as well of analysis, that is actively pursued by others within the community.

Other indirect artifacts include application prefetch files (commonly referred to as simply "Prefetch files") and entries in the index.dat file. Prefetch files are created by default on Windows XP, Vista, and 7 whenever an executable file is run on Windows. The Prefetch file contains information about the files loaded by the executable and is used to optimize execution of the program. Prefetch files are indirect artifacts because while they are not the direct result of an incident, they may be created by applications executed during the course of an incident. Index.dat files are created by Windows applications (such as Internet Explorer) that use the WinInet API for off-system communication. Entries in an index.dat file are not the direct result of an incident, but may be created by applications used in an incident that leverage the API (i.e., malware that uses the API to connect to an external site).

TIP

Internet History

Index.dat files are most often associated with a user's Internet Explorer (IE) browser history; when performing analysis on a system and attempting to discern what the user had been up to, an analyst will often look to the contents of the index.dat file, particularly if the user used the IE web browser.

However, malware authors may make use of the same API used by the browser in order to exfiltrate data from systems or allow their malware to communicate with a command and control (C2) server, and in doing so, will leave similar traces. What can be very telling about this kind of malicious use the WinInet API is when the malware is running with System privileges, such as within a Windows service. In such instances, the LocalService, NetworkService, or "Default User" (depending upon the specific privileges employed by the malware and the version of Windows infected) account will suddenly have indications of Internet activity populated in the index.dat file in that profile. This was true in the case of an exam I conducted of a system infected with ZeroAccess; the URLs for the click-fraud portion of the malware appeared in the index.dat file within the NetworkService profile.

Another example of an indirect artifact is the entries for Windows services beneath the Enum\Root key in the System hive. This artifact is a result of the function of the operating system and will be addressed in greater detail in Chapter 5.

WARNING

ZeroAccess

In November 2010, Giuseppe Bonfa wrote a series of articles (available at the InfoSecInstitute web site) describing his findings in reverse engineering the ZeroAccess/Max++ crimeware rootkit. One of the things he found was that the rootkit installed on a Windows system as a service, and when the service was started, it would delete not only its entry in the Services key, but also the relevant entries beneath the Enum\Root key. This is an indication of someone who is taking great pains to not only remain undetected on systems, but to also subvert deep forensic analysis of compromised systems. However, this is just one variant of the malware, and over time, others (including myself) have seen other variants of this malware that have displayed different characteristics.

Another way to look at this is that direct artifacts are those that only exist as a result of the incident occurring (i.e., SQL injection statements in web server logs, malicious executable files, log files being created on the compromised system), whereas indirect artifacts are those artifacts that would be generated – by design – as the result of any action (legitimate or malicious) occurring on the system. For example, with Windows services, administrators can install applications that create services (i.e., web server, antivirus applications) and the same artifacts would be generated if a malicious service were installed. Again, an indirect artifact is not a direct result of the incident or malicious action, but instead the result of the interaction with environment.

Remember that earlier we discussed the fact that different versions of Windows employ different implementations of technologies such as Task Scheduler, Windows Event Log? Well, this has an effect on the indirect artifacts that are available to an analyst. If the system you're examining doesn't have application prefetching enabled (either by default, or because it was purposely disabled), then you shouldn't expect to see any prefetch files. The same holds true for other technologies, as well, including but not limited to the Task Scheduler, System Restore Points, Volume Shadow Copies, etc. The artifacts that you can expect to find can be dependent not just on how the system is configured, but which version of Windows you're analyzing.

So by now you're probably wondering why I've presented all of this. Well, the point is that there are a lot of ways to compromise, do mischief, and remain persistent on a system. That is to say, there is not a simple, short list of artifacts to look for when examining a system or an image, and as such, we often have to look for indirect artifacts as indicators of the incident. Because often we don't really know what we're looking for, identifying indirect artifacts of the incident may lead us back to the direct artifacts. When performing your analysis, pursue and stay open to the indirect artifacts, as they will often provide clear indicators to the direct artifacts that we would not otherwise have observed or found.

NOTE

The Absence of an Artifact

All this discussion of direct and indirect artifacts, as well as using multiple artifacts to support your findings, should lead you to one inevitable conclusion; that is, *the absence of an artifact where you would expect to find one is in itself an artifact*.

Wait…what? What does this mean? Let's say that you're paranoid because you think someone's been going through your home while you're gone, and before leaving for work in the morning, you place a small piece of scotch tape over the door jamb. You then leave through the garage. Later that day, you return home and find what you think may be indicators that someone's been in your house, and you assume that the only way they could get in was through the front door. However, there are no fingerprints on the exterior doorknob, there are no indications that the door was forced open, and the piece of tape you left is still intact. Are there other artifacts that would indicate that someone came in through the front door? Or is the real issue that the absence of these specific artifacts instead indicates that access was *not* achieved through the front door?

Okay, so how does this apply to digital forensic analysis? Quite a lot, actually. The absence of artifacts showing, for example, a user logging and using the web browser on the system may indicate that the user never performed these actions, or that specific steps were taken to hide or destroy these artifacts. Either way, there will likely be other artifacts that indicate either of these (or other) scenarios.

Let's say that you're attempting to determine whether a user logged into a system from the console or via Terminal Services. One of the first artifacts you might look for is a record of the login in the Event Logs. If you don't find such a record, is it because auditing of logins wasn't enabled? Had the Event Logs been cleared? We sometimes don't think about these things, but many times when we don't find an artifact or series of artifacts that we would expect to find, this can tell us as much as (or more than) if we had found those artifacts.

Least frequency of occurrence

Back in the early days of the Internet, and even as late as the turn of the century, malware could and did run rampant across the Internet. One of the side effects of worm infections was that when a worm got into an infrastructure, it would often spread like wild fire, infecting and reinfecting systems over and over again. System A would become infected and then infect systems B, C, and D, who would then each infect the other systems over and over again, *ad infinitum*, *ad nauseum*. The result was that in fairly short order, systems would become so massively infected that they'd cease to function altogether, as the repeated infections consumed all available resources on the system. This was bad for the victim, and for the most part, bad for the attacker, because if the infected systems were offline or simply couldn't be accessed, what good were they to anyone? To address this issue and allow access to infected systems, malware authors began adding a throttling mechanism to their programs so that once systems were infected, they wouldn't be reinfected. Some created and checked for the existence of specific files, some used specific Registry keys or values, but the most prevalent method appears to have been to create a unique mutex in memory.

The end result of this, from a responder/analyst perspective, was that a malware infection became the least frequent activity to occur on a system. As malware authors and intruders began taking specific steps to ensure that their actions became less noticeable and "flew beneath the radar," these actions became more difficult to detect, as the infections did *not* result in massive amounts of file activity or memory consumption. Pete Silberman, an analyst with the consulting firm Mandiant, was the first in our community that I heard use of the term "least frequency of occurrence" to describe this phenomenon.

The same often applies to intrusions. With the exception of turning a compromised server into a "warez server" (essentially a repository of pirated movies, etc.), most intruders appear to take very conscious and specific steps to remain undetected, and avoid drawing attention to their activities by loading massive numbers of files on to the victim system, running a large number of programs, etc. Why copy an archive of tools and utilities over to a compromised system when the system itself has plenty of native tools that can be readily used for the same purpose?

One of the things I see quite often is analysts who create timelines (timeline creation and analysis will be discussed in Chapter 7) of activity on systems, and then attempt to locate indicators of malicious activity by looking for spikes in that activity. What most analysts don't seem to understand is that Windows systems are inherently "noisy" when it comes to activity on the system, particularly file system activity. During normal day-to-day operations, most users read and compose email, surf the web, maybe create reports and spreadsheets; however, a great deal of activity occurs automatically, under the hood. Consider Windows XP systems as an example; by default, a System Restore Point is created every 24 hours. This all occurs with no other interaction from the user beyond simply turning the system on. This also means that now and again, some System Restore Points are deleted. In addition, by default, a limited defragmentation process is run on the system every three days. We also need to keep in mind that in many instances, Windows Updates are set to run automatically, and many applications (Adobe Reader, Apple QuickTime and iTunes, Java, etc.) have their own update processes that run in the background. In short, just turning a Windows system on and walking away from it can lead to a great deal of activity over time, even with no user interaction with the system at all. So is it then any wonder that a malicious email attachment that is opened by the user, which then downloads malware that provides an attacker with remote access to the system is, in the grand scheme of things, often the least frequent activity on a system?

Documentation

In short, documentation is the bread and butter of what we do. There, I said it. And I said it knowing full well that technically oriented people (nerds) hate, more than anything else, to document anything.

But without documentation, where are we? If we didn't document our analysis goals, how do we make sure that we remain on track throughout our analysis, and actually achieve those goals? If we don't document our analysis, our reports would be nothing more than simply a 3 × 5 card with a couple of handwritten findings (which may not answer the customer's questions, because we didn't document our goals). In short, if you didn't document it, it didn't happen.

Documentation needs to be a core, central aspect of everything we do. From the point where an incident is detected, we need to begin documentation (we'll touch on this more in Chapter 2, and then go into more detail on the topic in Chapter 9). Most organizations have some sort of regulatory body that they need to report to particularly during or following an incident, and without clear, concise documentation along the way, responders go offtrack, systems get missed, and leaders and managers make bad decisions, all of which can lead to fines and a significant detrimental impact on the organization's brand name.

From the perspective of a consultant, documentation needs to start the instant that a customer contacts you. Most consulting firms have a list of questions (a "triage worksheet," if you will) that they use as a sort of script or guideline when talking to customers, and completing this worksheet serves as the initial documentation. Contracts are then written based on information collected during the initial call, and responders begin collecting and documenting information as soon as they arrive onsite (often before). Consider an incident requiring that data and images be collected from a large number of systems within a data center or in multiple locations. If you aren't documenting your activities, how likely do you think it would be that you either miss some systems or collect data from the same system twice or more?

Finally, without documentation, how do we learn and grow as analysts or as a community? Throughout our analysis, we may find something that we hadn't seen before, or we may have a question about the function of a specific tool or application. If we don't maintain documentation, we miss significant opportunities to improve our own processes, as well as to provide other analysts with the benefit of our experiences. Say you're on a team with 10 other analysts, and after eight hours of analysis, you find something that neither you nor any of the other analysts had seen before. Assuming all things (and analysts) being equal, if you don't document and share what you found (and how you found it), this is now going to cost your organization

80 hours for everyone to have that same experience and level of knowledge; however, if you were to document and share it with the other analysts during, say, a "brown bag" or catered working lunch, you've now reduced that time to less than an hour. Documenting and sharing our findings in this way allows us to learn from the past and for a group of analysts to quickly expand their knowledge and capabilities.

Maintaining documentation is relatively straightforward and simple. While there are applications available that were specifically designed for maintaining analyst case notes (such as Forensic CaseNotes, found online at http://www.qccis.com/forensic-tools), I've found that the simplest way to maintain case notes and analysis documentation is to start by opening MS Word. Word allows the analyst to create tables, outlines, and modify formatting so that notes are easier to read and understand, and also allows the analyst to insert pictures and diagrams that vastly improve the documentation. Many analysts (and their customers) have access to MS Word through their employer, and free and open source office suites such as OpenOffice (found online at http://www.openoffice.org/) can be used to read and edit Word documents. If you're looking for a word processing application with a wide range of capabilities and portability, MS Word or Writer from OpenOffice is an option to consider.

Convergence

Convergence refers to the fact that what we do in what appears to be vastly different aspects of our profession—the actual WORK we do—really isn't all that different. Here's what I mean—in June 2010, I attended the Open Source Conference that Brian Carrier (the author of *File System Forensic Analysis* and the TSK tools, although I'm sure he's famous for other things, as well) put on. While there, I was speaking to a member of law enforcement and he told me, "…we do child pornography and fraud cases; you do intrusion investigations and malware cases." When I heard this, my response was that people like me—that is, consultants—dealt with problems, and that the folks who called us for assistance had intrusion and malware problems. Hey, I thought that was a pretty witty and well-considered response. However, the more I thought about it, the more I discovered how off-base the original statement (that as a consultant, I dealt with "problems") really may have been.

Okay, you're probably thinking, "wait…what?" After all, what the law enforcement officer (LEO) said was pretty much on target with respect to his particular case load, right? Well, what happens during a CP case? After verifying that there were, in fact, the federally mandated number of contraband images and/or movies on the hard drive, the next thing that the LEOs can expect to hear is, "…it wasn't me, it was a virus." That's right, the "Trojan Defense," used in 2003 when then-19-year-old Aaron Caffrey was accused of hacking into computer systems and claimed that a Trojan had been installed on his system, allowing someone else to perform the acts of which he was accused (he was acquitted). At that point, LEOs must then examine the acquired image and determine if there was some form of malware installed on the system, and if so, was it capable of the actions that the defense claims. Well, doesn't the case then become a malware examination?

Or, if the claim is made that some unauthorized person gained access to the system and placed the contraband files on the system, doesn't the case then become an intrusion investigation? And wouldn't both also hold true for fraud cases, if those same claims were made?

We're at a point where there really isn't as much of a divergence between what various investigators do on a daily basis as some would like us to think. Yes, some analysts operate in vastly different environments, and with different requirements. But at the end of the day, we're using a lot of the same tools and processes, and ultimately looking for some of the same artifacts, in order to answer a lot of the same questions. Rather than divergence, what we do has reached a point of convergence, and as such, analysts from one aspect of our community (such as law enforcement, or the military or government) would likely benefit greatly from engaging with and sharing information with another aspect of the community, such as those in the private sector. And the reverse would be equally true, as well.

No, I'm not talking about sharing case information or details of investigations. What I am referring to is this; many analysts who are consultants in the private sector receive cases where the goal is to locate malware that *may be* on a system. As such, those analysts tend to develop detailed step-by-step processes and procedures for performing malware detection (see Chapter 6 for a more detailed discussion of this topic), but these processes and procedures have to be automated to some degree, as well, as the work these analysts do is often based on a contract with a set number of hours. As such, analysts that haven't encountered such examinations before, or don't encounter them often, would likely benefit from engaging with and learning from the private sector analysts.

This is just one example of how the digital forensic community can take advantage of this convergence phenomenon and grow as a community, rather than requiring all analysts to learn all of the same lessons.

Virtualization

Virtualization can have a significant impact on an investigation in a number of ways. If someone were to run a virtual system on their physical system, there's the issue during an examination of where the artifacts would be located. For example, several versions of Windows 7 (Professional, Ultimate, and Enterprise) allow users to download, install, and run Virtual PC (Microsoft's virtualization platform for PCs) and a Windows XP virtual machine (referred to as "XPMode"). The purpose of this is to allow users to continue to run applications that ran perfectly well on Windows XP but are not supported by Windows 7. However, it's relatively easy for the user to access and run applications from within the virtual machine, such that the artifacts of that activity would not appear within the confines (files, Registry, etc.) of the host system. With the Virtual PC application installed, users can also run other virtual machines, as well. For example, Microsoft has been known to provide minimal virtual machines for the purpose of testing older versions of the Internet Explorer web browser against new web sites, and these virtual machines can be downloaded, installed, run in order to facilitate malicious activity, and then deleted. Analysts who are not familiar with virtualization and what to look for can be left looking for artifacts that they may never find, unless they were to discover and access the actual virtual machine.

While an associate professor at the University of Advancing Technology (UAT), Diane Barrett gave a presentation titled "Virtual Traces." This presentation was the latest in which she addressed the use of virtualization on desktop systems and described artifacts left on a Windows system following the use of MojoPac and MokaFive (found on the web at http://www.mokafive.com/), both of which were, at the time, personal, portable environments that can allow users to take their favorite desktop applications, utilities, and even games with them where ever they go, and run them from any Windows system. At the time of this writing, MojoPac had been purchased by Citrix and MokaFive is now a commercial solution. Diane also mentioned the MetroPipe Portable Virtual Privacy Machine virtual environment, which is based on Damn Small Linux and purports to allow users to maintain their privacy while web surfing. These virtual systems, as well as innumerable others that are available, can be run on a live system and leave minimal traces of having been used. Someone can walk up to a computer system, plug in an iPod or thumb drive, run their virtual system and perform any number of activities (legal or otherwise), disconnect the device, and walk away. While there may be indications that the virtual environment was run on the host system, indicators of the malicious activity itself may remain embedded in the virtual machine that the user took with them. As stated on the WikiPedia page for MojoPac, "…all the browsing history for Internet Explorer and other browsers is stored on the USB device rather than the host."

Now, consider "cloud computing." This term, much-touted in the media, includes such offerings as infrastructure-as-a-service, platform-as-a-service, and software-as-a-service, and aside from these terms it also poses significant challenges to incident responders and forensic analysts. After all, how does one respond to an incident where the system of interest existed at one point, but was deleted and the sectors it consumed were overwritten? In a cloud environment, which is based on virtualization, how does a responder determine where those sectors are? Even if the responder is able to determine where the CPU and memory resources were "located," how does she address the issue of storage, when that storage can be in or spread across systems in another country?

TIP

It's About Implementation

The question of how responders and law enforcement address cloud environments is a valid one, for the reasons discussed in this chapter. The simple fact is that it comes down to implementation; how is the infrastructure designed, architected, and implemented? If you're considering moving into a "cloud" environment, and have to meet legal or regulatory requirements, be sure to get detailed information about the environment and implementation. Further, if you're promised some security measures, or need them to meet compliance, be sure that they're included in your contract.

However, virtualization can be very helpful to an analyst, as well. For example, virtual systems can be used for application and malware testing. As we will see later in this book, virtualization can not only assist the analyst "seeing what the user saw" by allowing them to boot the acquired image as if it were a live system, but also assist the analyst in accessing some data sources to which they might not otherwise have access. For example, being able to boot the system would give the analyst access not only to physical memory from the system, but also the ability to interact with the system just as the user did.

Setting up an analysis system

Another topic that we need to discuss before completing this chapter and moving into the rest of this book is more operational and less conceptual in nature; that is, setting up a system from which you can perform your analysis. I've used desktops, workhorse laptops, and at one point (while I was a member of the ISS Emergency Response Services, or ERS team), I even used a Mac OS X server system with Mac OS X and Windows XP installed via BootCamp. From my perspective and experience, the best way to develop skills in analyzing Windows systems is to use those systems, which is why I tend to opt for Windows as an analysis platform (I also use Windows as my work/admin platform, as well). This is not to say that you couldn't build a complete analysis platform using Linux; Rob Lee has done a great job putting together such a system in the SANS Investigative Forensic Toolkit (SIFT) (version 2.14 at the time of this writing) virtual machine, which is Linux-based and includes a number of very useful tools. However, my personal experience has shown me that to *really* analyze a Windows XP system (and the same thing applies to Windows 7) is to use that platform on a daily basis. As such, my recommendation for an analysis system would be something capable of running the 64-bit version of Windows 7, preferably the Ultimate or Professional editions.

NOTE

SIFT

I have used the SANS SIFT v2.0 Workstation virtual machine, as it can be very useful. In attempting to develop a solution to something of a unique issue, I downloaded (via the SANS Portal) and set up the SIFT VM, and then before starting it up, I added the .vmdk virtual disk file from a Windows XP VM that I already had available. I did this through VMWare Workstation, so I added the VM as an independent, non-persistent disk. When I booted the SIFT VM, I could "see" the Windows XP VM (via *fdisk*), and could not only mount the device read-only, but (with a little help from Rob Lee himself) also use the TSK tool *icat* to get a copy of the MFT from the device. This can be a very useful approach to data collection and analysis.

As far as a hardware platform goes, I have found great success using Dell Latitude laptops; they're on the beefier end of the spectrum, but still portable enough to carry around if you need to do so. If you're going to be primarily stationary in a lab, then getting a powerful desktop system would be the way to go, if you can afford it. In the end, it comes down to what you prefer and what you can afford. If you don't get a beefy system with a powerful processor (or four) and good amount of RAM, then things will just take a bit longer.

What about the operating system for our analysis platform? Well, I've spent a number of years working with Windows XP and I'm very comfortable with it, having become familiar with some of its nuances; however, over time, I've found that using Windows 7 provides me with a great deal more functionality, particularly when it comes to Volume Shadow Copies and Windows Event Logs (we'll be discussing both of these in greater detail later in this book), which are available on Vista, Windows 2008, as well as Windows 7 and 8. As we'll see later in the book, having access to the necessary Windows APIs can be extremely beneficial when you're trying to access data and conduct analysis. Using a 64-bit version of Windows 7 also ensures that I have the necessary capability to address analyzing both 32- and 64-bit editions of Windows (although that shouldn't be an issue when simply accessing specific files).

Now we're up to the point where we can discuss the software we'll be using. First, I want to make one thing clear; I'm not biased against commercial forensic analysis applications. Heck, I've even used some of them. I've used AccessData's FTK as well as Guidance Software's EnCase product, to include various versions of both. I like to use ProDiscover from Technology Pathways, in part because the built-in ProScript scripting language is based on Perl, and due in no small part to the fact that Christopher Brown has been kind enough to provide me with a license since version 3.0. However, I don't use many of the commercial tools on a regular basis simply because I don't need to—most of the things I do during analysis I cannot easily do, or do at all, using commercial forensic analysis applications. This is not to say that commercial forensic analysis applications do not have their place, as they do. In fact, they can be extremely useful. For example, I've used ProDiscover for running keyword searches (for files by name, or file contents) against images, after extracting timeline data so that I can conduct analysis while the search progresses. However, like any tool, a commercial forensic analysis application is only as strong or as valuable as the analyst who's using it, and what I tend to do as a major aspect of my analysis is to produce a timeline of system activity (which is discussed in detail in Chapter 7) from a variety of data sources from the system, and the commercial tools do not include the inherent capability for creating a timeline of system activity from these data sources. Very often, I will conduct a complete and thorough analysis using nothing more than open-source and freely available tools, and a file viewer. Remember, analysis isn't about the tools you use; it's about the goals and your analysis *process*.

> **TIP**
>
> **Open-Source Tools**
>
> Cory Altheide (of Google) and I co-authored the book *Digital Forensics with Open Source Tools* (ISBN: 9781597495868), which was published by Syngress Publishing, Inc., in April 2011. The book focuses primarily on open-source tools used for forensic analysis of Linux, Mac OS X, and Windows platforms. In addition, the book provides several scenarios describing how the tools are used and also presents some free, albeit not open-source tools. In previous editions of this book, I also spend a great deal of time discussing a number of open-source and freely available tools.

So what tools should you use? Well, it all depends on what to do. One of the first tools I start off with is 7Zip (available on the web from http://www.7-zip.org), a freely available archive utility that recognizes and unpacks file compressed via a number of compression algorithms (including gzip and tar). Next, I often look to the programming languages that are the foundation for many open-source tools (including my own RegRipper), Perl and Python. Distributions for both are freely available from ActiveState (found on the web at http://www.activestate.com). From there, you want to make sure that you have hex and text editors available for viewing file contents, as well as programming, if necessary. There are a number of freely available editors that you can find via searches on the Internet, and the ones you choose will likely depend primarily upon personal preference. For example, UltraEdit (not free, but available from http://www.ultraedit.com) is usually my script editor and file viewer of choice; however, the Crimson Editor (available from http://www.crimsoneditor.com/) also appears to be a good choice for creating and editing Perl scripts, while the HxD hex editor (available from http://mh-nexus.de/en/hxd/) makes a suitable hex viewer.

AccessData provides FTK Imager as a freely available download, and not long ago released version 3.0 of the tool, which not only allows you to acquire images, but also mount acquired images on your system as read-only volumes. As we'll discuss later in this book, this capability can greatly extend the range of your analysis. Loading an acquired image into FTK Imager allows you to quickly verify the integrity of the file system, view and extract files, extract a volume or partition, or even convert an image from either expert witness (EWF, also known as EnCases E0x format) or VMWare virtual disk (.vmdk) format to a raw, dd-style image.

Version 7.5 of ProDiscover Basic Edition is freely available from Technology Pathways (found on the web at http://www.techpathways.com/DesktopDefault.aspx?tabindex=7&tabid=14) and provides basic functionality for populating the Registry, Event Log, and Internet History Viewers, as well as conducting searches across the image. In addition, you can also extract files from the image, view the formatted contents of Recycle Bin Info2 or $I files, and view a directory via the Gallery View. This is a considerable amount of functionality available in a free tool.

Other tools you may want to install at this point include the version of strings. exe available from the MS/SysInternals site, as well as BinText (a GUI version of a "strings" tool) available from the McAfee/Foundstone site on the web. Both of these tools can be used to list strings found in file, including both "regular" file, as well as files that consist of unstructured data, such as the pagefile. This functionality can also be used as the basis for greater investigative capabilities.

Most of the tools and programs mentioned to this point provide basic functionality to the analyst and will allow you to get started conducting analysis quickly and easily. This list should not be considered all inclusive; throughout this book, I will be addressing and demonstrating the use of a number of other tools, so I won't present them all here in this chapter.

SUMMARY

Throughout this chapter, I've attempted to lay the foundation for your analysis by presenting some core analysis concepts, as well as provide some initial, first-step tools that can be installed on an analysis system. Both of these will provide the foundation for the rest of the book; we will not only be building on the analysis concepts throughout the following chapters, but we will also be discussing and demonstrating a number of additional tools that will assist us in our analysis.

Incident Preparation

CHAPTER OUTLINE

INFORMATION IN THIS CHAPTER

* Being Prepared to Respond
* Data Collection

INTRODUCTION

Much of what we read regarding incident response is that computer security incidents are a fact of life when we employ IT resources. It's long been said that it's not a matter of *if* your organization will experience a computer security incident, but *when* that incident will occur. If the media has made anything clear at all during the past several years, it's that no organization is immune to computer security incidents, whether that's a web page defaced, intellectual property copied, sensitive corporate emails exposed, or sensitive financial data compromised. Even computer security consulting firms have fallen victim to intrusions and breaches.

> **NOTE**
> **Annual Security Reports**
> Several consulting firms publish annual reports with respect to data collected in the course of incident response engagements. Each of these firms has different customers, utilizes different approaches, and presents their data in different formats. As such, we need to keep

these differences in mind when reading the reports; however, the reports can provide a vivid picture of the incident landscape, particularly when viewed over consecutive years.

The 2013 M-Trends report, published by Mandiant, stated that 63% of victims were notified of an incident by an external entity. The report goes on to state that the "median number of days that attackers were present on a victim network before detection" was 243.

The 2013 TrustWave Global Security Report Executive Summary states that the average time for an organization to detect an incident after it occurred was 210 days, and 64% of organizations took over 90 days to detect an incident. The full report states that 24% of incidents were detected via self-detection, while 25% were detected by law enforcement and 48% were the result of "regulatory detection" (keep in mind that a large number of the incidents detected were payment card industry (PCI) breaches). Of these breaches, 27% were detected in between 31 and 90 days, and 25% were detected in between 181 days and a year.

The 2013 Verizon Data Breach Investigations Report stated that 92% of breaches occurred as a result of actions from outsiders. Of the breaches included in the report, 69% were discovered by external parties, and 66% took "months or more to discover."

All of these percentages illustrate that incidents do occur, and do go undetected by the victims.

Most books on incident response discuss and demonstrate a variety of tools and techniques that are helpful (or even critical) in preparing for and responding to an incident, so these procedures should be both common knowledge and common practice. In reality, this is often not the case. When an incident does occur, responders—whether internal IT or incident response staff or third-party consultants that are called to respond—only have access to the data that is actually available. If a company has not prepared appropriately, they may not have access to critical data, may not know where sensitive information is stored, and may not know how to collect key time-sensitive data following the detection of an incident. This is true when internal staff is responsible for incident response, but is even more critical in cases where a company hires a third-party consulting firm to provide incident response services.

In such cases it can often take several days for the contracting process to run its course and for the responding consultants to actually get on a plane and travel to the customer's site. Once they arrive, they usually have to go about determining the layout of the infrastructure they're responding to, the nature of the incident, where critical assets are located, etc. All of this goes on while the upper level management of the organization is anxiously awaiting answers.

Given all of this, it behooves an organization to prepare for an incident and to be prepared to perform some modicum of response when those inevitable incidents are identified. In this chapter, we will discuss how organizations can better prepare themselves to respond to incidents, from the perspective of a consultant who has responded to incidents. The purpose of this is to ensure that response personnel—whether internal staff or third-party responders—have data that allows them to resolve the incident in a satisfactory manner. This chapter will not address overall infrastructure design, development of a complete computer security incident response plan (CSIRP), or "best practices" for network and system configuration, as all of these can require considerable thought, effort, and resources to implement in any environment; any book that tries to address all possible factors and configurations will not succeed. Rather, we will discuss some of the things that are easy for the local staff to do, that will have a considerable impact on improving incident response and resolution.

Being prepared to respond

As an incident responder, the vast majority of incidents I have seen have progressed in pretty much the same manner; our team would get a call from an organization that had been notified by an outside third party that an incident had occurred within their infrastructure, and during the initial call, we would ask the point of contact (PoC) a series of questions to determine the nature of the incident as best we could. Many times, those questions were met with the telephonic equivalent of blank stares, and in the extreme cases, due to the nature of the incident, with frantic requests to "just get someone here as fast as you can!" We would send responders on-site, based on what we knew about the incident, and by the time the responders made it on-site, little if anything had been done to prepare for their arrival. After introductions, the questions that had been originally asked on the telephone were asked again, and we (the responders—most often, just one person) had to work with local IT staff in order to develop an understanding of the network infrastructure and traffic flows, as well as the nature of the incident itself. Many times, much of the information (network maps, etc.) wasn't available, or the people who knew the answers to the questions weren't available, and considerable time could be spent trying to simply develop a clear and accurate picture of what had been reported or identified, and what had happened. This was never a quick process, and sometimes we would simply have to start arbitrarily collecting and analyzing data, which also takes time and in some cases, would prove to be fruitless in the long run, as the systems from which the data was collected were later found to not have been involved in the incident.

While the scenario I've described involved the use of outside consulting help, the situation is not all that different from what might occur with internal responders whenever an organization is not prepared to respond. Sounds pretty bad, doesn't it? So you're probably wondering, what's my point? Well, my point is that the clock doesn't start ticking once an organization becomes aware of an incident; in fact, it's already been ticking by that point, we just don't know for how long as the incident may have occurred well before it was identified or reported. And when it comes to incident response and digital forensic analysis, a great deal of what can (or can't) be determined about the incident is predicated on time; that is, how much time has passed between when the incident occurred and when pertinent data is collected and analyzed.

Several years ago at a SANS Forensic Summit, Aaron Walters (the creator of the Volatility Framework) used the term "temporal proximity" to describe this gap between the incident and response, and really brought to light just how critical time is with respect to incident response. Why is time so important? Consider what occurs on a live Windows system, even when it sits idle; there's actually quite a lot that goes on "under the hood" that most of us never see. Processes complete, and the space (bytes) used by those processes in memory is freed for use by other processes. Deleted files are overwritten by native, "organic" processes that are simply part of the operating system (i.e., the creation and deletion of System Restore Points on Windows XP and Volume Shadow Copies on Vista and Windows 7). On Windows XP systems, a System Restore Point is created by default every 24 hours, and often one may be deleted, as well. In addition, every three days a limited defragmentation of selected files on the hard drive occurs. On Windows 7 systems, not only are Volume Shadow Copies created and deleted, but every 10 days a backup is made of the main Registry hives. Windows systems are typically configured to automatically download and install updates; many common desktop applications (Adobe Reader, Apple's Quicktime application, etc.) provide the same functionality. In short, whether you see it or not, a *lot* of activity occurs on Windows systems even when a user isn't interacting with it. As such, as time passes, information that would give clear indications as to the extent of what occurred begins to fade and be obscured, and is finally simply no longer available. Given this, it is absolutely critical that those most capable of performing immediate incident response actually do so. As it can be some time before the scope of the incident and the need for assistance is really realized, it is critical that the local IT staff be able to react immediately to collect and preserve data.

Members of the military are well acquainted with incident response. Soldiers and Marines are trained in basic first aid procedures so that they can assist themselves or a buddy until more suitable medical response is at hand. They can respond immediately and apply bandages or a tourniquet to keep their buddy alive. Sailors are trained in damage control procedures so that they can respond to any issues impacting their ship, contain it, and keep the ship afloat until they can reach a safe port. Data available from annual reports illustrates that organizations would do well to take a similar approach, detecting and then immediately and decisively responding to incidents.

Questions

Once an incident has been detected, everyone has questions. Senior management most often wants to know how the intruder or malware got into the network, what data was taken, where it went, and the risk to which the organization may be exposed, and they want to know it immediately. The nature of the compromised data—and any legal, regulatory, or reporting requirements associated with it—is often of great concern to legal counsel and compliance staff, as well. Something to keep in mind is that there is often a significant gap between business needs during an incident, and the deeply technical information, the 1s and 0s, that responders tend to immerse themselves in. Therefore, it is critical for incident response staff to understand the types of questions that will be asked by key stakeholders in the company, so that the data collection and analysis process can answer those questions— especially when failure to do so may result in significant legal or financial penalties being incurred by the organization.

NOTE

Compliance

Regulatory bodies have had a significant impact on incident response over the last five or so years. When my team was conducting PCI breach investigations, one of the items added to the report was a "dashboard" that gave oversight staff a quick, at-a-glance view of the breach. One of the items in that dashboard was the "window of compromise," or an indication of the time between when the incident actually originated and when the breach was "closed." This was a very critical component of the investigations, as many organizations were able to quantify system uptime not in terms of days or weeks, but in transactions per minute, or per hour. Being able to accurately determine when the systems had actually been compromised and when PCI data could have been exposed had significant impact on the number of possibly compromised transactions (as well as notification and any regulatory repercussions), and as time went by, the likelihood of being able to accurately provide this information decreased.

If an outside consulting firm is called to provide emergency incident response, they will also have a number of questions, and how fast they respond and who they send will be predicated on the responses to those questions. These questions are often technical, or the answers that are being looked for are more technical than the PoC is prepared to provide. Examples of these questions can include such things as how many systems and locations are impacted, what operating systems (i.e., Windows, Linux, AS/400) and applications are involved, etc. As such, an organization can greatly facilitate both the response time and efficiency by having detailed information about the incident (or the personnel most able to provide that information) available for those preliminary discussions.

TIP

Triage Questions

Wherever I've been an incident responder, I've most often been a consultant. As such, the teams I worked with developed a triage worksheet or questionnaire, which was a list of questions we had written down and documented for each analyst to use for initial contact with a potential client. As calls could come in at any time and any analyst could take the call, I kept a copy of the worksheet (an MS Word document) on my computer desktop, and had several hard copies printed out and next to my phone for immediate access. The questions were the top dozen or so that we asked for *every* engagement: what is the nature of the incident, when was the incident identified, what systems were involved (and what are their current states), what operating systems were involved, how many locations were involved, had law enforcement been contacted, etc. Most often, depending on the responses to the questions, combined with our own experiences (every analyst knew that they were to complete the questionnaire as if they would be responding to the incident), we would ask further probing questions. However, the idea of having the questionnaire was to make that initial information collection as efficient as possible, and to give our staff as complete a view of the incident as possible in order to determine who was to respond, how many analysts and what skill sets would be needed, how long the analysts would be required, etc.

Third-party consulting firms are often contacted to perform emergency incident response for a variety of reasons. Perhaps the biggest reason is that while the internal IT staff is technically skilled at maintaining systems, applications, and the overall infrastructure, they do not possess the investigative experience and expertise in order to address the incident. While they may be able to troubleshoot an MS Exchange server issue or set up an Active Directory, they aren't often called upon to dump physical memory from a live Windows system and determine if there is any malware on that system. Another reason is that any investigation performed by the local IT staff may be viewed as being skewed in favor of the company, in a sort of "fox guarding the hen house" manner, and as such, the final answers to the questions being asked may be suspect. It is important to keep in mind that when a third-party consulting firm is called, they will ask you a number of questions, usually based on their experience responding to a wide range of incidents (malware, intrusions, data breaches, etc.) in a wide range of environments. And these will often be questions the local IT staff hadn't thought of, let alone experienced before, as they come from an entirely different perspective.

For example, the IT manager may "know" that a system (or systems) is infected with malware or has been compromised by a remote intruder, but the consultant on the other end of the phone is likely going to ask questions in order to better understand how the IT manager came to this understanding. The best thing to do is to ensure that those employees who have the necessary information to accurately respond to these questions are available, and to respond without making assumptions regarding where you think the questions may be leading. Consultants may have a much different breadth of experience than an IT manager, and responding with assumptions as to where the consultant may be taking their questions can take the response itself offtrack and lead to delays. If the organization was notified of the incident by an external entity, it is best to have the employee who took the call, as well as any other staff who may have engaged with the caller (legal counsel, etc.) available to answer questions. For more technical questions regarding the affected systems and the network infrastructure, having the appropriate employees available to respond to questions can be very valuable.

The consulting firm will use your responses to scope the incident. They will also use the responses to determine which skill sets are necessary to respond to the incident, who to send, and how many consultants they will need to send in order to resolve the incident in a timely manner. If accurate information is not available, too many responders may be sent, incurring addition cost for travel and lodging up front, or too few responders may be sent, which would incur not only additional costs (for travel, lodging, labor, etc.) but would also lead to delays in the overall response.

The importance of preparation

Did you see the first "Mission: Impossible" movie? After Ethan's (Tom Cruise's character) team is decimated, he makes his way back to a safe house. As he approaches the top of the stairs in the hotel, he takes off his jacket, takes the light bulb out of the fixture in the hallway, crushes the bulb in his jacket and spreads the shards in the now-darkened hallway as he backs toward the door, covering the only means of approach to his room. Does what he did make sense? He knew that he couldn't prevent someone from approaching his location, but he also knew that he could set up some sort of measures to detect when someone was approaching, because as they entered the darkened hallway, they wouldn't see the glass shards on the floor, and they'd make a very distinctive noise when they stepped on them, alerting him to their presence. And that's exactly what happened shortly thereafter in the movie.

Let's take a look at some examples of how being prepared can affect the outcome of an incident. In my experience as an emergency incident responder, the way the response process (internal to an organization) works has usually been that someone becomes aware of an incident, perhaps does some checking of the information they receive, and then calls a company that provides emergency computer security incident response services for assistance. Many times, they feel that the information they've received could be very credible, and (rightly so) they want someone on-site to assist as soon as possible. From that point, depending upon the relationship with the consulting company, it can be anywhere from 6 to 72 hours (or more) before someone arrives on-site.

For example, I've worked with customers in California (I'm based on the east coast) and told them, if you call me at 3 pm Pacific Standard Time, that's 6 pm Eastern Standard Time—the earliest flight out is 6 am the next day, and it's a 6-hour flight, depending upon the location in California. At that point, I wouldn't be on the ground at the remote airport until 18 hours after you called, assuming that there were no issues with getting the contract through the approval process, flight delays, and a direct flight was available. Once I arrive at the destination airport, I have to collect up my "go kit" (Pelican case full of gear weighing 65 lbs or more), get to the rental car agency and drive to your location (I've been on engagements where the site was a 2-hour drive from the airport). Once I arrive on-site, we have to get together and try to determine the scope of the incident, hoping that you have the appropriate staff available to address the questions I will have. I have responded to assist organizations that used part-time system administration staff, and the next scheduled visit from the system administrator was two days after I arrived on-site. As you can see, even under ideal conditions, it can be 24 hours or more before any actual incident response activities begin.

Now, most times when would I arrive on-site, considerable work would need to be done in order to determine the nature and range of the incident and figure out which systems were affected, or "in scope." (Note that this is an essential step, whether performed by outside consultants or your own internal staff.) When the incident involved the potential exposure of "sensitive data" (regardless of the definition you choose), there may have been a strong indication that someone had accessed the infrastructure and gained access to some sensitive data; what this means is that someone with no prior knowledge of the network infrastructure may have accessed it remotely and found this sensitive data (i.e., database or files containing credit card data or transaction information, personally identifiable information, medical records). As such, when trying to scope the incident, one of the first things I (and most responders) ask is, where does the data in question reside? Very often, this is not known, or not completely understood.

As a result, considerable time can be spent trying to determine the answers to the questions responders ask prior to as well as once they arrive on-site. It is important that these questions be answered accurately and in a timely manner, as responders usually arrive on-site after a contract is signed, and that contract often includes an hourly rate for that responder, or responders. The sooner incident response activities can commence, with accurate information, the less expensive those incident response activities are going to be in the long run. Where internal staff is performing response, these time delays may not translate (directly) into dollars spent on outside help; but any delay will still postpone the identification and collection of relevant data, perhaps to the point where the data is degraded or lost completely.

This is not to say that all organizations I've responded to are not prepared for a computer security incident, at least to some extent. During one particular engagement, I arrived on-site to find that rather than having an active malware infection, the IT staff had already responded to and removed the malware, and the IT manager was interested in having me validate their process. In fact (and I was very impressed by this), the staff not only had a documented malware response process, but they also had a checklist (with check boxes and everything) for that process, and I was handed a copy of the completed checklist for the incident. Apparently, once the first malware infections were found on several desktops within their infrastructure, the IT staff mobilized and checked other systems, found several infected systems in various departments (finance, billing, HR, etc.), and removed those infections from the systems. Unfortunately, there were no samples of the malware left to be analyzed, and all we had left was the completed checklist which included a name used by an antivirus (AV) vendor to identify the malware.

Now, something else that I did find out about this incident was that during a staff meeting following the response to the incident, the IT manager had announced proudly that his team had reacted swiftly and decisively to remove this threat to the infrastructure—at which point, corporate counsel began asking some tough questions. It seems that several of the systems were in departments where very sensitive information was stored and processed; for instance, the billing department handled bank routing information, and the HR and payroll departments handled a great deal of sensitive personal information about the company employees. As such, an infection of malware that was capable of either stealing this information or providing an attacker with access to that information posed significant risk to the organization with respect to various regulatory bodies. In addition, there were legislative compliance issues that needed to be addressed. It seems that the IT department had put a great deal of effort into developing their malware response process, but had done so in isolation from other critical players within the organization. As such, there was a chance that the organization may have been exposed to even more risk, as many regulatory and legislative compliance policies state that if you can't identify exactly which records (personally identifiable information, PCI information, etc.) were accessed, you must notify that regulatory body that *all* of the records could have been exposed. As the malware had simply been eradicated and no investigation of any kind had been conducted (root cause or otherwise), there was no information available regarding what data could have been accessed, let alone what (if any) data was actually accessed or exfiltrated from the infrastructure.

Now and again, I have had the opportunity to work with an organization that has taken great pains and put a lot of effort toward being prepared for those inevitable incidents to occur. I had another response engagement where as soon as I had arrived on-site and completed my in-brief, I was ushered to a room (yes, they provided me with a place to work without my having to ask!) where there were a dozen drives stacked up on a desk, along with a thumb drive and manila folder. It turns out that while the IT director was calling my team for assistance, his staff was already responding to the incident. They had collected and reviewed network logs and identified 12 affected systems, and replaced the drives in those systems—I was looking at the original drives sitting on the desk. The thumb drive contained the network logs, and the folder contained a print out of the network map (there was a soft copy on the thumb drive). With all of this, I began imaging the provided hard drives and reviewing the logs.

The incident that they'd experienced involved someone gaining unauthorized access to their infrastructure via Microsoft's Remote Desktop Protocol (RDP). They allowed employees to work from remote locations, requiring them to access the infrastructure via a virtual private network (VPN) and then connect to specific systems on the internal infrastructure via RDP. As such, they had VPN and domain authentication logs, as well as logs that clearly demonstrated the account used by the intruder. They had used these logs to identify the 12 systems that the intruder had connected to via the VPN, which corresponded to the 12 hard drives I was imaging. Their response was quick and decisive, and their scoping and analysis of the initial incident was thorough. They had also mapped exactly where, within their infrastructure, certain data existed. In this case, their primary concern was a single file, a spreadsheet that contained some sensitive data that was not encrypted.

The intruder had apparently connected to the VPN and used a single account to access the 12 internal machines using RDP. Once I began analyzing the drive images, it was a relatively straightforward process to map his activities across the various systems. As a result of this analysis, I was able to identify an additional 13 systems that had been accessed internally, via lateral inside the network. As these accesses were internal, indicators were not found within the VPN logs but were visible due to the fact that a profile for the user account the intruder was using was created on each system they accessed (on Windows systems, a user account—either local or a domain account—can be created, but a profile will not be created until the first time the user logs in via that account). I was also able to identify many of the actions that the intruder performed while accessing the various systems and when those actions occurred. These activities included running searches and accessing various files. However, none of the accessed files were spreadsheets, and specifically not the spreadsheet with which the IT director was most concerned. Ultimately, we were able to build a very strong case to present to the regulatory body that indicated that the sensitive data had not been accessed or exposed.

Logs

Throughout this book and in particular in Chapter 4, we will discuss logs that are available on Windows systems, both as part of the operating system and through applications installed on those systems. The two primary concerns during an incident with respect to logs are, where are they located and what's in them—both of which can have a significant impact on the outcome of your incident response activities. Logs often play a significant role in incident response because as mentioned previously, response happens after an incident occurs, and sometimes this can be a significant amount of time. The state of live systems can change pretty quickly, but logs can provide a considerable historical record of previous activity on the system—if they are available.

TIP

Device Logs

While we're concerned with logs on Windows systems, much of what is discussed in this section applies to other logs as well, such as those generated by firewalls and other network devices and systems.

One of the challenges of responding to incidents, whether as a consultant or an internal employee, is not having the necessary information to accurately and effectively respond to the questions your customer (or management) has regarding the incident, and therefore not being able to provide an accurate picture of what happened. Most organizations don't maintain full packet captures of what happens on their networks, and even if they did, this would still only be part of the picture, as you would still need to know what happened or actions were taken on the host. Windows systems have the ability to maintain records of what occurred on the host via the Event Logs (on Vista and Windows 7 systems, this is referred to as "Windows Event Logging"; Event Logs are discussed in more detail in Chapter 4); however, a number of times I have referred to the Event Logs only to find that either the specific events (i.e., logins) were not being audited, or Event Logging was not even enabled. This limits not just what data is being recorded but also how complete a picture an analyst can develop, and how effectively they can respond and answer the critical questions that are being asked by senior management. As such, one of the most effective steps in incident preparedness is to understand the logging mechanisms of your systems. A critical step that you can take quickly (and for free) to improve what information will be available when an incident is identified is to ensure that logging is enabled, that appropriate activities are being logged, and that the logs are large enough (or rotated often enough) to ensure sufficient data is available after an incident—which may be identified 6 or 12 months or more after the fact.

TIP

Application Logging

Some applications, in particular AV applications, will record events in the Application Event Log, as well as in text files managed by the application itself. It is important to remember that the Windows Event Logs are often limited to a specific size, and "roll over" in order to make room for new events. This means that older events may be removed from the Event Log; however, those events should still be available in the log files maintained by the application.

For example, Windows Event Logs have several characteristics that can be modified in order to enable more effective logging. One characteristic is the file size; increasing the size of the Event Logs will mean that more events will be recorded and available for analysis.

Another characteristic is what is actually being recorded. Recording successful and failed login attempts can be very useful, particularly in domain environments, and on servers or other systems which multiple users may access. In one analysis engagement, we found a considerable amount of extremely valuable data in the Event Log because "Process Tracking" had been enabled, along with auditing of successful (and failed) login attempts, as illustrated in Figure 2.1.

The actual settings you employ within your infrastructure depend heavily on what makes sense in your environment. Enabling auditing for success and failure process tracking events is very useful, as some processes run and complete very quickly, and are no longer visible mere seconds after they were launched. Enabling this auditing capability, as well as increasing the size of the logs (or, better yet, forward the logs from source systems to a collector system, per the instructions for

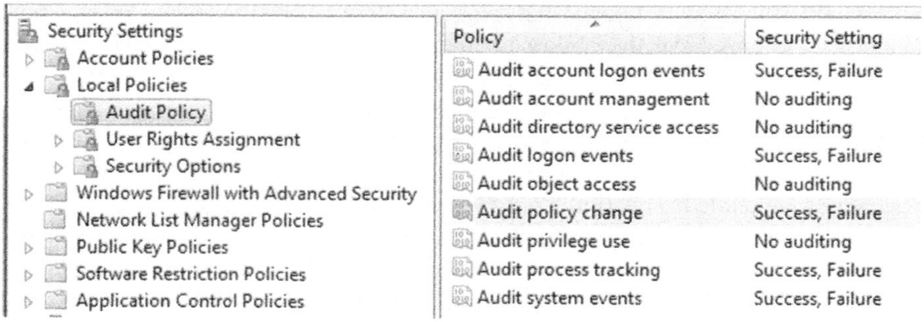

FIGURE 2.1

Windows 7 Audit Policy settings.

Windows 7 and higher systems found online at http://technet.microsoft.com/en-us/library/cc748890.aspx), will provide a persistent record of applications that have been executed on the system. Something to keep in mind when enabling this auditing functionality on servers as well as workstations is that, for the most part, there aren't a great number of processes that are launched on a Windows system. For example, once a server is booted and running, how many users log into the console and begin browsing the web or checking their email? Administrators may log in and perform system maintenance or troubleshooting, but for the most part, once the server is up and running, there won't be a considerable amount of interaction via the console. Also, on workstations and laptops, users tend to run the same set of applications—email client, web browser, etc—on pretty much a daily basis. As such, enabling this functionality can provide information that is invaluable during incident response.

There are other things you can do to increase both the amount and quality of information available from Windows systems during incident response. Some commercial products may offer additional features such as increased logging capabilities, log consolidation, or log searching. For example, Kyrus Technology, Inc. (http://www.kyrus-tech.com) has developed a sensor application called "Carbon Black" that is installed on Windows systems and monitors application execution on that system, sending its logs to a server for consolidation. That server can be maintained within the corporate infrastructure, or (for much smaller infrastructures) you can send the logs offsite to a server managed by the vendor. As of this writing, Carbon Black version 3 is available online at http://www.carbonblack.com/.

NOTE

Disclosure

I am providing my recommendation of Carbon Black after having seen a demonstration of the sensor and server, as well as being afforded the opportunity to work with both on my own small virtual network. I installed the sensor, which then reported its logs back to the Carbon Black server, which I installed and had access to on one of my own systems. I received no payment for any review of the application nor for any mention or discussion of it in this book. The simple fact is that I honestly believe that Carbon Black changes the dynamic of incident response, and is something that any organization that uses Windows systems should strongly consider deploying.

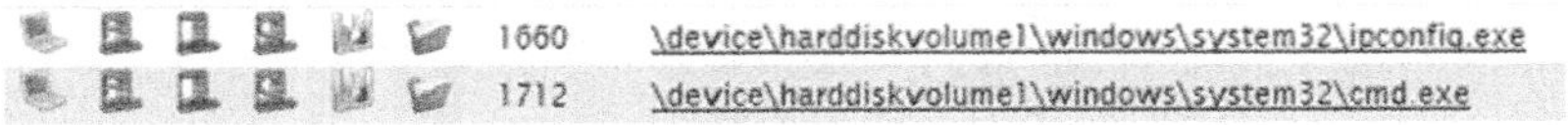

FIGURE 2.2

Excerpt of logged information available via Carbon Black server, prior to v.3.

Carbon Black is a lightweight (less than 100 kilobytes in size) sensor that you can install on Windows systems that you want to monitor. The sensor monitors the execution of applications, including child processes, file modifications, and loaded modules (as of this writing; future versions of Carbon Black will also record Registry key modifications and network connections). Carbon Black also records the MD5 hash of the executable file, as well as the start and end time for the process, and will provide a copy of the binary executable file, as well. All of these elements can also be searched within the logged information available via the server. A portion of the information available via the Carbon Black server is illustrated in Figure 2.2.

Again, this information can be extremely useful during incident response. As an example of this, and to get a little more familiar with what the data collected by Carbon Black looks like, I logged into a monitored Windows XP system (on my own internal "lab network") and created a "suspicious" application by copying the Solitaire game file (sol.exe) into an NTFS alternate data stream (ADS) attached to a file named "ads.txt." I then launched the game by typing "start.\ads.txt:game. exe" at the command prompt. Having already enabled Process Tracking within the audit policy for the system, I opened the Event Log on the system and found the event record that illustrated the application being launched. This record (event ID 593 indicates that the process has exited) is illustrated in Figure 2.3.

I then logged into the system to which the Carbon Black logs are sent, and accessed the user interface via the Chrome web browser (any web browser could have been used). I was able to quickly locate the log entry for the "suspicious" process, and even search for it based on the fact that I knew it was a child process of the "cmd.exe" process. The Carbon Black log entry is illustrated in Figure 2.4.

For the process illustrated in Figure 2.4, the exit time (although not displayed) correlated exactly with what is illustrated in the Event Log record in Figure 2.3. Now, this example was a bit contrived, in that it was a test and I knew what I was looking for via the Carbon Black interface. However, an analyst can use regular expressions as well as other search criteria (times, "new" processes, names of

FIGURE 2.3

Windows XP Event record for process launched from ADS.

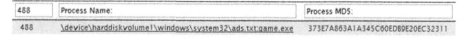

FIGURE 2.4

Carbon Black log entry for "suspicious" process.

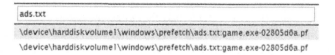

FIGURE 2.5

Results of Carbon Black file modification search (prior to v.3).

modified files, etc.) to locate potentially suspicious processes. Other search criteria can be used, such as the loaded modules (locate processes that have loaded a specific module, or DLL), MD5 hashes (of processes or loaded modules), and even file modifications. Figure 2.5 illustrates the results of a search for file modifications that include "ads.txt," via the Carbon Black interface.

As you can see, Carbon Black can be a powerful tool for use during incident response, and can be used to very quickly determine the extent and scope of an incident across monitored systems. Using various search criteria, a suspicious process can be found, and its source can quickly be identified (i.e., following the parent processes for a suspicious process leads to java.exe and then to firefox.exe might indicate a browser drive-by compromise). From there, additional searches can reveal any other systems that may have experienced something similar. While Event Logs may "roll over" and new entries push out older ones, the information logged by Carbon Black can be available for a much longer period of time, going back much farther into the past. Once monitoring of network connections has been added to the sensor, an analyst can search across all of the logs to see any other monitored systems that may have attempted to establish connections to a particular IP address, or created a specific Registry key (the significance of this will be a bit more clear once you read Chapter 6). That said, it's important to note that while Carbon Black is a great tool, its functionality and flexibility are based upon the fact that logging is configured, appropriate logging is occurring, and log data is being collected and preserved. These same principles apply whether you choose to use an add-on commercial product or native Windows functionality and tools.

Carbon Black (and other logging tools or products) may also have uses beyond incident response. One example of how Carbon Black has been used was in an organization that determined which components of the Microsoft Office Professional suite were being used by its employees, and that information was then used to reduce the overall corporate license for the software suite, saving the organization a significant amount of money on an annual basis.

Data collection

In addition to your preincident preparation, your response team needs to be prepared to begin collecting critical and / or volatile data once an incident is detected. The main purpose of immediate response is the timely collection of data. It is of paramount importance that IT staff who work with your systems on a regular basis also be trained so that they can begin collecting data from those systems soon after an incident is identified. Processes—particularly malicious processes—often do not run continually on systems. These processes may execute only long enough to perform their designated task, such as downloading additional malware, collecting the contents of Protected Storage from the system, or sending collected data off of the system to a waiting server. Malicious processes that may run on a continual basis include such things as packet sniffers and keystroke loggers.

However, it is unlikely that you will see continuous, ongoing malicious activity on your system. An intruder that has compromised your infrastructure does not go to one system, open a browser, and spend hours surfing the Failblog.org website. In fact, in a good number of instances, executables may be downloaded to a system, run, the data those processes collect sent off of the system to a waiting server on the Internet, and then the executables and their repository files are deleted. Of course, following this, the first forensic artifacts to decay are the network connections, and then as the system continues to function, MFT entries for the deleted files get reused, as do sectors on the disk that were once part of the files of interest. Therefore, collecting data as soon as the incident is identified can go a long way toward aiding the follow-on incident response and analysis efforts. In fact, with the proper procedures in place, having specific personnel implement a documented procedure for collecting data can obviate the need to do so later—such as days later (or longer), once the third-party responders arrive on-site.

TIP

Trusted Advisor

If you do not intend to perform your own incident response and analysis, the ideal approach to immediate response is to locate a firm providing incident response services and establish a relationship with them as your "trusted advisor." They can assist you in identifying the appropriate tools, procedures and documentation for collecting data from your available systems, as well as address issues such as configuration recommendations for future systems. They can also assist you in running drills or "mock incidents" in order to ensure that the procedures work properly and can be use effectively.

During immediate response, the first data that you will want to collect is the contents of physical memory. When collecting memory from live Windows systems, perhaps the easiest (and free) approach is the DumpIt utility from MoonSol (found online at http://www.moonsols.com/ressources/). DumpIt is a simple to employ application written by Matthieu Suiche; simply place a copy of the application on a thumb drive or external USB drive enclosure, and launch the application from the command prompt. You will be asked a confirmation question, and once you respond with "y," a raw dump of memory will be created on the media (therefore, the media needs to be writeable), as illustrated in Figure 2.6.

When the process completes, the word "Success" appears in green following "Processing...". The resulting file (in this example "Oliver-20110907-010837.raw") is named using the system name ("Oliver") and the UTC time at which the process

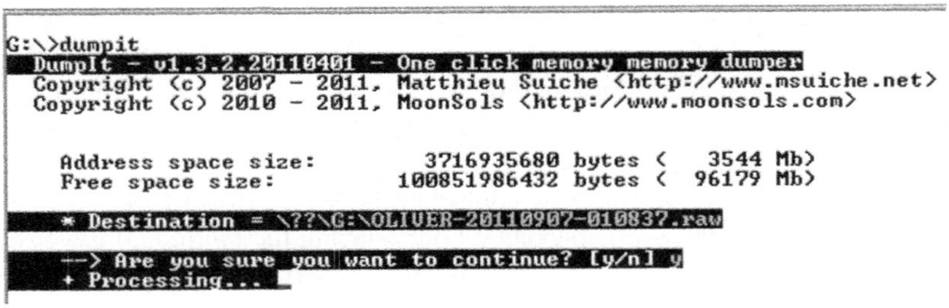

FIGURE 2.6

Example of MoonSol DumpIt use.

was initiated; in this case, the date and time in the filename correlate to 9:08 pm on September 6, 2011, Eastern Standard Time. What this means is that physical memory can be collected from multiple systems, or even multiple times from the same system, very easily and without having to use additional media. In fact, it's so easy that all you have to do is have a copy of DumpIt on a couple of USB external drives (or appropriately sized thumb drives), and you're ready to go. The sooner memory is collected after an incident has been identified, the better. Over time, not only do processes complete, but systems can be rebooted, or even taken out of service, and once the memory is gone, it's gone.

Collecting the contents of physical memory is just the start, however. Other freely available options for collecting the contents of physical memory include (but are not limited to) FTK Imager (found online at http://accessdata.com/support/product-downloads#), the Volatility winpmem tool (found online at https://volatility.googlecode.com/svn/branches/scudette/docs/pmem.html), or the BelkaSoft RAM-Capturer tool (found online at http://forensic.belkasoft.com/en/ram-capturer).

TIP

Dumping Windows Memory

I've mentioned several freely available tools for dumping the contents of physical memory from a Windows system, but while "free" usually means that the solution is accessible, it may not mean that it's necessarily the best option. Perhaps the best tools for performing this function are the KNTTools created by George M. Garner, Jr., and available online at http://www.gmgsystemsinc.com/knttools/. There is a fee associated with these tools, but based on discussions and exchanges with experts in the field, they are the best solution available for acquiring the contents of physical memory from Windows systems.

Regardless of the tool used, you should always test the tools on systems so that you understand how they're used, and what results you can expect to see. Also, be sure to perform the testing when downtime of the system is not an issue.

You can also use FTK Imager to collect copies of specific files from the system (MFT, Registry hives, Windows Event Logs, etc.), or initiate logical or full physical image acquisition from those systems, in fairly quick order.

NOTE

Spinning Plates

One of the challenges I've faced once arriving on-site is going to a server room or data center and acquiring data and images from multiple systems. In some cases, each system requires a different approach, particularly if the systems cannot be taken offline for some reason. Live acquisitions can be a challenge when the system has just a USB version 1.0 connector, as you watch the estimated completion time for the acquisition of a 250-gigabyte hard drive start at 2 hours and progress up over 56 hours. I've even encountered a boot-from-SAN system; while the device itself was "in scope," the multiterabyte SAN was not, so we performed a live acquisition of the *boot-from-SAN* system.

Whenever faced with situations like this, we often try to get as many systems started in the acquisition process as possible, keeping the plates spinning as it were, in order to reduce the overall amount of time required by using parallel processes. Often, the incident had been going on for several days (or weeks) before we were called, and the contracting process and our (consultant's) travel in order to get to the site added additional time to the clock. The overall process would have been far better facilitated had the local IT staff followed a documented procedure and initiated the acquisition process immediately.

FIGURE 2.7

FTK Imager "Export Directory Listing…" functionality.

For example, a great deal of analysis work can be performed rather quickly using a partial acquisition (rather than acquiring a full image) of data from a live system. Adding FTK Imager Lite to a USB external hard drive (often referred to as a "wallet" drive due to the size) will provide suitable storage space for acquired images and files in a small form factor, and when needed the drive can be connected to a system and FTK Imager launched. The IT staff member performing the acquisition can then choose to add either the physical drive of the system, or the logical volume for the C:\ drive (depending upon the response plan that's already been established and documented within the organization). From there, a directory listing that includes the last modified, last accessed, and creation dates (from the $STANDARD_INFORMATION attribute in the MFT; see Chapters 4 and 7 for more detail) for all files within the selected volume (as well as their paths) can easily be exported to the storage media using the "Export Directory Listing…" functionality, as illustrated in Figure 2.7.

Once the directory listing has been exported, specific files can then be exported through FTK Imager, allowing for rapid analysis and assessment of the state of the system. These files may include such files as Registry hives, Event Logs, Prefetch files, Jump Lists (Windows 7), application (Scheduled Task, AV, etc.) log files, etc.

TIP

F-Response

The acquisition process discussed previously in this chapter requires an IT administrator to physically touch each system, in order to plug the USB hard drive into that system. Depending upon the organization and how the infrastructure is designed, this may not be something that can be done in a timely manner. For example, systems may be located in a server room or data center on another floor or in another building within the city, or even in another city. F-Response (found online at http://www.f-response.com) is a dongle-based tool designed by Matthew Shannon that provides remote, read-only access to remote systems. Matthew wanted to have a way to perform incident response activities without having to coordinate with his customers to actually get someone physically on-site, and designed F-Response to meet his needs. Using the Enterprise version of F-Response, a responder can sit in a single location with network access to the various systems, deploy the F-Response agent, and connect to each system in read-only mode (all attempts to write to the remote hard drive are dropped by F-Response). From there, the responder can collect specific files or acquire a complete image using their acquisition-tool-of-choice (i.e., FTK Imager). F-Response also provides access to the contents of physical memory on Windows systems.

Another useful aspect of F-Response is that the agent can be deployed on systems ahead of time, as part of incident preparation activities. The agent installs as a Windows service, but by default it is not enabled to run automatically when the system is booted; therefore, it can be installed and waiting to be enabled when needed. The agent can also be installed using a name other than the default, so that it is not obvious that F-Response is installed (although because the service is not started automatically, anyone who logs in to the system and types "net start" at the command prompt will not see the agent listed as a running service anyway).

Training

In order for employees to perform their jobs effectively, they must be trained. Payroll and accounting staffs within organizations have training to attend, and then return to their organization and begin working in their field. The same is true with a lot of other departments within your business, as well as with professionals in other areas (emergency medical technicians, police officers, firefighters, doctors, nurses, etc.). Many organizations offer a variety of types of training to their employees, often ranging from the use of office suite applications, to professional development, and even basic first aid.

The same must also be true for those individuals responsible when an incident is identified by the organization. It does no good to have a CSIRP, but to not have designated staff trained in their activities when the plan needs to be implemented. Several regulatory bodies state that in order to be compliant (all "compliance vs. security" arguments aside), organizations subject to the regulations must not only have a CSIRP with all response personnel identified within the plan, but they must also receive annual training with respect to the CSIRP and the actions they are to take.

TIP

Mock Incidents

Mock incidents are a great way to test your response plan, either to see what needs to be improved or to simply provide training so that the plan and everyone's role is fresh in everyone's minds. I've provided mock incident and response team training to a number of organizations and seen firsthand just how revealing that first mock incident can be.

During one training event, we found two very interesting items. We'd placed an innocuous bit of software on a system chosen at random that would reach out to the web every 10 minutes and grab a web page, and then save that web page on the local hard drive in a file with the .DLL extension. The first thing that happened during the event was that an incident was declared and the firewall administrator was asked for the firewall logs, and he said that he'd have them to the incident manager in 10 minutes. Half an hour later, the incident manager hadn't received the logs, and when he tried to reach the firewall administrator, it turned out that he'd gone to lunch! When he returned, he said that he had thought that the request for the logs was part of a drill and hadn't actually intended to provide the logs. When he did try to retrieve the logs, we all found out that the logs weren't actually being archived.

The other finding involved the intrusion detection system (IDS). At one point during the exercise, the IDS administrator stated that this wasn't a valid test because, even given the domain and name of the web page being requested, he wasn't seeing anything in the logs. As it turned out, the "malware" had been placed on a subnet not covered by any IDS.

Running an exercise during which the CSIRP is tested or taken for a "shake-down cruise" (please excuse the naval vernacular, as I'm a former Marine officer) should include actually collecting the data that you've decided will be collected. Are you going to collect memory from Windows systems, and if so, how? Will it work? Challenges I've encountered include older systems with USB version 1.0 interfaces, which usually result in processes that should take a short time ultimately taking an inordinate amount of time to complete. How will you address such situations, and have you identified all of the pertinent systems that may have this issue (regardless of the issue)? How will you address virtual systems? How will you collect data from production systems that cannot be "taken down" (due to service level agreements, transaction processing, etc.)? All of these questions (and likely more) need to be addressed *before* an incident occurs; otherwise, critical, sensitive data will continue to be lost (either exfiltrated or degraded) while managers and staff members try to decide how to react.

Business models

So far in this chapter, I've loosely addressed business models from the perspective of the organization facing the incident, and hopefully been able to convince you, the reader, to some degree of the need for immediate response.

Much of the way that I've seen incident response "done" is akin to someone getting hurt, and then calling and waiting for a surgeon to arrive. What I mean is that an organization becomes or is made aware that they may have been subject to a breach or intrusion, and they call an incident response team for assistance, and do nothing until that team arrives on-site. This is what I refer to as the "classic emergency response service (ERS)" model. And as we've covered in this chapter thus far, it's not a particularly good or useful model, especially for the customer.

Why do I say that? Well, one of the things you see with the military is that soldiers and Marines are trained in basic first aid procedures, so that if they or a buddy become injured, they can provide immediate aid and assist their buddy until a medic or corpsman (someone with more specialized training) arrives. Navy sailors are trained in damage control, so that if anything should happen while the ship is at sea, they can respond immediately to an incident, contain and mitigate the risk, allowing the ship to remain afloat and make it to port of repairs. I can go on and on with more examples, but my overall point is that for years, and even to some degree now, incident response models have been based on organizations calling incident responders for help and waiting for them to arrive, while doing little to address the issue. Or worse, someone within the organization takes steps (running AV scans, wiping systems, etc.) that while attempting to address the incident, have simply made matters worse by eradicating crucial information that could be used to determine the extent of the incident. This is what I refer to as the "classic ERS" model of incident response.

Let's take a look at the other side of the coin. We've already discussed some of the costs associated with this model from the perspective of the organization that experienced the incident. From a consulting perspective, staffing a bench for the classic ERS model is difficult. How many analysts do you have available? Remember, the classic ERS model of incident response is sporadic—you have to wait for someone to call you for assistance, all while your sales and marketing function are "putting the word out" that this is what you do. If you have too many analysts on your bench, you're paying their salaries while you have no incoming work; if you have too few analysts, the ones you do have will be run at a high "burn rate" (meaning that they will be on the road a great deal) and you will likely be turning down work due to not having anyone available to send on-site. Do this too many times, and word gets around. This model can be very expensive for the consulting firm, and as such, that expense needs to be made up when work does become available.

So, why do we continue with this model? Why not move on to something new, something better? We understand the need for immediate response by this point in the chapter, and we also have an understanding that there's nothing "immediate" about the classic ERS model of incident response. Many organizations are subject to some sort of compliance regulations that state that they must have an incident response capability; for example, the PCI Data Security Standards (DSS) Chapter 12.9 states that the organization will maintain an incident response plan and be prepared to respond immediately to an incident. The best way to do that is to develop a relationship with "trusted advisor," or a consulting firm that can help guide you down the path to creating that capability, and will then be available to provide assistance, when needed. Incident response then becomes "immediate," as the initial responders are those who work with and maintain the infrastructure on a daily basis. This not only assists in the detection of incidents, but you get the added benefit of having your responders right there, with no travel required—and last minute plane tickets are expensive. Local IT staff trained in incident response can immediately begin collecting and analyzing data, and even begin containing and remediating the incident.

SUMMARY

When an incident is identified within an organization, it is critical that local IT staff be trained and knowledgeable in collecting pertinent data from Windows systems. Considerable time (hours, days, etc.) may pass before third-party consultants arrive on-site to begin performing incident response activities, and even then, the fact that they are not familiar with the organization's infrastructure can extend the overall response time. Being prepared for those inevitable computer security incidents to occur, simply by having documentation, as well as network and system data, available will make a significant difference in the ultimate outcome of the incident. This will be true regardless of whether an incident or data breach needs to ultimately be addressed a compliance oversight body, or by law enforcement interested in intelligence or evidence to pursue prosecution. Properly trained local IT staff can immediately collect data that would otherwise expire or be unavailable hours or days later. Local responders should be able to collect the contents of physical memory, as well as partial, logical or complete physical images from systems, and have that data ready and documented for the analysis effort that inevitably follows data collection.

Volume Shadow Copies

3

INFORMATION IN THIS CHAPTER

* What are "Volume Shadow Copies"?
* Live Systems
* Acquired Images
* Windows 8

INTRODUCTION

Every time a new version of the Windows operating system is announced or made public, a collective shudder ripples throughout the forensics community. What new features are going to be available in the next operating system version? What's going to remain the same? What new challenges will we face? Some changes are minor; for example, the binary structure of the Windows Registry hasn't changed between versions, from Windows 2000 all the way through to Windows 7, although how the Registry is used (where keys are located, what keys and values are created and modified, etc.) by the operating system and applications has changed in many cases. Other changes can be quite significant, such as those that change the very core of how Windows operates. In this chapter, we'll address one of those changes, specifically the introduction of Volume Shadow Copies (VSCs). However, we will discuss this topic not from the perspective of a developer or programmer, but instead from the perspective of an analyst, and how this technology might be utilized to further an investigation.

What are "volume shadow copies"?

VSCs are one of the new, ominous sounding aspects of the Windows operating systems (specifically, Windows XP, in a limited manner, and more so with Vista and Windows 7) that can significantly impact an analyst's examination. VSCs are significant and interesting as a source of artifacts, enough to require their own chapter.

With the release of Windows XP, Microsoft introduced the Volume Shadow Copy Service to provide functionality for backing up critical system files in order to assist with system recovery. With Windows XP, users and administrators saw this functionality as System Restore Points which were created automatically under various conditions (every 24 hours, when a driver was installed, etc.) and could also be created manually, as illustrated in Figure 3.1.

As illustrated in Figure 3.1, users can not only create Restore Points, but they can also restore the computer to an earlier time. This proved to be useful functionality, particularly when a user installed something (application, driver, etc.) that failed to work properly, or the system became infected with malware of some kind. Users could revert the core functionality of their systems to a previous state through the System Restore functionality, effectively recovering it to a previous state. However, System Restore Points do not back up everything on a system; for example, user data files are not backed up (and are therefore not restored, either), and all of the data in the SAM hive of the Registry is not backed up, as you wouldn't want users to restore their system to a previous point in time and have them not be able to access it, as a previous password had been restored. So, while System Restore Points did prove useful when a user needed to recover their system to a previous state, they did little to back up user data and provide access to previous copies of other files. From a forensic analysis, a great deal of historical data could be retrieved from System Restore Points, including backed up system files and Registry hives. Analysts still need to understand how backed up files could be "mapped" to their original file names but the fact that the files are backed up is valuable in itself.

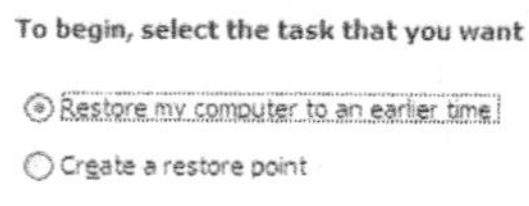

To begin, select the task that you want to perform:

⊙ Restore my computer to an earlier time

○ Create a restore point

FIGURE 3.1

Windows XP System Restore Point functionality.

> **TIP**
>
> **System Files in Restore Points**
>
> One use of system files being backed up to Windows XP System Restore Points is that when malware is installed as device driver (executable file with a ".sys" extension), it would be backed up to a Restore Point. If the installation process had included modifying the file time stamps so that the file appeared to have been created on the system during the original installation process, the true creation date could be verified via the master file table (MFT; see Chapter 4). Further, if there were six Restore Points, and the system file was not backed up in the older five Restore Points, and was only available in the most recent Restore Point, this would also provide an indication that the observed creation date for the file was not correct.

With the release of Vista, the functionality provided by the Volume Shadow Copy Service to support services such as Windows Backup and System Restore was expanded. In particular, the amount and type of data captured by System Restore was expanded to include block-level, incremental "snapshots" of a system (only the modified information was recorded) at a given point in time. These "snapshots"—known as VSCs—appeared in a different manner to the user. VSCs operate at the block level within the file system, backing up and providing access to previous versions of system and user data files within a particular volume. As with System Restore Points, the actual backups are transparent to the user, but with VSCs, the user can restore previous versions of files through the Previous Versions shell extension, as illustrated in Figure 3.2 (from a Windows 7 system).

FIGURE 3.2

Windows 7 "Previous Versions" shell extension.

Okay, so what does this mean to the forensic analyst? From an analyst's perspective, there is a great deal of historical information within backed up files. Accessing these files can provide not just historical data (previous contents, etc.) but additional analysis can be conducted by comparing the available versions over time.

Registry keys

As you'd expect, there are several Registry keys that have a direct impact on the performance of the Volume Shadow Copy Service (VSS; the service which supports the various functions that lead to VSCs). As this is a Windows service, the primary key of interest is:

```
HKLM\System\CurrentControlSet\Services\VSS
```

However, it is important to understand that disabling the VSC Service may affect other applications aside from just disabling VSCs, such as Windows Backup. As such, care should be taken in disabling this service on production systems. Also, forensic analysts examining Vista and Windows 7 systems that do not appear to have any VSCs available should check this key to see if the service had been disabled prior to the system being acquired.

There's another key within the System hive that affects VSC behavior, and that is:

```
HKLM\System\CurrentControlSet\Control\BackupRestore
```

Beneath this key are three subkeys: FilesNotToBackup, FilesNotToSnapshot, and KeysNotToRestore. The names should be pretty self-explanatory, but just in case, the FilesNotToBackup key contains a list of files and directories that (according to Microsoft; additional information is available online at http://msdn.microsoft.com/en-us/library/bb891959(v=vs.85).aspx) backup applications should not backup and restore. On a default Windows 7 installation, this list includes temporary files (as in those in the %TEMP% directory), the pagefile, hibernation file (if one exists), the Offline Files Cache, Internet Explorer index.dat files, as well as number of log file directories. The FilesNotToSnapshot key contains a list of files that should be deleted from newly created shadow copies. Finally, the KeysNotToRestore key contains lists of subkeys and values that should not be restored. It should be noted that within this key, values that end in "\" indicate that subkeys and values for the listed key will not be restored, while values that end in "*" indicate that subkeys and values for the listed key will not be restored from backup, but new values will be included from the backup.

Another Registry key to be very aware of is the following:

```
HKLM\Software\Microsoft\Windows NT\CurrentVersion\SPP\Clients
```

This key contains a value named "{09F7EDC5-294E-4180-AF6A-FB0E6A0E9513}," and the data within that value will tell you which volumes are being monitored by the Volume Shadow Service. The data for this value can contain

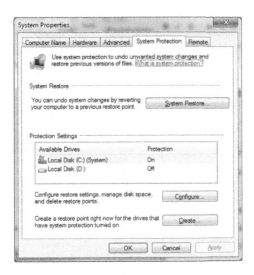

FIGURE 3.3

System Properties dialog.

multiple strings, each of which references a volume GUID and the drive letter for the volume, separated by a colon. This value will mirror what is listed in the Protection Settings section of the System Properties dialog, as illustrated in Figure 3.3.

TIP

Finding VSCs

I've run into and used the SPP\Clients key quite a bit during examinations. One of the steps I include in order to orient myself to an image prior to an examination, I will check (via FTK Imager or ProDiscover, usually) to see if there are any difference files available within the System Volume Information folder. In a number of cases, I've found none, and upon further examination, found that the VSS service was set to run automatically upon system boot. During examinations in which historical information would be very valuable, I will then verify the LastWrite time on the SPP\Clients key, and check the data of the "{09F7EDC5-294E-4180-AF6A-FB0E6A0E9513}" value. Using this information, I can then state my findings based on those values in my report; many times, I find from the client that deleting or clearing the value is actually part of the standard system configurations for the enterprise.

Live systems

Accessing VSCs on live Vista, Windows 2008, and Windows 7 systems is a relatively simple task, as Windows systems ship with the necessary native system tools to access VSCs. In order to see the available VSCs for the C:\ drive of the Vista

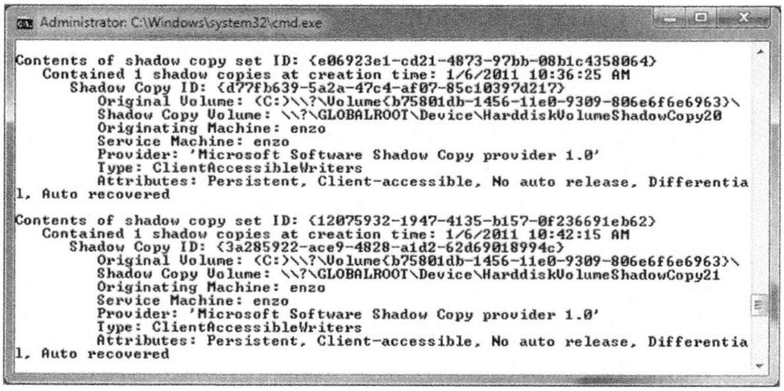

FIGURE 3.4

Sample output of the *vssadmin* command.

or Windows 7 system that you're logged into, type the following command into a command prompt using elevated privileges (you may need to right-click the command prompt window and choose "Run as Administrator"):

```
C:\>vssadmin list shadows /for=c:
```

Example results of this command are illustrated in Figure 3.4.

As you can see illustrated in Figure 3.3, we can use the *vssadmin* command to gather considerable information about available VSCs on the system.

WARNING

WMI

The Windows Management Instrumentation (WMI) class Win32_ShadowCopy (documentation found online at http://msdn.microsoft.com/en-us/library/aa394428 (v=VS.85).aspx) provides an interface for programmatically extracting much of the same information from Windows systems made available by the *vssadmin* command. However, according to information available at the Microsoft web site (see the "Community Content" section of the previously linked page) at the time of this writing, this class is not supported on the 64-bit version of Windows 2008. Testing using a Perl script indicates that this is also true for Windows 7; the script didn't work at all on 64-bit Windows 7, but ran very well on the 32-bit edition. A sample of what is available via Perl (or other methods for accessing WMI classes) appears as follows:

```
Computer: WIN-882TM1JM2N2
DeviceObject: \\?\GLOBALROOT\Device\HarddiskVolumeShadowCopy1
InstallDate: 20110421125931.789499-240
<snip>
VolumeName: \\?\Volume{d876c67b-1139-11df-8b47-806e6f6e6963}\
```

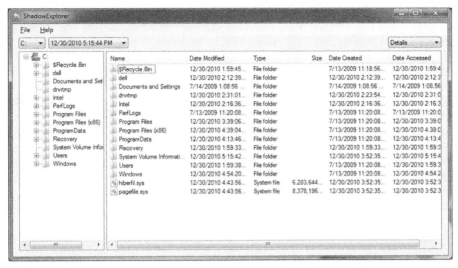

FIGURE 3.5

ShadowExplorer v0.8 interface.

Don't like the command line approach? Hey, that's okay—it's not for everyone. Head on over to ShadowExplorer.com and get a copy of ShadowExplorer (at the time of this writing, version 0.8 is available). Download and run the setup file on your system in order to install ShadowExplorer on the system in question. The web site describes ShadowExplorer as being useful to all users, but especially so to users with Windows 7 Home Edition, who don't have access to VSCs by default. Once you install and launch ShadowExplorer, you will see the interface as illustrated in Figure 3.5.

As illustrated in Figure 3.5, you can use the drop-down selector beneath menu bar to select the date of the VSC you would like access to; unfortunately, ShadowExplorer will only show you the VSCs available within the volume or drive (i.e., C:\, D:\) on which it is installed. Therefore, if your system has a D:\ drive, you'll need to rerun the installation program and install it on that drive, as well, in order to view the VSCs on that drive. Navigating through the tree view in the left-hand pane, locate the file for which you'd like to see a previous version, right-click the file and choose "Export" to copy that file to another location.

Going back to the command prompt, in order to access the VSCs on your live system and have access to the previous versions of files within those VSCs, you'll need to make a symbolic link to a VSC. To do that, go to the listing for a VSC, as illustrated in Figure 3.3, and select (you'll need to have Quick Edit mode enabled in your command prompt) the VSC identifier, which appears after "Shadow Copy Volume:." Then go back to the prompt and type the following command:

```
C:\>mklink /d C:\vsc
```

Do not hit the Enter key at this point. Once you get the far with command, right-click to paste the selected VSC identifier into the prompt and then add a trailing slash ("\"), so that the command looks like the following:

```
C:\>mklink /d C:\vsc \\?\GLOBALROOT\Device\
HarddiskVolumeShadowCopy20\
```

Remember to add the trailing slash to the command—this is very important! This is not something that is clearly documented at the Microsoft site, but has been found to be the case by a number of forensic analysts, to include Rob Lee, of SANS fame, and Jimmy Weg, a law enforcement officer from Montana. Now, go ahead and hit the Enter key, and you should see that the symbolic link was successfully created. Now you can navigate to the C:\vsc directory, and browse and access the files via the command prompt or Windows Explorer. Once you're done doing whatever you're going to do with these files (review, copy, etc.), type the following command to remove the symbolic directory link:

```
C:\>rmdir C:\vsc
```

This series of commands is going to be very important throughout the rest of this chapter, so it's important that we understand some of the key points. First, use the *vssadmin* command to get the list of VSCs for a particular volume; note that when you run the command from the command prompt, you do not have to be *in* that volume. For example, if you want to list the VSCs for the D:\ volume, you can do so using the following command, run from the C:\ volume.

```
C:\>vssadmin list shadows /for=d:
```

Once you know which VSC you'd like to access, you can use the *mklink* command to create a symbolic link to that VSC. Remember, you must be sure that the VSC identifier (i.e., \\?\GLOBALROOT\Device\HarddiskVolumeShadowCopy20\) ends with a trailing slash. Finally, once you've completed working in that VSC, you remove the symbolic link with the *rmdir* command.

ProDiscover

A number of commercial forensic analysis applications provide access to VSCs within acquired images, and ProDiscover is just one of those applications. However, ProDiscover is also the only commercial forensic analysis application to which I have access. As such, I briefly mention its ability to access VSCs on live systems here. For those who want more detailed information on how to use ProDiscover for this purpose, Christopher Brown posted a five-page PDF format paper at the Technology Pathways, LLC, web site that describes how to use ProDiscover IR (the Incident Response Edition) to access and acquire VSCs on remote live systems. This can be very valuable to an investigator who needs to quickly access these resources in another location, or to do so surreptitiously. The paper can be found on the web at http://toorcon.techpathways.com/uploads/LiveVolumeShadowCopyWithProDiscoverIR.pdf.

F-Response

If you're a user of the fantastic F-Response tool from Matt Shannon, particularly the Enterprise Edition (EE), you'll be very happy to know that you can use this product to access VSCs on remote systems. This may be important for a variety of reasons; a user within your enterprise environment may have "lost" an important file that they were working on, you may need to access an employee's system surreptitiously, or you may need to quickly acquire data from a system located in another building in another area of the city. While I generally don't recommend acquiring full system images over the network, even over a VPN, you can use tools like F-Response EE, which provides read-only access to the remote system drive, in order to collect specific information and selected files from remote systems very quickly. This will allow you to perform a quick triage of systems, and potentially perform a good deal of data reduction and reduce the impact of your response activities on your organization by identifying the specific systems that need to be acquired.

That being said, perhaps the best way to discuss F-Response EE's ability to provide access to VSCs is through a demonstration. Before describing the setup I used and walking through this demonstration, I need to make it clear that I used F-Response EE because Matt was gracious enough to provide me with a copy to work with; this process that I'm going to walk through can be used with all versions of F-Response, including the Consultant and Field Kit editions.

TIP

F-Response VSC Demo Setup

For my demonstration, I don't have a full network to "play with," so I opted to use the tools that I do have available. I booted my 64-bit Windows 7 Professional analysis system, and then started up a 32-bit Windows 7 Ultimate virtual machine (VM) in VMPlayer. I had set the Network Adapter in the settings for the VM to "bridged," so that the VM appeared as a system on the network. For the demonstration, the IP address of the running VM was 192.168.1.8, and the IP address of the host was 192.168.1.5. On both systems, the Windows firewalls were disabled (just for the demonstration, I assure you!) in order to simulate a corporate environment. Also, it is important to note that Windows 7 ships with the iSCSI initiator already installed, so I didn't need to go out and install it separately.

Again, this demonstration makes use of F-Response EE (thanks to Matt Shannon for allowing me the honor to work with this wonderful tool!). Once I logged into my analysis system, I plugged in my F-Response EE dongle and launched the F-Response License Manager Monitor to install and start the License Manager service. I then launched the F-Response Enterprise Management Console (FEMC) and started by configuring the credentials that I would be using to access the remote system. I clicked File→Configure Credentials... from the menu bar, and entered the appropriate username/password information to access the remote system (if you're in an Active Directory domain, check the "Use Current User

FIGURE 3.6

FEMC Direct Connect UI.

Credentials" option). Next, I clicked File→Configure Options… and configured my deployment options appropriately (for this demo, I didn't select the "Physical Memory" option in the Host Configuration section).

As I was going to connect to a specific system, I selected Scan→Direct Scan from the menu bar, and entered the IP address of the target system (i.e., 192.168.1.8), and clicked the Open button. Once the connection was made, F-Response was installed and started on the target system, as illustrated in Figure 3.6.

From there, I logged into the C:\ volume on the target host, and that host's C:\ drive appeared on my analysis system as the F:\ volume. I then ran the following command on my analysis system:

```
C:\>vssadmin list shadows /for=f:
```

In order to access the oldest VSC listed (HarddiskVolumeShadowCopy17, created on January 4, 2011), I entered the following command in a command prompt on my analysis system:

```
C:\>mklink /d d:\test \\?\GLOBALROOT\Device\
HarddiskVolumeShadowCopy17\
```

This command created a symbolic link on my analysis system called "d:\test" that contained the contents of a VSC created on the target system on January 4, 2011, and allowed me to access all of the files with that directory, albeit via the read-only access provided by F-Response EE.

> **WARNING**
>
> **Accessing VSCs on Live Systems**
>
> It is very important to remember that when you're accessing VSCs on live systems, that system, whether accessed remotely or locally, is still subject to operating normally. What this means is that if you're accessing the oldest VSC that you found, the system itself is still going about its normal operations, and that VSC could be overwritten to make

room for another VSC, as under normal conditions, the VSCs are subject to the "first-in-first-out" (FIFO) process. This actually happened to me while I was working on some of the demonstrations listed in this chapter. The remote live system continued to operate normally, and the VSC I was accessing was removed simply because I had taken too long to complete the testing (I was just browsing through some of the files). I had to back out of my demonstration and restart it. When I did, I found that the output of the *vssadmin* command was quite a bit different, particularly with respect to the dates on which the available shadow copies had been created.

Another very important aspect of accessing VSCs (and this applies to accessing VSCs within images, as well) is that you need to be very careful about the files you click or double-click on. Remember, if you double-click a file that is in a VSC on a remote system, your analysis system is going to apply its own rules to accessing and opening that file. This means that if you see a PDF file that you'd like to click on, you should be very sure that it wasn't what led to the remote system being infected in the first place. If it is a malicious PDF, and your system isn't protected (updated antivirus (AV) and PDF viewer, etc.), then your system may become infected, as well.

As I mentioned, there are a number of commercial forensic analysis applications and tools that provide analysts and responders with the ability to access VSCs on remote systems, and what we've discussed here are only a few of your (and my) available options. The application and methodology you choose to use depends largely on your needs, abilities, and preferences (and, of course, which tool or set of tools you can afford).

Acquired images

Since discussion of VSCs first started, one of the biggest and most often asked questions within the forensic analysis community has been, "how do we access VSCs within acquired images?" First of all, accessing VSCs within images is not the same thing as accessing those on live systems. Figure 3.7 illustrates what the VSCs "look like" within an acquired image.

As illustrated in Figure 3.7, the VSC difference files within the System Volume Information directory are binary files, and we need some means for translating

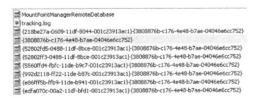

FIGURE 3.7

Acquired image of Vista system opened in FTK Imager v3.0.

this binary data into accessible information. On live systems, this is usually done through the use of the available API; therefore, one means of accessing the same data on an acquired image would be to boot the image through the use of LiveView and VMWare.

TIP

LiveView

LiveView, freely available online from http://liveview.sourceforge.net/, is a Java-based graphical tool developed by a student at Carnegie Mellon University. LiveView creates VMWare configuration files for acquired raw/dd-format images or physical disks and supports Windows versions from Windows 98 through Windows 2008 (Windows 7 is not listed among the supported operating systems).

However, even with the ability to "zero out" (not crack, but reset to a new value, possibly using a tool such as ntpwedit, found online at the time of this writing at http://cdslow.webhost.ru/en/ntpwedit/) the Administrator password so that you can log into the now-running system, this may still not be a viable option. So, the question becomes, with nothing more than an acquired image of a system that may contain VSCs, what are some options for gaining access to the data within those VSCs?

I asked myself this question seriously during the break between Christmas 2010 and the New Year, and I began researching it in order to find a solution. After all, I'd encountered several systems that contained VSCs, including Windows 7 and even a Vista system. In my case, neither instance required access to the VSCs in order to complete my analysis, but it was still clear to me that like other analysts, I could fully expect to see more of these systems. Subsequently, I was going to have to come up with a way to access the VSCs.

I began my search by going to Google… of course. I found a number of references to accessing VSCs within acquired images, but in each case, the materials included mounting the acquired image using EnCase (from Guidance Software) and the Physical Disk Emulator (PDE) module, as part of the process. Well, I don't have access to EnCase, nor to the PDE module, and I thought that there just *had* to be some way to access data within the VSCs of an acquired image, without using either one.

For my testing, I had an image acquired from a personal system that was running a 32-bit version of Windows Vista. This was an image of the physical hard drive, and as the system was a Dell laptop, the image contained several partitions including the Dell maintenance partition. As such, I used FTK Imager version 3.0 to extract the active operating system partition from the image, as I wanted to isolate the partition that contained the VSCs. The disk image was called "disk0.001," and the image of the active partition was called "system.001." My analysis workstation was a Dell Latitude E6510 laptop, running a 64-bit version of Windows 7 Professional. On that laptop, I had a copy of FTK Imager version 3.0.0.1443, as well as ImDisk 1.3.1.

VHD method

A "VHD" file is a virtual hard disk file used by virtualization software such as Microsoft's Virtual PC or Virtual Server (but can also be used by Oracle's VirtualBox application, as well). The VHD file represents a physical hard disk and can be used by a VM as if it were a physical hard disk. Additional information regarding VHD files can be found online at the Microsoft web site at http://technet.microsoft.com/en-us/library/cc708315%28WS.10%29.aspx.

As part of my research for this little project, I found vhdtool.exe at the Microsoft site (found on the web at http://code.msdn.microsoft.com/vhdtool). I also found that Microsoft's Virtual Server application includes a tool named "vhdmount" (information about this tool can be found online at http://technet.microsoft.com/en-us/library/cc708295%28WS.10%29.aspx) for mounting VHD files. In reading about vhdtool.exe, it has an option ("/convert") for converting a raw/dd-format image file into a fixed-format VHD file. I ran the tool against a copy of the system.001 file (the active OS partition image described above, on an external USB wallet drive) and although the file name was not changed to ".vhd," the tool reported that it had successfully modified the file (apparently by adding a footer). From there, the next step was to mount the new VHD file; I did this by opening the Computer Management console, selecting Disk Management and clicking Action, then Attach VHD from the menu bar. The system.001 file was recognized as a valid VHD file, resulting "Attach Virtual Hard Disk" dialog is illustrated in Figure 3.8.

Notice in Figure 3.8 that I had selected the option to mount the VHD file read-only. Even though I was using a working copy of the image file, and it had already been modified (via the use of vhdtool.exe, which I documented), I wanted to be sure to follow best practices in my procedures.

As a result of attaching the VHD file, the Disk Management console showed a 136.46 gigabyte (GB) partition mounted as Disk 2, and listed as the G:\ drive/volume, as illustrated in Figure 3.9.

Opening Windows Explorer, I could clearly see the files within in the G:\ volume; I confirmed this using the *dir* command to generate a file listing from the command prompt. The next step was to determine which VSCs were available, if any. To do this, I ran the following command from the command prompt:

```
vssadmin list shadows /for=g:
```

FIGURE 3.8

Windows 7 Disk Manager "Attach Virtual Hard Disk" dialog.

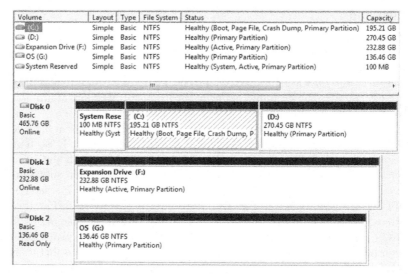

FIGURE 3.9

Disk Management console showing G:\ volume.

The output of this command indicated that there were a total of seven VSCs available in the image, with creation dates ranging from January 10, 2010 to January 20, 2010. I opted to mount the oldest VSC; to do so, I selected \\?\ *GLOBALROOT\Device\HarddiskVolumeShadowCopy23*, which appeared after "Shadow Copy Volume:" in the output of the above *vssadmin* command, and right-clicked to copy this string to the clipboard. I then returned to the command prompt and typed in the following command:

```
D:\>mklink /d d:\vsc23
```

After typing the above command, I right-clicked to paste the \\?\ GLOBALROOT... string that I'd copied to the clipboard at the end of the command, and then I made sure to add a closing "\" to the end of the command, and hit the Enter key. The result was that the symbolic link from the VSC to D:\vsc23 was successfully created.

TIP

Final Backslash

The final backslash at the end of the *mklink* command is critically important! Without it, you won't be able to access the mounted VSC properly.

At this point, I had the image file mounted as a VHD file, and the oldest VSC within the image also mounted and accessible from my analysis system (confirmed via the *dir* command). Using robocopy.exe (which is native to Windows 7) to preserve file metadata (time stamps), I copied the contents of a user's profile directory (albeit not the subdirectories) from both the mounted VHD file (the imaged Vista operating system partition) and the mounted VSC within the VHD file in order to run a quick comparison against the NTUSER.DAT files, and in particular the contents of the UserAssist key. I could have run RegRipper (specifically rip.pl or the "compiled" executable version of the tool, rip.exe) from the analysis system against the mounted VHD and VSC to obtain the information I was looking for, but copying the files gave me an excuse to run the *robocopy* command (until then, I hadn't ever used the command). To get information from the UserAssist keys from the two copied NTUSER.DAT hive files, I ran the following command:

```
C:\tools>rip.pl -r <path>\ntuser.dat -p userassist2>output.txt
```

Running the command against each hive file, redirecting the output to the appropriate text file, allowed me to then open the output files in an editor and compare them. From the NTUSER.DAT hive file from the oldest VSC within the image, I found the following entries:

```
Sat Jan 9 11:40:31 2010 Z
UEME_RUNPATH:C:\Program Files\iTunes\iTunes.exe (293)
Fri Jan 8 04:13:40 2010 Z
UEME_RUNPATH:Skype.lnk (5)
UEME_RUNPATH:C:\Program Files\Skype\Phone\Skype.exe (8)
```

Then, from the NTUSER.DAT hive file from the VHD image file itself, I found the following entries:

```
Thu Jan 21 03:10:26 2010 Z
UEME_RUNPATH:C:\Program Files\Skype\Phone\Skype.exe (14)
UEME_RUNPIDL:C:\Users\Public\Desktop\Skype.lnk (1)
Tue Jan 19 00:37:46 2010 Z
UEME_RUNPATH:C:\Program Files\iTunes\iTunes.exe (296)
```

What this clearly demonstrates is the changes that occur between various VSCs and the actual running system, as well as the forensic value of VSCs. As you can see from the above examples, in the space of 12 days, the user had run the Skype application six times, and in about 10 days, had run the iTunes application three times. As the UserAssist key records the date and time that the application was most recently run, all we would normally be able to determine from the image of the Vista was that as of January 21, 2010, the Skype application had been run a total of 14 times by the user. However, by accessing the VSCs, we're able to obtain historical information regarding previous times that the user had run the Skype application. This same concept applies to other Registry keys, as well, particularly those that maintain lists of subkeys and values. Specific keys that may be of interest during an examination may include "most recently used" or "MRU" lists; these keys usually contain a number of values, and the LastWrite time of the key corresponds to the date when the last file was accessed. However, we may be able to use data from hive files within VSCs to determine the dates and times when other files within the MRU list were accessed, as well. Being able to access this type of temporal information allows an analyst to infer certain things about a user's behavior on the system, particularly if (per this example) the fact that the user launched Skype six times in the space of approximately 12 days is pertinent to the goals of the examination (additional information regarding the user's activity could then be obtained from the application's log files). It should be clear from this that there is significantly more value to VSCs than simply previous versions of graphic image files.

TIP

Registry Analysis

A more detailed discussion of analysis of the Windows Registry hive files can be found in Chapter 5 of this book, as well as within *Windows Registry Forensics* [1].

Once I had completed all that I wanted to do (mostly just browsing), I removed the symbolic link that I'd created to the VSC using the following command:

```
D:\>rmdir d:\vsc23
```

As the symbolic link was created to a directory (i.e., *mklink /d*), I needed to treat the symbolic link as a directory in order to remove it (i.e., *rmdir* or *rd*). I then returned to the Disk Management console (see Figure 3.8), right-clicked on the "Disk 2" box to the left of the G:\ volume (displayed in the lower pane) and chose "Detach VHD" from the context menu.

TIP

Diskpart

The *diskpart* command (a reference for the command, albeit specifically for Windows XP, can be found online at http://support.microsoft.com/kb/300415) can be used to attach and detach VHD files from the command line. First, you need to simply type "diskpart" at the command prompt in order to being working in the diskpart shell. In order to attach a VHD file, use the following commands:

```
selectvdisk file=<path to VHD file>
attachvdisk
```

Using these commands, the VHD file is automatically mounted using the next available drive letter. In order to detach the VHD file, use the following command:

```
detachvdisk
```

In summary, the process you would follow to access VSCs using this method would be to:

- Convert a working copy of your image file to a VHD file using vhdtool.exe.
- Attach/mount the newly created VHD file to your Windows 7 analysis workstation, using either the Disk Management console, or diskpart.exe. Be sure to check the "Read-Only" box (see Figure 3.7) when mounting the VHD file.
- Determine how many VSCs you have available within the image, and for which dates, using vssadmin.exe (i.e., *vssadmin list shadows /for=n:*).
- Create a symbolic directory link to the VSC (or VSCs) of interest using mklink.exe (i.e., *mklink /d C:\mountpoint\\?\GLOBALROOT\Device\ HarddiskVolumeShadowCopyn*). Note: The trailing backslash in the *mklink* command is critically important!
- Perform whatever work is part of your analysis plan (i.e., copy files via robocopy, scan the mounted VSC with AV scanners)
- Remove the symbolic link with the *rmdir* command. When you've completed working with the VHD file itself, detach it via the Disk Management console or diskpart.exe.

I should note that mounting a working copy of your acquired image as a VHD file can be used for much more than accessing VSCs. For example, all of those tasks we mentioned performing against a mounted/linked VSC (scanning with AV, performing other malware detection steps, etc.) can be performed on just the mounted VHD file.

VMWare method

After I figured out how to access the VSCs within an acquired image via the VHD method, I began discussing this with others, and found out that folks like Rob Lee (of SANS and Mandiant fame) and Jimmy Weg (a law enforcement officer from Montana) have been using VMWare in a very similar manner to access VSCs. Discussing the VMWare method with both of them, I got an idea of the process that they used, and decided to try it on my own to see if I could get it to work. In order to work through this process you'll need the following:

- The ability to run a VMWare virtual machine, such as VMPlayer (freely available, and found online at http://www.vmware.com/products/player/) or VMWare Workstation (a 30-day evaluation version is available online from http://www.vmware.com). Using VMWare Workstation, you can create your own VMs.
- A Windows 7 VM (I used a 32-bit Windows 7 Ultimate VM for this demonstration).
- A copy of LiveView or ProDiscover Basic Edition (BE).

The first thing I did was downloadVMPlayer from the VMWare web site and get a copy of LiveView. Having only an image in raw/dd format, I needed a way to get the data within the image recognized as a disk or partition by the VMWare tools. LiveView provides that capability by generating a VMWare virtual machine disk format (.vmdk) file that points to the image; however, for this demonstration, I just wanted the vmdk file, and I didn't necessarily want to boot the VM.

TIP

ProDiscover

The ProDiscover forensic analysis application, from Technology Pathways, LLC, includes functionality for creating VMWare VMDK files (similar to LiveView). This functionality is included in the BE, a freely available version of the application. After you've installed ProDiscover BE, open the application, and under the Tools menu option, choose Image Conversion Tools and then "VMWare Support for "DD" Images…," as illustrated in Figure 3.10.

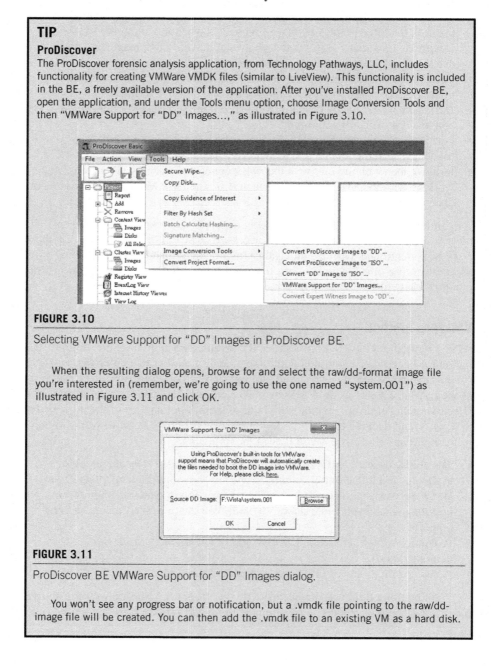

FIGURE 3.10

Selecting VMWare Support for "DD" Images in ProDiscover BE.

When the resulting dialog opens, browse for and select the raw/dd-format image file you're interested in (remember, we're going to use the one named "system.001") as illustrated in Figure 3.11 and click OK.

FIGURE 3.11

ProDiscover BE VMWare Support for "DD" Images dialog.

You won't see any progress bar or notification, but a .vmdk file pointing to the raw/dd-image file will be created. You can then add the .vmdk file to an existing VM as a hard disk.

Next, launch VMPlayer and select your VM, but do not start it; instead, edit the VM settings to add the newly created .vmdk file to the VM as an additional disk.

WARNING

Nonpersistent Disk

In the following section, we'll be adding an independent, nonpersistent disk to an existing VM via VMWare Workstation. The option to add a new hard disk that is nonpersistent is *not* available in VMPlayer, at least not at the time of this writing. As such, if you choose to use this method to access VSCs, you need to be sure to use a working copy of your image, or use other mechanisms to ensure that the image itself isn't modified.

When the Add Hardware Wizard opens and allows you to select a disk, choose "Use an existing virtual disk" and click Next, as illustrated in Figure 3.12.

In the "Select an Existing Disk" dialog, browse to the newly created .vmdk file (in our example, system.vmdk) and click Finish. At this point, if you get a message from VMPlayer (or Workstation) about converting the virtual disk format to a newer format, simply choose to keep the existing format. After you've added the new hard disk to the VM, boot it, log in, and open Windows Explorer to see the file system for the added disk. From here, you can view and access the VSCs using the same process we discussed previously in the chapter.

If you're using VMWare Workstation, when you get to the "Select an Existing Disk" dialog, you will be presented with some additional options, as illustrated in Figure 3.13.

When adding the new .vmdk file to as a hard disk to your VM, go to the Mode section of the dialog and select "Independent," and then "Nonpersistent." This will help ensure that any changes made to image file as a result of your analysis (or by

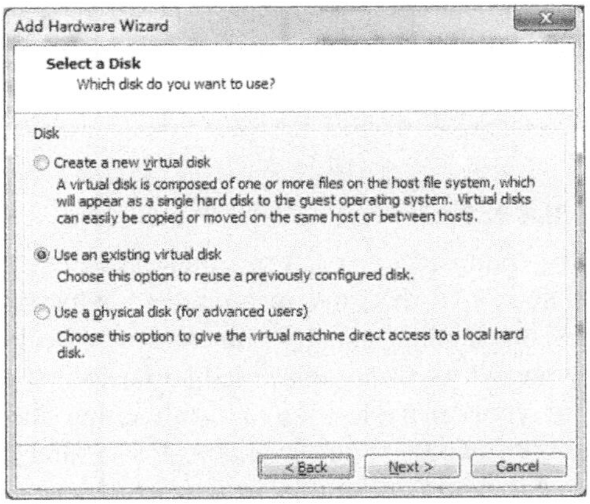

FIGURE 3.12

VMWare Workstation "Select a Disk" dialog.

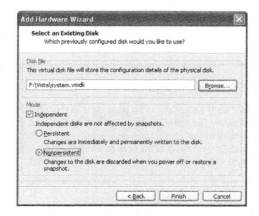

FIGURE 3.13

Adding an independent, nonpersistent disk.

the operating system) are not written to the image. This is simply an additional step you should take as part of sound analysis practices; you should already be working with a copy of your image, not the original image.

TIP

VMDKs and SIFT

I mentioned in Chapter 1 that I had used the SANS SIFT v2.0 Workstation VM that Rob Lee put together. I was working out the kinks in some ideas that I had and was going to try to access a raw/dd-format image of a Windows XP system, but this specific experiment required that I access the image as a .vmdk file. In short, I found that LiveView did a much better job of creating the necessary VMWare files for use with the SIFT Workstation than did ProDiscover BE. When I added the .vmdk file created via ProDiscover BE as an additional hard drive to the SIFT VM and ran the *fdisk* command, I got some very odd output. However, when I did the same thing, using the same image file, but using the VMWare files created through LiveView, everything worked just fine.

Automating VSC access

During conferences or training courses, I'm often asked by other analysts, "How can I fully exploit VSCs?" To that, my response is, "what do you want to do?", and that's where the conversation usually comes to a screeching halt. What does "fully exploit" really mean? As we've discussed so far in this chapter, once you've attached an image to your analysis system using either the VHD or VMWare method, you'll be able to access to the available VSCs, and from that point, you can use almost all of the techniques and processes that you already use to "fully exploit" the data available in the VSCs.

One way to collect information from available VSCs is to image the entire VSC. So, you have an image attached to your analysis workstation, and you can image an available VSC from the attached volume, using George M. Garner, Jr's Forensic Acquisition Utilities (found online at http://gmgsystemsinc.com/fau/). Download the archive and be sure to the use the appropriate version (32- or 64-bit) for your platform. You can then use the appropriate version of dd.exe to create a logical image of a VSC using the following command (substituting for the appropriate VSC number, of course):

```
C:\tools>dd.exe if=\\.\HarddiskVolumeShadowCopy20 of=D:\vsc20.img
-localwrt
```

One thing to consider about this method is that you will likely need a considerable amount of storage space. For a 70-GB volume, if there are nine VSCs, you will need a total of 700 GB of space; 70 GB for the original volume, and another 70 GB for each of the VSCs. This method for acquiring data from VSCs is resource-intensive, but there may be times when it is absolutely necessary. However, keep in mind that VSCs are not complete backups of the system at a point in time, and as such, acquiring an image of the entire VSC may be more effort than is required.

When it comes to accessing and collecting information from the VSCs, you can also use Windows native batch file functionality to automate a great deal of your data collection. Automation in this manner not only increases efficiency and reduces the chance of errors (i.e., typing the wrong command, or commands in the wrong sequence), but it's self-documenting, as well; simply keep a copy of the batch file (and any output) as your documentation. While we're discussing accessing VSCs within acquired images, you will see you can also use these same automation techniques to access VSCs on live remote systems, as discussed earlier in this chapter. Doing so will help you mitigate issues with the oldest VSCs being deleted through the normal function of the system while you're accessing it, as a batch file will run much quicker than typing all of the commands manually.

As we've discussed, once you've run the *vssadmin* command, you should see a list of the available VSCs in the output. You will see the list in the command prompt, or you can redirect the output of the command to a file and view the list that way. So let's say that you have four VSCs, listed as HarddiskVolumeShadowCopy20 through 23, and you'd like to run the same series of commands on each of these VSCs, in succession. You can do this using batch files, which is a capability native to Windows systems. For example, we can use the following command in a batch file (call it "vsc_sweep.bat," or something that you'd find meaningful) as the initial command that handles creating a symbolic link to each VSC:

```
for /l %i in (20,1,23) do mklink /d C:\vsc\vsc%i \\?\GLOBALROOT\
Device\HarddiskVolumeShadowCopy%i\
```

Once this command has completed, you should have four symbolic links created, C:\vsc\vsc20 through vsc23. At this point you can run through the directories, running whichever commands you choose. On April 13, 2010, a post to the "Forensics from the sausage factory" blog (http://forensicsfromthesausagefactory.blogspot.com) illustrated a command for using robocopy.exe to retrieve copies of specific files from the VSCs. That command, modified to work along with the previous command, looks as follows:

```
for %i in (20,1,23) do robocopyC:\vsc\vsc%i\Users C:\vsc_output\
vsc%i *.jpg *.txt /S /COPY:DAT /XJ /w:0 /r:0 /LOG: C:\vsc_output\
Robocopy_log_SC%i.txt
```

This command copies (via robocopy.exe) all of the files that end with .jpg and .txt extensions from the user profiles within the VSCs to a specific directory on the analysis computer, and logs the activity. As such, a copy of robocopy.exe must be located in the same directory as the batch file, and you should make sure that the C:\vsc_output directory exists before running the commands.

After you're done accessing the VSCs, you can remove the symbolic links using the following command:

```
for /l %i in (20,1,23) do rmdir C:\vsc\vsc%i
```

In April 2011, Corey Harrell (author of the "Journey into IR" blog at http://journeyintoir.blogspot.com) contacted me with the interesting idea of running RegRipper (more specifically, rip.exe) against successive VSCs in order to collect specific information. Using "&&" to append commands together in a single line in a batch file, Corey's idea was to collect information (Corey's original submission made use of recentdocs.pl RegRipper plugin) from a specific user's NTUSER.DAT hive file. The specific command (modified for use in this example) that Corey had put together was as follows:

```
for /l %i in (20,1,23) do (echo ----------------------
----------------- » output-file.txt && echo Processing
HarddiskVolumeShadowCopy%i» output-file.txt && C:\tools\
rip.exe -r c:\vsc\vsc%i\Users\user-profile\NTUSER.dat -p
userassist2»userassist.txt)
```

The batch file and various commands that we've discussed here are just a few simple examples of what you can do using batch file functionality that is native to Windows systems.

TIP

Batch Files

There are a number of very useful resources available online that provide references for batch file commands, such as http://www.computerhope.com/batch.htm and http://ss64.com/nt/. You can also find tutorials, such as http://commandwindows.com/batch.htm, that will assist you in writing batch files.

Corey also created a more comprehensive and functional batch file, which he graciously consented to allowing me to include in the additional materials associated with this book. The batch file is named "rip-vsc.txt" and can be found in the associated materials associated with this book (which can be found online at http://windowsir.blogspot.com/p/books.html). Corey spent some time in documenting and explaining the use of the batch file, by adding comments (lines that begin with "REM") to the file.

Internet Evidence Finder version 4 (available online at http://www.jadsoftware.com/go/?page_id=141) is a software application that can search files or hard drives for indications of a wide range of Internet-related artifacts, including Facebook, MySpace, mIRC, and Google chat, web-based emails, etc. The web page for IEF4 states that the application can also be used to search mounted VSCs.

ProDiscover

On March 3, 2011, Christopher Brown released version 6.9.0.0 of ProDiscover (all versions, including the BE). I've had a license for ProDiscover IR Edition since version 3, for which I'm very grateful to Chris. Over the years, I've had the privilege of watching the evolution of this product and used it to analyze a number of images. The latest update (as of this writing) provides access to VSCs, which (as we've discussed) can be extremely valuable to the examiner. I should note that in September 2011, Christopher released version 7.0.0.3 of ProDiscover.

To demonstrate accessing VSCs via ProDiscover IR, I have the application installed on a Windows XP SP3 system, and I have an image of a hard drive from a Dell laptop running Vista. First, I opened ProDiscover and created a new project, and then added the image of the hard drive to the project. Once the image was added (and I saved the project file), I clicked on the image file listing in the Content View to see the context menu illustrated in Figure 3.14.

Then, I clicked on "Mount Shadow Volume…" in the context menu and saw the "Mount Shadow Volume" dialog box illustrated in Figure 3.15.

As you can see in Figure 3.15, the mounted image has four partitions available, which, for those familiar with systems from Dell, is fairly common for default installations (when I purchase Dell systems for myself, the first thing

FIGURE 3.14

ProDiscover Mount Shadow Volume… functionality.

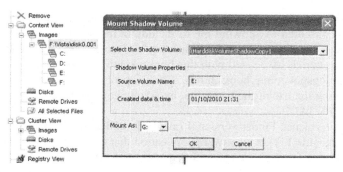

FIGURE 3.15

ProDiscover Mount Shadow Volume dialog.

FIGURE 3.16

VSC mounted in ProDiscover.

I do is completely reinstall the operating system) as they include, at the minimum, a Dell maintenance partition. Once the "Mount Shadow Volume…" functionality was selected, ProDiscover located the volume where the VSCs reside (in this case, E:\) and populated a drop-down list with the available VSCs. There are a total of seven VSCs available, and as we progress through the VSCs in the drop-down list, the "Created date & time" will change to reflect the correct date and time for the selected VSC. Finally, whichever VSC was selected will be added to the "Content View" display as the G:\ volume (note that C:\ through F:\ are already populated).

When I clicked "Okay," the selected VSC was mounted as the G:\ volume within the ProDiscover Content View interface. I then clicked on the volume letter, and the files were populated within the volume, as illustrated in Figure 3.16.

At this point, there's a great deal I can do with the available data in the VSCs. For example, I can navigate to the Users folder and select files to be copied out of the project for deeper examination, run ProScripts, etc. It all happened within the blink of an eye, right there while I was sitting in front of my analysis system. Along with the other functionality inherent to ProDiscover (parsing Vista and Windows 7 Recycle Bin files, locating and parsing email archives, etc.), being able to mount and access the VSCs puts a whole new level of capabilities in the hands of the analyst.

TIP

Other Image File Formats

Throughout this chapter so far we've discussed accessing VSCs with raw/dd-format image files. As such, I'm sure that at some point someone's going to ask, "...but I have an EnCase.EOx format image file, and it's compressed ... what do I do?" or "I have a snapshot of a VMWare virtual machine/vmdk file, how can I use the VHD method?" Those questions are easy to answer. For the expert witness format images (such as acquired via EnCase), you can open the image in FTK Imager and reacquire it to raw/dd format, making yourself a working copy of the image file. You can do the same thing with the vmdk file and then use vhdtool.exe to prepare the image for mounting, or search for tools to convert the vmdk file to vhd file format.

Windows 8

Throughout this chapter, we discussed VSCs from the perspective of Windows Vista and Windows 7, and what we've discussed also applies to Windows 2008 R2. But, as I've been asked numerous times, what about Windows 8?

Windows 8 appears to take a bit of a different approach to VSCs than Vista and Windows 7. I say this because while I've been working on writing and updating this edition, I have a Windows 8 system on which I can try the various techniques and tools discussed in this chapter and see how they work. I started by logging into my Windows 8 system, launching a command prompt with administrator privileges, and running the "vssadmin" command to list the available VSCs, and found that there were several listed (numbered 3 through 6) in the output of the command. I then launched FTK Imager on the system, added the C:\ volume as an evidence item, and found four difference files in the "System Volume Information" folder.

My next step was to use FTK Imager to acquire an image of the C:\ volume, and then use vhdtool.exe to convert the image file to VHD format (as described early in this chapter, this process simply adds a footer to the image file, without changing the extension). When I attempted to attach the newly created VHD to my Windows 7 analysis system, it was accessible as the G:\ volume, but I received a message stating that the volume would need to be formatted before it could be used. When I attempted to attach the VHD on the Windows 8 system, I received an error message stating "A virtual disk support provider for the specified file was not found." However, changing the file extension from ".001" to ".vhd" allowed the image file to be mounted as a read-only volume, in accordance with the VHD method procedure described earlier in this chapter.

Once the VHD was mounted as the H:\ volume, I was able to run the "vssadmin list shadows /for=h:" command to obtain a list of available VSCs within the image. I then used the *mlink* command to create a symbolic link from the oldest available VSC (do not forget the trailing slash!!) to a folder on the D:\ volume for my system. From that point, I was able to access the logical files within the VSC, and having demonstrated that, I used the *rmdir* command to remove the symbolic link.

TIP

VHD File Extension

When mounting an acquired image as a VHD on a Windows 8 system, be sure to change the file extension to ".vhd" after using vhdtool.exe to convert the raw/dd-format image file to a VHD format.

For the sake of simply being complete, I ran additional tests and attempted to access VSCs within a Windows 7 image from the Windows 8 analysis system, via the VHD method discussed in this chapter. Again, as long as I changed the file extension to ".vhd" after I ran the vhdtool.exe command to convert the image file, everything worked just fine, and I was able to list and access the VSCs available within the Windows 7 image.

SUMMARY

While VSCs may initially be somewhat mysterious to many analysts, they do provide a very valuable resource with respect to historical data. VSCs can be accessed via a number of methods, depending upon how you're accessing them (i.e., on a live system or within an acquired image).

Keep in mind, however, that accessing VSCs on live systems can be a bit tricky, in that you have to move quickly and decisively, as VSCs are subject to the FIFO cycle, and you may be attempting gather information from a VSC that gets deleted during that process.

Finally, remember to be extremely careful with respect to how you access files within VSCs, both on live systems and within acquired images, as double-clicking the wrong file can lead to your analysis system being infected or compromised.

Reference

[1]   Carvey H. Windows registry forensics. Burlington, MA: Syngress Publishing, Inc.; 2011.

File Analysis

CHAPTER OUTLINE

INFORMATION IN THIS CHAPTER

- MFT
- Event Logs
- Recycle Bin
- Prefetch Files
- Scheduled Tasks
- Jump Lists
- Hibernation Files
- Application Files

INTRODUCTION

As with any computer system, Windows systems contain a great number of files, many of which are not simply a standard, ASCII text format. Many of these files may not have any relevance to the analysis at all, and only a few may provide critical information to the analyst. There also may be a number of files that are unknown to the analyst, and due to their format, may not result in hits from keyword searches. These files can often provide an analyst with a great deal of insight into their examination, if they know that the files exist, if they understand the underlying data structures within the binary contents of the files and how to interpret and analyze them.

The purpose of this chapter is not to reiterate analysis techniques that have been discussed in detail in other resources. Instead, I'd like to discuss the existence of a number of files and artifacts, as well as analysis techniques that may be of value with respect to these files, that haven't been widely discussed in other venues.

As I mentioned, Windows systems contain a number of files of various formats. These files can also contain data consisting of or embedded in various structures, some of which are well documented, while others have been discovered through analysis. Many analysts start their examinations by running keyword searches in order to identify likely sources of information, but there are a number of files that may provide critical information related to these keywords even though they don't return any search hits.

Many times, the structure where the data exists within a file adds relevance or provides context to that data. For example, during a data breach investigation, I got several hits for potential credit card numbers within a Registry hive file (Registry analysis is discussed in detail in Chapter 5). Further analysis indicated that the credit card numbers were neither key names nor value data; instead, they were located in the unallocated space within the hive file. It turned out that the numbers detected in the search had been in sectors on the disk that had previously been part of another file, which had been deleted. As such, the sectors had been marked as available for use, and several of those sectors had been incorporated into the hive file as it grew in size (Registry hives "grow" 4 kilobytes at a time). What this demonstrates is that analysis must (and can) go beyond simply running a search, and it's critical that it actually does, in order to answer some very important questions. For example, consider the finding I just discussed: Would "I found credit card numbers in the Registry" really provide any value to the customer? Or would it be more important to develop an understanding of where those credit card numbers were found and how they got there? Understanding the structures of various files, and the value that understanding can provide, will be the focus of this chapter.

MFT

Within the NTFS file system, the master file table (MFT) serves as the master list of files and contains metadata regarding every file object on the system, including files, directories, and metafiles. This metadata can be extremely valuable during an examination, particularly if you suspect that file metadata has been manipulated in an effort to hide or mask activities (commonly referred to as "anti-forensics").

This chapter will not be a comprehensive treatise covering the complete structure of the MFT. Rather, we will focus on specific data structures (or "attributes") that can be extracted from MFT entries and limit our discussion to a brief description of MFT entries and two specific attributes. Further, while we will be discussing various tools that you can use to parse the MFT, we won't be doing so to the depth that you would expect to be able to write your own such tools from scratch. Perhaps the best source for additional, detailed information regarding the MFT, the structure of MFT entry attributes, and the forensic analysis of file systems in general is Brian Carrier's book, *File System Forensic Analysis* [1].

Each file and directory (folder) on a Windows system has a record in the MFT. Each record is 1024 bytes in length. As NTFS views each file as a set of attributes, the file's MFT record contains some number of attributes which hold metadata about the file or, in some cases, the file data (content) itself. The first 42 bytes of each record comprise the File Record Header, which provides information such as the link count (how many directories have entries for this file, which helps determine the number of hard links for the file); whether the record is for a file or directory; whether the file or directory is in use or deleted; and the allocated and used size of the file.

All file and directory records will have a $STANDARD_INFORMATION attribute ($SIA) which is 72 bytes in length (for Windows 2000 and later systems) and contains (among other things) a set of time stamps. These time stamps are 64-bit FILETIME objects, as defined by Microsoft, which represent the number of 100-nanosecond intervals since January 1, 1601. These time stamps are what we most often "see" when interacting with the system (via the command prompt when using the "dir" command, or via the Windows Explorer shell), and are written into the MFT record in Universal Coordinated Time (UTC) format on NTFS systems; this means that when we see these time stamps through Windows Explorer (or via the "dir" command at the command prompt), they are translated for display to the user in accordance with the time zone information stored in the Registry for that system.

NOTE

Displaying Time Stamps in Forensic Analysis Applications

Most commercial forensic analysis applications have the ability to display file MAC time stamps in accordance with the time zone settings on the analyst's system, although this functionality can be disabled. In ProDiscover Incident Response Edition, that setting can be found by clicking the File menu option, and choosing the Preferences option, which opens the Preferences dialog, as illustrated in Figure 4.1.

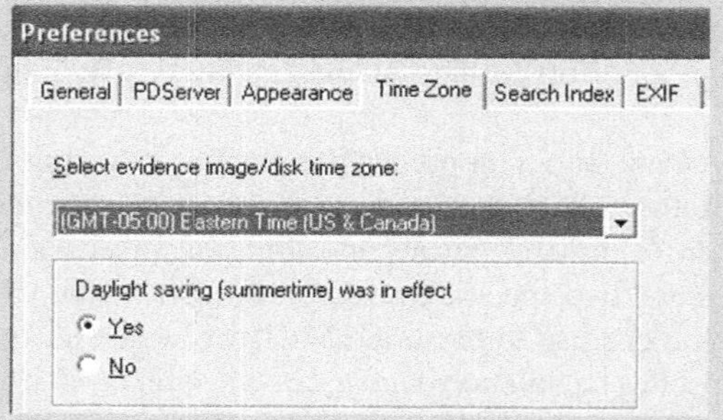

FIGURE 4.1

ProDiscover time zone settings.

The time stamps that are stored within the $SIA attribute are the last modified time, the last accessed time, the MFT entry modified (changed) time, and the creation ("born") time, and are referred to collectively as the "MACB" times, where each letter corresponds to each of the time stamps, respectively. Another way of referring to these times is "MACE times" (for file *m*odified, file *a*ccessed, file *cre*ated, and MFT *e*ntry modified); note that the last two times (MFT entry modified and file creation times) are transposed, with respect to the MACB format. For consistency, we will refer to these times as "MACB" times throughout the rest of this chapter. These time stamps are modified and updated during the course of normal operating system activity; for example, when a file is created, the time stamps are set to the current date and time. Whenever a change is made to the file itself (data is added, modified, or removed by the user or a service), the last modification time is updated. As we'll see in the "Last Access Time" sidebar, modification to this time stamp is subject to a couple of conditions.

WARNING

Last Access Time

Most analysts think that when a file is opened or accessed in some other way, the last access time for that file (in the $SIA attribute in the MFT) is modified to reflect the appropriate time. However, the last accessed time for a file on the NTFS file system on the hard drive is not always current. NTFS delays writing the updated last accessed time to disk for performance reasons, although the correct time is maintained in memory. Windows will update the value on disk once the time differs from the value in memory by an hour or more (I am referencing http://www.microsoft.com/resources/documentation/windows/xp/all/proddocs/en-us/fsutil_behavior.mspx?mfr=true).

In addition, there is a Registry value within the System hive file (i.e., *ControlSet00x\Control\FileSystem\NtfsDisableLastAccessUpdate*) that, when set to "1," disables updating of last access times. On Windows XP and 2003 systems, this Registry value does not normally exist in a default installation; however, the value can be added and set to "1," which is recommended to improve the performance of high-volume file servers. There are a number of online sources that are available that provide instructions for setting this value via the *fstuil* utility. As of Vista (and continuing to Windows 7 and 8), this value exists and is set to "1." This does not mean, however, that the last access times on files on these systems are never updated; in fact, file creation, move, or copy can cause this time to be modified; what it affects is "normal" user file accesses such as opening and viewing the file.

In addition, every file within the NTFS file system will have at least one $FILE_NAME ($FNA) attribute in its MFT record. This attribute contains 66 bytes of file metadata, plus the file name itself. An MFT record for a file can have more than one $FNA attribute, as the file system may require that for files with long file names, there is also a DOS 8.3 format name (this can be disabled via a Registry value). This simply means that if you have a file named "This is a long file named file. doc," there will also be an $FNA attribute containing the name "this_i~1.doc," which consists of eight characters, the dot separator, and the three-character extension. As such, this file would have a $SIA and two $FNA attributes. In addition to the file name, the metadata contained in the $FNA attribute includes a reference to the parent directory (which allows tools to completely reconstruct the full path to the file), as well as four time stamps, similar to and in the same format as those within the $SIA attribute. The primary difference with the $FNA time stamps is that Windows systems do not typically update these values in the same way as those in the $SIA attribute; rather, the $FNA times correspond to the original date for when the file was created, moved, or renamed. As such, accessing the MFT, parsing the various attributes for the specific files, and noting any anomalies between the $SIA and $FNA values is a technique that analysts use to determine the likelihood of the $SIA time stamps being purposely modified in an attempt to disguise the file.

MFT records will also contain several $DATA attributes. The $DATA attributes may contain the contents of the file itself, if the fie is resident. Some sources indicate that if the file is around 700 bytes in size or so, for systems with MFT records that are 1024 bytes in size, the file will be resident. In my own limited testing of such systems, I've found resident files up to 744 bytes in length. This can be very valuable, as these small files may be DOS batch files (often used to automate tasks by attackers), configuration files, or some other remnants left by an attacker or even a user. If an attacker deletes the file and you're able to acquire a copy of the MFT before the record is reused, you can retrieve the contents of the file. Another aspect to consider is if the file itself grows to the point where it becomes nonresident; the MFT record may contain "attribute slack," in that as the $DATA attribute becomes populated with the data runs that point to sectors on disk, the remaining available space that once contained the file contents may not be overwritten. As such, generating a hex dump of the record will clearly show some portion of the previously resident file contents. On systems where the MFT records are larger than 1024 bytes, such as 4096 bytes in size, there would be considerably more resident data available. On March 20, 2013, Kyle Oetken published an article on the Trace Evidence blog (found online at http://traceevidence.blogspot.com/2013/03/a-quick-look-at-mft-resident-data-on.html), in which he demonstrated the results of his own testing and clearly showed that the larger MFT records were able to hold considerable my resident data.

$DATA attributes can also refer to alternate data streams (ADSs). Working closely with MFT records, all of those things that analysts know about ADSs become abundantly clear, particularly how they don't have their own time stamps.

The MFT record attributes that we've discussed up to this point are not the only ones available. There are several others, but it is beyond the scope of this book to describe in detail the other attributes. One final attribute that I will discuss very briefly is the "extended attribute," or $EA. Much as the functionality that allows for ADSs was intended for compatibility with the Macintosh Hierarchal File System (HFS, which uses resource forks), the $EA attributes were intended for compatibility with the OS/2 High-Performance File System, and it really doesn't have a great use unless you have OS/2 systems in your environment. Midway through 2012, a variant of the ZeroAccess malware was found to be crafted to store its payload (a DLL file) in the $EA attribute of an MFT record; Corey Harrell discussed this in an article on his blog, which can be found online at http://journeyintoir.blogspot.com/2012/12/extracting-zeroaccess-from-ntfs.html. As such, a technique that can be used to look for malware that uses this technique is to scan the MFT and report any records that contain an $EA record (the $EA attribute type is 224 in decimal format, 0xE0 in hex format). Corey includes a means for not only locating $EA attributes within MFT records in his blog article, but also a technique (using free tools) to extract the information stored within those attributes.

There are several free, open source tools available that can be easily retrieved from the Internet that will allow us to extract the $SIA and $FNA attributes from the MFT. One such tool is David Kovar's Python script named "analyzeMFT.py" (information about this script is available online at http://www.integriography.com/, and the code is available on GitHub at https://github.com/dkovar/analyzeMFT/). David originally created analyzeMFT.py as a Python script, and then Matt Sabourin created an objected-oriented version of the script, allowing the functionality to be accessed by other scripts.

I've also written my own tools (i.e., Perl scripts) for parsing the time stamps (and other information) for files and directories listed in the MFT. This Perl script is included with the materials provided in association with this book and provides a good framework from which I've been able to write other Perl scripts, with additional functionality. As you'll see later in this chapter, the script displays information from the MFT File Entry Header, as well as the $SIA and $FNA attributes in an easy-to-view format.

TZWorks provides a tool called *ntfswalk* (found online at https://www.tzworks.net/prototype_page.php?proto_id=12) that allows the analyst to access the MFT records for a given volume, filter those records, and display various statistics about the records. The use of this tool requires that the analyst mount an acquired image, which can be done quite easily using methods such as those described in Chapter 3.

TIP

Accessing the MFT

Just accessing the MFT can prove to be a challenge for the analyst, or at the very least, cumbersome. You may not want to mount the acquired image, as it may instead simply be easier to retrieve the MFT and parse it. There is an excellent blog post available online at http://epyxforensics.com/node/43 that describes how to use the Sleuthkit tools *mmls* and *icat* to extract the MFT from an acquired image, and parse it with analyzeMFT, on Ubuntu Linux. I used the technique described in the blog post to extract the MFT, on Windows 7. I first ran the following command against a physical image acquired from a Windows system:

```
D:\Tools\tsk > mmls -t dos -i raw f:\win7.001
```

Once I had the offset to the partition I was interested in, I then ran the following command:

```
D:\Tools\tsk > icat -o 2048f:\win7.001 0 > d:\case\win7\MFT.raw
```

The result was that a copy of the MFT from the first partition in the acquired image was extracted from the image and placed in my case folder.

When analyzing the information derived from the MFT, it is important to keep in mind that other user actions (besides simply reading from or writing to a file) can have an effect on the file time stamps within the $SIA entry, as well, and several are described in Microsoft KnowledgeBase (KB) article 299648 (found online at http://support.microsoft.com/?kbid=299648). For example, copying or moving a file between directories within an NTFS partition retains the last modification date on the file, but the copy operation will reset the creation date to the current date, whereas the move operation retains the original creation date of the file. Refer to the KB article for details, but keep in mind that when transferring files, whether or not time stamps are updated (and which time stamps are actually updated) depends on a number of factors, including whether the file is being copied or moved, and whether it is being transferred to a different location within the same drive partition, or from one partition to another.

NOTE

Testing

I have yet to find any clear, thorough documentation regarding how file time stamps are affected by all possible operations; as such, analysts should always test their hypotheses when faced with unusual conditions or situations. For example, if you suspect that a file was copied from a FAT32-formatted USB thumb drive to an NTFS partition, how would you expect the time stamps for both (the original and copied) files to appear? How about a file copied between NTFS shares? It is always a good idea to simulate the conditions of your hypothesis as best as possible and run your own tests for verification.

Not only do the aforementioned actions affect the time stamps in the $SIA attribute, but these values (within the $SIA) can be manipulated arbitrarily, as well. Essentially, if a user has write access to a file, they can modify the time stamps of that file to arbitrary values, and those modifications are written to the time stamps in the $SIA attribute (technically, per http://msdn.microsoft.com/en-us/library/cc781134, these are also written to the directory entry). This is an anti-forensic technique that is often referred to as "time stomping," named for a tool used to perform this function, which allowed the user of that tool to set the time stamps to arbitrary times (at the time of this writing, the graphical version of timestomp.exe is available online at http://sourceforge.net/projects/timestomp-gui/files/Windows/). Consider the effect on an investigation of finding illegal images on a system confiscated in 2011, only to find that the files had creation dates in 2014 and last access dates in 1984. Even one or two files with time stamps similar to this would be enough to cast doubt on other files. One of the drawbacks of using timestomp.exe, however, was that the application reportedly had a resolution of 32 bits for the times, leaving the upper 32 bits of the 64-bit FILETIME object all zeros. This makes the use of this technique relatively easy to detect.

Another technique for modifying time stamps on files is copying the time values from another file, particularly one that was part of the original Windows installation, such as kernel32.dll (found in the *C:\Windows\system32* directory). This technique avoids the resolution issue faced by timestomp.exe, does a better job of hiding the file from analysis techniques (see Chapter 7), and is easily accessible via native application programming interface (API) functions.

NOTE

Time Stomping

As I mentioned, while I was writing this chapter, I was not able to find a copy of timestomp.exe; however, using Perl, I can easily modify file time stamps by copying time stamps from another file on the system. After installing ActiveState's ActivePerl, I then installed the Win32API::File::Time Perl module using the following command:

```
C:\Perl > ppm install win32api-file-time
```

Once the module was installed, I could use this module to access two specific native Windows API functions, using the following lines of code (excerpted from the Perl script):

```
my ($atime, $mtime, $ctime) = GetFileTime ($file);
SetFileTime ($file2, $atime, $mtime, $ctime);
```

In order to demonstrate this functionality, I added a couple of checks for file time stamps using the Perl *stat()* function to the script, ran it against file (C:\temp\test.txt), copying the time stamps from kernel32.dll. The output of the script appeared as follows:

```
C:\Windows\system32\kernel32.dll
Creation Time: Tue Feb 28 08:00:00 2006
Last Access: Mon May 30 21:14:22 2011
Last Write: Sat Mar 21 10:06:58 2009
```

```
C:\Temp\test.txt
Creation Time: Mon May 30 17:36:12 2011
Last Access: Mon May 30 17:36:12 2011
Last Write: Mon May 30 17:36:12 2011
C:\Temp\test.txt
Creation Time: Tue Feb 28 08:00:00 2006
Last Access: Mon May 30 21:14:22 2011
Last Write: Sat Mar 21 10:06:58 2009
```

The script first displays the output of the Perl *stat()* function for the file kernel32.
dll (all times are displayed in local system time, and my system is set to Eastern
Standard Time with daylight savings), as well as the current settings for the target file,
test.txt. After changing the time stamps on the target file, it then displays the new time
values. As you can see, the last accessed time for kernel32.dll was modified when the
script was run (the Perl script was run on a Windows XP SP3 system), and the time
stamps on the test.txt file were modified in accordance with the time stamps copied
from kernel32.dll.

In order to verify this information, I extracted the MFT from the system (using FTK
Imager) and extracted the information using mft.pl; the information for the test.txt file
appears as follows (times are displayed in UTC or "Zulu" format):

```
70319 FILE Seq: 15 Link: 1 0×38 3 Flags: 1
0×0010 96 0 0×0000 0×0000
M: Sat Mar 21 14:06:57 2009 Z
A: Tue May 31 01:14:22 2011 Z
C: Tue May 31 01:14:23 2011 Z
B: Tue Feb 28 11:59:59 2006 Z
0×0030 112 0 0×0000 0×0000

FN: test.txt Parent Ref: 67947 Parent Seq: 49
M: Mon May 30 21:36:12 2011 Z
A: Mon May 30 21:36:12 2011 Z
C: Mon May 30 21:36:12 2011 Z
B: Mon May 30 21:36:12 2011 Z
0×0080 48 0 0×0000 0×0018
```

The first set of "MACB" time stamps were extracted from the $SIA attribute, and
the second set were extracted from the $FNA attribute. As you can see, the time stamps
extracted from the $SIA attribute reflect what was seen using the Perl *stat()* function
(taking the time zone settings into account), while the time stamps from the $FNA attribute
reflect the original times.

Extracting the $SIA and $FNA time stamps for comparison and analysis is
only one example of how understanding the MFT can be beneficial to an analyst.
Understanding additional elements of the MFT, as well as the structure of each
individual MFT record, can provide additional details with respect to the status of
various files.

File system tunneling

Another aspect of Windows file systems that can affect the time stamps that you observe during your analysis (and isn't often discussed) is file system tunneling. This process applies to both FAT and NTFS file systems and is described in Microsoft KB article 172190 (found online at http://support.microsoft.com/kb/172190). "File system tunneling" refers to the fact that within a specific time period (the default is 15 seconds) after a file is deleted, file table records (FAT or MFT) will be reused for files of the same name. In short, if you have a file named "myfile.txt" that is deleted or renamed, and a new file of the same name is created shortly after the deletion or rename operation, then the file table record is reused, and the original file's creation date is retained. According to KB article 172190, this "tunneling" functionality is meant to maintain backward compatibility with older 16-bit Windows applications that perform "safe save" operations.

To demonstrate file system tunneling, I created a text file named "test3.txt" on my Windows XP SP3 system that is 31 bytes in size and waited few days. Using the Perl *stat()* function, the $SIA time stamps appear as follows, in UTC format:

```
c:\temp\test3.txt 31 bytes
Creation Time: Mon May 30 21:41:48 2011 UTC
Last Access: Mon May 30 21:41:48 2011 UTC
Last Write: Mon May 30 21:41:48 2011 UTC
```

I then deleted test3.txt and immediately (within 15 seconds) recreated the file using the *echo* command (i.e., *echo "A tunnel test" > test3.txt*) at the command prompt. The new version of test3.txt is 18 bytes in size, and the time stamps appear as follows (again, in UTC format):

```
c:\temp\test3.txt 18 bytes
Creation Time: Mon May 30 21:41:48 2011 UTC
Last Access: Fri Jun 3 20:39:18 2011 UTC
Last Write: Fri Jun 3 20:39:18 2011 UTC
```

As you can see, the creation date of the new file remains the same as the original test3.txt, even though the new file was "created" on June 3, 2011. Using FTK Imager, I then exported the MFT and parsed it with the mft.pl Perl script; the $SIA and $FNA information for the test3.txt file appears as follows:

```
39630 FILE Seq: 60 Link: 1 0x38 3 Flags: 1
0x0010 96 0 0x0000 0x0000
M: Fri Jun 3 20:39:18 2011 Z
A: Fri Jun 3 20:39:18 2011 Z
C: Fri Jun 3 20:39:18 2011 Z
B: Mon May 30 21:41:48 2011 Z
0x0030 112 0 0x0000 0x0000
FN: test3.txt Parent Ref: 67947 Parent Seq: 49
M: Fri Jun 3 20:39:18 2011 Z
A: Fri Jun 3 20:39:18 2011 Z
C: Fri Jun 3 20:39:18 2011 Z
B: Mon May 30 21:41:48 2011 Z
```

As you can see from the above excerpt from the MFT, the "born" or creation dates in both the $SIA and $FNA attributes remain the same as the original file, but all other time stamps are updated to the current date and time, with respect to the file creation. Remember, all I did was create the file (from the command line)—I didn't access (open) or modify the file in any way after creating it.

More than anything else, I've found the information discussed thus far to be very useful in establishing when files were really created on a compromised system. By comparing the creation dates from the $SIA and $FN attributes for suspicious files, I've often found clear indications of attempts to hide the existence of those files from detection and closer inspection. This will become a bit clearer when we discuss timeline analysis in Chapter 7.

NOTE

NTFS $I30 Index Attributes

On September 26, 2011, Chad Tilbury, a SANS instructor, posted an entry to his blog titled "NTFS $I30 Index Attributes" (the blog post can be found online at http://forensicmethods.com/ntfs-index-attribute and had originally been posted to the SANS Forensic Blog). Chad does an excellent job of describing the index attributes, how they can be used to identify the names of deleted files, and how they can be parsed. Many times during incidents malware files may be deleted, often through actions taken by an intruder, or inadvertently by an administrator or responder. Index attributes may provide indications of the deleted files, including time stamps associated with those files; as Chad points out, the time stamps are similar to those found in the $FILE_NAME attribute of an MFT record. Chad also demonstrates the use of Willi Ballenthin's indxparse.py Python script for parsing index attributes. Willi's discussion of the indxparse.py script can be found online at http://www.williballenthin.com/forensics/indx/index.html.

TriForce

Early in 2013 (very early, in fact, on January 4), David Cowen described, via his blog, a means of analyzing several NTFS artifacts together that he refers to as the "TriForce"; he uses "tri," as this technique involves the MFT, the $LogFile, and the USN Change Journal ($USNJrnl). The $LogFile is an NTFS metadata file that is used by Windows to restore metadata consistency after a system failure. From David's blog post, the $LogFile "...*contains the before and afters or undo/redo for each change to the MFT. It contains the full entry of what is being changed (File records, $STDINFO blocks, etc...) and the metadata contained within them (with the exception of resident files on windows 7 journals whose contents appear to be nulled out). The $logfile is great for getting a very granular level exactly what changes have occurred to a file system.*" The update sequence number (USN) change journal maintains a persistent log of all changes made to files within a volume. David's TriForce analysis technique takes advantage of the fact that the individual records within the three files examined all contain elements that can be used to relate the artifacts to one another. In fact, this very likely isn't too different from what the NTFS file system does itself, when it needs to, and is simply being applied to digital forensic analysis. David's blog post can be found online at http://hackingexposedcomputerforensicsblog.blogspot.com/2013/01/happy-new-year-new-post-ntfs-forensic.html. Be sure to also read the article that David posted three days later (January 7) that goes much deeper into describing the various artifacts used by TriForce, and how they can be correlated.

NOTE

TriForce, Patent Pending

As of this writing, David Cowen has submitted the TriForce technique for a patent, so technically it's patent pending. David's blog post announcing this can be found online at http://hackingexposedcomputerforensicsblog.blogspot.com/2013/08/daily-blog-53-triforce-is-now-patent.html.

Event logs

Windows systems are capable of recording a number of different events in the Event Log, depending upon the audit configuration (we will discuss in Chapter 5 how to determine the audit configuration). The Event Log files on Windows 2000, XP, and 2003 systems are made up of event records that are stored in a well-documented binary format (which can be found online at http://msdn.microsoft.com/en-us/library/aa363646(v=VS.85).aspx). Part of this format includes a "magic number" that is unique to individual event records (including the header record, which contains information about the Event Log file itself), as illustrated in Figure 4.2.

As illustrated in Figure 4.2, the "LfLe" "magic number" can be used to identify event records within the Event Log file. The 4 bytes immediately prior to the event record (0xE0 in Figure 4.2) tell us the size of the event record in bytes. This information is not only useful in parsing through the Event Log file on a binary level, extracting each record in turn (and writing tools to help us do this), but it can also

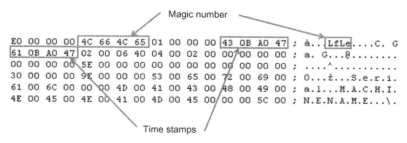

FIGURE 4.2

Partial Windows XP event record format.

be used to extract event records from relatively unstructured data, such as unallocated space (or the page file), which will be described later in this section.

Many analysts have discovered that when extracting Event Log files from an acquired image and opening them in the Event Viewer on their analysis system, they will often encounter a message stating that the Event Log is "corrupt." This is usually not due to the Event Log files actually being corrupted, but instead is often due to the fact that some message dynamic linked library (DLL) files may not be available on the analysis system. As such, I've written several tools to assist me collecting information pertinent to my analysis from Event Log files. The first is the Perl script evtrpt.pl, which collects information about the event records, such as the frequency of events based on event sources and identifiers (IDs), an excerpt of which, from an Application Event Log, appears as follows:

```
Source                  Event ID      Count
------------------      --------      -----
SecurityCenter          1800          2
SecurityCenter          1807          192
Symantec AntiVirus      12            17
Symantec AntiVirus      14            17
Symantec AntiVirus      16            12
Symantec AntiVirus      53            3
```

This information is a quick way to determine the type and number of the various event records within the Event Log, based on event sources and IDs. This is a great way of providing an overview of the Event Log content, and whether or not I can expect to find any records of value to my analysis. Having this information available has let me see some things very quickly. For example, if I'm working a malware detection issue and see that there are several event records with the source "Symantec AntiVirus" (or for another antivirus (AV) product, such as "McLogEvent" for McAfee), I know that the system had the application installed at one point and that may help provide insight for my analysis. In particular, if I opt (as part of my malware detection process, something we will discuss in Chapter 6) to mount the image as a volume and scan it with an AV product, I know not to use the product that was installed on the system. Similarly, while I most often start my analysis of the Event Logs by looking at what is actually being audited via the audit policy, there have been times when, although logins are being audited, the system has been running for so long that no one has needed to log into it. As such, I have found Security Event Logs with no login events available in the visible event records.

Evtrpt.pl also provides the date range of all of the event records within the file, as follows:

```
Date Range (UTC)
Thu Jan 18 12:41:04 2007 to Thu Feb 7 13:39:25 2008
```

The date range information can be very useful, as well. There have been times when I've been asked to provide information regarding which user was logged into the system on a certain date or within a specific timeframe. Evtrpt.pl provides me with a quick view into whether or not digging deeper into the Event Logs is of value, or perhaps I should decrease the priority of the logs as source of information and focus my analysis on more profitable targets.

NOTE

AV Logs

Most AV products produce some sort of logs; many produce text-based logs that are easy to view and parse, particularly if you load them into Excel. Many AV products will also write their logs to the Application Event Log, but for some, this can also be a configurable option. I have analyzed systems on which I have easily located the AV application logs, but have not seen any corresponding entries in the Application Event Log.

Another tool that I like to use is for parsing Event Log records is the Perl script evtparse.pl. This Perl script reads through the Event Log files on a binary level, locating and parsing the records without using any of the native Windows API functions. This has a couple of benefits: one is that you don't have to worry about the Event Log file being deemed "corrupted," as will sometimes occur when using tools (such as the Windows Event Viewer) that rely on native Windows API functions. The other is that the Perl script is platform-independent; it can be used on Windows, Linux, and even MacOS X. The script is capable of parsing event records into either comma-separate value (CSV) format, suitable for opening Excel, or into a format suitable for timeline analysis (which will be discussed in greater detail in Chapter 7).

Parsing the values is only half the battle, though. There are a number of resources available that provide information and details regarding what the various event records, either individually or correlated together, can mean. One of my favorite resources is the EventID web site (http://www.eventid.net). The $24 annual registration fee is well worth the expense, as I can log into the site and run searches to not only get additional information about MS-specific events, but also see information with respect to issues that others (mostly system administrators) have observed or encountered, as well as links to pertinent Microsoft KB articles. All of this can be very revealing, even if it only provides me with additional leads or places to look. Application-specific event records are usually best researched at the vendor's web site, as blogs and forum posts can provide a great deal of information about various events generated by these applications.

Another resource for finding information about Security Event Log entries is the Ultimate Windows Security Log Events site (found online at http://www.ultimate-windowssecurity.com/securitylog/encyclopedia/default.aspx). This site provides an easily searched list of Security Event Log entries, with some explanations to provide context. The site provides information regarding Security Event Log entries for Windows XP and 2003 systems, as well as corresponding entries for Vista and Windows 2008 systems.

> **TIP**
>
> **Event Log Analysis**
>
> When conducting analysis on a Windows system, I don't have specific event records that I search for every time; rather, what I look for depends heavily on the goals of the examination and the system's audit configuration. While many of the systems I've analyzed have had fairly default configurations (minimal changes, if at all, beyond the default, out-of-the-box settings), I have found great value in those systems where settings had been modified, to include the Event Log size being increased. I once had the opportunity to analyze a Windows XP system on which not only were both successful and failed logon events being recorded, but Process Tracking was also enabled. When analyzing this system, I created a timeline (discussed in detail in Chapter 7) of system activity, and the additional detail provided by the Event Log configuration was invaluable.

The Event Logs themselves are not always the sole source of event records on a system. Event log records, like other data, may be found within the page file or within unallocated space. I was once asked to analyze a system from which very few event records were found in the Event Logs and the Security Event Log had an event ID 517 record, indicating that the Event Log had been cleared. As such, one of the steps in my analysis was to attempt to recover deleted event records. My first step was to use the Sleuthkit (found online at http://www.sleuthkit.org/) tool blkls.exe to extract all of the unallocated space from the acquired image into a separate file. I then loaded that file into BinText (available online at http://www.mcafee.com/us/downloads/free-tools/bintext.aspx) and saved the list of strings located within the file. I then wrote a Perl script to go through the list of strings and locate all those that contained the event record "magic number" (i.e., "LfLe"); when BinText reports the strings that it locates, it also provides the offset within the file where that string is located (strings.exe available from Microsoft will do the same thing if you add the "-o" switch to the command line—the utility can be downloaded from http://technet.microsoft.com/en-us/sysinternals/bb897439). For every string that BinText located that began with "LfLe," the Perl script would go to the offset within the file containing the unallocated space, "back up" 4 bytes (a "DWORD") and read the size value. As the event record structure begins and ends with this 4-byte size value, the script would then read the total number of bytes, and if the first and last DWORDs in the sequence were the same, the event record was assumed to be valid, extracted, and parsed. Using this technique, I was able to recover over 330 deleted event records. Another way to do this would be to simply have a slightly modified version of either the evtrpt.pl or evtparse.pl script parse through unallocated space 4 bytes at a time, looking for the event record magic number, and then processing each event found to be a valid record. However you go about doing this, it can be a very valuable technique, particularly if you're trying to construct a timeline, as discussed in Chapter 7. The point of this is to illustrate how understanding the various data structures on Windows systems can lead to the recovery of additional data that may significantly affect your overall analysis.

TIP

Interesting Artifacts

While I do not have a list of specific event IDs that I look for during every analysis engagement, there are some records of interest that I do look out for when required by the goals of the engagement. As mentioned previously in the chapter, a Security Event Log entry with event ID 517 indicates that the Event Log was cleared. Further, on most systems, some Windows services being started will result in an event with the "Service Control Manager" source and an ID of 7035 being generated by the system shortly after the system is booted. As such, services started by a user hours or days after the system was last started may indicate normal system administration activity, or provide indications of a compromise, such as an intrusion or malware being installed. Further, a number of organizations may use tools such as psexec.exe (available online at http://technet.microsoft.com/en-us/sysinternals/bb897553) to access and remotely manage systems; however, intruders will sometimes use psexec.exe or similar tools (such as rcmd.exe, the remote command utility available from Microsoft) to remotely access systems. The use of such tools usually results in a service being started in the context of the user account used to launch the tool, and is preceded by a network logon (Security event ID 540, type 3).

Windows Event Log

With Vista, Microsoft modified a great deal about how events are recorded, as well as the types of events recorded, the location where the events are recorded, and the structure of those recorded events. This new mechanism is referred to as the "Windows Event Log," rather than just "Event Log" as seen on Windows XP and 2003 systems. On Vista through Windows 7 systems, the Windows Event Logs are stored in the C:\Windows\system32\winevt\Logs folder (by default) and are stored in a binary extensible markup language (XML) format.

On a system with a default installation of Windows 7 and only MS Office 2007 installed, I found 134 different .evtx files in the *winevt\Logs* directory. There are two types of Windows Event Logs: Windows logs and Application and Services logs. Figure 4.3 illustrates these logs, visible via the Event Viewer.

You can see a number of the Event Logs that you'd expect to see on a Windows system in Figure 4.3. For example, there are the Application, System, and Security event logs, which correspond to appevent.evt, sysevent.evt, and secevent.evt, respectively, on Windows XP/2003 systems. The Security Event Log records many of the same events as you may be used to seeing on Windows XP systems, including logons and logoffs (depending upon the audit configuration, of course); however, there is a difference—many of the event ID you would be interested in are different for the same event. For example, on Windows XP, an event ID of 528 would indicate a logon; for Windows 7, that same event would have an event ID of 4624. The difference between these two event IDs is 4096; this holds true for a number of Security events. The Ultimate Windows Security site has a fairly exhaustive listing of both Windows XP and Windows 7 Security Event Log records that you might expect to see, which can be found online at http://www.ultimatewindowssecurity.com/securitylog/encyclopedia/default.aspx.

FIGURE 4.3

Windows 7 Windows Event Logs (via Event Viewer).

You will also see the Setup and Forwarded Events logs in Figure 4.3. According to Microsoft, the Setup log contains events related to application setup; however, reviewing the various entries on live system reveals that the statuses of Windows Updates are also recorded in this log. The Forwarded Events log is intended to store events forwarded from other systems.

The remaining logs are Applications and Services Logs and store events for a single application or component, rather than events that would affect the entire system. These logs have four subtypes: Operational, Admin, Analytic, and Debug. By default, on a normal Windows 7 system, you're likely to see Operational and Admin logs, although now and again you'll see Analytic logs. Admin events are targeted at end users and system administrators, and provide information that an administrator may use to fix an issue or take some other action. Operational logs are generally used to diagnose an issue. For example, the Microsoft-Windows-WLAN-AutoConfig/Operational log provides information about wireless networks that the system has associated with, and through which network adapter, as illustrated in Figure 4.4.

Events such as this can be instrumental not just in diagnosing problems, but can also provide clues to examiners during an investigation. For example, this information can help an analyst determine if a user is connecting to a WiFi access point in a nearby building in order to exfiltrate data, or determine where a user may have taken the laptop by submitting access point MAC addresses to a geo-location lookup service such as WiGLE.net.

The Debug and Analytic logs are intended for developers and used to diagnose problems that cannot be handled through user intervention.

TIP

VHDs and VMs

I've done a bit of testing of virtual hard drives (VHDs) while writing this book (see Chapter 3), mounting and removing them from my Windows 7 system. As such, the Microsoft-Windows-VHDMP/Operational.evtx log has a number of events visible that are associated with the "surfacing" (mounting) of VHD files (event ID 1), and "unsurfacing" (removing) of those files (event ID 2). However, this log applies only to the mounting and removal of VHD files. The Microsoft-Windows-Virtual PC/Admin log maintains records of the use of Virtual PC to create and start virtual systems or machines (VMs), including "XP Mode," a version of Windows XP available to maintain compatibility with applications that may not run well (or at all) on Windows 7. This log also maintains information about applications installed in XP Mode, but launched from Windows 7. Both of these may provide valuable information during exams, particularly when you're looking for files that may not be in the Windows 7 file system, but may have been accessed from a VHD or VM.

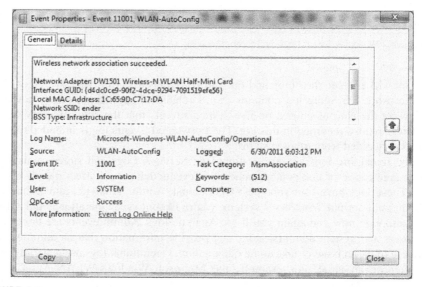

FIGURE 4.4

Event from the WLAN-AutoConfig/Operational Log (Windows 7).

All this aside, what are some of the ways to get at the data within the Windows Event Logs? One means for parsing Windows Event Logs that I've found to be very effective is to install Microsoft's free Logparser tool (available online at http://www.microsoft.com/download/en/details.aspx?displaylang=en&id=24659) on a Windows 7 analysis system, and then either extract the Windows Event Log files from the acquired image, or mount the acquired image as a volume. From there, I then use the following command to extract all of the event records from, in this example, the System Event Log extracted from an image:

```
logparser -i:evt -o:csv "SELECT RecordNumber,TO_UTCTIME(TimeGene
rated),EventID,SourceName,ComputerName,SID,Strings FROM D:\Case\
System.evtx" > output.csv
```

This command accesses the extracted System Event Log file and parses the various individual items from each record found in the file. If you were to extract more than just the System Event Log from an acquired image, you may want to run the command against all of the files without having to enter each one individually. You can do this using the "*" wildcard, as illustrated in the following command:

```
logparser -i:evt -o:csv "SELECT RecordNumber,TO_UTCTIME(TimeGener
ated),EventID,SourceName,ComputerName,SID,Strings FROM D:\Case\*.
evtx" > output.csv
```

Using this command lets you open the output file using Excel, and sort that file on any of the columns (time stamp, Event ID, etc.), which depending upon the type of analysis you're doing, may be very helpful.

When using this command, it's important to remember that Logparser relies on the APIs (available via DLLs) on the analysis system. As such, you won't be able to use it to parse Vista, Windows 7, and Windows 8 Event Logs if you're running Windows XP on your analysis system, as the Event Log APIs on Windows XP aren't compatible with the Vista/Windows 7 Windows Event Log format. Similarly, you can't use Logparser to parse Windows XP or 2003 logs on a Vista/7 analysis system. Sending the output of the Logparser command to CSV format allows for easy viewing and analysis via Excel, in addition to providing additional columns for you to add references or your own notes. The format also allows for easy parsing, as we will see in Chapter 7.

TIP

Converting Event Logs

While attempting to use Logparser running on a Windows 7 system to parse Windows XP Event Logs won't result in anything useful, you can use wevtutil.exe (native to Windows 7) to convert the XP Event Logs to Windows 7 Windows Event Log format, using a command line similar to the following:

```
D:\tools > wevtutil epl appevent.evt appevent.evtx /lf:true
```

Andreas Schuster, whose blog can be found at http://computer.forensikblog. de/en/, has put a good deal of effort into deciphering and decoding the Windows Event Log format, and creating a Perl-based library and tools collection for parsing the events from a log. As of this writing, the version of his library is 1.1.1 (last updated on November 28, 2011). You can download and install Andreas' library, or you can use tools that have the library and tools already installed, such as the SANS Investigative Forensic Toolkit (SIFT) Workstation that Rob Lee developed. SIFT version 2.14 was available online at http://computer-forensics.sans.org/community/ downloads when this chapter was being written.

Recycle bin

Windows systems have a great deal of event recovery built into them. Microsoft understands that users make mistakes or may delete a file that they later wish they hadn't. As such, the Windows Recycle Bin acts as a repository for files deleted by the user through normal means, such as hitting the Delete key or right-clicking the file and selecting "Delete" from the context menu (files deleted from remote shares or from the command line are not sent to the Recycle Bin).

TIP

Bypassing the Recycle Bin

According to http://support.microsoft.com/kb/320031, the Recycle Bin can be bypassed by right-clicking on the Recycle Bin, choosing Properties, and checking the "Do not move files to the Recycle Bin" checkbox, as illustrated in Figure 4.5.

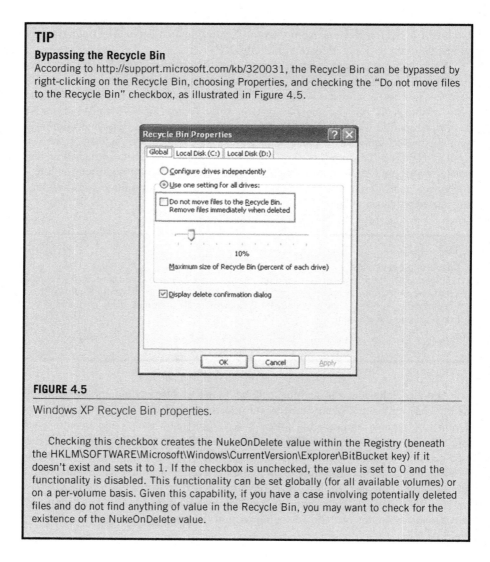

FIGURE 4.5

Windows XP Recycle Bin properties.

Checking this checkbox creates the NukeOnDelete value within the Registry (beneath the HKLM\SOFTWARE\Microsoft\Windows\CurrentVersion\Explorer\BitBucket key) if it doesn't exist and sets it to 1. If the checkbox is unchecked, the value is set to 0 and the functionality is disabled. This functionality can be set globally (for all available volumes) or on a per-volume basis. Given this capability, if you have a case involving potentially deleted files and do not find anything of value in the Recycle Bin, you may want to check for the existence of the NukeOnDelete value.

FIGURE 4.6

Windows XP Recycle Bin in FTK Imager.

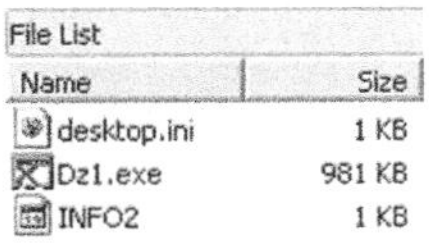

File List	
Name	Size
desktop.ini	1 KB
Dz1.exe	981 KB
INFO2	1 KB

FIGURE 4.7

Deleted file in the Windows XP Recycler directory.

On Windows XP systems, deleted files are moved to the Recycler directory, within a subdirectory based on the security identifier (SID) for the user. Figure 4.6 illustrates the subdirectory for the Administrator user on a Windows XP system.

When a file is deleted on a Windows XP system and moved to the Recycle Bin, the file is renamed in accordance with a standard format, which is outlined in the "How the Recycle Bin Stores Files" Microsoft KB article (found online at http://support.microsoft.com/kb/136517). The name is changed so that the first letter is "D" (for "deleted"), the second letter is the drive letter from which the file originated, which is followed by the number of the deleted file, and the name ends with the original file extension. Figure 4.7 illustrates a deleted executable file that originated from the Z:\ drive.

As illustrated in Figure 4.7, the Recycle Bin also maintains an index file (named "INFO2") that keeps track of the original file name and location of deleted files, as well as when the files were deleted. The Perl script recbin.pl can be used to extract specific data from the INFO2 file, as illustrated here:

```
C:\tools > recbin.pl -f d:\cases\info2
1 Mon Sep 26 23:03:27 2005 C:\Documents and Settings\jdoe\Desktop\
lads.zip
2 Mon Sep 26 23:05:28 2005 C:\Documents and Settings\jdoe\LADS_
ReadMe.txt
3 Mon Sep 26 23:05:28 2005 C:\Documents and Settings\jdoe\lads.exe
4 Mon Sep 26 23:23:58 2005 C:\Documents and Settings\jdoe\My
Documents\Morpheus Shared\Downloads\Toby Keith - Stays In Mexico.
mp3
```

As you can see, recbin.pl parses through the INFO2 file and returns the index of the deleted file, the date and time the file was deleted, and the original file name of the deleted file.

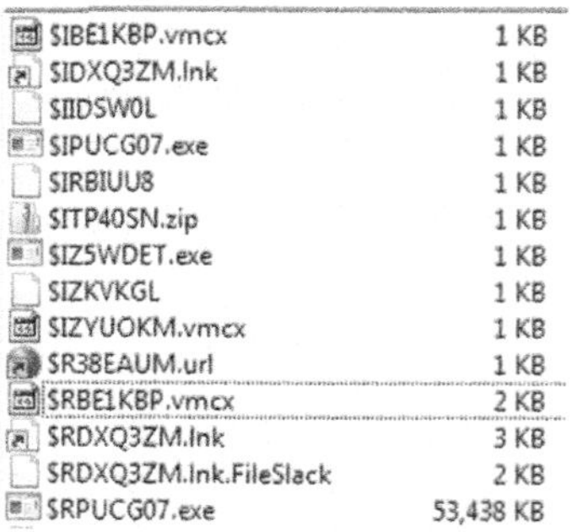

$IBE1KBP.vmcx	1 KB
$IDXQ3ZM.lnk	1 KB
$IIDSW0L	1 KB
$IPUCG07.exe	1 KB
$IRBIUU8	1 KB
$ITP40SN.zip	1 KB
$IZ5WDET.exe	1 KB
$IZKVKGL	1 KB
$IZYUOKM.vmcx	1 KB
$R38EAUM.url	1 KB
$RBE1KBP.vmcx	2 KB
$RDXQ3ZM.lnk	3 KB
$RDXQ3ZM.lnk.FileSlack	2 KB
$RPUCG07.exe	53,438 KB

FIGURE 4.8

Files populating the Windows 7 Recycle Bin, via FTK Imager.

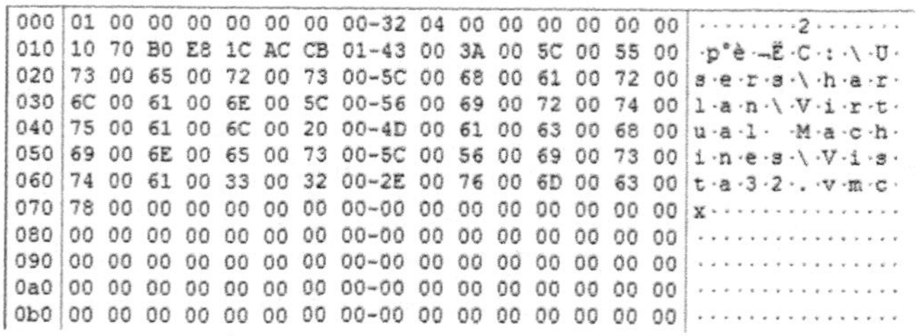

```
000 01 00 00 00 00 00 00 00-32 04 00 00 00 00 00 00  ·······2······
010 10 70 B0 E8 1C AC CB 01-43 00 3A 00 5C 00 55 00  ·p°è·¬Ë·C·:·\·U·
020 73 00 65 00 72 00 73 00-5C 00 68 00 61 00 72 00  s·e·r·s·\·h·a·r·
030 6C 00 61 00 6E 00 5C 00-56 00 69 00 72 00 74 00  l·a·n·\·V·i·r·t·
040 75 00 61 00 6C 00 20 00-4D 00 61 00 63 00 68 00  u·a·l· ·M·a·c·h·
050 69 00 6E 00 65 00 73 00-5C 00 56 00 69 00 73 00  i·n·e·s·\·V·i·s·
060 74 00 61 00 33 00 32 00-2E 00 76 00 6D 00 63 00  t·a·3·2·.·v·m·c·
070 78 00 00 00 00 00 00 00-00 00 00 00 00 00 00 00  x···············
080 00 00 00 00 00 00 00 00-00 00 00 00 00 00 00 00  ················
090 00 00 00 00 00 00 00 00-00 00 00 00 00 00 00 00  ················
0a0 00 00 00 00 00 00 00 00-00 00 00 00 00 00 00 00  ················
0b0 00 00 00 00 00 00 00 00-00 00 00 00 00 00 00 00  ················
```

FIGURE 4.9

Partial contents of Recycle Bin index file, via FTK Imager.

Beginning with Vista, Microsoft changed the format of the files within the Recycle Bin. When files are deleted through the Windows Explorer shell, by default they will be moved to the Recycle Bin ("$Recycle.Bin" on disk), into a subfolder named for the user's SID. The file itself will be given a new file name, which starts with "$R," and is followed by six characters and ends in the original file's extension. A corresponding index file will be created which starts with "$I," and contains the same remaining characters and extension as the "$R" file. Several deleted files and their index files are illustrated in Figure 4.8.

Figure 4.8 illustrates several deleted files and their corresponding index files. Figure 4.9 illustrates the binary contents of an index file.

Each index file is 544 bytes in size. As you can see in Figure 4.9, the first 8 bytes of the file appear to be a header, and the second 8 bytes is the size of the original file, in little-endian hexadecimal format. Bytes 16 through 23 comprise the 64-bit FILETIME object for when the file was deleted, and the remaining bytes of the file are the name and path of the original file, in Unicode format. This structure makes the file relatively easy to parse and provide similar information as what is provided via the recbin.pl Perl script; once the index file (the one that begins with "$I") is parsed, you can then recover the actual file contents from the corresponding file that begins with "$R."

The recbin.pl tool described above can also be used to parse the index ($I) files found in the Recycle Bin on the newer versions of the Windows operating system:

```
C:\tools > recbin.pl -f d:\cases\$I2Y3QW9.tar
C:\Users\harlan\Desktop\Parse-Win32Registry-0.60.tar deleted on Sun
May 6 13:49:01 2012 Z
```

It's important to note the differences between the two files parsed using the recbin.pl tool. On XP systems, the INFO2 file contains records for all of the deleted files; on Vista systems and above, each $I index file contains only the record for the corresponding $R file.

Prefetch files

By now, most analysts recognize the forensic value of application prefetch, or just "Prefetch," files. As with other artifacts, Prefetch files can provide some interesting indicators, even if a user or intruder takes steps to hide their activity.

Since Windows XP, Windows systems have been capable of prefetching. All Windows systems can perform boot prefetching, but only Windows XP, Vista, Windows 7, and Windows 8 perform application prefetching *by default* (Windows 2003, 2008, and 2008 R2 can perform application prefetching following a Registry modification).

TIP

Enable Application Prefetching

To enable application prefetching, navigate to the *CurrentControlSet\Control\Session Manager\Memory Management\PrefetchParameters* key in the System hive, and locate the "EnablePrefetcher" value. If this value is set to 1 ("Prefetch only application launch files") or 3 ("prefetch both application and boot files"), application prefetching is enabled. I've recommended to a number of organizations that the application prefetch capability be enabled on server systems in order to enable the creation of these valuable artifacts, in the event of a breach or intrusion occurring.

Application prefetching is intended to enable a better user experience within Windows systems by monitoring an application as it's launched, and then "prefetching" the necessary code to a single location so that the next time the application is launched, it launches faster. This way, the system doesn't have to seek across the file system for DLLs and other data that it needs to start the application—it knows exactly where to find it. These Prefetch files are created in the C:\Windows\Prefetch directory and end with the ".pf" extension. Each

Prefetch file name also includes the name of the application, a dash, followed by a one-way hash constructed using, among other things, the path to the application and any arguments used.

TIP

SSD Drives

According to the "Engineering Windows 7" blog (found online at http://blogs.msdn.com/b/ e7/archive/2009/05/05/support-and-q-a-for-solid-state-drives-and.aspx), if Windows 7 detects that it is running on a solid-state drive (SSD), certain functionality such as SuperFetch (which is responsible for producing application prefetch files) is automatically disabled. See the linked blog entry for a more detailed explanation, as well as a list of additional functionality that may be disabled or modified if Windows 7 detects that it is running from an SSD drive. This is also supported by Microsoft KB article 2727880 (found online at http://support.microsoft.com/kb/2727880). I should note that as of this writing, at least one member of the DFIR community has reported installing Windows 7 on a system with an SSD drive, and found that Prefetch files were, in fact, enabled and created. No information regarding the type of SSD drive, any troubleshooting or investigative steps, nor how the operating system identified the drive itself has been made available.

To see an example of the creation of application prefetch files, particularly if you're running Windows XP, open a command prompt and change to the C:\ Windows directory, and type "Notepad." Close the Notepad window that appears and then return to the command prompt and change to the C:\Windows\system32 directory. Then type "Notepad" again and close the Notepad window that appears. Now, if you go to your Prefetch directory, you should see two different Prefetch files that start with "Notepad.exe" and include two different hashes, as illustrated in Figure 4.10. This is also why you will sometimes see multiple Prefetch files for rundll32.exe.

Prefetch files contain metadata that can be useful to an analyst during an examination. For example, they contain the date that the application was last launched, as well as a "run count," or how many times that application has been launched. The Prefetch file also contains information about the volume from which the application was launched, as well as a list of DLLs and other files accessed by the application (in Unicode). There are a number of tools available that will allow you to parse this information from the files; due to the usefulness of this information, I wrote a Perl script called "pref.pl" to parse and display this information (this script is included in the ancillary materials available online). I found an odd Prefetch file on a system

Name	Size	Type	Date Modified
NOTEPAD.EXE-189578DA.pf	14 KB	PF File	5/30/2011 9:38 AM
NOTEPAD.EXE-336351A9.pf	14 KB	PF File	5/30/2011 9:38 AM

FIGURE 4.10

Two Prefetch files for Notepad.exe.

and ran the pref.pl Perl script against the file; an excerpt of the metadata information available in the Prefetch file is shown here:

```
C:\tools > pref.pl -f c:\windows\prefetch\0.8937919959151474.EXE-
12EB1013.pf -p -i
c:\windows\prefetch\0.8937919959151474.EXE-12EB1013.pf Thu May 26
16:46:19 2011
(1)
EXE Name : 0.8937919959151474.EXE
Volume Path : \DEVICE\HARDDISKVOLUME1
Volume Creation Date: Fri Jan 1 22:24:09 2010 Z
Volume Serial Number: A424-CE42
\DEVICE\HARDDISKVOLUME1\WINDOWS\SYSTEM32\NTDLL.DLL
\DEVICE\HARDDISKVOLUME1\WINDOWS\SYSTEM32\KERNEL32.DLL
\DEVICE\HARDDISKVOLUME1\WINDOWS\SYSTEM32\UNICODE.NLS
\DEVICE\HARDDISKVOLUME1\WINDOWS\SYSTEM32\LOCALE.NLS
\DEVICE\HARDDISKVOLUME1\WINDOWS\SYSTEM32\SORTTBLS.NLS
\DEVICE\HARDDISKVOLUME1\DOCUME~1\User\LOCALS~1\
TEMP\0.8937919959151474.EXE
\DEVICE\HARDDISKVOLUME1\WINDOWS\SYSTEM32\USER32.DLL
\DEVICE\HARDDISKVOLUME1\WINDOWS\SYSTEM32\GDI32.DLL
```

As you can see in the above output excerpt, there is a considerable amount of metadata available. For example, we can see the last time that the application was launched and the run count (i.e., "Thu May 26 16:46:19 2011" and "(1)," respectively), as well as information about the volume where the application.exe file was found, and the actual path to the executable file (i.e., "\DEVICE\HARDDISKVOLUME1\ DOCUME~1\User\LOCALS~1\TEMP\0.893791995915174.EXE").

I've also found other interesting information in the output from pref.pl. In one instance, I found another very oddly named Prefetch file, named "KARTCICYYIR. EXE-2CC557AD.pf"; using pref.pl, an excerpt of the output I saw appeared as follows:

```
\DEVICE\HARDDISKVOLUME1\DOCUME~1\ABC\LOCALS~1\TEMP\KARCICYYIR.EXE
\DEVICE\HARDDISKVOLUME1\PROGRAM FILES\SOPHOS\SOPHOS ANTI-VIRUS\
SOPHOS_DETOURED.DLL
\DEVICE\HARDDISKVOLUME1\WINDOWS\SYSTEM32\BDYAWUIS.DAT
\DEVICE\HARDDISKVOLUME1\WINDOWS\SYSTEM32\CONFIG\SOFTWARE
\DEVICE\HARDDISKVOLUME1\WINDOWS\SYSTEM32\MRYDUTAG.DAT
\DEVICE\HARDDISKVOLUME1\WINDOWS\SYSTEM32\MBQTAEPO.DAT
\DEVICE\HARDDISKVOLUME1\WINDOWS\SYSTEM32\CMD.EXE
```

Again, as with the first example, this is only an excerpt of the output, but it shows the artifacts that were most interesting and immediately caught my attention. You can see in the above output excerpt not just the path the actual executable file, but also that it appeared to be accessing three .dat files, as well as the Software Registry hive. This is an excellent example of how Prefetch files can be valuable to an analyst, as it illustrates the concept of secondary artifacts that we discussed in

Chapter 1. The Prefetch file parsed in the above example was a secondary artifact created during a malware infection; that is, it was created by the operating system as the malware executed and interacted with its "ecosystem" or environment. As it turns out, the Application Event Logs from the system from which the Prefetch file was retrieved included an event record that indicated that the malware file itself ("KARTCICYYIR.EXE") had been detected by the installed AV application and deleted. However, the benefit of secondary artifacts is that they often are not deleted when an intruder "cleans up" after herself, or when malware is deleted; Registry keys and values, Prefetch files, etc. often remain. The metadata in this Prefetch file not only gives us a clear indication of when the executable was launched, but also from where (via the volume path and serial number in the previous example output). The metadata also gives us an indication of other files that may be associated with the malware, providing us with some context (we'll discuss the concept of context with respect to digital forensic analysis at greater length in Chapter 7) as to the creation of those files.

As you can see, viewing the module paths, as well as the path to the executable file, embedded within these files can be very revealing during analysis. Executable files, generally speaking, are not normally run from paths that include "Temp," such as "Local Settings\Temp," or "Temporary Internet Files." With the notable exception of the prefetch file for the Internet Explorer (IE) web browser, it may not be likely that most files would contain module paths that similarly include "Temp" in the path. Also excepting the prefetch file for IE, most prefetch files are not likely to contain module paths that point to files ending in ".dat" or ".bat." Looking for indicators such as these are a great way to expedite analysis, as well as help locate indications of programs that had been run on the system, even well after the executable file itself has been removed from the system.

Near the end of September 2013, Jared Atkinson posted an article to his blog (found online at http://www.invoke-ir.com/2013/09/whats-new-in-prefetch-for-windows-8.html) that described something new in Prefetch files on Windows 8. In short, these files contain space for a total of eight time stamps for when the application was previously run. Jared also shared some of the testing he'd conducted to demonstrate that repeatedly running the application will cause the spaces for the time stamps within the .pf file to be populated. This additional, historical information can be extremely useful to an analyst.

The pref.pl Perl script provided with the materials associated with this book includes the ability to differentiate between Prefetch files from Windows XP, and those from Vista, as well as Windows 7 and 8.

TIP

NTOSBOOT

When examining Prefetch files, do not overlook the NTOSBOOT-BOODFAAD.pf file. This file can be parsed just like any other Prefetch file, and some analysts have reported finding references to malware within the file path strings embedded within this Prefetch file.

Scheduled tasks

Windows systems are capable of a great deal of functionality, including being able to execute tasks on a user-determined schedule. These are referred to as Scheduled Tasks, and are accessible via several means, including the at.exe command and the Scheduled Task Wizard, as illustrated in Figure 4.11.

Scheduled Tasks allow various programs to be executed once, or on a regularly scheduled basis. This can be very useful; for example, regular housekeeping functions can be scheduled to occur at regular, specific intervals. One example of this is if you install iTunes or another Apple product, you will likely see the file "AppleSoftwareUpdate.job" in the C:\Windows\Tasks directory on your system, as illustrated in Figure 4.12.

That being said, the existence of a scheduled task does not always correlate directly to a user creating the task, as these tasks can be created programmatically, through the appropriate API calls (which, with the appropriate credentials, can be accessed remotely). As such, the existence of a scheduled task may be associated with a software installation, or in some cases, a malware infection or compromise. Windows systems require that, in order to create a scheduled task, the user context have Administrator level credentials. When the task executes, the running task itself

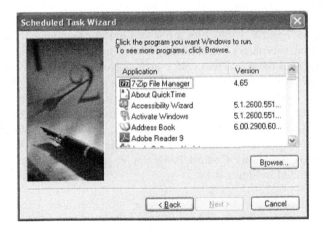

FIGURE 4.11

Windows XP Scheduled Task Wizard.

Name ▲	Schedule	Next Run Time
Add Scheduled Task		
AppleSoftwareUpdate	At 10:13 PM every Tue of every week, starting 12/27/2...	10:13:00 PM ...

FIGURE 4.12

AppleSoftwareUpdate task.

has System level privileges. This can be very useful to administrators, particularly when System level privileges are needed temporarily; an administrator can create a scheduled task to launch the command prompt (i.e., cmd.exe) and have it run immediately. Once the command prompt appears, it will be running with System level privileges, allowing the administrator access to areas of the system restricted to that privilege level. Microsoft KB article 313565 (found online at http://support. microsoft.com/kb/313565) provides instructions for how to use at.exe to create scheduled tasks; while this article was written for Windows 2000, the commands work on later versions of Windows.

On Windows 2000, XP, and 2003, the scheduled tasks themselves are found within the C:\Windows\Tasks folder and have the ".job" file extension. These files have a binary format, a description of which is available online at http://msdn.microsoft.com/en-us/library/cc248285%28v=PROT.13%29.aspx. The information available via this site allows for tools to be written to parse the .job file format to extract information that may be of particular value. For example, the fixed length portion of the format contains an 8-byte SYSTEMTIME time stamp that indicates when the task was most recently run, and the variable length data section includes a Unicode string that indicates the name of the author of the task. This can be valuable to an analyst, as anything useful to an administrator can also be useful to an intruder; scheduled tasks have been used as a persistence mechanism (see Chapter 6) for malware, as well as means for activating Trojans, backdoors, or legitimate remote access services to allow an intruder access to the system.

On Windows 7 and 8, ".job" files are stored in the "\Windows\System32\Tasks" folder, as well as subfolders beneath it, in XML format, which means that you can open them and read them in a text editor such as Notepad. An example of a portion of a Windows 7 .job file (opened in ProDiscover) is illustrated in Figure 4.13.

Windows 7 and 8 ship with a number of scheduled tasks already installed; for example, the RegIdleBackup task backs up the Registry (to the "\Windows\System32\config\RegBack" folder) every 10 days, and limited defragmentation is scheduled for once a week. These tasks can be viewed on a live Windows 7 system via the Task Scheduler Control Panel applet (available within Administrative Tools), as illustrated in Figure 4.14.

```
ÿþ<Task xmlns="http://schemas.microsoft.com/windows/2004/02/mit/task">
  <RegistrationInfo>
    <Source>$(@%systemroot%\system32\defragsvc.dll,-800)</Source>
    <Author>$(@%systemroot%\system32\defragsvc.dll,-801)</Author>
    <Description>$(@%systemroot%\system32\defragsvc.dll,-802)</Description>
    <URI>Microsoft\Windows\Defrag\ScheduledDefrag</URI>
  </RegistrationInfo>
```

FIGURE 4.13

Portion of Windows 7 .job file (via ProDiscover).

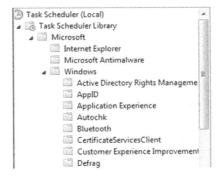

FIGURE 4.14

Portion of the Windows 7 Task Scheduler applet.

Again, on Windows 7 and 8, these tasks (described within XML ".job" files) are stored in subdirectories beneath the "\Windows\System32\Tasks" folder.

Another means for creating scheduled tasks, aside from at.exe or using a wizard, is to use schtasks.exe. This tool was introduced with Windows XP (Microsoft KB article 814596, found online at http://support.microsoft.com/kb/814596, describes how to use schtasks.exe to create scheduled tasks on Windows 2003), and is available on all systems up through Windows 7. While at.exe produces tasks or "jobs" that are named "AT#.job," much like the wizard, schtasks.exe allows tasks to be created with more descriptive names.

WARNING

at.exe Versus schtasks.exe

When performing live response and using a batch file to collect volatile information from Windows systems, be sure to use both at.exe and schtasks.exe within the batch file to list the available tasks. It turns out that tasks created by one tool will not be "seen" by the other, when used to list the tasks.

Another useful bit of information available to the analyst is the Scheduled Tasks log file, named "SchedLgU.txt." This file is 32 kilobytes (KB) in size, by default, and is located in the "\Windows\Tasks" directory on Windows 2003; it's in the "\Windows" directory on Windows XP. Many times, this file will simply contain entries that state that the Task Scheduler service started (or exited) at a specific date and time; this can be useful to establish a record (albeit short term, as the file isn't very large and older entries get overwritten) of when the system was running. This log may also hold a record of various tasks that have executed, along with their exit code. In some instances, I have found indications of tasks having completed that were associated with an intrusion, and corroborated with external data source (network traffic, etc.). In such cases, the task was created from a remote system using compromised domain administrator credentials, and once the task completed, it was deleted; however, the entry still remained in the SchedLgU.txt file, and we were able to correlate that information to other events. A complete discussion of timeline creation and analysis is covered in Chapter 7.

On Windows Vista systems and above, the Microsoft-Windows-TaskScheduler/ Operational Event Log maintains records of Scheduled Tasks that have started, completed, etc.

Jump lists

Jump lists are Task Bar artifacts that are new as of Windows 7; they are not available on versions of Windows prior to Windows 7, but are available on Windows 7 and 8. In short, jump lists are lists of files that the user has recently opened, organized according the application used to open them, so in this way, they are similar to the RecentDocs Registry key (Registry analysis will be discussed in Chapter 5). Users can view their recently accessed documents and files by right-clicking on the program icon in the Task Bar. Figure 4.15 illustrates a jump list for VMWare's VMPlayer application, viewed via the desktop.

What the user sees depends upon the program; for example, the Jump List of Internet Explorer will show URLs, whereas the jump list for MS Word will show documents that the user has opened. Users can also choose to keep specific items persistent in the jump list by "pinning" them; that is, clicking on the push-pin to the right of the item, as illustrated in Figure 4.15. While the items under the Recent list may change over time, items that the user chooses to "pin" will persist in the jump list. These jump lists may also appear alongside programs listed in the Start menu, as well.

FIGURE 4.15

VMPlayer jump list.

From an analyst's perspective, the user's Jump Lists are maintained in the *AppData\Roaming\Microsoft\Windows\Recent\AutomaticDestinations* folder within the user profile, as illustrated in Figure 4.16.

As you can see in Figure 4.16, the Jump List files are named with 16 hexadecimal characters, followed by ".automaticDestinations-ms." The first 16 characters of the Jump List file name pertain to the specific application used and are fixed across systems. For example, "b3f13480c2785ae" corresponds to Paint.exe, "adecfb853d77462a" corresponds to MS Word 2007, and "918e0ecb43d17e23" corresponds to Notepad.exe. These characters comprise the "application identifier" or "AppID," and identify the specific application, including the path to the executable file. Mark McKinnon of RedWolf Computer Forensics, LLC, posted a list of the AppIDs to the ForensicsWiki, at http://www.forensicswiki.org/wiki/List_of_Jump_List_IDs. The AppIDs for specific applications appear to persist between platforms, the same version of an application will have the same AppID, regardless of the system on which it's been installed.

Several analysts within the community have noted that the Jump List files follow a specific file structure. In fact, at a Microsoft cybercrime conference in the fall of 2008, Troy Larson, the senior forensic investigator at Microsoft, stated that jump lists were based on the compound document "structured storage" binary file format (the format specification can be found online at http://msdn.microsoft.com/en-us/library/dd942138(v=prot.13).aspx) that was used in Microsoft Office prior to version 2007. This structured storage file format was also referred to as a "file system within a file," in that the format was used to create a mini-file system within the contents of a single file, complete with "directories" and "files." Given this, Rob Lee (of SANS) offered up one way to view the contents of a jump list using MiTeC

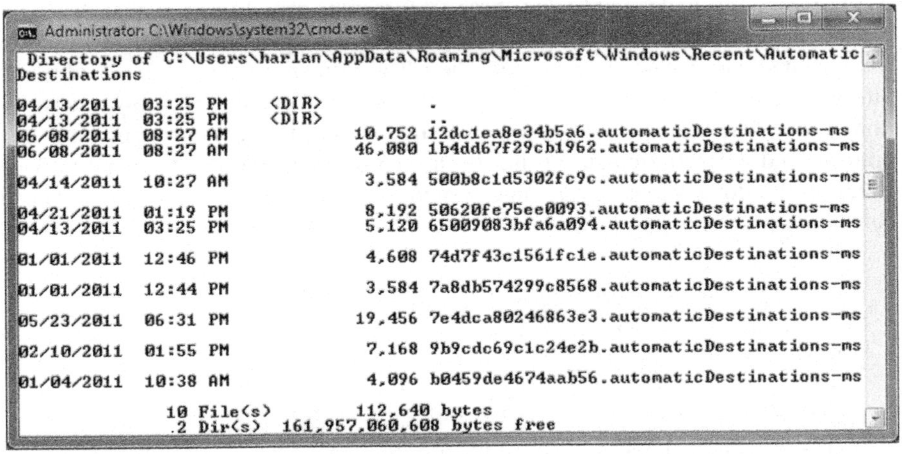

FIGURE 4.16

Contents of user's AutomaticDestinations folder.

FIGURE 4.17

Jump list file open in the MiTeC Structured Storage Viewer.

Structured Storage Viewer (available online at http://mitec.cz/ssv.html), as illustrated in Figure 4.17.

Each of the numbered streams visible via the Structured Storage Viewer are, in turn, based on the file format associated with Windows shortcut files; shortcut files, when by themselves, usually end with the ".lnk" extension and have the nickname "LNK" files. Microsoft has made the binary format of these files, referred to as shell link files, available online at http://msdn.microsoft.com/en-us/library/dd871305(v=prot.13).aspx.

As these streams follow the binary format of shortcut files, they contain a considerable amount of information that can be valuable to an analyst. For example, the format contains last modified, last accessed, and creation time stamps (in UTC format) for the target file; that is, when a jump list stream is created, the MAC time stamps of the target file are used to populate these values within the jump list stream, in much the same manner that they are when a Windows shortcut is created. Analysts need to understand what these time stamps represent, and that the jump lists streams do not contain time stamps that indicate when the streams themselves were created, last accessed, or last modified. The format can also contain additional information, such as command line arguments used, if any, and possibly a description string. One example of a jump list stream that may contain command line options (and a description string) has been seen in the use of the Terminal Service client on Windows 7 to access remote systems, as illustrated here (extracted using a custom Perl script):

```
Stream: 1
M: Tue Jul 14 00:01:53 2009
A: Tue Jul 14 01:14:27 2009
C: Tue Jul 14 00:01:53 2009
C:\Windows\System32\mstsc.exe /v:"192.168.1.24"
Connect to 192.168.1.24 with Remote Desktop Connection
```

Other streams extracted from within the jump list file contain the same time stamps as seen above, as they represent the last modified, last accessed, and

FIGURE 4.18

LNK file information visible in WFA.

creation dates for the file C:\Windows\System32\mstsc.exe. Remember, starting with Vista, updating of last access times on files has been disabled, by default.

The streams identified within the jump list file can also be extracted and viewed with a shortcut/LNK file viewer. For example, using the Structured Storage Viewer, we can extract a stream, rename the extension to ".lnk," and then point the MiTeC Windows File Analyzer (interestingly enough, named "WFA.exe") at the directory where we saved the stream. The .lnk files within the directory will be parsed and the extracted information displayed, as illustrated in Figure 4.18.

The information available from the LNK streams within the jump list file will depend upon the shortcut viewer application you choose. For example, the MiTeC Windows File Analyzer application does not have a column for a description string or command line options when parsing shortcut files.

So how would this information be valuable to an analyst? Well, for the jump list to be created and populated, the user has to take some action. In the previous example, the user accessed the Remote Desktop Connection selection via the Windows 7 Start menu. As such, the existence of this information within the jump list may provide clues (possibly when combined with other information) as to the user's intent. The "user" may be a local user with legitimate access to the system, or an intruder accessing the system via some remote, shell-based access such as Terminal Services. In addition, jump list artifacts may persist well after the user performs the indicated actions or even after the target file has been deleted.

NOTE

DestList Stream

Figure 4.17 illustrates several streams within an "automatic" Jump List file, including two numbered streams and a third one named "DestList." There isn't much information available about the structure of the DestList stream; however, research indicates that following a 32-byte header, the elements of the DestList stream follow a consistent format. Each element is associated with one of the numbered streams within the Jump List file, and is 114 bytes long, plus a Unicode string. The following table provides information regarding the identified items within each element, along with the offset, size, and description of each item:

Offset (Dec/Hex)	Size	Description
72/0 × 48	16 bytes	NetBIOS name of the system; zero padded to 16 bytes
88/0 × 58	8 bytes	Stream number; corresponds to the appropriate numbered stream with the jump list
100/0 × 64	8 bytes	FILETIME object
112/0 × 70	2 bytes	Number of characters in the Unicode string that follows; the string is actually (size * 2) bytes long

Each offset listed within the first column of the table is indexed from the beginning of the element within the stream. The first element is found immediately following the 32-byte header, and each subsequent element is adjacent to the last, with no separator. The 8-byte FILETIME object within the element is most likely used to sort the elements into a "most recently used" (MRU) or "most frequently used" (MFU) list; this is further supported by research, by accessing several files through several applications (MS Word, Adobe Reader, MS Paint, etc.), recording the times, and then parsing the entire Jump List file, including the DestList stream. This research was initially conducted by Jimmy Weg, a law enforcement officer and forensic analyst in Montana, and further validated by other analysts, including some of my own analysis.

The Jump Lists that we've looked at thus far have been from the "AutomaticDestinations" folder. Users can create custom jump lists based on specific files and applications, which populate the "CustomDestinations" folder (in the *AppData\Roaming\Microsoft\Windows\Recent* folder within the user profile), with jump list files that end with the extension, ".customDestinations-ms." As with the previously discussed jump lists, the files begin with a 16-character "AppID" name that is associated with a specific application; limited testing indicates a correlation between the two types of jump lists, with the same 16 characters associated with the same application between them. According to Troy Larson, these jump lists consist of one or more streams in the shortcut/LNK file format, without the benefit of each stream separated into individual streams, as is the case with the automatic destination jump lists.

There are a number of tools available to assist in parsing jump lists for inclusion in your overall analysis. Mark Woan has made not only a shortcut file analyzer (lnkanalyzer) freely available at http://www.woanware.co.uk/?page_id=121, but he has also made a jump list viewer application (JumpLister) available at http://www.woanware.co.uk/?page_id=266. Both tools require that .Net version 4.0 be installed on your system. The folks over at TZWorks.net have a Jump List parser application available named "jmp" (found online at https://tzworks.net/prototype_page.php?proto_id=20) that is capable of parsing both the automatic* and customDestinations-ms Jump Lists.

Using the Microsoft specifications for the compound document binary and shortcut file formats, I wrote my own Jump List parsing tool (in Perl, of course!). This code consists of two Perl modules, one for parsing just the Windows shortcut file format, and the other for parsing the AutomaticDestinations Jump List files as well as the DestList stream. This allows me a great deal of flexibility in how I can implement the parsing functionality, as well as how I choose to display the output. For example, using the two modules (literally, via the Perl "use" pragma), I wrote a script that would read a single AutomaticDestinations Jump List file, parse the DestList stream, parse the numbered streams, and then display the entries in MRU order, as illustrated here:

```
Fri Apr 15 11:41:56 2011
C:\Windows\System32\mstsc.exe /v:" 192.168.1.12"
Tue Apr 5 16:26:19 2011
C:\Windows\System32\mstsc.exe /v:"192.168.1.10"
Wed Mar 16 18:45:58 2011
C:\Windows\System32\mstsc.exe /v:"ender"
Mon Feb 7 14:09:40 2011
C:\Windows\System32\mstsc.exe /v:" 192.168.1.7"
```

This example output is from the Jump List file for the Remote Desktop Client and illustrates connections that I made from my Windows 7 system to various systems in my lab, several of them virtual systems. This information could very easily have been displayed in a format suitable for inclusion in a timeline (see Chapter 7).

WARNING

Jump List Parser

The Perl modules and scripts that I wrote for parsing Jump Lists are somewhat rough—perhaps a better term would be "alpha"—and at the time of this writing, not suitable for release, and are therefore *not* provided with the materials associated with this book. Also, I am concerned that even though Windows 7 has been available for some time, Jump Lists are relatively new and not well understood for their forensic value; as such, releasing a tool that provides information from Jump Lists without the analyst really understanding the nature or context of that information would simply lead to confusion. I do hope to release the tool at some point in the future, after I've had a chance to clean up the code and make it more usable.

ProDiscover (all but the free Basic Edition) also includes a built-in full featured Jump List Viewer, as illustrated in Figure 4.19.

To populate the Jump List Viewer, open your ProDiscover project, right-click on the Users profile directory, and choose "Find Jump List Files..." from the drop-down menu. ProDiscover will scan through the subdirectories, looking for, cataloging, and parsing the various automatic and custom Jump List files (sans the DestList stream in the automatic Jump List files, as of ProDiscover version 7.0.0.3). As of this writing, ProDiscover version 8.2 is available.

FIGURE 4.19

ProDiscover Jump List Viewer.

The key aspect to remember about Jump Lists is that the customDestinations-ms Jump Lists are *usually* created by specific user activity; that is, the user pins an item to the Task Bar or to the application. I say "usually" because I have seen applications installed on a system that come with one or two pinned items (URLs to visit for assistance with the product, etc.) that are visible via the shell. AutomaticDestinations-ms Jump Lists are created automatically by Windows as the user interacts with the application via the Windows Explorer shell. In most cases, the user isn't even aware that the Jump Lists are being populated, which can be very beneficial to an examiner. Within the automaticDestinations-ms Jump List files, the individual numbered streams contain Windows shortcut streams (again, the follow the binary format for LNK files specified by Microsoft) that point to each of the target files or resources, as well as a stream named "DestList" that acts as an MRU list.

Hibernation files

Laptop systems running Windows XP, Windows 7, or Windows 8 (I say this because it's not often that you'll see a server operating system such as Windows 2008 R2 installed on a laptop) may often be found to contain hibernation files. These files are basically the compressed contents of Windows memory from when the system (usually a laptop) "goes to sleep." As such, a hibernation file can contain a great deal of very valuable historic information, including processes and network connections from some point in the past. This information can be used to address issues of malware that may have been installed on the system and then deleted, or demonstrate that a user was logged in or that an application had been running at some point in the past. As with some other artifacts, hibernation files are often not included in "cleanup" processes, such as application uninstalls, or when AV deletes detected malware.

The Volatility Framework, found online at http://code.google.com/p/volatility/, can provide you access to the contents of a Windows hibernation file and allow you to analyze it just as if it were a memory dump. In order to install the Volatility Framework on your system, consult the Volatility Framework wiki for the appropriate instructions (as of the time of this writing, Jamie Levy, a volunteer with the Volatility project, has graciously compiled detailed installation instructions for version 1.4 of the framework).

Detailed discussion of memory analysis is beyond the scope of this book, particularly when there are other, much better suited resources that cover the subject, such as the *Malware Analyst's Cookbook* [2]. However, information found through analysis of the hibernation file can prove to be extremely valuable; analysts have found pertinent information, including keys for encrypted volumes, within hibernation files.

Application files

There are a number of application-specific files that may be found on Windows systems that may be crucial to an analyst. Application logging and configuration information may be critical to an analyst, but the value of those sources of information will depend in large part on the nature and goals of the examination. In the rest of this chapter, we will discuss some of the files that you may run across during an examination, based on some of the various applications that may be installed on the system being examined. In each case, we will also look to applications or tools that may be used to parse and further analyze these files. However, do not consider the rest of this chapter to be a comprehensive and complete list of those files; something like this is just impossible to produce. Application developers develop new tools and storage mechanisms for log and configuration data; for example, some browsers have moved away from text or binary files for bookmark and history/cache storage and have moved to SQLite databases.

> **TIP**
>
> **Accessing SQLite Databases**
> One of the best tools I've found for accessing SQLite databases is the SQLite database browser, found online at http://sqlitebrowser.sourceforge.net. The browser is free, as well as easy to use and set up. While it does provide command line functionality for accessing SQLite databases, it also provides a graphical user interface (GUI) that provides much easier access to the database for browsing, etc.

With new applications being developed all the time and current applications changing, including adding new features, it would be impossible to keep up on all of that information, even if only from a digital forensic analysis perspective. My goal here is to have you consider alternate sources of data to corroborate your findings, or to fill in gaps. For example, application logs can be very useful, as in many cases, entries are only added when the system is running and a user is logged in and using the application. As such, this information can be correlated with Event Log entries or used in the absence of such information. While there is really no way to thoroughly address all applications or even provide an overview, my hope is to provide information about some of the types of files that you might consider including in your analysis.

An aspect of Windows systems that some analysts may not consider is the Windows Error Reporting (WER) service, which captures information about kernel-mode (operating system) and user-mode (application) crashes. Analysts have used information regarding crashes on a system in some cases to provide indications of an attempt to install malware. In other cases, crash reports have been used to get a list of processes running and modules installed at the time of the application hang or crash, illustrating that a particular bit of malware was (or was not) running at a particular time. The WER logs are written to subfolders beneath the *C:\ProgramData\Microsoft\Windows\WER* folder. Beneath the *ReportArchive* subfolders, you will most likely find files named "Report.wer"; these are flat text files that contain some basic information about an application that may have had an issue or crashed, as well as a description of the issue itself. Within the *ReportQueue* subfolders, you will find Report.wer files, as well as XML files that contain more information about devices and drivers that were loaded, etc. If you're performing timeline analysis (discussed in detail in Chapter 7), for example, and you find that a WER report was written near the time of an incident, you'll likely want to open the appropriate files in a viewer (Notepad++ works just fine) and see what information they may contain.

Antivirus logs

Logs produced by AV applications will be discussed in greater detail in Chapter 6, but I wanted to present at least a cursory discussion of the topic in this chapter, for the sake of completeness. AV logs can be extremely valuable to a forensic analyst in a number of ways. During one particular intrusion incident, I examined the AV logs and found that on a specific date (shortly after the files were created), an AV scan had detected and deleted several files identified as malware. Several weeks later, files with the same names appeared on the system again; however, this time, the files were not detected as malware. This information was valuable, in that the logs provided me with names of files to look for, and also allowed me to more accurately determine the *window of compromise*, or how long the malware had actually been on the system. This information was critical to the customer, not only because it was required by the regulatory compliance organization, but also because it reduced their *window of compromise*, but did so with hard data (the creation dates for the second set of files was verified through MFT analysis).

Another use for the AV logs is to help the analyst narrow down what malware might be on the system. For example, Microsoft's Malicious Software Removal

Tool (MSRT) is installed by default on many systems and updated through the regular Windows Update process. MSRT is an application meant to protect the system from specific threats (again, discussed in greater detail in Chapter 6), rather than provide more general protection in the manner of AV products. As such, checking the mrt.log file (located in the Windows\debug directory) will let you know when the application was updated, and the results of any scans that had been run. An example log entry is illustrated here:

```
Microsoft Windows Malicious Software Removal Tool v3.20, June 2011
Started On Wed Jun 15 21:13:25 2011
Results Summary:
----------------
No infection found.
Microsoft Windows Malicious Software Removal Tool Finished On Wed
Jun 15 21:14:45 2011
Return code: 0 (0×0)
```

As you can see, the mrt.log file includes the date of when MSRT was updated; this can be compared to the table in Microsoft KB article 891716 (found online at http://support.microsoft.com/kb/891716) to determine what the system *should* be protected against. Note that KB article 891716 also provides example log excerpts that illustrate malware being detected.

As I've analyzed more and more Windows 7 (and even Vista) systems, I've had an opportunity to dig into the Windows Defender logs. According to Microsoft, Defender is intended to be "your first line of defense against spyware and unwanted software." As such, logs from this application can be useful in determining what the system should be protected against, as well as perhaps provide indications of issues and even possible infections that may have occurred on the system. The Windows Defender log file can be found in the *C:\ProgramData\Microsoft\Windows Defender\Support* folder and can be examined to verify information about when the application was updated.

Skype

Skype is a useful communications utility that has been around for some time, and in the spring of 2011, Microsoft purchased Skype (for a reported $8.5 billion). Skype is not only available on Windows, Linux, and MacOS X computers, but it can be downloaded and run from Apple products (iPhone, iTouch, iPad), as well as from some smart phones and tablets running the Android operating system. As such, it is a pretty pervasive utility for not only making video calls, but also for something as simple as instant messaging, for sharing information outside what may be considered more "normal" channels (as opposed to AOL Instant Messenger, or Internet relay chat).

I've had Skype available on a Windows XP system for some time, in part to test the application and see what tools were available for parsing any log files produced by the application. The current version (as of this writing) of Skype that I'm using

Record Number	Action Type	Action Time
93	Outgoing Call	6/2/2010 7:56:02 PM
94	Outgoing Call	6/2/2010 7:56:02 PM
103	Outgoing Call	6/2/2010 7:56:02 PM
123	Incoming Call	6/10/2010 3:02:03 PM
149	Incoming Call	6/28/2010 9:48:46 AM
157	Outgoing Call	6/28/2010 9:50:39 AM
164	Outgoing Call	6/28/2010 9:53:34 AM
168	Chat Message	6/28/2010 12:13:03 PM
169	Chat Message	6/28/2010 12:13:49 PM
170	Chat Message	6/28/2010 12:13:51 PM
171	Chat Message	6/28/2010 12:13:54 PM

FIGURE 4.20

Portion of Skype Log View UI, accessing main.db.

is 5.3, and the communications logs are maintained in the main.db file located within my user profile, in the "\Application Data\Skype*username*" subdirectory. Two tools available for parsing information from the database file are Skype Log View (available online at http://nirsoft.net/utils/skype_log_view.html) and Skype History Viewer (available online at http://skypehistory.sourceforge.net). Figure 4.20 illustrates a portion of the user interface for Skype Log View (run on my live system) with the contents of the main.db file displayed.

This information can be very useful to an analyst, illustrating not just communications between parties, but also who initiated the call, when the call was initiated, etc. This can also show when the system was in use and may support or refute a user's claims regarding when they were accessing the system.

Apple products

Many of us may have products from Apple, including an iPod or iTouch, an iPhone, or even an iPad. Many of us may also use iTunes to sync and make backups of our devices. In April 2011, two researchers (Alasdair Allan and Pete Warden, article located online at http://radar.oreilly.com/2011/04/apple-location-tracking.html) found that as of the release of iOS 4, the iPhone and iPad would track approximate longitude and latitude information, along with time-stamp information. On the iPhone, this information is reportedly recorded in the file "consolidated.db."

When a user syncs their Apple device to a Windows system via iTunes, the backup information is placed in the user's profile, in the path, "Application Data\Apple Computer\MobileSync\Backup" (on Windows XP; on Windows 7, the path is "\Users*user*\AppData\Roaming\Apple Computer\MobileSync\Backup"). When I sync my iTouch to my Windows XP system, I have a subdirectory in that path with a name that is a long string of characters, as illustrated in Figure 4.21.

The backup information is maintained in that subdirectory in multiple files, also with long strings of characters for names. Within that directory, the Info.plist file is an XML file (you can open it in a text editor) that contains information about the device being backed up, and the Manifest.mbdb and Manifest.mdbx files

FIGURE 4.21

Path to MobileSync\Backup subdirectory.

contain file name translations, between the long strings of characters and the original file names.

The iPhoneBackupBrowser (authored by "reneD" and available on the web at http://code.google.com/p/iphonebackupbrowser/) is a freely available tool that allows you to access the backup information, reportedly beginning with iTunes 9.1.1, and parse the Manifest.mbdb file in order to map the backup file names to their original names. The wiki at the Google Code site includes information about the format of the Manifest.mbdb file, as well as the Manifest.mbdx index file (so you can write your own parser, if need be). The iPhoneBackupBrowser application itself reportedly runs better on Windows 7 than Windows XP, due to some of the APIs accessed. Once you download the tools and place them into a directory, you can run mbdbdump.exe (works just fine on Windows XP) against the Manifest.mbdb file by passing the path to the directory where the file is located to the tool, as follows:

```
D:\tools\iphone > mbdbdump [path to directory] > output.txt
```

The resulting output file contains the parsed contents of the Manifest.mbdb file, allowing you to search for specific files, such as the "consolidated.db" file. Once you determine which of the files with the long file names is the "consolidated.db" file, you can use free tools for accessing SQLite databases, such as the SQLite Browser (mentioned previously in this chapter) or the SQLite Manager add-on for Firefox (available at https://addons.mozilla.org/en-US/firefox/addon/sqlite-manager/) to peruse the contents of the database and extract the location information. The researchers stated in their article that the information recorded for each location may not be exact; however, from an overall perspective, it can show routes and that the phone or tablet was in a particular proximity at a specific time.

TIP

iTouch Backup

Even though I ran my initial tests against the backup of an iTouch, rather than an iPhone, some of the available information was pretty telling. Parsing through the mbdbdump. exe output, I could clearly see installed applications, as well as files that likely contained configuration information, such as wireless networks I'd connected to via WiFi. All of this information may be valuable to an analyst or investigator.

An analyst can use information within these backup files in order to develop more detailed information regarding specific devices attached to the system, as well as possibly gain further insight into the user's movements, not just geographically but also around the web.

NOTE

Android Devices

Apparently, Apple products may not be the only devices to record location information. In April 2011, Cory Altheide (of Google) pointed me to Packetlss's Android-locdump site (available online at https://github.com/packetlss/android-locdump), in which the author of the site describes which files on some Android devices (no specific devices were named) apparently maintain location information for WiFi sites and cell phone towers. I checked my BackFlip (Motorola MB300 handset, running kernel version 2.6.29) and didn't find the files mentioned at the site (the site does mention that you will need to be "root" or superuser to see the files). The site also includes a Python script for parsing the information in the cache.wifi and cache.cell files into more readable format. As with Apple products, the information in these files may be extremely valuable to an investigator, and they may exist on a Windows system if the user copied them or backed up the information on their handset or device.

Image files

I own a work phone and a personal cell phone, both of which can be described as "smart" phones, and both of which contain cameras. I also own an iTouch, which contains a camera. I can connect all of these devices directly to my computer and copy pictures and videos directly to a folder. There are very few similar devices available these days that do not contain a camera of some type, and most of the ones available are capable of producing very high-quality digital images and videos. Not only that, many of the devices have global positioning system (GPS) capabilities; a friend of mine once took a picture with their Droid phone, swiped their hand across the screen, and pulled up a Google map with a push-pin on the location where the digital photo was taken. This simply illustrates that digital images can contain a significant amount of metadata; the question is then, how can you access that data?

One excellent tool for doing exactly that is Phil Harvey's EXIFTool (found online at http://www.sno.phy.queensu.ca/~phil/exiftool/). The term "EXIF" stands for "exchangeable image file," which is a standard that specifies the formats of various tags used by digital cameras (as well as smart phones and scanners), and Phil's tool is capable of extracting embedded EXIF (metadata) information from within a number of image file formats. The tool can be used from the command line, an example of which follows:

```
D:\tools > exiftool -a -u -g1 D:\pictures\img_3791_2165.jpg
---- ExifTool ----
ExifTool Version Number: 8.60
---- System ----
File Name: img_3791_2165.jpg
```

```
Directory: D:/pictures
File Size: 4.0 MB
File Modification Date/Time : 2010:07:18 15:32:06-04:00
File Permissions : rw-rw-rw-
---- File ----
File Type : JPEG
…snip…
---- IFD0 ----
Make : Canon
Camera Model Name : Canon EOS DIGITAL REBEL XTi
Orientation : Horizontal (normal)
```

I added "…snip…" to the above output to indicate that I'd removed some information to make it easier to view; neither the tool nor the camera added that to the output. I am able to verify the relevant output because I have seen the camera, and know that it is, in fact, a Canon EOS Digital Rebel XTi camera.

Further along in the output of the tool, we see the following additional information:

```
Canon Image Type : Canon EOS DIGITAL REBEL XTi
Canon Firmware Version : Firmware 1.1.1
Owner Name : unknown
Serial Number : 2271247134
Canon Model ID : EOS Digital Rebel XTi/400D/Kiss Digital X
…snip…
Internal Serial Number : H3624774
```

From this, we can see that we have two possible candidate serial numbers to uniquely identify the camera. So, if the user had copied the image from the camera and the camera was available to be analyzed, you could use this and other information (image file hashes, information from the computer system Registry indicating that the camera had been connected to the system, etc.) to definitively tie the image to the devices, and to the user.

What other information might be available within images? Well, many smart phones come with global positioning capability enabled, and GPS information may be embedded within the images. Phil's tool is capable of extracting that information, as well as a great deal of additional information that may be embedded within a number of image file formats.

TIP

File Metadata

Phil Harvey's EXIFTool is reportedly capable of reading metadata from file formats other than just images. For example, the web site for the tool indicates that it can read metadata embedded in MS Office 2007 (and above) file formats (.docx, .pptx, and .xlsx file extensions), making it a very versatile and potentially valuable tool. Another tool capable of reading metadata from MS Office 2007 file formats is read_open_xml.pl, available from http://blog.kiddaland.net/downloads/. Information derived from the use of either of these tools can be very useful, depending upon your investigation.

A final thought on metadata such as we've discussed in this section: while metadata can be very useful and even immensely valuable to an analyst, the simple fact is that not all files have metadata, and not all files that do have metadata necessarily have all metadata fields populated; if the metadata isn't there, it isn't there. For example, some images captured on via cell phone cameras may not have GPS coordinates as part of the image EXIF data. This may be due to the fact that the cell phone is not a "smart" phone and did not have a GPS receiver, or that the software used to capture the image did not embed the data, or there could be other reasons.

SUMMARY

Windows systems contain a number of files in a variety of both open and proprietary formats. Depending on the type of case that you're working or what you're looking for, these files will be of varying importance. However, my intention in this chapter has been to make you aware of some of the various files (and formats) available, and how their contents have been used to further examinations. One particularly important aspect of this chapter has been to help you understand that in many cases, a file can be much more than just a binary stream of data. For example, if you understand the structure of the data, and how the various elements of the structure are used by an application, or even the operating system, you will then have some context associated with that data. I once worked with another analyst who had identified a particular string—a file name—within a Windows portable executable (PE) file (the structure of these files is discussed in *Windows Forensic Analysis, Second Edition* [3]). Before reporting this finding to the customer, further analysis needed to be completed; for example, did this file name refer to a DLL within the import table of the PE file, or was it the name of a file used as a data repository? The answer to this question, while relatively easy to determine, can have a significant impact on the overall examination.

References

[1] Carrier B. File system forensic analysis. Pearson Education, Inc., <http://www.amazon.com/System-Forensic-Analysis-Brian-Carrier/dp/0321268172>; 2005.0-321-26817-2.

[2] Ligh MH, Adair S, Hartstein B, Richard M. Malware analyst's cookbook and DVD. Wiley Publishing, Inc., <http://www.amazon.com/Malware-Analysts-Cookbook-Techniques-Malicious-ebook/dp/B0047DWCMA/ref=sr_1_1?s=books&ie=UTF8&qid=1390435955&sr=1-1&keywords=malware+analyst%27s+cookbook>; 2011.978-0-470-61303-0.

[3] Carvey HA. Windows forensic analysis, 2nd ed. : Syngress Publishing, Inc., <http://www.amazon.com/Windows-Forensic-Analysis-DVD-Toolkit-ebook/dp/B002ZFXTXI/ref=sr_1_2?s=books&ie=UTF8&qid=1390435996&sr=1-2&keywords=windows+forensic+analysis>; 2009.978-1597494229.

Registry Analysis

CHAPTER
5

INFORMATION IN THIS CHAPTER

- Registry Analysis

119

INTRODUCTION

The Registry is a key component of every Windows system, and as Windows systems have become more complex, progressing from Windows 2000 to XP and on to Windows 7 and 8, the value of the Registry as a source of forensic data has likewise increased. As such, what is available to an analyst through analysis of the Registry needs to be better understood. As the versions of Windows have progressed, each new version has brought with it new data that can be critical to an investigation. As applications come to rely more on the Registry, and the "user experience" is monitored and optimized, even in part by the Registry, more useful data is available to be incorporated into an examination.

The Windows Registry has always been a central component, not just of Windows systems, but of the forensic analysis of those systems. The Registry contains a great deal of configuration information that can significantly impact your analysis. For example, a Registry single value can determine whether or not file last accessed times are updated through normal user activity, or if files automatically bypass the Recycle Bin when the user simply selects the file and hits the "Delete" key, or if application Prefetch files (see Chapter 4) are created, or which domain name service (DNS) server the system will use for name resolution. All of these like very basic aspects or configuration settings for a Windows system, but each one can have a significant impact on your analysis. If the user's Recycle Bin folder is empty, do you assume that they emptied it, or do you check the NukeOnDelete value? A single Registry value can tell you which volumes, if any, are being monitored for the creation of Volume Shadow Copies (VSCs, see Chapter 3), or if the Internet Explorer (IE) browser history gets automatically cleared when the user closes the application.

The Registry also records a great deal of user activity. For example, on Windows 7 systems, if the user clears the IE browser history, an entry gets created in the user's hive file with the date and time that they cleared it. The user's UserAssist subkeys (discussed in detail later, in the User Hives section) provide something of a record of the applications that the user has launched via the Windows Explorer shell, and when they last launched that application. The Registry also records information about folders, devices, network resources, and files the user accessed, and in some cases, when they accessed each of the files. Much of this recorded information persists well after the user removes the application that they launched. For example, I have analyzed systems and found that the user installed an application, ran it multiple times, and deleted that application; all of these actions, from launching the setup routine to launching the uninstall routine, and everything in between, was recorded right there in the Registry. All of this can be very valuable to an examiner, and provide a great deal of context and granularity to the examination.

In this chapter, we will not be discussing the Registry in detail, as other resources have already laid the groundwork on this subject. Details of the Registry are covered in Ref. [1] and even more so in Ref. [2]. Much of what was covered in these two books (particularly the binary structure of the Registry, as well as

Registry analysis techniques and tools) applies across all versions of Windows, including Windows 7 and 8. Ligh et al. [3] provide considerable information regarding how the Registry can be a valuable forensic resource when analyzed in conjunction with or as part of Windows physical memory and malware analysis. With this considerable treatment of the topic, there is really no significant value in repeating what's already been said; as such, in this chapter, we will assume that the reader (that's you) has a basic understanding of the Registry—where the hives are located within the file system, the difference between a "key" and a "value" some of the tools used to collect information from the Registry (including but not limited to RegRipper), etc.—and focus on information available in the Registry that is specific to Windows 7.

Also, I'd like to take something of a different approach in this chapter; rather than providing a list of keys or values of interest, I'd like to discuss the Registry in terms of addressing analysis questions through case studies or investigative processes. Many resources leave it up to the analyst to flip back and forth between the various pages, trying to track information between hives; instead, I think it may be useful to present all of the components of a case study together. Hopefully, this approach will be valuable to analysts.

Finally, one of the questions I hear continually from the community after the release of a new version of Windows is, "what's new?" I'm not really sure how it is useful to provide a long list of what's "new"—new file paths, new Registry keys and values (and data), new data structures, etc.—that no one is going to ever be able to remember. For example, I hear the question, "what's new in Windows 8?" fairly often, and in many cases, the folks asking that question may not yet have done a deep analysis of a Windows 7 system, so where do I start? The fact is that each version of Windows, with different service packs and applications installed, presents both its own challenges and its own opportunities. While some folks have conducted research into specific artifacts associated with, for example, the use of the Photos tile on the Windows 8 desktop, I would suggest that it's far more important (and beneficial) to build on your analysis *process* than it is to focus on any one particular artifact, or set of artifacts. With this chapter, my hope is to develop an appreciation for the value of the Windows Registry as a forensic resource so that more analysts will include it in their analysis process, and share their findings with others.

Registry analysis

All of the information presented and discussed in the first two chapters of the book *Windows Registry Forensics* applies across all versions of Windows, particularly the analysis concepts, the binary structure of the Registry (including key and value cells), and the tools that can be used to extract and view information from the Registry, such as RegRipper (available online from http://windowsir.blogspot.com/p/books.html). This book also covers the use of RegRipper in some detail, including how to set it up, how to use it, and even how to create your own plugins for extracting and translating information of interest from the Registry. As such, there's really no need to repeat content and graphics of what the Registry "looks like" with respect to the native Registry Editor or files on the system, or when the hive file is opened in another, nonnative viewer, such as the MiTeC Windows Registry Recovery (WRR) tool (which can be found online at http://www.mitec.cz/wrr.html). Other tools for extracting and viewing information from Registry keys and values, or monitoring accesses to the Registry on a live system (such as Process Monitor, found online at http://technet.microsoft.com/en-us/sysinternals/bb896645) work equally well on Windows XP, Windows 7, and Windows 8 systems.

As an example, the information from Chapter 3 of *Windows Registry Forensics* regarding using tools such as pwdump7.exe in order to extract and view the password hashes in the security accounts manager (SAM) hive applies equally as well to Vista, Windows 2008, and Windows 7. However, it is important to keep in mind that the LAN Manager password hash field will (in most cases) say "no password" or "blank" (depending upon the tool used), as the "NoLMHash" value (discussed in MS KB article 299656, found online at http://support.microsoft.com/kb/299656) exists and is set to "1" by default on those versions of the Windows operating system.

Instead, the approach I'd like to take in this chapter is to address analysis questions through case studies, or investigative steps that you can take to answer some common questions when it comes to Registry analysis. In several instances (albeit not all), these case studies will correlate data from multiple hive files, so it makes sense to present the information all together in a single process flow, rather than spreading that information across multiple chapters.

TIP

Registry Structure

A key concept discussed in Chapter 4 is applicable in this chapter as well; that is, locating data in a Registry hive file using something like strings.exe or the BinText application tells us that the string is there. But understanding the structure of the data where the string exists within the "container," and how that data is used by an application provides us with *context* to that information. This can be extremely valuable, as the location of the string can have a significant impact on your examination. For example, if the string that you're interested in is a key name, that information will take your examination in a vastly different direction than if the string were a value name, or if the string was actually located within unallocated space within the hive file. Understanding how this context applies to Registry analysis leads to good choices during analysis, which in turn can lead the analyst to a shorter path to achieving their analysis goals.

This is an important concept to keep in mind. As such, we also discuss the context of data with respect to surrounding data at other points in this book, including within Chapter 7, when we explore creating and analyzing timelines (TLNs) of system activity.

Registry nomenclature

Before we begin our discussion of Registry analysis and dive into some case studies, one thing I think is important to reiterate is Registry nomenclature. Many

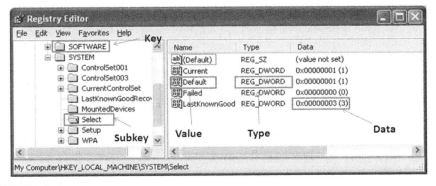

FIGURE 5.1

Registry viewed via RegEdit.exe.

analysts may not completely understand the names of various objects within the Registry, or why they're important. Figure 5.1 illustrates a fairly standard view of the Registry on a live system via the native Registry Editor tool.

As you can see in Figure 5.1, the Registry is made up of keys, values, and value data. It is important for analysts to understand the differences between these various objects, as they have different properties associated with them. For example, Registry keys (the folders visible in the left-hand pane in Figure 5.1) contain subkeys and values, and also have a property referred to as the LastWrite time. This is a 64-bit FILETIME (a description of the FILETIME object can be found online at http://support.microsoft.com/kb/188768) time stamp that refers to the last time the key was modified in some way. This can include the key being created (creation or deletion being the extreme form of modification), or subkeys or values within the key being added, deleted, or modified. This is an important distinction, as Registry values do not have LastWrite times; however, some Registry values may contain time stamps within their data that refer to some other function or action having occurred. The value of the Registry key LastWrite times, as well as time stamps recorded within the data of various values will be discussed through case studies in this chapter, and are also discussed in Chapter 7.

NOTE

Unicode RLO Control Character

Registry key and value names are stored within their structures in ASCII format. This is easy to verify by opening a hive file in a hex editor, locating either a key or value, and following the structure until you locate where the name is stored. However, the Unicode "right-to-left override" (RLO) control character (U + 202E) can be inserted into the name, either prepended to the beginning of the name, or inserted anywhere within the name. When this is done, everything following the name is reversed when viewed in Unicode-aware applications, such as the Registry Editor (RegEdit). So, you can create a Registry key, name it "etadpupg," and then insert the RLO control character at the beginning of the name (in RegEdit, select the name, right click, select "Rename" from the drop-down menu, and when the name is surrounded by a box, right click again and choose "Insert Unicode Control Character," and choose the appropriate character). Once you've modified the name, you should see "gpupdate" displayed. However, what you see in RegEdit isn't what the computer sees—the computer and operating system think that the name of the key is the RLO control character followed by "etadpupg." This technique has been used as a persistence mechanism for malware; the malware author has the installation routine for the malware create a Windows service using the RLO control character as part of the name, so that when the Registry is viewed using tools such as RegEdit, it can be very difficult to tell which services are legitimate, and which is the malicious service. The RegRipper *rlo.pl* plugin will help you detect the use of this technique to disguise the persistence of malware within the Registry; the plugin works for all hives, and can detect both key and value names that were hidden using this technique.

The registry as a log file

Microsoft refers to the "structured storage" file format (known as "common object model (COM) structured storage" or "object linking and embedding (OLE) structured storage"; the format used for Word documents up to and including MS Office 2003, as well as Jump List and Sticky Notes files on Windows 7, and the binary format specification can be found online at http://msdn.microsoft.com/en-us/library/dd942138(v=prot.13).aspx) as a "file system within a file," and if you think about it, the same thing can be said about a Registry hive. Keys are often viewed as "folders," as they contain other keys as well as values. As such, values can then be viewed as "files," with the value data comprising the file contents. Taking this a step further, we can view a Registry hive file as a log file, as various system and user activity is recorded within the hive files, along with modifications to time stamps (i.e., Registry key LastWrite times). This is important to keep in mind, as some of the most valuable data can be derived from the Registry when combining value data with available time stamps, much like one would do when conducting log file analysis.

All that being said, I think we're ready to take a look at some of the analysis that can be done through the Registry.

USB device analysis

Tracking the use of USB devices—in particular, thumb drives or external drive enclosures (also referred to as "wallet" drives)—can be a very important aspect of an investigation. For example, determining that a specific removable device was connected to a system, along with information such as who was logged into the system at the time, and what data was accessed during that time period, may provide indications that an employee copied sensitive corporate data onto that device. Alternately, combining information about external device connection with events relating to a malware infection may not only identify a thumb drive as the source of the infection, but also which specific device introduced the malware. Windows 7 and 8 systems record a great deal of information with respect to USB devices that users connect to those systems, most of which is stored in the Registry. Starting with the Registry, an analyst may discover some very interesting information with respect to devices that were connected to a Windows 7 system. For example, it may be possible to not only discover which types of devices were connected to the system, but also to uniquely identify those devices (via a unique instance identifier, or serial number) and determine *when* the devices were connected to the system. In order to do this, however, we need to not only extract information from multiple locations within a hive file, but we also need to look to information within multiple hive files (System, Software, and NTUSER. DAT). What we will do in this section is walk through a couple of examples of connecting devices to a Windows 7 system, and extracting the information and artifacts of those connections for analysis.

TIP

Analysis Checklists

For analyzing USB thumb drives and drive enclosures that have been connected to Windows systems, Rob Lee, faculty fellow at the SANS Institute, created checklists that can be used in your USB device analysis. The checklist for USB keys and thumb drives is available online at http://blogs.sans.org/computer-forensics/files/2009/09/USBKEY-Guide.pdf, and the checklist for drive enclosures is available online at http://blogs.sans.org/computer-forensics/files/2009/09/USB_Drive_Enclosure-Guide.pdf.

In our first example, we will start with a thumb drive. In this case, I used a 1 gigabyte (GB) thumb drive that I purchased at Best Buy several years ago. The device has a "Geek Squad" logo on it, as well as a "U3 Smart" logo (I removed the U3 components from the device a while back).

TIP

U3-Enabled Devices

To see artifacts left by U3-enabled devices, see Chapter 4 of *Windows Forensic Analysis Second Edition.*

The Geek Squad thumb drive had never been connected to my target Windows 7 system before. I connected it to the system at approximately 8:13 am eastern daylight time (EDT) (equates to 12:13 pm UTC), and disconnected approximately 40 minutes later. Then I reconnected the thumb drive to the same Windows 7 system at approximately 9:14 am EDT (approximately 1:14 pm UTC), and used Forensic Toolkit (FTK) Imager version 3.0.0.1442 to extract the System and Software hive files, as well as the NTUSER.DAT from my user profile, from the system. I then shut the system down.

So the first place to start looking for information about the device is in the USBStor keys within the System hive. This has long been known as an initial location where information about USB removable storage devices (thumb drives, "wallet" drives, and as we'll see later in the System hive section, other devices recognized as removable storage) is maintained. The full path to this key on a live system is:

```
HKLM\System\CurrentControlSet\Enum\USBStor
```

TIP

Locating the Current ControlSet

You will notice when viewing the System hive file (using the Registry Editor or another viewer such as WRR) extracted from an acquired image, you won't see a key named "CurrentControlSet." Instead, you will see two (or possibly three) keys with names such as "ControlSet001" and "ControlSet003." To determine which of these was treated as the current ControlSet, go to the Select key and look at the value "Current." This will tell you which ControlSet you should look to as the CurrentControlSet.

In this case, we'll be looking at the subkey beneath the ControlSet001 key. Following the path and looking at the subkeys beneath the USBStor key, we see an entry for the Geek Squad device, which is illustrated in Figure 5.2.

As you can see in Figure 5.2, immediately beneath the USBStor key we see the device instance identifier (device class ID, or just "device ID") for the device, and then immediately beneath that key we see the unique instance ID key for the device itself. This unique instance ID is, in fact, the serial number maintained in the device descriptor (*not* the storage section) of the Geek Squad thumb drive.

WARNING

Device Mapping

This unique instance ID is used on Windows 7 and Vista systems to map the device found beneath the USBStor key to other elements that are critical to our analysis, such as which drive letter was used to mount the removable device. On Windows XP systems, a value named *ParentIdPrefix* was created and used to perform this mapping. While this value is not created by Vista and above systems, the unique instance ID (or serial number) is used instead.

If we view the relevant Registry keys with WRR, we can right click on the device ID and choosing Properties, we can see the LastWrite time for the device ID key, as illustrated in Figure 5.3.

FIGURE 5.2

USBStor subkeys, seen via WRR.

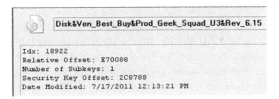

FIGURE 5.3

USBSstor device subkey properties seen via WRR.

From Figure 5.3, we see that the LastWrite time of the device ID key corre-lates to the time that the device was first connected to the system since the last time the system was rebooted. What this means is that after the system is booted, a device can be (and in this case, was) connected to the system multiple times; the LastWrite time of the device ID key correlates to the *first* time that the device was connected to the system following the most recent reboot. Prior to the system being shut down, the device can be disconnected and reconnected multiple times, but the LastWrite time of this key will—in most cases—reflect when the device was first connected during that boot session. However, this may not always be the case; some analysts have reported finding cases where multiple devices had been con-nected to a Windows system, and all of the devices listed beneath the USBStor key had the same LastWrite time. There is speculation within the community that this anomaly may be the result of a Service Pack or patch having been installed, or of a Group Policy Object (GPO) that modifies the access control list (ACL) on the keys; further analysis of the system itself (perhaps using the TLN creation techniques dis-cussed in Chapter 7 of this book) would be recommended.

TIP

Driver Events

When a USB device is connected to a Windows 7 system for the first time, an entry is written to the C:\Windows\inf\setupapi.dev.log file (per http://support.microsoft.com/kb/927521, this file contains information about Plug and Play devices and driver installation), and events with identifier (ID) 20003 and 20001 and source "UserPnp" are written to the System Event Log. There may also be event IDs 10000 and 10002 (source is "DriverFrameworks-UserMode"), indicating the installation or update of a device driver. These events will contain an identifier or name of the device that can be correlated to information extracted from the Registry. When drivers are loaded to support a USB device, several events are generated in the Microsoft-Windows-DriverFrameworks-UserMode/Operational Event Log, with IDs of 1003, 2003, 2010, 2004, 2105, etc., all containing a name or identifier for the device. When the device is removed from the system, a series of events (IDs 2100, 2102, 1006, 2900, etc.) are written to the DriverFrameworks-UserMode/Operational Event Log, as the driver host process for the device is shut down. As such, the System Event Log can be useful in correlating information about USB devices being connected to a Windows 7 system for the first time, and the Microsoft-Windows-DriverFrameworks-UserMode/Operational Event Logs, if available, can provide information regarding when devices were connected and removed from the system, allowing you to see how long the device had been connected.

At this point, we also have the unique instance ID (or serial number) of the device, which can uniquely identify the device. I say "can," simply because there is no guarantee that each and every USB thumb drive with a serial number has (or must have) a unique serial number. Some analysts have reported seeing several devices from the same manufacturer, all with the same serial number. Further, some devices do not have serial numbers within their device descriptors and are assigned a unique instance ID by the Windows system to which they're connected. We can tell the difference between a serial number and a unique instance ID assigned by the operating system, as the one assigned by the operating system has an "&" as the second character. As you can see in Figure 5.2, our example serial number listed in the figure (0C90195032E36889&0) has an "&" as the *second to last character*, but a unique instance ID assigned by the operating system will have an "&" as the second character. This allows the device to be uniquely identified on that system. The algorithm used to create a unique instance ID for a device that does not have a serial number is not publicly available but is important for analysts to know and understand the distinction in unique instance IDs.

Next, we navigate to the Enum\USB subkey within the same ControlSet, and locate the subkey whose name is the serial number (or unique instance ID) of the device in question. The key for the device we're interested in, visible in WRR, is illustrated in Figure 5.4.

Right clicking on the key named for the unique instance ID (in this example, the serial number for the device) and selecting Properties, we can see the LastWrite time of the key, illustrated in Figure 5.5.

The LastWrite time of the unique instance ID/serial number key correlates to the *last* time that the device was connected to the system. This finding appears to be fairly consistent across Windows systems.

Next, we need to navigate to the MountedDevices key at the root of the System hive, and within the values, locate the volume globally unique identifier (volume GUID) that contains the device serial number within its data. In our example, the data for the volume GUID "\??\Volume{b7d8834c-b065-11e0-834c-005056c00008}" contains the device unique instance ID (i.e., serial number), as illustrated in Figure 5.6.

NOTE

The Mysterious Q:\ Volume

Early in 2013, I started to see questions in some of the online forums regarding a value beneath the MountedDevices key that pointed to a Q:\ volume. The values beneath the MountedDevices key are well understood as being useful in USB device discovery and analysis, and in some cases, analysts were surprised to see volumes up to perhaps G:\ or H:\ listed, and an entry for Q:\ seemed out of order. Further, the data associated with this value appeared to contain a volume GUID, rather than what was "normally" seen for these values. That is, this volume did not appear to be a partition on an existing drive, nor did the data point to a removable device or another device, such as a DVD-ROM drive.

It turns out that MS KB article 2028653 (found online at http://support.microsoft.com/kb/2028653) provides some useful information regarding the Q:\ volume; specifically, this is an artifact of the "Click-to-run" feature for installing MS Office 2010.

Additional information regarding the "Click-to-run" feature can be found on the MS Office 2010 Engineering blog (found online at http://blogs.technet.com/b/office2010/archive/2009/11/06/click-to-run-delivering-office-in-the-21st-century.aspx).

USB
ROOT_HUB
ROOT_HUB20
VID_0403&PID_C580
VID_04B4&PID_6560
VID_08EC&PID_0016
0C90195032E36889

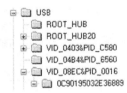

FIGURE 5.4

Enum\USB subkeys visible via WRR.

0C90195032E36889
Idx: 18527
Relative Offset: E06C98
Number of Subkeys: 3
Security Key Offset: 2C8788
Date Modified: 7/17/2011 1:14:52 PM

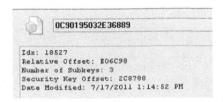

FIGURE 5.5

Enum\USB subkey properties visible via WRR.

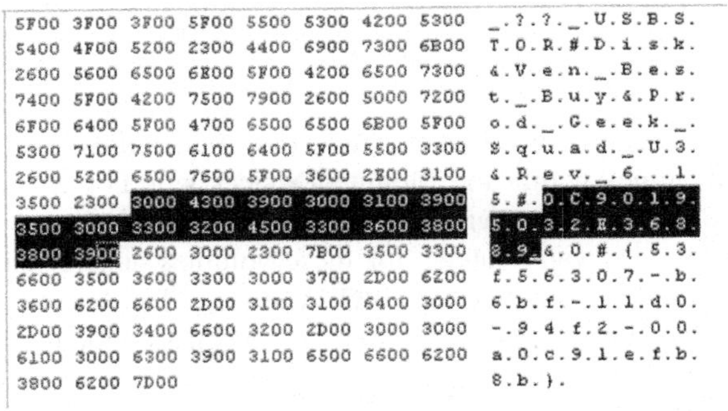

5F00 3F00 3F00 5F00 5500 5300 4200 5300 _.?.?._.U.S.B.S.
5400 4F00 5200 2300 4400 6900 7300 6B00 T.O.R.#.D.i.s.k.
2600 5600 6500 6E00 5F00 4200 6500 7300 &.V.e.n._.B.e.s.
7400 5F00 4200 7500 7900 2600 5000 7200 t._.B.u.y.&.P.r.
6F00 6400 5F00 4700 6500 6500 6B00 5F00 o.d._.G.e.e.k._.
5300 7100 7500 6100 6400 5F00 5500 3300 S.q.u.a.d._.U.3.
2600 5200 6500 7600 5F00 3600 2E00 3100 &.R.e.v._.6...1.
3500 2300 3000 4300 3900 3000 3100 3900 5.#.0.C.9.0.1.9.
3500 3000 3300 3200 4500 3300 3600 3800 5.0.3.2.E.3.6.8.
3800 3900 2600 3000 2300 7B00 3500 3300 8.9.&.0.#.{.5.3.
6600 3500 3600 3300 3000 3700 2D00 6200 f.5.6.3.0.7.-.b.
3600 6200 6600 2D00 3100 3100 6400 3000 6.b.f.-.1.1.d.0.
2D00 3900 3400 6600 3200 2D00 3000 3000 -.9.4.f.2.-.0.0.
6100 3000 6300 3900 3100 6500 6600 6200 a.0.c.9.1.e.f.b.
3800 6200 7D00 8.b.}.

FIGURE 5.6

Volume GUID data seen in WRR.

As you can see in Figure 5.6, the device serial number is selected within the value's binary data. Also within the data, we can see the device ID ("Ven_Best_Buy&Pord_Geek_Squad_U3"), as well. Now, as it turns out, the MountedDevices key also contains a value named "\DosDevices\F:," which contains the same data as the volume ID value seen in Figure 5.6. This tells us that the device had been mapped to the F:\ volume on the system; this information can be very useful during an examination (for mapping to file paths, volumes listed in Windows shortcuts/shell link (LNK) files and jump lists, etc.). What this also indicates is that no other device had been mapped to the F:\ volume after the Geek Squad device was removed from the system; had another device been connected and mounted as the F:\ volume, we would likely see another device's information in the data, as opposed to that of the Geek Squad device.

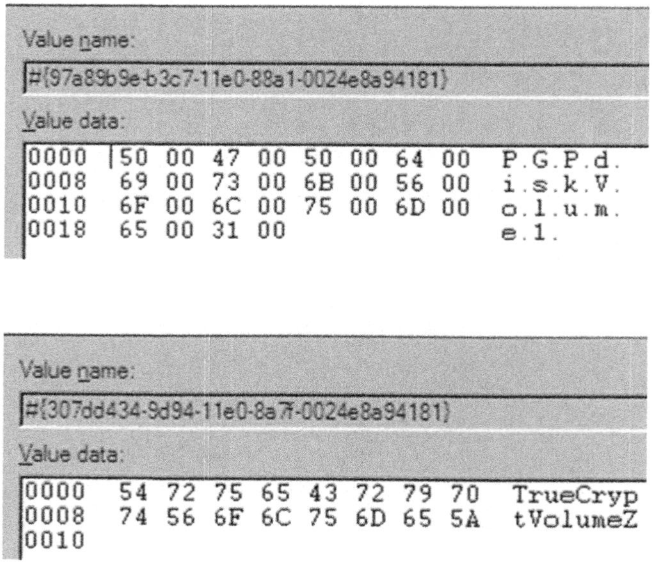

Value name:

#{97a89b9e-b3c7-11e0-88a1-0024e8a94181}

Value data:

```
0000  50 00 47 00 50 00 64 00    P.G.P.d.
0008  69 00 73 00 6B 00 56 00    i.s.k.V.
0010  6F 00 6C 00 75 00 6D 00    o.l.u.m.
0018  65 00 31 00                e.1.
```

Value name:

#{307dd434-9d94-11e0-8a7f-0024e8a94181}

Value data:

```
0000  54 72 75 65 43 72 79 70    TrueCryp
0008  74 56 6F 6C 75 6D 65 5A    tVolumeZ
0010
```

FIGURE 5.7

PGPDisk and TrueCrypt volumes listed within the MountedDevices key.

This is a good time to mention that you may find indications of a variety of other types of volumes within the MountedDevices key. For example, TrueCrypt and PGPDisk volumes can be seen listed here, as well, as illustrated in Figure 5.7.

As you can see, the value names for these volumes appear listed a bit differently, beginning with "#" rather than "\??\Volume." The use of TrueCrypt and PGPDisk volumes may be part of legitimate business practices; forensic analysts will often use both of these methods to protect data being stored or shipped. However, it may also indicate specific attempts to hide data.

TIP

DeviceClasses

Within the System hive, the DeviceClasses subkeys maintain some very good information about USB devices. If you navigate to the ControlSet001\Control\DeviceClasses key (or whichever ControlSet is marked "current"), and then locate the "{53f56307-b6bf-11d0-94f2-00a0c91efb8b}" subkey (the GUID refers to devices identified as disks), then beneath this subkey, you will find a subkey that starts with "##?#USBSTOR" and contains the device ID ("VEN_BEST_BUY&PROD_GEEK_SQUAD_U3") and unique instance ID ("0C90195032E36889") for the thumb drive in question. If you look for the "{53f5630d-b6bf-11d0-94f2-00a0c91efb8b}" subkey (refers to volumes) beneath the DevicesClasses key, you should find a subkey that starts with "##?#STORAGE#VOLUME#_??_USBSTOR," and also contains the device ID and serial number of the thumb drive. In both cases, the LastWrite time for the keys containing the device ID and unique instance ID of the device corresponds to the *first* time that the device was connected to the system during the most recent boot session.

This may not seem like very valuable information, but the fact that these keys are available provides additional, correlating information for an analyst. This information can be particularly helpful when someone has taken steps to cover their tracks, and has perhaps deleted the contents of the USBStor key mentioned earlier in this chapter in an attempt to hide the fact that they connected a device to the system, as remnants may still exist in other locations within the Registry.

Now we can navigate to the Software\Microsoft\Windows\CurrentVersion\ Explorer\MountPoints2 key within the NTUSER.DAT hive file for a user, and locate the subkey with the same name as the volume GUID ("{b7d8834c-b065-11e0-834c-005056c00008}"). Right clicking that key and choosing "Properties" we can see that the LastWrite time for that key corresponds to the *last* time that the device was connected to the system, as illustrated in Figure 5.8.

The information illustrated in Figure 5.8 not only allows us to see when the device was last connected to the system but also under which user context it was connected.

By now, you should be able to see that there is a great deal of information available within the Windows 7 Registry regarding USB thumb drives. Starting with the ControlSet00x\Enum\USBStor subkeys (where "*x*" refers to the ControlSet marked as "current" within the Select key) in the System hive, we can determine the device class and unique instance IDs of devices connected to the system. We can use the unique instance ID to then map to the MountedDevices key (at the root of the System hive) and determine the volume GUID, and possibly the drive letter to which the device was mounted. Then using this information, we can determine both when the device was first connected during the most recent boot session (LastWrite times from USBStor and DeviceClasses subkeys), as well as when the device was last connected to the system (LastWrite time from USB subkey in the System hive, and MountPoints2 subkey in the NTUSER.DAT hive).

FIGURE 5.8

MountPoints2 volume GUID subkey LastWrite time (via WRR).

Interestingly enough, there's even more information available about USB-connected devices in the Windows 7 Registry. For instance, continuing with our previous example and navigating to the "Microsoft\Windows Portable Devices\Devices" key in the Software hive, we see a subkey named as follows:

```
WPDBUSENUMROOT#UMB#2&37C186B&0&STORAGE#VOLUME#_??_
USBSTOR#DISK&VEN_BEST_BUY&PROD_GEEK_SQUAD_U3&REV_6.15#0C901950
32E36889&0#
```

The LastWrite time for this key (viewed via WRR) correlates to the *first* time that the device was connected to the system during the most recent boot session. Also, the key has value named "FriendlyName," whose data is "Test."

Next, if we navigate to the "Microsoft\Windows NT\CurrentVersion\EMDMgmt" key within the Software hive, we see a key named as follows:

```
_??_USBSTOR#Disk&Ven_Best_Buy&Prod_Geek_Squad_U3&Rev_6.15#0C9019503
2E36889&0#{53f56307-b6bf-11d0-94f2-00a0c91efb8b}TEST_1677970716
```

Information available online indicates that the EMDMgmt key is associated with ReadyBoost, a technology available beginning with Vista systems (and included in Windows 7 and 8) that allows the system to use a USB-connected device as a source of RAM. Within the name of the key, we can see the device ID, the unique instance ID, and the word "TEST" is actually the name of the FAT16 volume on the device. As with the Devices key discussed previously, the LastWrite time on this key appears to correlate to the first time that the device was connected to the system during the most recent boot session. In addition, the key contains several values, as illustrated in Figure 5.9.

As you can see in Figure 5.9, the available values could potentially provide some valuable information, in particular the "LastTestedTime" value. If this value and the "CacheSizeInMB" value were populated with nonzero data, this might indicate that the device was used as a ReadyBoost drive, and provide information regarding when it was last tested. If nothing else, this key and its values provide an additional indication of certain devices that had been connected to the system, even if they hadn't been tested by ReadyBoost.

Another piece of information available from the EMDMgmt key, particularly for USB hard drive enclosures ("wallet drives") is the volume serial number for the mounted volume. Now, this is not the drive or disk signature seen in the

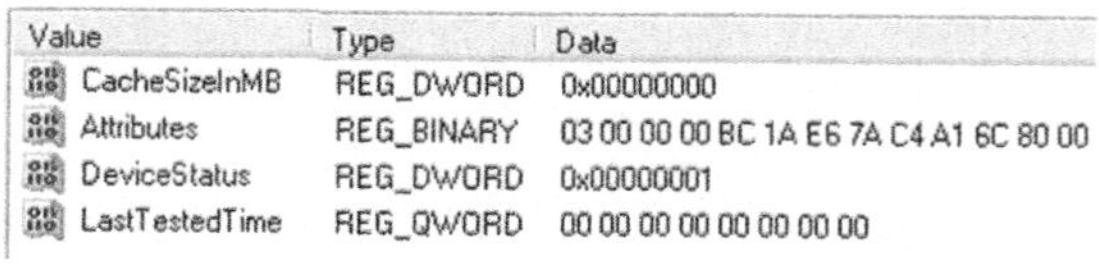

Value	Type	Data
CacheSizeInMB	REG_DWORD	0x00000000
Attributes	REG_BINARY	03 00 00 00 BC 1A E6 7A C4 A1 6C 80 00
DeviceStatus	REG_DWORD	0x00000001
LastTestedTime	REG_QWORD	00 00 00 00 00 00 00 00

FIGURE 5.9

EMDMgmt subkey values, visible in WRR.

MountedDevices key. A volume serial number is used to identify a volume and is changed whenever the volume is formatted.

As an example, I have a SimpleTech 500-GB drive that I had attached to my Windows 7 system at one point; the EMDMgmt subkey for the device is "RIG___ ST500_1354504530." The volume name is "ST500," and I can view the volume ID using the following command:

```
G:\>vol
Volume in drive G is ST500
Volume Serial Number is 50BC-1952
```

If I open the Windows calculator tool (calc.exe) and switch to the scientific view, I can convert the value from the EMDMgmt subkey (i.e., "1354504530") from decimal to hexadecimal; when I do this, I get "50BC1952."

WARNING

ReadyBoost and SSD drives

According to an MS TechNet article (available online at http://technet.microsoft.com/en-us/magazine/ff356869.aspx), if it is installed on a system with an solid state drive (SSD) drive, "Windows 7 disables ReadyBoost when reading from an SSD drive." As such we would not expect to see ReadyBoost artifacts, such as the EMDMgmt subkeys.

Remember, I said that the volume serial number is *not* the same thing as the drive signature; these are often confused, or considered to represent the same artifact. A drive signature is a 4-byte value stored at offset 0 × 1B8 within the master boot record (MBR). A volume serial number is a unique value assigned by Windows to a volume when the volume is formatted. The drive signature for the wallet drive in question, which is available via the MountedDevices key, is "23 48 3D D4." I verified this by plugging the device back into the system, and then viewing the physical disk via FTK Imager; I saw the drive signature within the 4 bytes starting at offset 0 × 1B8 (440 in decimal) within the drive MBR.

WARNING

USBStor Subkey LastWrite Times

There have been a number of posts to online forums asking about a specific observation regarding LastWrite times on the USBStor subkeys. Several analysts have reported seeing all of the subkeys with identical LastWrite times; not within seconds or minutes, but the same time stamps. Several analysts have asked how it would be possible for a user to connect all of the devices at the same time. It is important to remember that the LastWrite times on these keys do NOT indicate when the device was last connected to the system. Also, other analysts have reported creating TLNs (see Chapter 7) of system activity and observing that the key LastWrite times appear to have been updated shortly after an update or Service Pack was installed on the system.

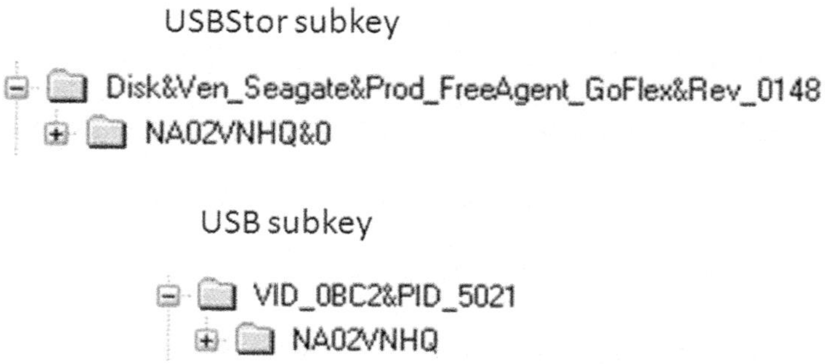

USBStor subkey

⊟ ▢ Disk&Ven_Seagate&Prod_FreeAgent_GoFlex&Rev_0148
　　⊞ ▢ NA02VNHQ&0

USB subkey

⊟ ▢ VID_0BC2&PID_5021
　　⊞ ▢ NA02VNHQ

FIGURE 5.10

USBStor and USB subkeys for external hard drive enclosure.

```
00000001a0 | 00 00 00 00 00 00 00 00-00 00 00 00 00 00 00 00
00000001b0 | 00 00 00 00 00 00 00 00-B6 19 F4 04 00 00 00 01
00000001c0 | 01 00 07 FE FF FF 3F 00-00 00 02 4C 38 3A 00 00
```

FIGURE 5.11

Drive/disk Signature.

The process for tracking "wallet" or external drives (also referred to as "drive enclosures") on Windows 7 systems is just a bit different. As an example, I connected a Seagate FreeAgent GoFlex external USB drive to my Windows 7 system (the serial number written on the label was NA02VNHQ), and as you'd expect, an entry was created in both the USBStor key as well as the USB key within the System hive. The keys that were created are illustrated in Figure 5.10.

As you can see in Figure 5.10, the unique instance ID subkey for the device is, in fact, the serial number of the device. Also, as with thumb drives, the LastWrite time of the unique instance ID key beneath the USB key correlates to the last time the device was connected to the system.

The biggest difference between drive enclosures and other USB removable storage devices is that we do not use the unique instance ID to determine the volume ID from the MountedDevices key. Remember, this should allow us to then determine which user may have had access to the device. Instead, we have to use the drive or disk signature, which is the 4 bytes located at offset 440 ($0 \times 1B8$) within the MBR of the drive. As I have access to the drive, I can use a hex editor or forensic analysis software the view the disk signature, as illustrated in Figure 5.11.

With the disk signature (which is set by the operating system whenever the drive is formatted), we can then parse the contents of the MountedDevices key using the mountdev.pl RegRipper plugin and find the volume GUID for the drive enclosure, which appears as follows:

```
\??\Volume{5d3e617b-b2c7-11e0-8563-005056c00008}
Drive Signature=b6 19 f4 04
```

Once we have this information, we can then parse the contents of the MountPoints2 key within the user's NTUSER.DAT hive using the mp2.pl RegRipper plugin, in order to determine when the device was last connected to the system. In this case, that information appears as follows:

```
Wed Jul 20 15:07:15 2011 (UTC)
{5d3e617b-b2c7-11e0-8563-005056c00008}
```

As it turns out, this is not only the same LastWrite time for the unique instance ID key found beneath the USB key, it's also the last time I actually plugged the device into the system, although this time is displayed in Coordinated Universal Time (UTC). As with other USB removable storage devices, the first time that the device was connected to the system can be found by examining the Windows Event Logs (as discussed earlier in this chapter) or the setupapi.dev.log file.

Thumb drives and external "wallet" drives (those in drive enclosures) are not the only devices that can be attached to Windows systems. Other devices may be connected, including smartphones and even devices capable of capturing video and still images, such as the Apple iTouch. This can be particularly important during an exam if images are found to contain EXIF metadata (see Chapter 4), and the analyst finds that a device (smart phone, iTouch, digital camera) of the type identified in that data had also been connected to the system. In order to demonstrate what these devices might "look like" to an analyst examining the Registry from an acquired image from a Windows system, I connected an Android smart phone (Motorola Backflip) and an Apple iTouch to a Windows 7 system, disconnected them, repeated the connection–disconnection process later, and then finally rebooted the system. In order to view artifacts from this activity, I extracted the Registry hive files from the system and parsed them using RegRipper, or more specifically, the command line tool, rip.pl. Using the usbstor.pl plugin, we see the following:

```
C:\tools > rip.pl -r f:\system -p usbstor
Launching usbstor v.20080418
ControlSet001\Enum\USBStor

...

Disk&Ven_Motorola&Prod__MB300&Rev__001 [Wed Jul 20 13:24:27 2011]
S/N: TA538029DP&0 [Wed Jul 20 13:24:27 2011]
FriendlyName Motorola: MB300 USB Device
```

Now, this device was first plugged into the Windows 7 system at 9:24 am, July 20, 2011 EST. This can be verified by examining the setupapi.dev.log file, as well as the Windows Event Log, as mentioned previously in this chapter. We also know that the LastWrite time on the device ID and unique instance ID keys do not specifically correlate to when the device was last connected to the system; in this case, the LastWrite times correlate to the first time the device was connected to the system during the most recent boot session, but only because this was the first time that the device had been connected to the system.

Something else interesting is that I don't see any indication of the Apple iTouch in the output from the usbstor.pl plugin. However, using the usbdevices.pl plugin, we see the following:

```
C:\tools > rip.pl -r f:\system -p usbdevices
Launching usbdevices v.20100219
...
Apple iPod [VID_05AC&PID_129E\
b9e69c2c948d76fd3f959be89193f30a500a0d50]
Class: WPD
Service: WUDFRd
Location Information: Port_#0003.Hub_#0004
Mfg: Apple Inc.
```

This shows us that the Apple iTouch is identified as an iPod, with unique instance ID (or serial number) "b9e69c2c948d76fd3f959be89193f30a500a0d50." During testing, the iTouch was last connected to the system at 11:02 am, July 11, 2011 EST, and the LastWrite time for the unique instance ID, when viewed via WRR, is "7/20/2011 3:02:37 PM," which correlates to the last time the device was connected to the Windows 7 system, expressed in Universal Coordinated Time (UTC).

Using the mountdev.pl plugin to examine the MountedDevices key within the System hive, we see the following:

```
C:\tools > rip.pl -r f:\system -p mountdev
Launching mountdev v.20080324
Get MountedDevices key information from the System hive file.
...
Device:_??_USBSTOR#Disk&Ven_Motorola&Prod__MB300&Rev__001#TA538029
DP&0#{53f5630
7-b6bf-11d0-94f2-00a0c91efb8b}
\??\Volume{5d3e6180-b2c7-11e0-8563-005056c00008}
```

This indicates that the smart phone was mounted to the system with the volume GUID "{5d3e6180-b2c7-11e0-8563-005056c00008}." The iTouch, however, does not appear to have been recognized as a removable storage device, and does not appear to have been mounted as a volume. Using the devclass.pl plugin to look at the devices mounted as disks indicates the following:

```
C:\tools > rip.pl -r f:\system -p devclass
Launching devclass v.20100901
DevClasses - Disks
```

```
ControlSet001\Control\DeviceClasses\
{53f56307-b6bf-11d0-94f2-00a0c91efb8b}

...

Wed Jul 20 13:24:27 2011 (UTC)
Disk&Ven_Motorola&Prod__MB300&Rev__001,TA538029DP&0
```

As mentioned previously in this chapter, the smart phone was first connected to the system at 9:24 am, July 20, 2011 EST. We also know from previous discussions that the LastWrite time for the device key listed under the DevicesClasses disk device subkey will tell us when the device was first connected during the most recent boot session; in this case, Wed Jul 20 13:24:27 2011 (UTC).

With the volume GUID for the smart phone, we can now run the mp2.pl plugin against the NTUSER.DAT hive file extracted from the system, in order to parse the MountPoints2 key. Running the plugin, we see the following:

```
C:\tools > rip.pl -r f:\ntuser.dat -p mp2
Launching mp2 v.20090115
MountPoints2
Software\Microsoft\Windows\CurrentVersion\Explorer\MountPoints2

...

Volumes:

...

Wed Jul 20 15:11:34 2011 (UTC)
{5d3e6180-b2c7-11e0-8563-005056c00008}
```

Again, as discussed previously in this chapter, the LastWrite time for the volume GUID key for the smart phone (i.e., Wed Jul 20 15:11:34 2011 (UTC)) indicates (and does in fact correlate to) when the device was last connected to the system.

We can then use the port_dev.pl plugin to parse the contents to the "Microsoft\Windows Portable Devices\Devices" key from the Software hive, and when we do, we see the following:

```
C:\tools > rip.pl -r f:\software -p port_dev
Launching port_dev v.20090118
Microsoft\Windows Portable Devices\Devices
Device:
LastWrite: Wed Jul 20 12:56:48 2011 (UTC)
SN:
Drive: Apple iPod

...

Device: DISK&VEN_MOTOROLA&PROD__MB300&REV__001
LastWrite: Wed Jul 20 13:24:30 2011 (UTC)
SN: TA538029DP&0
Drive: F:\
```

The output of the port_dev.pl plugin indicates key LastWrite times that correlate to the first time that each device was connected to the system during the most recent boot session. It also indicates that the smart phone had been mapped to the F:\ volume, which is not something that we got from the contents of the MountedDevices key (from the System hive), as another device (not part of the testing) had been connected to the system and mounted as the F:\ drive *after* the smart phone had been disconnected from the system. This can be determined by comparing the two sets of output and their associated time stamps.

Finally, the EMDMgmt key (full path within the Software hive is Microsoft\Windows NT\CurrentVersion\EMDMgmt) contains a subkey named "_??_USBSTOR# Disk&Ven_Motorola&Prod__MB300&Rev__001#TA538029DP&0#{53f56307-b6bf-11d0-94f2-00a0c91efb8b}_946156644" which corresponds to the smart phone (including the device model and serial number). Again, the EMDMgmt key is specific to ReadyBoost, and this device was not tested for its suitability for ReadyBoost functionality. However, the EMDMgmt key does provide indications of devices that had been connected to the system, which can be particularly useful when a user deletes some of the other Registry keys in an attempt to hide their activities.

TIP

Deleted Registry Keys

When Registry keys are deleted, much like files, they aren't really gone. Instead, the space that they consume within the hive file is simply marked as being available, and can be overwritten. As discussed in Chapter 2 of *Windows Registry Forensics*, Jolanta Thomassen's regslack.exe (provided along with the materials associated with this book, found online via http://windowsir.blogspot.com/p/books.html) utility does a great job of recovering deleted keys and values, in addition to illustrating free space within the hive file.

As we began this section on USB device analysis, I mentioned a couple of checklists for this type of analysis that Rob Lee had created. Hopefully, you took the time to download those checklists and take a look at them. Regardless, I put together similar checklists based on the information provided in this section, including where within the Registry to look for specific pieces of information, and where appropriate, which RegRipper plugin can be used to retrieve and display that information. These checklists are included with the materials associated with this book, and can be found online at http://windowsir.blogspot.com/p/books.html.

System hive

Many times, Registry analysis may not involve multiple keys or hives, but will instead involve just a single hive, or even just a single key. As one would think, the System hive maintains a great deal of information regarding the system, including devices that have been attached, services and drivers that should (or should not) be running, etc. As such, analysts may find a good deal of very useful information within the System hive. So far in this chapter, we've already discussed some of the information available that can be used to determine when USB devices had been connected to the system, and we also included references to the MountedDevices key in that discussion.

Again, in this chapter, I do not want to provide a voluminous list of keys and values; instead, my goal is to present possible solutions to questions commonly posed as such, we will not be going through each hive, a key at a time. Instead, we will focus on providing solutions.

Services

Analyzing available services can be an important part of investigations for a number of types of incidents, include compromises, data breaches, and even malware infections. Windows services serve as a great persistence mechanism for malware (something that will be discussed in more detail in Chapter 6), as many services start automatically when the system is started (no user login or other interaction required), and services often run with elevated privileges. An attacker may compromise a system and leave a backdoor running as a Windows service, knowing that if the service is set to start when the system boots, that backdoor will be available as long as the system is running. As such, analyzing the available services may prove to be fruitful.

When you open the System hive in WRR, locate the "current" ControlSet, and expand the "services" key, you'll likely see a great number of subkeys; not all of these are actually services. Many of the subkeys you'll see are for device drivers installed with the operating system or with applications. As you click your way down through the available services (I'll stop on BITS, or "Background Intelligent Transfer Service"), you'll see the values for each key, with information similar to what is illustrated in Figure 5.12.

From these values, you can see considerable information, including the Start value. In this case, a value of 3 indicates that the service is set to a Manual

Value	Type	Data
DisplayName	REG_SZ	@%SystemRoot%\system32\qmgr.dll,-1000
ImagePath	REG_EXPA...	%SystemRoot%\System32\svchost.exe -k netsvcs
Description	REG_SZ	@%SystemRoot%\system32\qmgr.dll,-1001
ObjectName	REG_SZ	LocalSystem
ErrorControl	REG_DWORD	0x00000001
Start	REG_DWORD	0x00000003
DelayedAutoStart	REG_DWORD	0x00000001
Type	REG_DWORD	0x00000020
DependOnService	REG_MULTI...	RpcSs‖EventSystem‖
ServiceSidType	REG_DWORD	0x00000001
RequiredPrivileges	REG_MULTI...	SeCreateGlobalPrivilege‖SeImpersonatePrivilege‖Se1
FailureActions	REG_BINARY	80 51 01 00 00 00 00 00 00 00 00 03 00 00 00 14

FIGURE 5.12

Service key values, via WRR.

start—i.e., on demand, usually via some user- or application-initiated action. Other services may have a Start value of 2, indicating that they are set to an Automatic start when Windows boots. We can also see the DisplayName (previous versions of Windows, particularly XP, actually had names and description fields in the Registry, rather than references to strings in dynamic link library (DLLs)), and the ImagePath, which can be used to help identify suspicious services.

NOTE

ImagePath Value

Some malware may maintain persistence by referencing a malicious executable in the ImagePath value. However, malware may use a more subtle persistence method by loading a malicious DLL into a valid executable. In these cases, the ImagePath will reference a legitimate Windows file—frequently %SystemRoot%\system32\svchost.exe—while the malicious DLL will be referenced in the service's Parameters subkey under the ServiceDLL value.

More information about the various values and their meaning can be found in MS KnowledgeBase article 1030000, found online at http://support.microsoft.com/kb/103000.

There is also more information regarding Windows services available in the System hive. If we navigate to the Enum\Root key within the appropriate ControlSet, we'll see a number of subkeys whose names all start with "LEGACY_." You should recognize the remaining portions of the names as being the same as some of the services and drivers we saw listed beneath the "services" key. These keys are created automatically by the operating system as part of normal system function. Many of the LEGACY_* keys will also have a subkey named "0000," as illustrated in Figure 5.13.

In this case, the LEGACY_IMDISK (ImDisk is a virtual disk driver available online from http://www.ltr-data.se/opencode.html/#ImDisk) key illustrated in Figure 5.13 refers to a legacy driver; we can see this listed in the Class value beneath the "0000" subkey. Now, the really interesting thing is that the LastWrite time for the LEGACY_IMDISK is "Tue Jan 4 11:35:45 2011 (UTC)" (extracted using the RegRipper legacy.pl plugin), which correlates to the *first* time that the device driver was launched, and the LastWrite time for the LEGACY_ IMDISK\0000 key is "Wed Jan 5 16:50:32 2011 (UTC)," which refers to the *last* time the device driver was launched. Not only can this be very useful during

FIGURE 5.13

Enum\Root\LEGACY_IMDISK keys, via WRR.

malware and data breach investigations (particularly when you need to identify a "window of compromise," or how long the system has been compromised), but the *really* interesting thing is that the ImDisk driver is no longer installed on the system. After installing it and using it briefly, I uninstalled the driver, yet the "LEGACY_" key for that driver persisted on the system. This information can clearly be extremely useful during an investigation.

Bluetooth

Along with all manner of devices, a means of connecting those devices that is becoming more and more ubiquitous is Bluetooth. We already have Bluetooth headsets that connect to our smart phones, and we can connect our smart phones to our vehicles via Bluetooth. I've also seen a number of laptop systems that come with Bluetooth radios installed, and when Windows 7 (in particular) is installed, certain components are installed from the installation media without requiring any input from the user.

I ran across a case not long ago where I found an unusual Prefetch file (see Chapter 4 for details on Prefetch files) whose name started with "fsquirt.exe." As I was doing my research on this apparent issue (I didn't know if this was a legitimate application or malware), I found a good bit of information at the Microsoft web site (found online *at* http://msdn.microsoft.com/en-us/library/windows/hardware/dn133848(*v=vs.85*).*aspx*) that describes fsquirt.exe as the MS Bluetooth File Transfer wizard. As I dug further in my research, I found that some users would connect to their smart phones and play music from their smart phone through their computer speakers. However, this file transfer wizard intrigued me, and I eventually found a system with a Bluetooth radio and fsquirt.exe, and I launched the wizard. The wizard allows the user to select files that they want to transfer *to* the device that they've connected to (via Bluetooth) via a common file selector dialog (see the User hives section that addresses the *ComDlg32* key later in this chapter), which means that files that are selected, or at least the directory that the user chooses, will very likely show up beneath this key. See Chapter 8 for more information on the use of Bluetooth as a means of data exfiltration.

If you're analyzing an image of a system, and don't have access to the system itself, it's still pretty simple to tell if the system had a Bluetooth radio; however, your results can vary depending upon the drivers used. The RegRipper *bthport.pl* plugin will check for the Registry key referenced in the above MSDN article (i.e., HKLM\System\ControlSet00*x*\services\BTHPORT\Parameters\Devices), and extract the device IDs (media access control (MAC) addresses) and names for any devices seen by the Bluetooth radio, albeit not necessarily connected. An entry to the ForensicArtifacts.com web site (found online at http://forensicartifacts.com/2012/10/bluetooth-connected-device-artifcacts-broadcom-widcomm/) includes information specific to Broadcom/Widcomm drivers; those artifacts are found in the Software hive. I have not written a RegRipper plugin for these artifacts, as I have yet to see a system with these artifacts, and I don't have access to any test data that includes these Registry keys.

FIGURE 5.14

Portion of keys at the Software hive root, via WRR.

Software hive

As the Software hive contains information regarding installed software, as well as the system-wide configuration of that software (the user's hive will contain user-specific settings), analysis of this hive can prove to be very valuable during an examination.

Application analysis

Many times, analysts want to know what applications are installed on the system in order to begin the process of determining user activity, to see what applications the user may have had access to, to determine if there was a violation of corporate acceptable use policies, or to tie specific activities to an application. The simplest way to start going about this is to check the available keys at the root of the Software hive, as illustrated in Figure 5.14.

As you can see from Figure 5.14, the system in question has the 7-Zip archive utility installed, as well as some Broadcom, Dell, and Intel applications. This information can provide the analyst with some indications of installed applications.

Next, the Uninstall key (the key path is "\Microsoft\Windows\CurrentVersion\ Uninstall" within the Software hive) should also be examined. The subkeys beneath the Uninstall key may appear to be GUIDs or readable names, and many will contain values that provide information regarding installation date, install path and source, as well as the string used to uninstall the application. As with those keys at the root of the Software hive, the Uninstall keys are most often the result of applications that are installed via an installation package, such as the Microsoft installer. Applications that are simply executable files copied to a directory do not generally create installation or uninstall keys, although some will leave traces in the Registry once they have actually been executed. One such example is the MS SysInternals utilities; these tools have an end-user license agreement ("EULA") that must be accepted before the tool will run, and running the tool will create an entry in the Registry for that tool.

Applications installed via a Microsoft installer package (a file that ends in "*.msi") are logged or recorded in the Software hive in the path "\Classes\Installer\ Products." Each subkey beneath the Products key has a name with a long sequence of hexadecimal characters, and the ProductName value will tell you the name of the

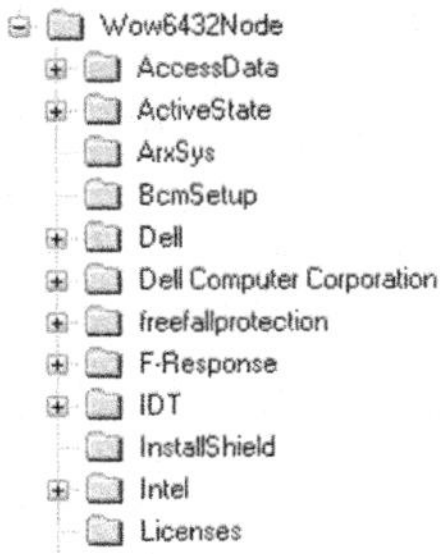

FIGURE 5.15

Wow6432Node key, via WRR.

product that was installed. The msis.pl RegRipper plugin will extract this information for you, and sort the various installed packages by their key LastWrite times (which correlates to the package installation date/time). An example of this information collected from one Windows 7 system appears as follows:

```
Thu Apr 21 16:51:24 2011 (UTC)
VMware Player;C:\Users\harlan\AppData\Local\Temp\vmware_1303404464\
vmware player.msi
Wed Apr 13 18:54:38 2011 (UTC)
ActivePerl 5.8.9 Build 829;F:\tools\ActivePerl-5.8.9.829-
MSWin32-x86-294280.msi
```

These are not the only places that an analyst should look for installed applications. On 64-bit Windows 7 systems, 32-bit applications may appear beneath the WOW6432Node key at the root of the Software hive, as illustrated in Figure 5.15.

In addition, the analyst should also check the root of the NTUSER.DAT hive for indications of installed applications, and the Uninstall key within the user hive (key path is "\Software\Microsoft\Windows\CurrentVersion\Uninstall") should also be examined. These keys will contain information regarding application data specifically installed by and available to a particular user.

TIP

Browser Analysis

Many times when the subject of browser or web history analysis comes up in online forums, one of the first responses you'll usually see is "check the TypedURLs key in the user hive"; however, this key applies to IE, and there are several other browsers that users can download and install. As such, the first step in browser analysis is to determine which browser the user was using during the time frame in question (tips on determining the browser in use, from system or user file associations or other information found in the Registry are discussed in greater detail below). Do not assume that simply because the system is Windows, or because the TypedURLs key is populated with values, that at the time in question, the user was using IE.

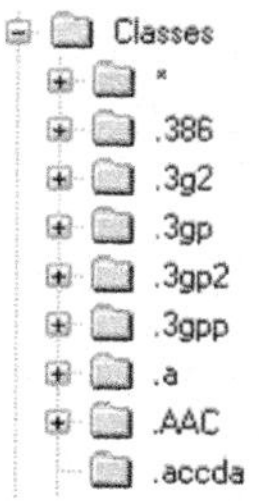

FIGURE 5.16

Classes subkeys from Software hive.

Yet another way for an analyst to gather information regarding applications on a system is through what I have referred to as "file extension analysis." This technique has proven itself to be useful for finding not only installed applications (in the sense that the application had an installer, such as an MSI file, or a setup.exe file) but also for stand-alone applications (that do not necessarily appear in the Registry) that the user has associated with certain file types. We want to start by accessing the Software hive, navigating to the Classes key, and looking at each of the subkeys that starts with a ".", as illustrated in Figure 5.16.

From each of these file extensions, we can determine considerable information. For example, if we open each of the keys (as illustrated in Figure 5.16) and look for the "Default" value, for most of them we'll see what type of file the extension refers to; for example, the "Default" value for the .3g2 key is "WMP11.AssocFile.3G2." If we then go to the "Classes\ WMP11.AssocFile.3G2" key and then navigate to the "shell\open\command" subkey, we'll see that the command used to access or execute files that end in the .3g2 extension appears as follows:

```
"%ProgramFiles(x86)%\Windows Media Player\wmplayer.exe" /prefetch:6
/Open "%L"
```

What this tells us is that the files ending in the .3g2 extension are associated with the Windows Media Player, and when the user double-clicks one of these files, the Windows Media Player will open automatically to run the file.

The way you would find this information on a live system is by opening a command prompt and typing the command "assoc." A lot of file extensions would go flying by, so let's say that you just wanted to see just one ... say ".jpeg". So you'd type the command "assoc | find ".jpeg"", and you'd see ".jpeg = jpegfile" returned. Then you'd type the command "ftype jpegfile" and see something similar to the following:

```
%SystemRoot%\System32\rundll32.exe "%ProgramFiles%\Windows Photo
Viewer\ PhotoViewer.dll", ImageView_Fullscreen %1
```

This is great information, but it's for a live system. In order to determine similar information from an acquired image, you'd want to run the assoc.pl

RegRipper plugin against the Software hive from the system, using the following command:

```
C:\tools> rip.pl -r f:\software -p assoc
```

The assoc.pl plugin processes information from the Software hive in a manner similar to running the "assoc" and "ftype" commands mentioned above. You will also want to check the keys at the root of the user's USRCLASS.DAT hive file, as well. I had installed the Google Chrome browser in my Windows 7 system, and the "Default" value for the ".https\shell\open\command" appears as follows:

```
"C:\Users\harlan\AppData\Local\Google\Chrome\Application\chrome.
exe" -- "%1"
```

Also at the root of my USRCLASS.DAT file is a key named ".shtml," and the "Default" value is "ChromeHTML"; mapping back to the Software hive, the value for the "Classes\ChromeHTML\shell\open\command" is the same as what appears above, indicating that if I double-click a file the ends in ".shtml" (or ".https"), the file will be opened via the Chrome browser.

From an analyst perspective, this is great information, as it provides indications of applications installed on the system. However, it also helps us answer another question; many times I will see a question in lists and online forums similar to, "does anyone know what application uses a file with this extension?" Many times, this question is a result of some analysis that has already been performed, and the analyst has apparently run across an unfamiliar file. In cases such as this, searching via Google may provide a number of possible solutions, but analysis of the Registry from the system that is being examined will likely provide the most accurate information.

Finally, another means for seeing what applications the user may have accessed involves examining the contents of the UserAssist subkeys, which is discussed in detail in the User hive section later in this chapter. This can be a valuable avenue of investigation, as the contents of these keys persist even though the application itself may have been uninstalled or deleted.

NetworkList

Windows systems have always maintained information regarding network connections, including wireless access points (WAPs) to which the system (usually a laptop) has connected. Tools used to manage these connections maintain historical information regarding the connections, and we can often see these within the user interface for the application. As you might expect, this information is maintained in the Registry, and on Vista and Windows 7, there is considerable information available to the analyst.

To start examining this data, we first have to navigate to the following Registry key within the Software hive:

```
Microsoft\Windows NT\CurrentVersion\NetworkList\Signatures
```

Value	Type	Data
ProfileGuid	REG_SZ	{F9A38942-A362-4D6D-B9BB-A4AD8F11C28C}
Description	REG_SZ	linksys
Source	REG_DWORD	0x00000408
DnsSuffix	REG_SZ	<none>
FirstNetwork	REG_SZ	linksys
DefaultGatewayMac	REG_BINARY	00 0F 66 58 41 ED 00 00

FIGURE 5.17

Values from a NetworkList\Signatures\Unmanaged subkey.

Beneath this key, you will usually see two subkeys; Managed and Unmanaged. "Managed" refers to connections for which the system is managed by a domain controller; "Unmanaged" refers to connections for which the system is not managed by a domain controller. Beneath both of these keys, you will find subkeys with names that are a long series of letters and numbers; what we're looking for is the values within each of these subkeys. An example of these values is illustrated in Figure 5.17.

From the available values, you can see how they can be valuable. For example, the "Description" and "FirstNetwork" values refer to the service set identifier (SSID) of a WAP. The "DefaultGatewayMac" value is the MAC address of the WAP, which we can use in WiFi geolocation mapping.

TIP

WiFi Geolocation Mapping

Over the years, there have been a couple of databases compiled for use in WiFi geolocation; that is, providing a mapping between wireless router MAC addresses (usually compiled via "wardriving" or submissions) and the coordinates (latitude and longitude) of the physical location of the router. Some of these services focused primarily on mapping major metropolitan areas. One such service that is publicly available can be found at WiGLE.net. In order to access the information available at WiGLE.net, I wrote a Perl script (macl.pl is available with the materials associated with this book) that would take a MAC address, or list of addresses, and provide various output formats. As an example of what the script can do, I extracted the MAC address of a wireless router from the Registry of one of my systems, and after passing MAC address as one of the arguments to the script, was able to obtain coordinates for where the WAP is located. One of the script options is to provide the output as a URL for Google Maps. The map location for the wireless router in question is illustrated in Figure 5.18.

As you can see, information such as this can be extremely useful to law enforcement for mapping locations of devices used by suspects or missing individuals. I've heard that analysts in private industry have also used similar techniques and found former employees who visited a competitor's location (presumably with their company-issued laptop) prior to resigning their employment and going to work for that competitor. The time stamp information associated with the connection to the WAP near the competitor's site was then used as a basis to determine what the employee accessed (files, databases, etc.) prior to giving notice.

One thing to keep in mind, however, is that over time, open access to databases such as WiGLE.net may change or be disabled, requiring license payment and/or some sort of access token to be used via an application programming interface (API). As such, the macl. pl code may stop working; however, other resources may be used to obtain geolocation

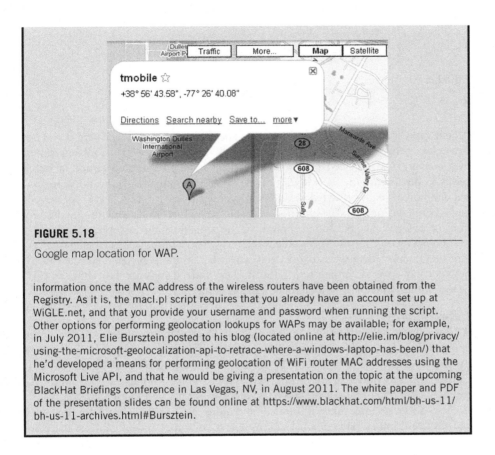

FIGURE 5.18

Google map location for WAP.

information once the MAC address of the wireless routers have been obtained from the Registry. As it is, the macl.pl script requires that you already have an account set up at WiGLE.net, and that you provide your username and password when running the script. Other options for performing geolocation lookups for WAPs may be available; for example, in July 2011, Elie Bursztein posted to his blog (located online at http://elie.im/blog/privacy/using-the-microsoft-geolocalization-api-to-retrace-where-a-windows-laptop-has-been/) that he'd developed a means for performing geolocation of WiFi router MAC addresses using the Microsoft Live API, and that he would be giving a presentation on the topic at the upcoming BlackHat Briefings conference in Las Vegas, NV, in August 2011. The white paper and PDF of the presentation slides can be found online at https://www.blackhat.com/html/bh-us-11/bh-us-11-archives.html#Bursztein.

Value	Type	Data
ProfileName	REG_SZ	linksys
Description	REG_SZ	linksys
Managed	REG_DWORD	0x00000000
Category	REG_DWORD	0x00000000
DateCreated	REG_BINARY	D8 07 02 00 06 00 10 00 0C 00 02 00 0F 00 20 00
NameType	REG_DWORD	0x00000047
DateLastConnected	REG_BINARY	D8 07 02 00 01 00 12 00 0B 00 02 00 30 00 5A 00

FIGURE 5.19

Windows 7 NetworkList key profile values.

Finally, we can use the "ProfileGuid" value to map to the appropriate profile in the "NetworkList\Profiles" key. The data for the ProfileGuid value should correspond to one of the available profiles beneath the Profiles key. The values for the profile identified in Figure 5.17 are illustrated in Figure 5.19.

As we can see in Figure 5.19, the "ProfileName" and "Description" values should match the "Description" and "FirstNetwork" values that we saw in Figure 5.17. The

Value	Type	Data
ab ServiceName	REG_SZ	{D4DC0CE9-90F2-4DCE-9294-7091519EFE56}
ab Description	REG_SZ	DW1501 Wireless-N WLAN Half-Mini Card

FIGURE 5.20

Values for NetworkCards\12 key.

"NameType" value refers to the type of connection of the profile, where 0×47 is a wireless network, 0×06 is a wired network, and 0×17 is a broadband (a.k.a., 3G) network (as indicated by the MS TechNet blog post located online at http://blogs.technet.com/b/networking/archive/2010/09/08/network-location-awareness-nla-and-how-it-relates-to-windows-firewall-profiles.aspx). The "DateCreated" and "DateLastConnected" values are 128-bit SYSTEMTIME structure, a description of which can be found online at http://msdn.microsoft.com/en-us/library/ms724950(*v=vs.85*).*aspx*. These values refer to when the profile was created (the system first connected to the network) and when the system was last connected to the network; however, according to Microsoft, these time stamps can be "either in UTC or local time, depending on the function that is being called."

NetworkCards

All versions of the Windows operating system also maintain information about network interface cards (NICs) within the Registry. For example, a quick look in the Software hive ("HKLM\Software") at the "\Microsoft\Windows NT\CurrentVersion\NetworkCards" key shows two subkeys (named "12" and "8," respectively), one of which contains the values illustrated in Figure 5.20.

The ServiceName value illustrated in Figure 5.20 is the GUID for the NIC, and the Description value is what is seen when you type "ipconfig/all" at the command prompt on a live system; in fact, it's actually listed after "Description" in the output of the command. We can then go to the System hive, and navigate to the "ControlSet00*n*\services\Tcpip\Parameters\Interfaces" key (where "*n*" is the number of the ControlSet identified as current), and locate the subkeys named for the ServiceName value we found beneath the NetworkCards key. This key will contain a great deal of pertinent network settings and information that refers to the interface, such as whether dynamic host configuration protocol (DHCP) was enabled (or the interface had a hard-coded IP address), the DHCP server, default gateway, etc. This information can be useful, particularly when attempting to identify the system being analyzed in association with other external sources, such as network packet captures, firewall/web server/network device logs.

Scheduled tasks

Vista, Windows 7, Windows 8, and Windows 2008 R2 systems manage Scheduled Tasks a bit differently from previous versions of Windows. Starting with Windows Vista, Microsoft introduced Task Scheduler 2.0, which stored information regarding scheduled tasks in the Registry's Software hive beneath the following key (note that these Windows versions ship with a number of default tasks):

```
Microsoft\Windows NT\CurrentVersion\Schedule\TaskCache
```

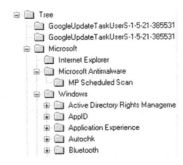

FIGURE 5.21

TaskCache\Tree subkeys, via WRR.

Value ▲	Type	Data
Id	REG_SZ	{CA4B8FF2-A4D2-4D88-A52E-3A5BDAF7F56E}
Index	REG_DWORD	0x00000003

FIGURE 5.22

Values in RegIdleBackup key, via WRR.

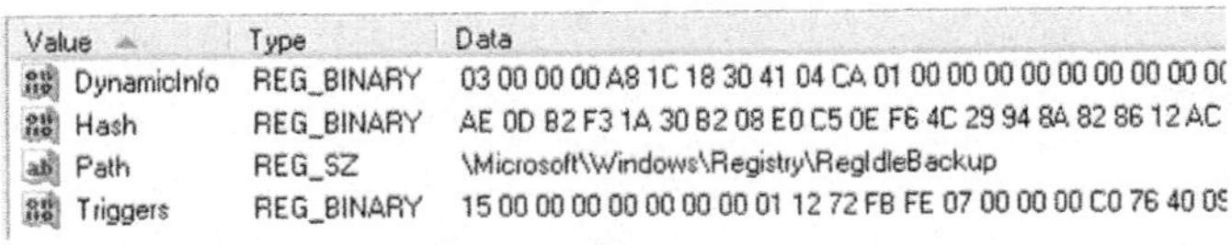

Value ▲	Type	Data
DynamicInfo	REG_BINARY	03 00 00 00 A8 1C 18 30 41 04 CA 01 00 00 00 00 00 00 00 00 0(
Hash	REG_BINARY	AE 0D B2 F3 1A 30 B2 08 E0 C5 0E F6 4C 29 94 8A 82 86 12 AC
Path	REG_SZ	\Microsoft\Windows\Registry\RegIdleBackup
Triggers	REG_BINARY	15 00 00 00 00 00 00 00 01 12 72 FB FE 07 00 00 00 C0 76 40 0S

FIGURE 5.23

Values beneath a TaskCache\Tasks*GUID* key.

The XML files that contain the scheduled task settings and instructions are located in the C:\Windows\System32\Tasks folder (and subfolders; refer to Chapter 4 for a detailed discussion of Scheduled Task information maintained within the file system). Most of the human-readable information regarding scheduled tasks within the Registry is found beneath the Tree subkey, as illustrated in Figure 5.21.

On a default installation of Windows 7, most of the scheduled tasks will have keys listed beneath the Tree\Microsoft\Windows subkey. For each scheduled task, there will be an "Id" value which contains a GUID, and an index value. The values for the Microsoft\Windows\Registry\RegIdleBackup task are illustrated in Figure 5.22.

We can then use the GUID value to navigate to the TaskCache\Tasks key, and locate the subkey with the ID GUID as its name. Beneath this key, you will find the values illustrated in Figure 5.23.

Most notable are the Path and Hash values. The Path value clearly provides the path to the scheduled task file. The Hash value is a bit more interesting, as the hash is of the XML task file itself and used to verify the integrity of that file. Bruce Dang (of Microsoft) gave a presentation at the 27th Chaos Communications Congress (the video of which is available online at http://www.vimeo.com/18225315), during which he discussed Microsoft's efforts in analyzing the Stuxnet malware. During that presentation, Bruce stated that the hash algorithm used at the time to identify changes in the scheduled task files was the cyclic redundancy code (CRC)-32 algorithm, for which it is very easy to generate collisions. Analysis of the malware determined that one of the vulnerabilities it would exploit was to modify a scheduled task and pad the file so that when the Task Scheduler verified the task's hash prior to running it, the hash would match what was stored in the Registry. According to Bruce, Microsoft decided to replace the algorithm with the secure hash algorithm (SHA)-256 algorithm; this fix appears to have been provided in security update MS10-092, found online at http://support.microsoft.com/kb/2305420. Note that the KnowledgeBase article states that any Scheduled Tasks that have already been corrupted by malware may be validated following the installation of this security update; as such, the article recommends that the actions associated with the tasks be verified, which is excellent advice.

One piece of advice if you're going to watch Bruce's video while at work; wear headphones, or don't play it at work. Some of the language used in the video is not appropriate for a work environment.

TIP

WOW6432Node

As long as you're examining a Software hive, don't forget to take a look in the WOW6432Node key. This key is used for Registry redirection of calls from 32-bit applications on 64-bit systems, and can contain some very useful information. For example, I've found values within the "\Wow6432Node\Microsoft\Windows\CurrentVersion\Run" key in the Software hive from a 64-bit Windows 7 system, and these values were not also included in the "\Microsoft\Windows\CurrentVersion\Run" key. I've also found a significant number of subkeys beneath the "\Wow6432Node\Microsoft\Windows\CurrentVersion\Uninstall" key, indicating applications and updates that had been installed on the system.

User hives

As with other Registry hives, there are some similarities between keys and values found in the user profile hives on the more familiar (to analysts) Windows XP systems and newer Windows 7 and 8 systems. Some keys and their values remain relatively unchanged; one such key is the ubiquitous Run key, as the path and use (in both the Software and NTUSER.DAT hives) has remained essentially the same. Some keys have changed slightly; for example, beneath the "Software\Microsoft\Windows\CurrentVersion\Explorer\ComDlg32" key on Windows 7 and 8 we no longer find the

FIGURE 5.24

ComDlg32 subkeys, via WRR.

familiar LastVisitedMRU (most recently used) and OpenSaveMRU keys we were used to from Windows XP. Instead, we find other keys, as illustrated in Figure 5.24.

As you can see from Figure 5.24, there are some new keys, as well as some keys with different names. Instead of values beneath the keys illustrated in Figure 5.24 containing ASCII strings within their data, as of Windows Vista, the values are binary data types that contain Unicode strings in some cases; in others, the value data contains shell items (shell items were discussed earlier in this chapter). The data beneath the CIDSizeMRU and FirstFolder keys contain Unicode strings, while the values in the subkeys beneath the OpenSavePidlMRU key contain shell items. The data beneath the LastVisitedPidlMRU and LastVisitedPidlMRULegacy keys contain Unicode strings followed by shell item ID lists. The RegRipper *comdlg32.pl* plugin is capable of parsing the contents of these keys from both XP and Vista and above systems.

What I hope to do in the rest of the chapter is discuss some of the keys that are new to Windows 7, and different from Windows XP. In many cases, the keys that are new as of Windows 7 persist on Windows 8; Windows 8 contains a number of new Registry artifacts of its own. Have no illusions, I will not be able to address every new key and every change, as something like that is simply beyond the scope of this book. Instead, I will try to address some of the significant changes that are important to analysts and investigators. I will focus primarily on those keys and values associated with the operating system itself, as it is impossible to address every possible application. So, please consider this a start, but I hope one in which you find significant value.

WordWheelQuery

With Windows XP, searches that the user ran via the Search functionality accessed via the Start menu appeared in the ACMru key within the user's hive. When Vista was deployed, analysts found that searches performed by the user were no longer maintained in the Registry, but were instead stored in a file. Shortly after the release of Windows 7, analysts found that user searches were again stored in the Registry, this time in the following key:

```
Software\Microsoft\Windows\CurrentVersion\Explorer\WordWheelQuery
```

The values within this key are stored in Unicode format, and maintained in an MRU list, as illustrated in Figure 5.25.

Value	Type	Data
MRUListEx	REG_BINARY	01 00 00 00 00 00 00 00 FF FF FF FF
0	REG_BINARY	63 00 63 00 74 00 75 00 6E 00 65 00 00 00
1	REG_BINARY	70 00 72 00 6F 00 67 00 72 00 61 00 6D 00 00 00

FIGURE 5.25

WordWheelQuery values.

As with other MRU list keys, the LastWrite time for the key in questions corresponds to when the most recent search was conducted. As illustrated in Figure 5.25, the search terms are stored as binary values, with the actual terms listed in Unicode. As such, item "1" (the byte sequence "70 00 72 00 6F 00 67 00 72 00 61 00 6D 00 00 00") indicates that the user searched for the term "program." When viewing the Properties for the WordWheelQuery key via WRR, we see that the LastWrite time for the key is "3/13/2010 1:34:03 PM," which indicates the date and time (in UTC format) that the user searched for item 1. We know this because the first 4 bytes (or DWORD) in the MRUListEx value ("01 00 00 00") indicate that the value named "1" was the most recent search term. The RegRipper wordwheelquery.pl plugin will assist in enumerating this information.

TIP

Historical Registry Data

This is as good a place as any to point out how historical Registry data can be accessed and used. Windows 7 maintains VSCs, which can provide access to previous versions of files, to include Registry hives. Accessing VSCs from an analyst's perspective (i.e., from within an acquired image) is discussed in detail in Chapter 3 of this book. What this means is that while Registry keys that maintain MRU lists (such as the WordWheelQuery key, RecentDocs) only provide information about the most recent activity, historical information can be retrieved by mounting the appropriate VSCs and running queries for the same Registry keys and values. For example, the value named "0" in Figure 5.25 is "cctune," but the MRUListEx value indicates that the MRU value is "1," and as such the LastWrite time for the key indicates when the user searched for the term in value "1." The date and time for which the user ran the search for "cctune" may be determined by mounting the appropriate VSC from the acquired image and querying the WordWheelQuery key. This can be a very useful analysis technique, and can be used to provide greater detail and context to TLNs (discussed in detail in Chapter 7).

Shellbags

When conducting research on Windows forensic analysis, you may see mention of "Shellbags," and wonder exactly what this refers to. "Shellbags" are a set of Registry keys and values that, on Windows XP, store user-specific preferences for Windows Explorer display options. One of the nice things about Windows systems is that when you open Windows Explorer to a particular file path and position and size the window that you have open, Windows "remembers" these settings, so that the next time you go to that directory or folder, you are presented with the same settings. This information is maintained in the Registry hives within the user profile. This way, if you log into a system as "userA," you would likely have different settings than if you logged in using another account. An example of how this Registry information can affect a system, from a user perspective is available in MS KnowledgeBase article 813711 (found online at http://support.microsoft.com/kb/813711); this article describes a situation in which changes in size, view, icon and position of folders is not remembered on Windows XP systems. As such, these settings can be said to contain user preferences for displaying certain information, settings the user would have had to set within the Windows XP shell.

On Windows 7 (and presumably on Windows 8), the information recorded in the shellbags artifacts are a bit different. Instead of recording the view settings each time that a folder is opened, modified and then closed, "Windows 7 remembers one size and location for all your folders and libraries" (this is quoted from the Windows 7 Help and Support file, under "Folders: Frequently Asked Questions"). Regardless, it appears that on Windows 7 and 8 systems, the shellbags artifacts provide considerable insight into resources that a user has accessed.

On Windows XP systems, the shellbags artifacts are located in the NTUSER.DAT Registry hive file. Within the NTUSER.DAT hive, the path to the keys that we're interested in is "Software\Microsoft\Windows\ShellNoRoam\BagMRU." Beneath this key is a tree of subkeys whose names are numbers; that is, 0, 1, 2. These keys are nested, and this is what allows paths to the resources (folders, etc.) to be developed from the information within these keys. Most of these keys will have values that are also numbered (i.e., the names are 0, 1.), as well as an MRUListEx value (that tells us which of the values was "most recently used"), and a NodeSlot value. Each of the numbered values contains a "shell item," or a binary "blob" of data that means something specific to the operating system, and of which there are a number of different types. Some shell items contain nothing more than a volume letter or a GUID that points to a Control Panel or virtual folder, while other shell items refer to folders within the file system. Various shell items can contain a good bit of additional metadata, as well, include (but not limited to) time stamps.

TIP

Shell Items

Shell items are used pervasively throughout Windows systems, more so as the operating system has been developed. Shell items can be found in Windows shortcuts (LNK files), within Jump Lists on Windows 7 and 8 (refer to Chapter 4 for a detailed discussion of Jump Lists), within shellbag artifacts, as well as other locations within the Registry. For example, as of Windows Vista, the ComDlg32 subkeys within the NTUSER.DAT Registry hive contain shell items. As of Windows 8, the Registry key that records images that the user has viewed via the Photos tile on the desktop includes a value that contains shell items.

A detailed discussion of the various types of shell items and how they are or can be parsed is beyond the scope of this book. For more information, see the Shell Items page at the ForensicsWiki, found online at http://www.forensicswiki.org/wiki/Shell_Item. Joachim Metz has put in considerable effort and gone to great lengths to consolidate and maintain information about shell items on this page.

The NodeSlot value within the BagMRU subkeys points to a subkey beneath the "Software\Microsoft\Windows\ShellNoRoam\Bag" key path. So, if one of the subkeys beneath the BagMRU key contains a NodeSlot value whose data is 0 × 02, then this value points to the "Software\Microsoft\Windows\ShellNoRoam\Bag\2" key, and additional information may be found within the Shell subkey. Specifically, on Windows XP systems (and I haven't seen this on any other versions of Windows), if there is a value within the "Software\Microsoft\Windows\ShellNoRoam\Bag\2\Shell" subkey (keeping with our example) whose name begins with "ItemPos," that value invariably contains a number of concatenated shell items that, when parsed, amounts to a directory listing. This information can be very valuable to an examiner.

On Vista systems and above, the shellbags artifacts are located in the USRCLASS. DAT Registry hive file, found in the "AppData\Local\Microsoft\Windows" folder within each user profile. Within the USRCLASS.DAT hive, the path to the shellbag artifacts is "Local Settings\Software\Microsoft\Windows\Shell\BagMRU," and as with the BagMRU subkeys on Windows XP, the numbered subkeys are nested, and when parse appropriately will build complete paths to the resource accessed by the user. As with Windows XP, the number values beneath the subkeys contain shell items of various types. Interesting enough, or perhaps to be expected, shell items under Windows XP can be very different than those under other versions of the operating system, while the shell items under Vista are similar to those under Windows 7 and 8. A notable difference on Vista systems and above, however, is that the NodeSlot value within the BagMRU subkeys does not have the same value as it does with Windows XP systems. I have yet to find corresponding values, based on the NodeSlot value beneath the BagMRU subkeys, that contain listings of files embedded in shell items.

TIP

Tracking User Activity

User actions that result in a persistent change to the system can be useful to an investigator. The key is for analysts to understand what actions may lead to the creation or modification of an artifact (or specific set of artifacts), and developing supporting, corroborating information through the inclusion and analysis of additional data sources. For example, the existence of a Prefetch file (discussed in Chapter 4) indicating that the Windows defragmentation utility had been launched doesn't implicitly indicate that the user launched the utility; in fact, Windows systems run a limited "defrag" on a regular basis. However, the existence of artifacts related to the user launching the utility, preceded by file deletions and/or applications being removed from the system, would provide indications of user intent.

Analysts can access the information within the shellbags artifacts through the use of the Windows shellbag parsers, such as the sbag.exe tool, available online from http://tzworks.net/prototype_page.php?proto_id=14.

Using the sbag.exe tool is quite simple; it's a command line interface (CLI) tool and requires only the path to the hive file of interest. The tool is easily able to

71	01/07/11 00:05:50.383	Win2008	01/05/2011	17:07:00	01/05/2011	17:13:40	01/05/2011
77	06/21/11 21:20:51.048	New folder	01/18/2011	01:24:50	01/18/2011	01:24:50	01/18/2011
78	06/21/11 21:20:51.048	user	01/18/2011	01:24:50	01/18/2011	01:24:50	01/18/2011
79	06/21/11 21:20:51.048	user23	01/18/2011	01:25:00	01/18/2011	01:25:00	01/18/2011
83	06/21/11 21:20:51.048	ProDiscoverRelease6800Basic.zip	01/21/2011	15:18:54	01/20/2011	23:25:48	01/21/2011
104	06/21/11 21:20:51.048	Shadow_Analyser_Beta_U52.zip	02/09/2011	18:41:04	02/10/2011	01:24:04	02/09/2011
20	07/20/11 16:16:41.134	D:					
34	04/21/11 17:19:03.427	fau-1.3.0.2390a.zip	01/04/2011	11:43:10	01/04/2011	11:43:26	01/04/2011

FIGURE 5.26

Extract of output from sbag.exe.

distinguish between the various versions of Windows and parse the appropriate key paths. Therefore, you can easily dump the shellbags information from a hive file extracted from an acquired image using the following command:

```
C:\tools> sbag f:\usrclass.dat
```

With the amount of information that can be available, it's a good idea to redirect the output to a file. The output of the tool produces 10 pipe-separated columns which include the bag number (i.e., "NodeSlot"), LastWrite time of the key being parsed, the path, embedded creation, modification and access times, and the full path for the folder accessed. The pipe-separated output can be opened in Excel for analysis; a portion of output from sbag.exe, open in Excel, is illustrated in Figure 5.26.

This information can be very valuable to an analyst, illustrating access to specific resources, along with the date and time that those resources had been accessed. For example, the parsed shellbag information can illustrate access to zipped archives and folders that no longer exist on the system, removable storage devices, and even network shares. As with other artifacts located in the Registry, the shellbags provide indications of access to resources that persist after the resource (i.e., folder) is no longer available.

Some interesting artifacts I've found in USRCLASS.DAT hives from Windows 7 systems are file names, as you can see illustrated in Figure 5.26. Specifically, fau-1.3.0.2390a.zip, ProDiscoverRelease6800Basic.zip, and Shadow_analyser_beta_U52.zip are visible listed in the figure. This is interesting because the available information regarding the BagMRU keys is that the data within the values refers to folders. However, keep in mind that when a user views the contents of a zipped archive in Windows Explorer on Windows Vista and above, the zipped archive is viewed as a folder.

Also, if you run sbag.exe against an NTUSER.DAT hive file from a Windows 7 system, you may see files listed beneath a key with a name that appears as follows:

```
\Software\Microsoft\Windows\Shell\Bags\1\Desktop\
ItemPos1920x1080×96(1)
```

This key (and ones like it) appears to contain information (via the key's values) about icons available on the desktop, which can include … well, any file.

From the NTUSER.DAT from a Windows 7 system, I found references to "{CLSID_RecycleBin}," "Crimson Editor SVN286.lnk," and "Google Chrome. lnk." On a Windows XP system, I found references to a considerable number of PDF files. Information such as this can be correlated with the contents of the user's RecentDocs key, and perhaps application (image viewer) MRU lists in order to determine where particular files that the user accessed were located.

NOTE

Tools

As of this writing, sbag.exe (and sbag64.exe) version 0.32 was available from TZWorks. net. Running sbag64.exe against a test hive file (USRCLASS.DAT hive from a Windows 7 system), I noticed that several entries were missing. When I ran the RegRipper *shellbags. pl* plugin (specifically written for Vista and above systems) against the hive, I found that there were a total of 632 lines of data (actual shellbag entries, not output headers), whereas when I ran sbag64.exe against the same hive file, there were 608 lines of data. A quick comparison showed that 21 of the missing lines were for shell items that refer to devices; in this case, two Apple iPods (for one, the shellbag artifact was "Apple iPod\ Internal Storage\DCIM\800AAAAA") and a Canon EOS digital camera (the shellbag artifact was "Canon EOS DIGITAL REBEL XTi\CF\DCIM\334CANON"). It appears that sbag.exe does not parse shell items that refer to devices, nor any of the shell items that comprise paths beneath those shell items.

It is very important for analysts to understand the capabilities of the tools that they use and employ in pursuit of their exams. Knowing the capabilities (and deficiencies) of various tools is extremely important, as is understanding the data structures that the tools parse and present to the analyst.

MenuOrder

In November 2011, Kurt Aubuchon posted to his blog (the article can be found online at http://kurtaubuchon.blogspot.com/2011/11/start-menu-and-ie-favorites-artifacts.html) that on most versions of Windows, if a user rearranges the contents of their Start Menu, and/or their Favorites menu or Favorites Center for the IE web browser, this information will be recorded in the user's NTUSER.DAT Registry hive file. This information will be recorded in the key path "Software\Microsoft\ Windows\CurrentVersion\Explorer\MenuOrder" key, beneath the "Start Menu2" and "Favorites" subkeys, respectively. Beneath the various subkeys will be a value named "Order," whose binary data is one or more shell items to reference the files listed in the respective folders.

This information can be very valuable to an analyst. For example, on one system, I found that a user had the Cain password cracking utility referenced in their Start Menu. All that was available was a shell item that referenced file named "Cain.lnk"; it did not contain the contents of the shortcut file, it only referenced the name of the file. However, this provided an indication of potentially malicious intent by the user, as well as an indication that the user had perhaps not been completely truthful with respect to the software they downloaded from the Internet and installed on their system (in violation of corporate acceptable use policies).

The RegRipper.pl *menuorder.pl* plugin will parse and display any information listed beneath these keys.

MUICache

The MUICache key first came to my attention several years ago when I was looking into some interesting malware artifacts; specifically, one antivirus vendor indicated in several write-ups that malware was creating entries beneath these keys. This was not, in fact, the case—instead what was happening was that the entry was being created by the operating system as a result of how the malware was being executed for testing.

On Windows 7 systems, the MUICache key is located in the USRCLASS. DAT hive within the user profile, in the path "Local Settings\Software\Microsoft\ Windows\Shell\MuiCache." The values beneath this key, specifically ones that do not begin with "@", appear to provide indications of applications that had been run on the system. An example of the partial contents of an MUICache key is illustrated in Figure 5.27.

As you can see Figure 5.27, the MUICache key contains a list of applications that have, at some point, been run on the system by the user. However, since each program entry is a value, there is no time stamp information associated with when the program may have been executed. The value of this key during an investigation is that the running of the program can be associated with a particular user, even after the program itself has been removed (deleted or uninstalled) from the system. Further, comparing visible values beneath the MUICache key from USRCLASS. DAT hives in VSCs can provide a time frame during which the user ran the program. Finally, on more than one occasion, I've found indications of oddly named programs beneath this key that, when the program file was found and examined, turned out to be malware.

The RegRipper *muicache.pl* plugin will display a subset of the values listed in the MUICache key for Windows XP, as well as Vista, and above systems.

C:\Program Files\AIM6\aim6.exe	REG_SZ	AIM
C:\Program Files\AIM6\anotify.exe	REG_SZ	AOL
C:\Program Files\Apple Software Update\SoftwareUpdate.exe	REG_SZ	Apple Software Update
C:\Program Files\Dell\QuickSet\quickset.exe	REG_SZ	QuickSet
C:\Program Files\Google\Picasa3\Picasa3.exe	REG_SZ	Picasa
C:\Program Files\Google\Picasa3\PicasaPhotoViewer.exe	REG_SZ	Picasa Photo Viewer
C:\Program Files\HP\Digital Imaging\bin\hpqdirec.exe	REG_SZ	hpqdirec.exe
C:\Program Files\Internet Explorer\iexplore.exe	REG_SZ	Internet Explorer
C:\Program Files\iTunes\iTunes.exe	REG_SZ	iTunes

FIGURE 5.27

Partial contents of MUICache key.

UserAssist

The purpose and use of the UserAssist subkeys have been discussed at length in a number of resources; suffice to say at this point that the contents of this key provide some very valuable insight into user activity, as the key appears to be used to track certain user activities that occur via the shell (Windows Explorer). When users double-click icons to launch programs, or launch programs via the Start menu, this activity is documented in the UserAssist subkeys, along with a date and time of the most recent occurrence of the activity, and the number of times the user has performed that activity. Each subsequent time the user performs the activity, the time stamp and counter are updated accordingly. The value names beneath the subkeys are "encrypted" using a Rot-13 ("rotate 13") translation cipher, which can be easily decrypted. The RegRipper *userassist.pl* plugin decrypts the value names beneath the subkeys and parses the time stamps and count (number of times the activity has occurred) from the binary data. Didier Stevens' UserAssist tool (found online at http://blog.didierstevens.com/programs/userassist/) does this, as well. In order to run the RegRipper plugin on an NTUSER.DAT file within an image mounted as a volume, simply use the following command line:

```
C:\tools>rip -r F:\users\jdoe\NTUSER.DAT -p userassist
```

The output from this command would appear at the command prompt (you would need to redirect the output from STDOUT to a file in order to save it), and an excerpt of a sample output appears as follows:

```
Wed Apr 13 19:06:47 2011 Z
D:\Tools\RFV.exe (3)
Wed Apr 13 19:06:39 2011 Z
D:\Tools\bintext.exe (1)
Wed Apr 13 19:06:29 2011 Z
D:\Tools\PEview.exe (1)
Wed Apr 13 18:59:08 2011 Z
F:\tools\PEview.exe (1)
F:\tools\RFV.exe (1)
F:\tools\bintext.exe (1)
F:\tools\PEDUMP.exe (1)
```

As you can see, the information is presented sorted in order of occurrence with the time stamps listed in UTC format. The applications launched are followed by their run count in parentheses.

TIP

Adding UserAssist Data to TLNs

We discuss TLN creation and analysis in Chapter 7 of this book, but this is good point to mention that you can output the information from the UserAssist keys to TLN format using the userassist_tln.pl plugin, via the following command line:

```
C:\tools>rip -r F:\users\jdoe\NTUSER.DAT -p userassist_
tln>events.txt
```

The information from the UserAssist keys can be used to demonstrate access to the Date Time Control Panel applet, installing or launching applications, etc. Most often, it's a good idea to include what you find in the UserAssist subkeys with other data, such as information from the RecentDocs key, in order to corroborate and validate your findings. In this way, you may find that a user launched MSWord, created a document, and metadata (file metadata was discussed in Chapter 4) from within the document may correlate back to the user.

Photos

As I mentioned, Windows 8 brings with it some new Registry artifacts. On March 8, 2013, Jason Hale posted his findings regarding the use of the Photo tile on the Windows 8 desktop to view image files (the blog post can be found online at http://dfstream. blogspot.com/2013/03/windows-8-tracking-opened-photos.html). In his post, Jason described that when a user views image files via the Photos tile on the Windows 8 desktop, Registry values are recorded within a very long key path in the user's USRCLASS. DAT hive file. I'll leave the key path in the blog post, but I do think that the values created beneath each subkey are very interesting; there's a file path (can show if the image was viewed from external media), a LastUpatedTime (appears to indicate when the file is opened), and a Link value that, according to Jason, contains a stream that follows the Windows shortcut binary format, minus the first 16 bytes from the documented format.

This information can be correlated with other sources within both the Registry and the file system, in order to assist the examiner in performing a more comprehensive analysis. The RegRipper *photos.pl* plugin was written specifically to parse and display most of the value data (with the notable exception of the Link value data) within the keys.

Since this blog post, Jason has published several other blog posts that address other artifacts specific to Windows 8 systems. For example, on September 9, 2013, he published an article regarding the Search Charm History from Windows 8 and 8.1 that is well worth reading.

NOTE

XPMode

In order to provide compatibility with older applications that ran under Windows XP and may not run within the Windows 7 environment, Microsoft provides a free download a custom virtual environment called "Windows XP Mode," or just "XPMode." XPMode can be installed and run on Windows 7 Professional, Ultimate, and Enterprise systems using Microsoft's Virtual PC (VPC) (http://windows.microsoft.com/en-US/windows7/products/features/windows-xp-mode). Applications installed in XPMode can be run from the Windows 7 host environment through a Windows shortcut or "LNK" file. As this interaction occurs via the shell, it appears in the user's UserAssist subkeys within the Windows 7 environment. Using the RegRipper plugin userassist2.pl to extract and translate the values and their data, indications of the use of applications launched via XPMode appear as follows:

```
Wed Apr 13 19:25:57 2011 Z
{A77F5D77-2E2B-44C3-A6A2-ABA601054A51}\Windows Virtual PC\
Windows XP Mode Applications\RFV (Windows XP Mode).lnk (1)
```

Information from the UserAssist subkeys may also correlate to other activity that the analyst has available that is separate from the system being examined. For example, information from the UserAssist subkeys may indicate that the user launched the Terminal Server Client, and the Terminal Server Client key, as well as the Jump Lists for the application (discussed in Chapter 4), would provide indications of which system the user had attempted to connect to. The Windows Event Logs on the remote system might indicate that the user successfully logged in, and network device logs might provide additional information regarding the connection, such as correlating information regarding the date and time of the connection, total number of bytes transferred.

Another great thing about the contents of the UserAssist subkey information is that it persists beyond activity associated directly with applications. Let's say that a user downloads and installs an application, runs it a couple of times, then deletes the application and any data files created. Weeks or even months after the deleted files are overwritten and unrecoverable, the information within the UserAssist subkeys is still available. I once performed an examination in which this was precisely the case. We were able to determine that the user had installed Cain & Abel, a password recovery tool available online from http://www.oxid.it/cain.html. The user had installed and run the tool to collect password information, viewed several of the output files, and then deleted the application files themselves.

> **TIP**
>
> **Historical UserAssist Data**
>
> Information within the UserAssist subkeys provide us with indications of user activity, but only the most recent occurrence of that activity. For example, if we see that a user launched a particular application 14 times, we can see the date and time that they did so, but we have no information regarding the previous 13 times that they launched that application. By mounting available VSCs within the acquired image (see Chapter 3 for techniques for mounting VSCs) in order to access previous versions of the Registry hives, we may be able to determine the dates and times when the user previously launched the application.

Virtual PC

When a Windows 7 system (Professional, Ultimate, or Enterprise) has VPC and XPMode installed, a user may be using it to run legacy applications from the special Windows XP environment. On a Windows 7 system with XPMode installed, I wanted to run an application that I could not run in Windows 7, so I ran it from the Windows XP environment. Once installed in the XPMode environment, the application appeared on the Windows 7 Start menu under "Windows XP Mode Applications." A reference to the application also appeared in "Software\Microsoft\ Virtual PC" key path within the NTUSER.DAT hive, as illustrated in Figure 5.28.

Beneath the final key in the path ("c6d3bf33.Windows.XP.Mode"), several values were added, as illustrated in Figure 5.29.

The AppPath value visible in Figure 5.29 illustrates where the application executable file is located within the XPMode environment. This information can

FIGURE 5.28

Software\Microsoft\Virtual PC, via WRR.

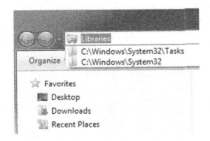

FIGURE 5.29

Partial contents of c6d3bf33.Windows.XP.Mode key.

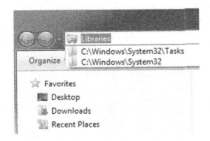

FIGURE 5.30

Typed paths in Explorer Address Bar.

be very useful, as it can also be correlated with information found beneath the UserAssist subkeys, in order to determine how many times the user accessed the application, and the most recent time and date that they did so.

TypedPaths

A Registry key that is new to Windows 7 is the TypedPaths key, found in the user's hive file, in the path, Software\Microsoft\Windows\CurrentVersion\Explorer\TypedPaths. Values within this key are populated when the user types a path into the Windows (not Internet) Explorer Address Bar, as illustrated in Figure 5.30.

The first value added is named "url1," and as each new value is added, that value appears to be named "url1" and previous values are "pushed down." As such, the LastWrite time of the TypedPaths key would correlate to when the "url1" value was added to the list.

Additional sources

As you can see from this chapter so far, a great deal of potentially valuable information can be retrieved from the Registry on a Windows 7 system. However, while we've focused on information that can be derived by analyzing an image acquired from a system, most of what we've discussed so far has involved what would correlate to the Registry visible via the Registry Editor on a live system. As it turns out, Windows 7 has much more Registry data available, if you know where to find it and how to access it. Knowing the structure of Registry keys and values, we can search the pagefile, unallocated space, and even the unallocated space within hive files for additional information.

RegIdleBackup

Earlier in this chapter, we discussed Registry keys associated with Scheduled Tasks. Figure 5.23 illustrates a task named "RegIdleBackup," which is a default task that ships with Windows 7. If we locate the file for that scheduled task and open it in Notepad, we'll see that the task backs up the SAM, Security, Software, and System hives to the C:\Windows\System32\config\RegBack folder every 10 days. So whenever you acquire an image from a Windows 7 system, you should expect to find backups of the Registry hives, and on an active system, those backups should be no more than 10 days old. The information may be very helpful to the analyst, possibly showing historical Registry information, or showing keys that were deleted from the hive file after the last backup was made.

TIP

Diff

If you install ActiveState Perl and then install the Parse::Win32Registry module (via the command "C:\perl > ppm install parse-win32registry"), a script called regdiff.pl will be installed in the Perl\site\bin folder. You can use this script, or the regdiff.bat batch file that is also installed, to "diff" the current active hives against the backed-up hive files, to see what changed since the last backup was made.

Volume shadow copies

In Chapter 3, we discussed how to access VSCs within images acquired from Vista and Windows 7 systems. Using these mounting techniques, multiple previous versions of the Registry hives (including the NTUSER.DAT and USRCLASS. DAT hives) can be accessed and parsed using tools such as RegRipper (and the associated rip.pl/.exe command line tool) in order to retrieve historical data from those hives. This technique can be added to analysis in order to search previous versions of hive files for earlier versions of data, or for keys and values that were subsequently deleted from the Registry. Information such as this may prove to be extremely valuable to the analyst or the investigator.

> **TIP**
> **Evidence Eliminators**
> Users may sometimes elect to run "evidence eliminator" tools in order to hide their illicit
> activities. Depending upon which tool is used (I've seen a tool called "Window Washer"
> run on systems), the Registry keys or values that get deleted may vary. Besides searching
> the unallocated space within hive files for deleted keys, another method for recovering this
> information would be to compare the current version of the hive files to previous versions of
> those files.

Virtualization

As discussed in Chapter 1, virtualization is available to a much greater degree on
Windows 7 systems than in previous versions of the operating system. For example, not only is VPC freely available for download and installation on several versions of Windows 7, but a special virtual environment called "XPMode" can also
be installed on those versions. This special version of Windows XP not only allows
the user to more easily run legacy applications that may not run on Windows 7, but
users can also access and interact with the Windows XP environment. For example,
a user can access the XPMode virtual machine as "XPMUser" and install applications, surf the web, and none of that activity will appear within the host Windows 7
environment.

In addition to XPMode, users can create and use other virtual guest systems
within VPC. Users may do this in order to hide their illicit activities within the virtual guest system; if the virtual system is run via VPC, then analyzing that virtual
hard drive (.vhd) file would be essentially no different from analyzing an image
acquired from a physical system; these systems would have their own Registry files.
The same is true for VMWare.vmdk files, as well. Virtual systems can prove to be
extremely valuable sources of information.

Memory

Beyond these sources, and beyond the scope of this chapter (memory analysis is
a chapter, or perhaps even a book unto itself), Registry information may be available in Windows memory, either in a dump of physical memory or in a hibernation
file (which is essentially a frozen-in-time snapshot of memory) and is accessible
using the open source Volatility framework, which can be found online at http://
code.google.com/p/volatility/. Brendan Dolan-Gavitt (a.k.a, "moyix"; his blog is
located online at http://moyix.blogspot.com/) has done considerable work in locating and extracting Registry data from memory and his work is incorporated in the
Volatility framework. One of the key aspects of accessing Registry data within
memory is that there are several volatile keys, which are keys that exist only in
memory and not on disk. In fact, the structures that identify volatile keys themselves only exist in memory. While this is not usually an issue, as many volatile
keys are created and used for legitimate purposes by the operating system (such as

the "CurrentControlSet" key within the System hive), it is possible that a volatile key could be created and used for malicious purposes (i.e., Registry-based mutex indicating that the system was infected with a particular bit of malware, temporary staging area for stolen data). As such, looking for available Registry information should be part of an analyst's investigative process whenever they have a memory dump or hibernation file available. If you are interested in information regarding memory analysis specifically for malware analysis, be sure to consult the *Malware Analyst's Cookbook*.

Tools

Before we close out this chapter, I wanted to make a couple of comments regarding tools. Throughout this chapter, I've mentioned a number of RegRipper plugins, and specific information regarding RegRipper and how to go about creating plugins can be found in *Windows Registry Forensics*. However, it's worth mentioning again here that there are two ways to go about listing the available plugins, which hive each is intended to be run against, and a brief description of what each plugin does.

The first way to do this is to use rip.pl (or the "compiled" Windows executable, rip.exe) with the appropriate switches. For example, typing "rip.pl –l" at the command prompt will list all of the available plugins in order, in a table format. An example of this format is illustrated as follows:

```
180. winzip v.20080325 [NTUSER.DAT]
Get WinZip extract and filemenu values
181. win_cv v.20090312 [Software]
Get & display the contents of the Windows\CurrentVersion key
182. wordwheelquery v.20100330 [NTUSER.DAT]
Gets contents of user's WordWheelQuery key
183. xpedition v.20090727 [System]
Queries System hive for XP Edition info
```

Adding the "-c" switch to the previous command tells rip.pl to format the output in a comma-separated value format, suitable for opening in Excel, as illustrated in the following command:

```
C:\tools > rip.pl -l -c > plugins.csv
```

The other way to view the available plugins is to use the GUI-based Plugin Browser, illustrated in Figure 5.31.

After selecting the directory where the plugins are located, you will see each plugin listed beneath the "Browse" tab, and as each plugin is selected (by clicking on the plugin name), the plugin information (i.e., name, version, hive, and the short description are all included in the code for each plugin) will appear to the right. The Plugin Browser is part of the RR.zip archive that contains the tools that are part of the *Windows Registry Forensics* book, and can be found online at http://windowsir. blogspot.com/p/books.html.

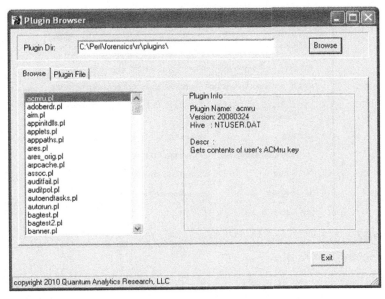

FIGURE 5.31

Plugin Browser interface.

Another tool that definitely deserves attention is the "Registry Decoder." In September 2011, Andrew Case released the Registry Decoder (the announcement for the release of the tool can be found online at http://dfsforensics.blogspot.com/2011/09/announcing-registry-decoder.html), which is an open source (Python) project that was initially funded by the National Institutes of Justice, and was released to the public.

The Registry Decoder consists of two components; the online acquisition component safely acquires copies of Registry hives from live systems by using the System Restore Point functionality on Windows XP, or the Volume Shadow Service on Vista and Windows 7. Creating the Restore Point or VSC ensures that there is a current, read-only copy of the hives that are not in use by the operating system. The second component provides a GUI for offline analysis of Registry hives. Figure 5.32 illustrates the results of a plugin run across a Windows 7 Software hive file loaded into the Registry Decoder.

The Registry Decoder allows an analyst to create a case and load multiple hive files (including those extracted from VSCs) and process those hives (i.e., run searches, "diff" hives, run plugins across all of the "mounted" hives, generate reports). Registry Decoder can process acquired images, Registry hives, and even acquired databases. Once the information is loaded, the tool performs a one-time preprocessing of all of the information, and generates databases and metadata files that contain all of the information needed for analysis. Andrew was interviewed by

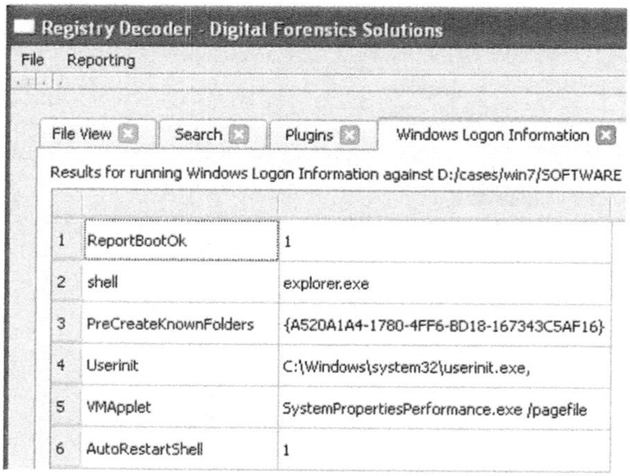

FIGURE 5.32

Partial Registry Decoder UI.

Ovie Carroll regarding the Registry Decoder, and you can listen to the interview, which contains a great deal more information regarding the tool, in September 26, 2011 CyberSpeak podcast (found online at http://cyberspeak.libsyn.com/cyber-speak-sep-26-2011-registry-browser).

Both components of the Registry Decoder can be downloaded from http://code.google.com/p/registrydecoder/.

SUMMARY

The Registry contains a great deal of forensically valuable data, and understanding what is available, as well as how to access and interpret it, can provide a great deal of context and additional (perhaps even critical) investigative detail to an analyst. While the Registry does contain a great deal of information, it cannot be used to answer every question; for example, analysts have asked in online forums where records of file copy operations are maintained in the Registry, and the simple answer is that they aren't. However, the good news is that there are a great number of questions that can be answered through Registry analysis, but there is so much information that no one resource can be written to document it all. As further research and analysis is conducted, new artifacts are discovered and cataloged, and often the best approach, beyond referencing resources such as this book (as well as the other books and resources mentioned in this chapter), is to collaborate with other analysts, and conduct some of your own research.

Again, all of the materials associated with this book can be found online via http://windowsir.blogspot.com/p/books.html.

References

[1] Carvey HA. Windows forensic analysis. 2nd ed. Syngress Publishing, Inc. <http://www.amazon.com/Windows-Forensic-Analysis-DVD-Toolkit-ebook/dp/B002ZFXTXI/ref=sr_1_2?s=books&ie=UTF8&qid=1390435996&sr=1-2&keywords=windows+forensic+analysis>; 2009. 978-1597494229.

[2] Carvey HA. Windows registry forensics. Syngress Publishing, Inc. <http://www.amazon.com/Windows-Registry-Forensics-Advanced-Forensic-ebook/dp/B004JN0CDO/ref=sr_1_1?s=books&ie=UTF8&qid=1390439699&sr=1-1&keywords=windows+registry+forensic>; 2011. 978-1597495806.

[3] Ligh MH, Adair S, Hartstein B, Richard M. Malware analyst's cookbook and DVD. Wiley Publishing, Inc. <http://www.amazon.com/Malware-Analysts-Cookbook-Techniques-Malicious-ebook/dp/B0047DWCMA/ref=sr_1_1?s=books&ie=UTF8&qid=1390435955&sr=1-1&keywords=malware+analyst%27s+cookbook>; 2011. 978-0-470-61303-0. .

Malware Detection

6

CHAPTER OUTLINE

INFORMATION IN THIS CHAPTER

- Malware Characteristics
- Detecting Malware

INTRODUCTION

If you own or use a computer, at some point malware is just going to be a part of your life. This is especially true for system and network administrators, who are often responsible for managing and maintaining hundreds of systems. However, this is also true for small businesses, which are often without the benefit of a dedicated system administrator, and even home users. We all know friends and family who have suffered the frustration of having systems infected with malware; in most cases, the complaints are about how the system has slowed down or about annoying pop-ups and messages that appear on the screen. What most folks don't realize is that the truly insidious malware is what we *aren't* seeing on the screen: the key loggers; the malware that grabs the contents of web browser form fields whenever we log into our online banking account; or the Trojan that captures your keystrokes when you order something online, before the data is encrypted and sent to the server on the other end of the web browser session.

The presence of malware on a system can have a significant impact on an organization. For example, the presence of malware may indicate a violation of acceptable use policies within that organization, in addition to potentially exposing the organization to risk in the eyes of compliance and regulatory bodies. Further, understanding the nature of the malware (based on the identification of the malware through the analysis of associated artifacts) can help an organization address business issues, such as reporting and notification.

This chapter is not about malware reverse engineering; there are extremely high quality books available that address that topic far better than I ever could, such as *Malware Analyst's Cookbook* [1]. The purpose of this chapter is to provide analysts and responders with an understanding of malware characteristics in order to aid in detecting suspicious and malicious files within an acquired image; if not the malware itself, then indications of malware having executed on the system. We will discuss various techniques for performing a thorough examination for malware and malware artifacts, as well as provide a checklist of these techniques.

Malware Characteristics

While I was a member of an emergency computer incident response services team, I began to notice that, as a team, we were receiving calls regarding, as well as responding to a good number of malware infection incidents. As such, I felt that it would be valuable, and indeed important, to develop a framework for not only better understanding malware in general but also to come up with a way for all of the consultants on our team to respond intelligently and speak authoritatively about malware, and be able to explain what they were seeing to our customers. After all, as consultants we were approaching the problem from a technical perspective: which systems were infected, what network traffic was being observed, etc. However, the customer was coming at the problem and concerned about the issue from a business perspective:

how does this affect me from a legal or compliance perspective, what data was stolen (if any), and where did it go? During some examinations, this will be the primary target of your analysis; during others, the malware will be a secondary artifact, installed on a system following a compromise. As such, I wanted to develop a framework that allowed our consultants (and others) to easily address the situation and bridge the technology-business gap. Customers very often aren't so much concerned with the technical aspects of the malware as they are with what data may have been exposed as a direct (or indirect) result of the infection, what risk they may be exposed to, and what issues they may have with respect to compliance and regulatory bodies.

What I came up with (and blogged about several times at http://windowsir.blogspot.com) were four simple malware characteristics that could be used to understand, respond to, and eradicate malware, as well as answer the customer's questions. These characteristics are the initial infection vector (how the malware got on the system); the propagation mechanism (how the malware moves between systems, if it does that); the persistence mechanism (how the malware remains on the system and survives reboots and when the user logs out); and artifacts (what traces the malware leaves on a system as a result of its execution) that you can look for during an examination. I've found that when understood and used by responders (either consultants that fly in or on-site IT staff) these characteristics also provide a framework for locating malware on a system, as well as collecting information about a malware sample found on a system.

For the types of cases where malware is likely to play a role (e.g., intrusion incidents), most customers want to know things like what data, if any, was exposed, as well as if the malware was specifically targeted to their organization. Developing a more complete picture of malware and the effects on its ecosystem (not just the system it's installed on, but the entire infrastructure) can guide us in answering those questions. Understanding how the malware behaves allows us to understand its capabilities. For example, some malware behaves differently if it finds that it's in a virtual environment or depending upon the version of Windows it's running on. There is also malware that will install itself differently on systems depending upon the level of privileges available. Knowing things like how malware gets on a system or how it communicates off of the system (if it does) helps us understand where else we should be looking for artifacts; subsequently, we learn more about the malware when these artifacts are found (or when they're not found! see Chapter 1) and ultimately provide better answers to our customers.

It's important for everyone to understand the characteristics of malware. If you think back to Chapter 1, we talked about convergence—the fact that no one area of computer/digital forensic analysis is really as separate from others as we might think. When law enforcement officers (LEOs) have to deal with an issue of contraband (often called "illicit") images or fraud, it's very likely that someone will ask about or make the claim that malware (a Trojan) was responsible for the observed activity, or at least contributed to it. As such, LEOs are no longer simply dealing with cataloguing contraband images, as they now have a malware investigation to complete. As such, turning to those who address malware detection and user activity analysis issues on a regular basis would likely provide a great deal of assistance and expertise.

WARNING

The "Trojan Defense"

The claim by defendants that "a virus did it" is nothing new. In 2003, Aaron Caffrey was accused in the United Kingdom for hacking into computer systems in the United States; he claimed that someone had hacked into his system and run an attack script; essentially, "a Trojan did it." Even though no indication of a Trojan (although the attack tools were found) was found, Caffrey was acquitted.

That being said, let's go ahead and take a look at the four malware characteristics in greater detail.

Initial infection vector

Not to be circular, but the initial infection vector is how the malware initially infected or made its way onto a system or infrastructure. There are a number of ways that systems can be infected; the user opens or double clicks on an email attachment that is really a malicious document, clicks on a link to a malicious or infected web site, other browser "drive-bys," etc. Systems can also be infected when removable storage devices (thumb drives, their iPod, etc.) that are infected are connected to their systems. Peer-to-peer (P2P) file sharing infrastructures are other popular means by which systems can get infected. The more interconnected we become, and the more devices that we have that can be updated and synchronized by connecting them to our computer systems, the more we are open to infection from malware.

Another prevalent infection mechanism is social networking sites, such as MySpace and Facebook. In their book *Cybercrime and Espionage*, Will Gragido and John Pirc mentioned a quote reportedly attributed to the infamous bank robber, Willy Sutton; when asked why he robbed banks, Mr. Sutton reportedly replied "because that's where the money is." Well, this provides us a glimpse as to why those who spread malware use email and target social media/networking sites—if they're looking to infect a large number of systems, then they have to go where the users are, and in particular where they can find massive numbers of users. If the goal is to create masses of infected systems (for botnet activity, collecting user's personal data, etc.), then casting as wide a net as possible would likely be the best way to achieve your goal. The motivations of the malware authors are often predicated by the predilections of their target prey or "user community," in that the vast majority of users like to browse the web, click links, use email, open email attachments, etc.

Speaking of email and attachments, the February 2011 Symantec.cloud MessageLabs Intelligence report (found online at http://www.symanteccloud.com/globalthreats/overview/r_mli_reports) indicated that "malicious PDF files outpace the distribution of related malicious attachments used in targeted attacks, and currently represent the attack vector of choice for malicious attackers." Didier Stevens (whose blog can be found at http://blog.didierstevens.com/) has spent considerable effort writing tools to detect malicious contents in PDF files, and his tools have even been included in online malware analysis sites, such as VirusTotal (found online at http://www.virustotal.com). These demonstrate not only that those who proliferate malware gravitate to using infection vectors that tend to be "popular" (i.e., applications may be targeted not so much because they are vulnerable to exploit, but because they are so widely used) but also that the security community will often follow suit in providing appropriate and novel detection mechanisms.

Targeting users isn't the only way to gain access to systems. Vulnerable Internet-facing applications and servers are discovered and exploited through scanning. For example, vulnerable web servers (as well as applications running on those servers) can provide access to systems through such means as SQL injection attacks. Systems can also be exploited via functionality inherent to the operating system, such as automatically executing the commands in an autorun.inf file on a USB thumb drive that is inserted into or connected to the system. In short, there are more vectors that allow malware to infect a system than simply getting a user to click a link or open a file.

The initial infection vector of malware is important to understand, as it is very often one of the questions that the customer wants answered: "How did this malware originally get on my system or into our infrastructure?" For some, this information is needed in order to clearly establish a "window of compromise," that is, what was the initial infection vector, when did the initial infection occurs, therefore how long have we been infected? Identifying the initial infection vector can also be used to find gaps in protection or detection mechanisms or user awareness training.

TIP

Phishing Training

Aaron Higbee is the CTO and a cofounder of the Intrepidus Group and responsible for the PhishMe.com site, which allows someone to send phishing emails into their own infrastructure in order to baseline or test their user awareness training with respect to clicking on links and attachments offered through email. The idea is that following (or even prior to) user awareness training with respect to the dangers and risks of phishing attacks, an organization can use the PhishMe.com site to validate and reinforce their training.

The initial infection vector can also help determine if the malware infection is a targeted attack. In some instances, a malware infection is simply opportunistic, such as when a user (coincidentally) visits a compromised web site infected with a downloader; the downloader gets on the user's system through a vulnerability or misconfiguration in their browser, and then downloads additional malware. For example, about two years ago, a friend of mine contacted me for advice because his laptop was infected with malware. It seemed that his son (a fourth grader) was doing homework, which required that students go to the National Geographic web site and complete a task. As it turned out, the site had been compromised and every visit to the web site using a Windows system (apparently, regardless of the actual web browser used) resulted in an infection. The intent of such attacks is to infect any and all visitors to the site. However, some infections occur when a user is sent an email with an attachment or link that is designed to be interesting to them, and appears to come from a known, trusted source. These types of attacks are often preceded by considerable open-source intelligence collection, and target victims are selected based on their employer and projects that they may be working on or know something about. These attacks are referred to as "spear phishing," during which specific individuals are sought to launch an attack against. As such, the answer to the question of "was this a targeted attack?" would be yes.

Propagation mechanism

Once malware has infected an infrastructure, there is generally some means by which that malware moves to other systems. This may be via network-based vulnerability exploitation (such as with Conficker), making use of operational business functionality by writing to available network shares, or by parsing the user's Address Book or Contact List and sending out copies of itself or other malware to everyone listed with an email address.

Malware's propagation mechanism can be particularly insidious when it takes advantage of the day-to-day operational business infrastructure within the organization in order to spread, such as writing to existing network shares. Many organizations have home directories for users as well as file shares that users will access or be automatically connected to when they login, and if the malware writes to these shares, the user systems may end up being infected. When the malware propagates using the infrastructure in this manner, it makes incident response and malware eradication efforts difficult. The affected functionality is most often required and critical to business operations, and taking that infrastructure offline for an indeterminate amount of time is simply not an acceptable response measure. Additionally, taking some systems offline for "cleaning" without understanding how they were infected in the first place may result in the systems becoming re-infected shortly after connecting them back to the network, making effective eradication and cleanup procedures impossible. Without understanding the infection or propagation method used, it is impossible to take appropriate measures—such as installing patches, making configuration changes, or modifying permissions—in order to prevent re-infection.

Depending on which system(s) you're looking at within an infrastructure, the propagation mechanism (how the malware moves between systems) may appear to be the initial infection vector. In some instances, malware may initially make its way into an infrastructure as a result of a browser "drive-by" or as an email attachment. This initial infection may then be described as a "Trojan downloader," which in turn downloads a worm that infects systems within the infrastructure through some vulnerability or other mechanism. If you're looking at the fifth or tenth system infected by the worm within the infrastructure, the initial infection vector for that system would appear to be the worm. However, if you missed "patient 0" (the originally infected system), you would not be able to "see" how the infrastructure was originally infected.

In other instances, the propagation mechanism may, in fact, be the same as the initial infection vector, in that the means by which the malware infected the first system was also used to infect subsequent systems. An example of this may be when an employee takes their laptop home and it becomes infected with a network worm while attached to the home wireless network. When the employee then brings the laptop back to the office and connects it to the network, the worm propagates using the same method as the initial infection vector.

The propagation mechanism needs to be identified and understood, not simply because it impacts the infrastructure but also because the manner in which the malware spreads to other systems may impact and lead to the infection of other, external organizations, such as vendors and business partners, or even customers. In the case of malware that spreads through email attachments, customers may also be impacted. At the very least, this can bring undue attention to an organization, negatively impacting the brand image of that organization, and possibly even exposing vulnerabilities within that infrastructure to public scrutiny.

Another reason the propagation mechanism needs to be understood is that this mechanism will very likely play an important role in the response to the incident. Depending upon the situation, patches may need to be applied or configuration modifications may need to be made to devices or to the infrastructure itself. As such, correctly understanding the propagation mechanism so that it can be addressed as part of an overall security response plan will ensure that resources are correctly applied to the issue.

Persistence mechanism

Jesse Kornblum pointed out in his paper *Exploiting the Rootkit Paradox* (found on the web at http://jessekornblum.com/publications/ijde06.html) that malware most often wants to remain persistent on the infected system. (In his paper, he was specifically referring to rootkits, but the concept applies to malware in general.) What use is a Trojan or backdoor that disappears and is no longer accessible after the system is rebooted, particularly if this happens regularly? As such, most malware has some mechanism that allows it to be automatically restarted when the system is rebooted, when a user logs in, or via some other trigger. Again, this is a general statement, as some malware has been identified that takes advantage of the fact that the system itself must remain online and is unlikely to be rebooted; therefore the malware doesn't employ what would be defined as a "traditional" persistence mechanism. Instead, an attacker uses some vulnerability or identified technique to inject the malware into the server's memory; should the system be taken offline or rebooted for some reason, the attacker hopes that they can re-infect the system using the same or a similar method. In this case, the malware remains persistent in memory as long as the server remains online and functioning. However, our discussion in this chapter focuses on detecting malware within an acquired image, so some form of persistence mechanism is assumed.

Perhaps one of the most popular malware persistence mechanisms employed by malware authors is to make some use of the Registry, using what's commonly become known as an "autostart" mechanism. While the Registry contains a great deal of configuration and user tracking information, it also contains a considerable number of locations from which applications can be automatically started, without any interaction from the user beyond booting the system, or possibly logging in. For example, when a Windows system is booted, Windows services are started, and entries within the "Run" key in the Software hive are parsed and launched, and a number of other Registry keys and values are also parsed. The Registry can also be modified to ensure that the malware is launched even if the system is started in Safe Mode.

NOTE

Unicode RLO Control Character

We discussed the Unicode "right-to-left override" (RLO) Control Character (U + 202E) in detail in Chapter 4, and how it can be used by malware to "hide" itself in the Registry. On July 31, 2013, the antivirus (AV) vendor Sophos posted an article that describes a variant of the ZeroAccess malware (the article can be found online at http://nakedsecurity.sophos.com/2013/07/31/zeroaccess-malware-revisited-new-version-yet-more-devious/) that uses the Unicode RLO control character not only for file names within the file system but also for its persistence mechanism (i.e., creating an entry in the System hive as a Windows service). As mentioned in Chapter 4, the RegRipper *rlo.pl* plugin can be used to detect the presence of the RLO control character in key and value names within any Registry hive file.

When a user logs in, the "Run" key within the user's hive is parsed, and the applications launched, with no error checking or notification to the user if something fails. I've seen malware launch via the dynamic linked library (DLL) Search Order "issue," so that the malware launches when the Windows Explorer shell loads in the user context (this was discussed in detail on the Mandiant blog post found online at https://www.mandiant.com/blog/malware-persistence-windows-registry/). There are a number of autostart mechanisms that can be engaged to launch malware when a user takes a specific action, such as launching a command prompt, running a specific program, or launching any graphical user interface (GUI)-based application.

WARNING

Memory Scraper

I once encountered an interesting piece of malware found on back office point of sale (POS) servers. This malware used a Windows service as its persistence mechanism, but rather than launching immediately when the system booted, the service started a timer to wait or "sleep" for a random amount of time. When the timer had expired the service would "wake up" and run a series of other tools, the first of which would extract the virtual memory used by any of eight named processes (all of which were associated with processing credit card information). The malware then launched a Perl script (that had been compiled into a standalone executable file with the Perl2Exe application) to parse the virtual memory dump, looking for track 1 and 2 data (the data found in the magnetic stripe on the back of your credit card). This was an interesting approach to data theft; first, it targeted the only location within the credit card processing system at the local site where the data was not encrypted (i.e., in memory). Second, it waited for a random period after the system was booted, because when the system was booted, there was no credit card data in memory. By waiting for a random amount of time (in one instance, 41 days), the malware author ensured that there was data in memory to collect and parse.

Not all persistence mechanisms reside within the Registry, however. In fact, once analysts become aware of the Registry as a source for malware persistence, it's just their luck that the very next case involves malware that uses a persistence mechanism that does *not* reside within the Registry. Some malware may be identified as a file infector, for example, and therefore doesn't need to use the Registry to maintain persistence on an infected system. Instead, such malware would infect executable files or data files, so that the malware would be run whenever the executable was launched, or the data file accessed.

An example of malware whose persistence mechanism that does not require the Registry was originally identified as "W32/Crimea" (the write up can be found online at http://home.mcafee.com/VirusInfo/VirusProfile.aspx?key=142626) in July 2007; this malware was placed on a system as a DLL, and persistence was achieved by modifying the import table (within the header of the portable executable (PE) file) of the file imm32.dll (a legitimate Windows "PE" file) to point a function in the malicious DLL. As such, any process that loaded imm32.dll became infected.

One means for malware to remain persistent on a system that really came to light in the summer of 2010 had originally been documented by Microsoft as normal system behavior in 2000. Nick Harbour, a malware reverse engineer for the consulting firm Mandiant, was the first to publicly describe this specific issue in an M-unition blog post titled "Malware Persistence without the Windows Registry" (the blog post can be found online at http://blog.mandiant.com/archives/1207). In particular, a malicious DLL was added to the C:\Windows directory and named "ntshrui.dll," which also happens to be the name of a legitimate DLL and shell extension that is found in the C:\Windows\system32 directory. However, unlike other shell extensions listed in the Registry, this shell extension does not have an explicit path listed for its location, and when Explorer.exe launches to provide the user shell, it uses the established and documented DLL search order to locate the DLL by name only (no other checks, such as for MD5 hash or digital signature verification, are performed), rather than following an explicit path. As such, the Explorer.exe process starts looking in its own directory for the DLL first and finds and loads the malicious DLL. In this way, the malware relies on how the system operates, rather than adding a key or value to the Registry as its persistence mechanism.

Yet another persistence mechanism to consider is Windows Scheduled Tasks functionality. Scheduled tasks allow administrators to run tasks or "jobs" at designated times, rather than every time the system is booted or when a user logs in. For example, if you use Apple products such as iTunes, Safari, or QuickTime on your Windows system, you can expect to see a scheduled task that launches the software update application on a weekly basis. As such, it's relatively easy to get malware on a system and schedule it to run at specifically designated times. Methods for determining which scheduled tasks had launched, and their exit status, for various versions of Windows were discussed in Chapter 4.

Yet another example of a persistence mechanism that does not rely on the Registry is to use other startup locations within the file system. For example, the Carberp Trojan, which at one point was reportedly replacing Zeus/ZBot as the preeminent malware for stealing a user's online banking information, does not appear to use the

Registry for persistence. The Symantec write up for one variant of this Trojan (which can be found online at http://www.symantec.com/security_response/writeup.jsp?docid=2010-101313-5632-99&tabid=2) indicates that the malware remains persistent by placing an executable file in the "\Start Menu\Programs\Startup" folder within a user's profile, which causes the file to be launched when the user logs onto the system. Further, on September 23, 2011, Martin Pillion wrote a post titled "Malware Using the Local Group Policy to Gain Persistence" to the HBGary blog (the blog and Martin's post don't seem to be available online at the time of this writing) which described the use of the Windows Local Group Policy (the article specifically addresses Windows 7) functionality for running scripts during specific events (Logon, Logoff) as a persistence mechanism. In the article, Martin stated that this was particular due to the fact that the Microsoft AutoRuns tool (updated to version 11 on September 20, 2011 and found online at http://technet.microsoft.com/en-us/sysinternals/bb963902; at the time of this writing, version 11.7 is available) reportedly did not check these locations.

Additionally, malware doesn't have to *be* or reside on a system in order to remain persistent on that system. In networked environments, "nearby" systems can monitor infected systems and ensure that the malware spread to those systems is running. This is a particularly insidious approach to use, as many organizations only perform detailed monitoring at their network perimeter and egress points. Unusual or suspicious traffic seen at the perimeter will lead back to the systems that are communicating out of the infrastructure; however, the systems that are ensuring that malware is running on those systems will likely not be seen by the monitoring. Therefore, IT staff will respond to the systems identified via egress monitoring, "clean" or even re-provision those systems, which (depending on the method used) may become re-infected shortly after being placed back on the network. This sort of approach ensures that the malware remains persistent on the infrastructure as a whole, rather than focusing on persistence on a specific host. In order to detect this sort of "lateral movement" within an infrastructure, IT staff and responders need to ensure that the Windows Event Logs are configured to record login attempts (both successful and failed), configured to a size such that events are not quickly overwritten, and that the Event Log records are actually retrieved and reviewed prior to being destroyed. Means for analyzing Windows Event Logs were discussed in Chapter 4.

WARNING

Multiple Persistence Mechanisms

One has to be careful when determining what the persistence mechanism is for a particular bit of malware. I once responded to a malware infection incident that wasn't particularly widespread, but did seem to be particularly persistent. The local IT staff had determined that the persistence mechanism for the malware was apparently a Windows service. However, when they deleted the service and corresponding file on disk and then rebooted the system, the malware was back. Close examination of one of the systems indicated that there was a second Windows service involved that monitored the first service. If this service did not detect the other malware service when the system started, it would "re-infect" the system.

When analyzing Windows Event Logs for indications of lateral movement within the infrastructure, what responders should typically look for are network logins for accessing resources; on Windows XP and 2003 systems, these events appear in the Security Event Log with event ID 540, type 3, and on Windows 7, they appear in the same Event Log with event ID 4624, again as a type 3 login. These events would typically then be followed by and event ID 7035 event, indicating that a particular service was sent a start command. In the case of lateral movement, that service might be PSExec, XCmdSvc, or ATSvc. The first two services allow for remote code execution, and the third allows for the creation of scheduled tasks. Descriptions of security events for Windows 7 and Windows 2008 R2 can be found in Microsoft Knowledge Base (MS KB) article 977519, found online at http://support.microsoft.com/kb/977519.

The purpose of this section has not been to list all possible persistence mechanisms; instead, my goal has been to open your eyes to the possibilities for persistence on Windows systems. One aspect of this has been obvious over time—that is that responders will continue to learn from intruders and malware authors as they identify and use new persistence mechanisms. As Windows systems provide more functionalities to the user and become more complex, new persistence mechanisms are invariably discovered and employed; as such, the goal for responders and analysts is to recognize this and keep malware's need for persistence in mind, as understanding that there *is* a persistence mechanism in the first step to identifying that mechanism.

Artifacts

Artifacts are those traces left by the presence and execution of malware, which are not themselves specifically used by the malware to maintain persistence. Malware persistence mechanisms appear to be similar to artifacts, and based on this definition, can be considered to be a subset of the more general "artifacts" description. However, the best way to look at this is that persistence mechanisms are artifacts used for a specific purpose, while the more general use of the term applies to other artifacts not specifically used for persistence. For example, some malware creates or modifies Registry keys or values in order to remain persistent on an infected system, whereas that same malware may also create Registry values to maintain configuration information, such as servers to contact, values for encryption keys, or even bits of code to run.

That being said, not all artifacts are directly created by the malware itself; some artifacts are created as a result of the ecosystem in which the malware exists (remember when we talked about "indirect artifacts" in Chapter 1). I know, you're asking yourself, "what?" That's just a fancy way of saying that some artifacts aren't created by the malware, but are instead created as a result of the malware's interaction with the infected host. For example, some malware creates a Windows service in order to ensure its persistence; as a result, when the service is launched, Windows will create subkeys under the HKLM\System\CurrentControlSet\Enum\Root key

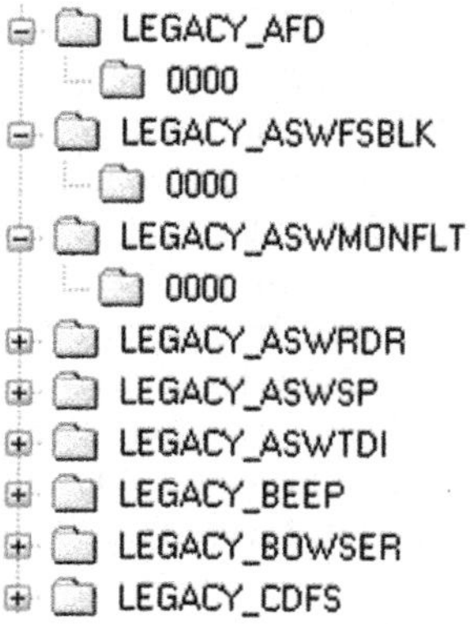

LEGACY_AFD
    0000
LEGACY_ASWFSBLK
    0000
LEGACY_ASWMONFLT
    0000
LEGACY_ASWRDR
LEGACY_ASWSP
LEGACY_ASWTDI
LEGACY_BEEP
LEGACY_BOWSER
LEGACY_CDFS

FIGURE 6.1

Enum\Root\Legacy_* keys.

that refer to the service name, prepended with "Legacy_*," as illustrated in Figure 6.1.

This is an interesting artifact, but how is it useful? Well, several analysts have noted that the LastWrite time for the "Legacy_*\0000" keys closely approximates to the last time that the service was launched, while the LastWrite time for the "Legacy_*" (again, where the "*" is for the service name) closely approximates to the first time that the service was launched. This information was developed largely through observation and testing and has been extremely useful in determining when a system was initially infected.

WARNING

Malware Evolution

One aspect of analysis that examiners need to keep in mind is that malware authors may learn of our analysis methods and attempt to use those processes against us. For example, the ZeroAccess rootkit (a.k.a. Smiscer or Max++), which was reverse engineered by Giuseppe Bonfa, was found to delete its Legacy_* service keys (these keys were discussed earlier in this chapter) that the operating system created beneath the HKLM\ System\CurrentControlSet\Enum\Root key. The write up that includes the discussion of the Legacy_* service key being deleted can be found online at http://resources.infosecinstitute. com/zeroaccess-malware-part-2-the-kernel-mode-device-driver-stealth-rootkit.

The key to sharing information amongst analysts is to have an analysis *process*, and not to rely solely on individual artifacts. It is likely that when a malware author employs a method for their new variant to avoid detection, something else will occur and new artifact may be created. Employing an analysis process that casts a wide net will allow you to detect these new artifacts, as well as notice the *absence of artifacts where you would expect to find them*. Openly sharing with other analysts allows everyone to improve their processes.

Another example of artifacts created by the operating system is Prefetch files, specifically as a result of application prefetching performed by the operating system.

TIP

Application Prefetching

As was discussed in Chapter 4, server systems such as Windows 2003 and 2008 are capable of performing application prefetching, although it is not enabled by default. Enabling this functionality as part of incident preparedness planning may provide useful artifacts during incident response and analysis.

Prefetch files are found in the C:\Windows\Prefetch directory on Windows systems where application prefetching is enabled; by default, Windows XP, Vista, Windows 7 and 8 have application prefetching enabled by default (Windows 2003 and 2008 are capable of application prefetching, but this functionality is not enabled by default). Details regarding the creation and analysis of these files were covered in Chapter 4, but suffice to say here that Prefetch files have provided useful indications of malware being executed, even after that malware has been deleted from the system.

TIP

Prefetch and Data Exfiltration

Prefetch files can contain significant data with respect to data exfiltration. For example, some intruders may use rar.exe to archive stolen data prior to shipping it off of the system; as such, the Prefetch file for rar.exe may contain references to the directory paths and file names of the data that was included in the archive. See Chapter 4 for a discussion of parsing Prefetch files, particularly as they apply to Windows 8; on Windows 8 systems, application Prefetch files can contain up to eight different last execution times.

Malware artifacts can also be based on the version of Windows that the malware infects/installs itself on, or based on the permissions under which the malware is installed. There is malware, for example, that when it infects a system via a user account with Administrator privileges, it uses the Run key in the Software hive for persistence, and files may appear in the C:\Windows\Temp directory; however, if the account through which the system is infected is a normal user (lower privilege account), the malware will use the Run key in the user's hive for persistence and write files to the Temp directory in the user profile. As such, when an analyst looks at the entries in the Run key within the Software hive, they won't see anything that would indicate an infection by that particular malware and should also be sure to check (all of) the user profiles.

NOTE

Self-inflicted Artifacts

One thing to be careful of when reading AV vendor malware write ups and descriptions is self-inflicted artifacts; that is, artifacts created as a result of the method used to dynamically execute and analyze the malware. For example, to get a better view of how the malware operates, an analyst may launch the malware with a virtual machine. When doing so, artifacts will be created based on how the malware is launched. You may see entries in the UserAssist or MUICache data under the "Registry values added" section of the write up. This sort of thing is simply the nature of the business; AV company customers will, in many cases, send the vendor samples of malware without the benefit of intelligence regarding how the malware made it onto the system (the initial infection vector) the first place. This is also something to be aware of if you're doing your own malware dynamic analysis.

Another important aspect of malware artifacts to keep in mind is that if you're aware of artifacts specific to various malware families, and if you employ an analysis process that "casts a wide net" in looking for anomalies, you're very likely going to find indications of malware that is not detected by AV applications. For example, a new variant of malware may not be detected by the installed AV product, but an analyst looking at the StubPath values in the "Installed Components" subkeys (within the Software Registry hive) may find that an entry points to a file within the Recycle Bin (on Windows 7, "$Recycle.Bin"). Earlier in this chapter, I mentioned finding memory scraping malware used to collect credit card track data from back office POS server systems. One of the components of the malware was a Perl script "compiled" via Perl2Exe; when this component was launched, the various modules compiled into the executable code were extracted as DLL files and written to a Temp folder on the system, and when it finished executing, these files were not removed. Using this artifact information, we had a running log of how many times and when the malware had executed.

Understanding the characteristics that we've discussed so far when attempting to locate malware within an acquired image can often have a significant impact on your examination. For example, some families of malware may have different file names or propagation mechanisms associated with each variation within the family, but there will also be characteristics that are consistent across all variants. For example, while the malware family known as "Conficker" (family description found online at http://www.microsoft.com/security/portal/Threat/Encyclopedia/Entry.aspx?name=win32%2fconficker) had differences across all variants, the malware had a consistent persistence mechanism, using a random name for a Windows service that started as part of svchost.exe. As such, Conficker infections could be determined by locating the persistence mechanism, and from there locating the DLL file that comprised the infection. Understanding these characteristics, in particular the persistence mechanism and artifacts, can also assist in helping to locate malware that is not identified by AV scanning applications, as locating the artifacts can lead you to the malware itself.

Detecting Malware

Detecting malware within an acquired image is perhaps one of the most amorphous and ethereal tasks that an analyst may encounter. Many analysts have cringed at receiving instructions to "find all of the bad stuff," because the question remains, how do you go about doing this effectively, and in a timely manner? The answer to that is simple—you don't, and you can't. After all, isn't "bad" a relative term? Without context, a good deal of effort can be dedicated to finding something that is actually normal activity, or isn't the "bad" thing you're looking for. I know of one analyst who was told to "find bad stuff," and found hacker tools and utilities, as well as indications of their use. After reading the report, the customer stated that those tools were actually part of the employee's job, which was to test the security of specific systems within the infrastructure. Sometimes, we have to take a moment to get a little context and find out just what "bad" is, so that we have a better understanding of what to look for.

The goal of detecting malware within an acquired image should be one of data reduction. Malware authors are sometimes lazy, but they can also be very insidious, and take great pains to protect their files from detection. There are a number of techniques that malware authors can and do use to hide their programs from detection, even going so far as to make their programs look as much like a normal Windows program as possible. Malware authors will use specific techniques (giving the file a "normal" looking name, placing the file in a directory where such a file would be expected to be found, etc.) to hide their programs, sometimes even based on the techniques used by analysts to detect these files.

> **NOTE**
>
> **Unicode and File Names**
> We've discussed the use of the Unicode "RLO" control character several times so far in this book, mostly in the context of the Registry. As pointed out, however, this control character can also make file names within the file system "look" normal. Unicode characters from other character sets can also be used to make file names look normal, by replacing the letter "o" or "s" with an equivalent character from a completely different character set. In this way, the file name looks normal when viewed through Windows Explorer, but the operating system sees it as a completely different file than what the user might expect.

Given the challenge of finding one (or a small number) of well-disguised files within an acquired image containing thousands of files, the best approach that an analyst can take is to use a thorough, documented process to reduce the number of files that need to be analyzed to a more manageable number. Having a documented process allows the analyst, as well as other analysts, to see exactly what was done, what worked, and what needs to be done to improve the process, if anything. The following sections of this chapter lay out some steps that an analyst can use as a methodology and include in their analysis process in order to detect the presence of malware within an acquired image, or provide a thorough process for ensuring that malware does not exist with an image. However, while each section will describe that particular step thoroughly, this is not intended to be an all inclusive list. Some of these steps are sure to be familiar, while others may be new, but given enough time, someone will very likely come up with additional steps.

Log analysis

One of the first steps in detecting malware within an acquired image is to determine what AV application, if any, was already installed and/or run on the system. If the system did have AV installed, the analyst would need to determine if it was running at the time that the system was acquired (or when the incident occurred; some malware actually disables AV and other security products on Windows systems) and when that application was last updated. This can be done easily by examining logs generated by AV applications; many maintain logs of updates, as well as the results of regularly scheduled and on demand scans. Some AV applications even write their events to the Application Event Log; however, in some cases, this may be a configurable option, and may be disabled, or simply not enabled; therefore, if you check the event sources for the various Application Event Log records and do not see an indication of an AV application (McAfee AV products use the source "McLogEvent"), do not assume that one hasn't been installed.

WARNING

Application Event Logs

When analyzing a system, keep in mind that Application Event Logs, like the other Event Logs on Windows systems, do not simply keep recording events *ad infinitum*. Instead, once the logs have reached their specified size, older events are discarded to make room for new ones. The maximum size of the Event Logs can be controlled by modifying a Registry value, but in my experience, this is not something that's done very often, particularly on desktop systems. As such, analysts should look for both Application Event Log records and AV application log files, as the AV log files may have considerably more historical data available.

One of the first things I will usually look for on a Windows system is the log file for the Microsoft Malicious Software Removal Tool (MRT). MRT is a targeted microscanner that is installed in the background on Windows systems, and is updated with signatures on an almost monthly basis. The term "microscanner" refers to the fact that MRT is not a full-blown AV application, but is instead intended to protect Windows systems from very specific threats. MS KB article 890830 (found on the Microsoft Support site at http://support.microsoft.com/kb/890830) provides information about installing and running MRT (there are command line switches that can be used to run scans), as well as an up-to-date list of the threats that MRT is intended to detect. MRT logs the results of its scans to the file mrt.log, which is located in the C:\Windows\debug directory. The log contains information such as the version of MRT run (usually following an update), when the scan started, when the scan completed, and the results of the scan. An example of an entry from the MRT log file retrieved from a Windows XP SP3 system appears as follows:

```
Microsoft Windows Malicious Software Removal Tool v3.15, January
  2011
Started On Wed Jan 12 21:50:26 2011
Engine internal result code = 80508015
Results Summary:
----------------
No infection found.
Microsoft Windows Malicious Software Removal Tool Finished On Wed
  Jan 12 21:51:29 2011
Return code: 0 (0 × 0)
```

This information can be very useful to an analyst, particularly when claims are made of particular malware being found on a system; for example, I've received a number of images along with the statement that the systems had been infected with Zeus. According to KB article 890830, detection of Win32/Zbot (also known as "Zeus" or "Wnspoem") was added in October 2010. If an analyst receives an acquired image and there is a suspicion that this particular malware had infected the system, then this is one artifact that can be used to determine whether there were any indications of particular malware on the system. As I include AV log analysis as part of my methodology for these types of examinations, I document my findings with respect to when MRT was updated, and what I find in the mrt.log file. This helps address issues of what malware may or may not be on the system.

TIP

MRT Registry Key

Whenever MRT is updated, the "Version" value of the *Microsoft\RemovalTools\MRT* Registry key in the Software hive is updated with a globally unique identifier (GUID) that indicates the version of MRT, as illustrated in Figure 6.2.

Name	Type	Data
(Default)	REG_SZ	(value not set)
EULA2	REG_DWORD	0x00000001 (1)
Version	REG_SZ	258FD3CF-9C82-4112-B1B0-18EC1ECFED37

FIGURE 6.2

MRT version value.

This GUID can be looked up in MS KB article 891716 (found on the web at http://support.microsoft.com/kb/891716), and used in conjunction with key LastWrite time to determine when MRT was last updated and which threats it should detect.

Later versions of Windows (starting with Vista) tend to have Microsoft's Windows Defender application installed, although this program can also be installed on Windows XP. Windows Defender is a program that reportedly protects Windows systems from pop-ups, spyware, and "unwanted programs." As such, it may also be worthwhile to examine the application logs, as well, to see if there are any indications of unusual or suspicious activity.

TIP

Windows Defender Logs

MS KB article 923886 (found on the web at http://support.microsoft.com/kb/923886) provides very useful information regarding Windows Defender logs. The KB article describes where to go within the file system and which files and other data to collect when seeking support assistance with respect to Windows Defender. The KB article also describes the command you can use on Windows XP, Vista, and Windows 7 to automatically gather all pertinent information into a compressed.cab file, to be sent to Microsoft Support for analysis.

During an examination, you may find that other AV applications may have been installed and run on the system. Check the Registry, "Program Files" directory, and even the Prefetch files for indications of these applications and their use. Often, both home user and corporate employee systems may have AV applications installed; home user systems may have freely available AV scanners installed, and corporate systems will likely have an enterprise-scale commercial AV scanner installed and as such, you may need to determine if the logs are maintained on the local system or in a central location. I have received a number of hard drives and acquired images which indicate that shortly after an incident or malware infection was suspected, the administrator logged into the system and either updated the installed AV and ran a scan, or installed and run an AV application. Like other examiners, I've also clearly seen where more than one AV scanner was run on the system. What you would want to do is locate the logs (if possible) from these scans and determine what, if anything, these scanners may have found. Even if the administrator installed the AV application, ran a scan, and then deleted the application, you may still be able to find indications of scan results in the Application Event Log.

So why is it so important to determine which AV applications have already been run on a system? Within the information security industry, and specifically within the digital forensics and incident response (DFIR) community, it's understood that just because a commercial AV scan didn't find any malware on a system, that doesn't definitively indicate that there was no malware on the system. As such, many of us rely on a methodology, rather than one specific commercial AV application, in order to attempt to detect malware within an acquired image. Along those lines, what an analyst does not (and I mean *NOT*) want to do is hinge their findings on one AV scan, and in particular, one done using the same AV application that had been installed on the system. And to answer the question that just popped into your mind, yes, I have seen reports that have indicated that no malware was found on a system based on a single AV scan, and when the analyst went back and checked later, they found that the AV application they used was the same version and malware signature file as what had been installed on the system. What is the point of redoing something that was already done, especially when it didn't provide findings of any significance?

As such, the first step of any malware detection analysis should be to determine what, if any, anti-malware or -spyware applications were already installed on the system, what were the versions of these applications, and when they were last updated. The version of the application itself can be very important, as AV vendors have stated that the reason why known malware hadn't been detected on a customer's infrastructure was that while the signature file was up to date, the scanning engine itself was out of date and was not properly utilizing the signatures.

Once this information has been documented, determine if there are any logs available, and if so, examine them for any indication that malware had been detected. I've had a number of opportunities to examine systems onto which malware had originally been detected and quarantined by the AV application when it was first introduced to the system. The intruder later returned to the system and uploaded a new version of the malware that the AV application did not detect, but used the same file name for the new version of the malware. As such, a search for the file name originally detected by the AV application turned up the version of the malware that the AV application didn't detect.

I've analyzed a number of systems that had multiple AV applications installed. In some cases, AV application was installed and later disabled (perhaps the license expired), and then another application was installed. In other cases, once an issue was reported, an IT administrator was installed and ran one or more (I've seen indications of up to three different scanners being run, in addition to the installed AV product) AV products prior to making the system available for acquisition and analysis. Documenting this information as part of your analysis can be very important, as it can help the customer understand their IT protection process and identify any gaps. Also, if you intend to perform your own AV scans (discussed later in this chapter), it wouldn't necessarily be a good idea to run the same AV product and version as was already run on the system. Think about it—what would be the point or advantage in reporting that you'd run the same AV product against the system as was already installed on the system, and then billing the customer for that "work?" Finding and documenting the protection mechanisms already installed on the system can help you understand what the system *should have been* protected against, as well as help direct your analysis efforts.

I've also seen instances in which an AV application detected the presence of malware, but that application had been specifically (however unintentionally) configured to take no action other than to record the detection event. As such, the logs (as well as the Application Event Log) provided clear indication that there was in fact malware on the system (including the full path to the files) but that it hadn't so much as quarantined by the AV application. In one instance, the AV application logs indicated that the creation and subsequent deletion of malware files (presumably, after the intruder was done with them) had been detected, but again, no action other than to record these events had been taken. This proved to be extremely valuable information that provided insight into other actions taken by the intruder. In other instances, AV scanning applications have additional functionality beyond the traditional signature-based detection. For example, McAfee AV products can detect and/or block (that is to say that they can be configured to detect but not block) suspect actions, such as trying to run an executable file from a Temp directory, or from a web browser cache directory. So, while malware itself may not be explicitly detected by an AV product, the actions taken to download and install that malware may be detected, and possibly even prevented or simply inhibited.

> **WARNING**
>
> **Mixing Protection Mechanisms**
>
> I once responded to an incident in which a user's system was thought to have been infected with some form of malware. The organization used a network monitoring product that watched for domain name service (DNS) queries for known-bad malware/botnet sites, and reported on these as an indication of an infected system. As it turned out, the organization also had rolled out a campus-wide installation of a host-based anti-spyware application to all of their user systems, one which "blackholed" known malicious sites by modifying the hosts file (found in the C:\Windows\system32\drivers\etc directory, and described in MS KB article 172218, found on the Microsoft Support site at http://support.microsoft.com/kb/172218) to redirect the queries for the domains and hosts to local host (i.e., 127.0.0.1). The final result of the engagement was that the user had installed an additional anti-spyware application on his system, one which extracted all of the host names from the hosts file and issued DNS queries for each one, regardless of the fact that they were blackholed. The combination of these three tools, while thought to be providing overlapping layers of protection, actually triggered what was thought to be a significant incident.

Dr. Watson logs

Another source of potentially valuable data is the Dr Watson log file. Dr Watson is a user-mode debugger found on Windows XP (but not Windows 7) that launches and generates a log file when an error occurs with a program. This log file (drwtson32.log) is located in the "All Users" profile, in the \Application Data\Microsoft\ Dr Watson\ subdirectory, and when subsequent application errors occur, data is appended to the file. The appended data includes the date, the application for which the error occurred and a list of loaded modules for the application, and a list of the processes that were running at the time of the error. I've looked to the information in this file to not just help determine if malware had been installed on the system but also reviewed the list of processes (as well as modules loaded in the "offending" or crashed process) to see if the malware process was running at the time that the information in the log was captured. This has been very useful when attempting to verify the "window of compromise" (how long the system had been compromised) during data breach investigations.

AV scans

Once you've determined and documented which, if any, AV applications had been installed and/or run on the system prior to acquisition, another step you may decide to do is to mount the image as a volume on your analysis workstation and scan it with other AV products. Not all AV applications seem to be created equal; in some instances, I've run multiple big name AV applications across a mounted image and not found anything. Then after running a freely available AV application, I got a hit for one of the files associated with the malware, and was able to use that as a starting point for further investigation. So it doesn't hurt to use multiple AV applications in your detection process.

Mounting an acquired image is relatively straightforward, using a number of freely available tools. For example, the ImDisk virtual disk driver (found on the web at http://www.ltr-data.se/opencode.html/#ImDisk) installs as a Control Panel applet and allows you to mount Windows images new technology file system (NTFS) or file allocation table (FAT) read-only on your Windows system. AccessData's FTK Imager version 3.1.3 (found on the web at the AccessData web site at the URL http://accessdata.com/support/product-downloads) includes the capability to mount acquired images as read-only volumes, as well. As mentioned in Chapter 3, the `vhdtool.exe` utility (available from Microsoft) will allow you to convert a copy of your image to a Virtual Hard Drive (VHD) file and mount it read-only on your Windows 7 or 8 system. Regardless of the tool used, the purpose is to make the file system within the image accessible as a drive letter or volume (albeit in read-only mode) on your analysis system.

Once you've mounted the image as a volume, you can scan it with AV scanners in the same manner as you would a "normal" file system. Many AV products allow scans to be configured to only be run against specific volumes or drive letters (some even allow you to scan specific directories), making it relatively simple and straightforward to scan only the mounted volume(s). If you do not have access to commercial AV products, there are a number of free AV products available for download and use (be sure to read the license agreement thoroughly!!), several of which are simply limited (in the sense that they provide scanning but not other capabilities, such as real-time monitoring) versions of the full commercial AV products. For example, there is a free version of the AVG AV scanner available at http://free.avg.com, and you have the option to upgrade to a full version of the application that provides additional protection, while downloading files or chatting online. Other AV products such as Eset (producer of the NOD32 AV product, available at http://www.eset.com) provide a limited time trial version of their software; again, be sure that you read and understand the license agreement before using any of these options.

There are a number of other AV products available for use, and many (such as Microsoft's Defender product, mentioned earlier in this chapter) are freely available, while other vendors provide limited time trial versions of their full, professional products. This part of the chapter is not intended to provide a breakdown or "shootout" between the various available products, but to instead demonstrate that there are options available. The point is that it's always better to run a scan using an

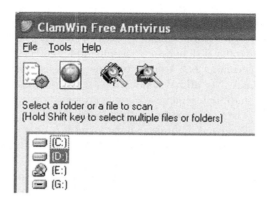

FIGURE 6.3

Partial ClamWinPortable v.0.97 GUI.

AV product that had not been installed on or run on the system, and it's not usually a bad idea to run multiple AV scans using disparate products.

One free, open-source AV product that is very useful and includes a portable (run from a thumb drive) version is ClamWin (illustrated in Figure 6.3), found on the web at http://www.clamwin.com.

ClamWin can be installed on, updated, and run from a thumb drive, making it a useful option for using amongst multiple systems, without having to install the full application on your analysis system.

Another option available, particularly when specific malware variants are suspected, is microscanners. These are not general-purpose AV scanning products, but are instead targeted scanners to look for specific malware variants. One such product is McAfee's AVERT Stinger product, available online at http://www.mcafee.com/us/downloads/free-tools/how-to-use-stinger.aspx. Downloading the file and running it on your analysis system open the user interface (UI) as illustrated in Figure 6.4.

If you click on the purple "List Viruses" button in the Stinger UI (Figure 6.4), a dialog listing all of the malware that the microscanner is designed to detect will be listed. Again, while not as comprehensive as a more general AV product, microscanners offer a useful capability. At the same time, don't forget other scanner products, such as those specifically designed to detect spyware and adware, as these can provide some useful coverage, as well. Finally, be sure to document the applications that you do use, as well as their versions and results. Both pieces of information will help demonstrate the thoroughness of your detection process.

AV write ups

There's something that I think is worth discussing with respect to malware write ups from AV vendor companies. These write ups provide descriptions and a wealth of information about the malware that these companies have found, been given access to, and analyzed. However, there's very often a gap when it comes

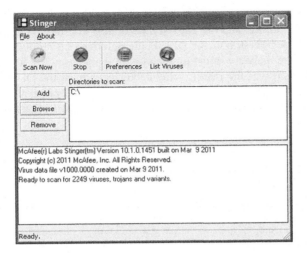

FIGURE 6.4

McAfee Stinger UI.

to what incident responders and forensic analysts need to know about malware, and what's provided by the AV companies. This gap is due in large part to the fact that AV companies are not in the business of supporting incident responders; rather, they're in the business of supporting their business. Now, don't take this as an indictment of AV companies, because that's not what I'm doing. What I am saying here is that malware write ups from AV companies are a good resource, but should be considered within that context, as sometimes they are not complete and do not provide a comprehensive or completely accurate picture of the malware. For example, there is malware that infects files that are "protected" by Windows File Protection (WFP), but often there is no reference to WFP or the fact that it was subverted in the malware write up. While WFP is not intended as a security or AV mechanism and is easily subverted (code for this is available on the Internet), this fact is important to know as it may help us detect the malware where the AV product fails, as AV products are most often based on signatures within the malware files themselves, and not on specific artifacts on the system. Another aspect of malware write ups that can be confusing is that there's often no differentiation between artifacts produced by the malware infection, and those produced by the ecosystem (operating system, installed applications, etc.) that the malware infects. One example of this is the MUICache key within the Registry; several years ago I found a number of malware write ups that stated that the malware added a value to this key when it infected a system, when, in fact, the value was added by the operating system based on how the malware was executed in the test environment. Another example is the ESENT key within the Registry on Windows XP systems. When someone asked what this key was used for, Google searches indicated that there were malware samples that modified this key when executed. It turned out that Windows XP systems were mistakenly shipped with a checked (or debug) version of the esent.dll file, and the key itself (and all of its subkeys and values) was a result of that debug version of the DLL being deployed on production systems. As such, it wasn't the malware infecting the system that caused the Registry modifications as much as it was the result of the debug version of the DLL. This could be confusing when an analyst was examining a Windows Vista or Windows 7 system and found the malware in question, but did not find a corresponding ESENT key within the Registry.

WARNING

Googling

Analysts should beware of conclusively identifying any malware sample as a particular virus based on the name or location of the malicious file, a Registry key used for persistence, etc. There are literally hundreds of thousands of malware samples and variants floating around, and a relatively limited number of autostart/persistence locations, innocuous-looking file names, etc., that tend to get used and reused by malware authors. Analysts should not base their analysis on "I Googled the file name and this is what I found," as doing so can easily lead to a misidentification of the malware, and an incorrect report of the malware's capabilities provided to a customer. Remember, the customer is very likely going to have to make some tough business decisions regarding risk and compliance based on your findings, and providing incorrect information about the nature of the malware found on their systems will lead to the wrong decisions being made. In some cases, all it would take is for the intruder to design his malware to use the same file names and locations as some very well-known malware (perhaps something known to fairly innocuous) that has completely different functionalities and poses a completely different set of risks to infected systems; this would have a significant impact on the information provided to the customer, if the analyst relied on the "Googling" to identify the malware.

Digging deeper

Windows systems contain a lot of executable files, many of which are completely legitimate, and it's neither productive nor efficient to examine each and everyone of those files to determine if it's malicious. While these files can be hashed and comparisons can be run, this method of identifying "known good" files can be cumbersome, particularly on Windows systems, as software installations and system patches tend to change a number of files, so that while they are still completely legitimate, they may trigger false positives in the hash comparison tool that you're using. Also, system administrators and home users rarely maintain an accurate set of system file hashes for you to use as a baseline for comparison.

There are a number of other techniques available to analysts, beyond log analysis and AV scans, that allow us to perform some significant data reduction and narrow the field of interesting files quite a bit. We can use these techniques to help us detect malware within an acquired image that would be missed by other detection means.

We'll discuss several of these techniques throughout the rest of this chapter, but there are a couple of things that should be clear. First, this should not be considered a complete list; I will attempt to be comprehensive, but there may be techniques discussed in which you may find limited value, and you may have your own techniques. Second, these techniques will be discussed in no particular order; do not assume that a technique presented first is any more valuable than another. Finally, whichever techniques you decide to use should be included in a documented malware detection process. A sample checklist is provided as an MS Word document along with the additional materials provided with this book (the link to these materials can be found online at http://windowsir.blogspot.com/p/books.html).

Packed files

Compression or "packing" is a means for reducing the size of a file, but more importantly, PE files can be packed to hide their true nature and to "hide" from AV scanners. However, it is uncommon—albeit not unheard of—for legitimate files to be packed. Therefore any packed files found during a scan would bear closer inspection. One tool that is freely available for checking for packed files is PEiD (version 0.95 was available at the time of this writing; as of April 4, 2011, the project appears to have been discontinued). The PEiD UI is illustrated in Figure 6.5.

Choosing the Multi Scan button on the PEiD UI allows you to run a scan of files within a directory, as well as recurse through subdirectories, and only scan PE files, as illustrated in Figure 6.6.

PEiD also supports command-line switches (be sure to read the readme text file that comes as part of the distribution), but the difference from other command line interface (CLI) tools is that running application via command line switches sends the output to GUI dialogs, as seen in Figure 6.6. Without an option for redirecting the output to files, PEiD cannot effectively be incorporated into batch files. Regardless, this is still an invaluable tool to have available.

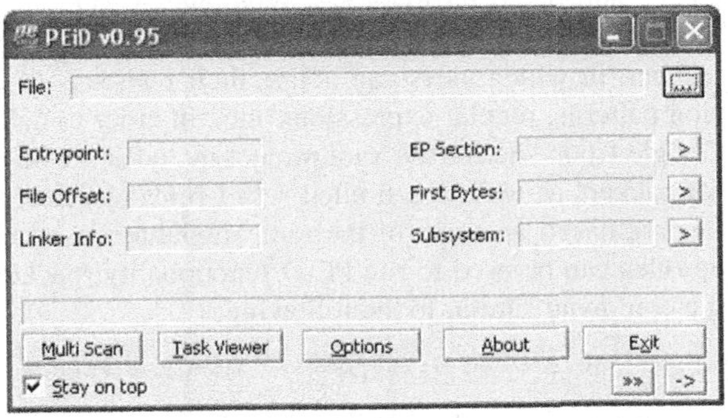

FIGURE 6.5

PEiD UI.

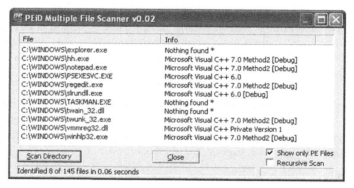

FIGURE 6.6

PEiD multiscan output.

NOTE

Using PEiD

PEiD's capability for detecting packed files is signature based, and the configuration file that ships with the tool (userdb.txt) contains only one signature. As such, users will need to provide their own signatures; fortunately, Jim Clausing has provided a list of packer signatures, which is available via the SANS Incident Handler's site (found online at http://handlers.sans.org/jclausing/userdb.txt).

If you would prefer a CLI tool, you might consider the Yara project, found online at http://code.google.com/p/yara-project/. Yara started out as an open-source project to help identify and classify malware samples, but the author's (Victor Manuel Alvarez of Hipasec Sistemas) work has expanded the project. While it remains open source and based on Python, a Windows executable file is available for download, making it much more accessible to a wider range of users. Yara is a rules-based scanner, in which users can define their own sets of rules, based on strings, instruction patterns, regular expressions, etc., in order to detect and classify malware. The Google Code site for the Yara project includes a wiki page with sample rules files for packers as well as a limited set of rules to detect some malware. The packers rules are based on some of the same signatures used by PEiD, which means that those rules can be used to run PEiD functionality (packer scans) from a batch file, using a command similar to the following:

```
C:\tools > yara packer.txt C:\Windows > d:\case\yara-packer.txt
```

In the above Yara command, the file "packer.txt" is simply a file that contains a limited number of rules for detecting packers, available on the Yara project wiki (i.e., copy and paste the rules into a file). The book *Malware Analyst's Cookbook* contains several "recipes" (i.e., Python scripts) for converting ClamAV (*Note*: This

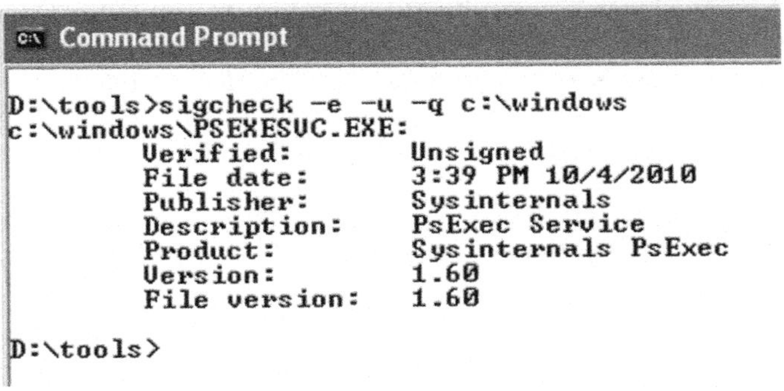

FIGURE 6.7

Sigcheck.exe.

is not the ClamWin AV product discussed earlier in this chapter and is instead available at http://www.clamav.net.) AV signatures and the full set of PEiD packer signatures to Yara rules files. If you work with or encounter malware at all, having a copy of the *Malware Analyst's Cookbook* available can be quite valuable.

Digital signatures

Examining executable image files for valid digital signatures using a tool such as sigcheck.exe (available from the SysInternals site on MS TechNet) is a valuable approach for detecting malware. This is an excellent technique to use, in that an analyst can scan systems for executable files that do not have digital signatures as illustrated in Figure 6.7.

As with many CLI tools, simply typing "sigcheck" at the command prompt will display the syntax for the various command line switches. Figure 6.7 illustrates a scan of just the C:\Windows directory, looking for unsigned executable files, regardless of their extension. CLI tools are very useful in that they can be very easily included in batch files in order to facilitate scanning and processing of the results. For example, adding appropriate switches will tell sigcheck.exe to recurse through subdirectories, and send the output to comma-separated value (.csv) format, which is suitable for ease of analysis. This is illustrated in the following command line:

```
C:\tools > sigcheck -e -v -u -q -s c:\windows > d:\case\dig_sig.csv
```

However, it's worth noting that like many methods used by responders and analysts, someone is going to find out about them and find a way to use that method against the responders and analysts. In June 2010, malware known as "StuxNet" was publicly mentioned and described, and one of the notable aspects of the malware was that it contained a valid digital signature. On July 16, 2010, a post to the Microsoft Malware Protection Center (MMPC) blog titled "The StuxNet Sting" (found online at http://blogs.technet.com/b/mmpc/archive/2010/07/16/the-stux-net-sting.aspx) stated that the StuxNet malware files had been signed with a valid digital signature belonging to Realtek Semiconductor Corp. This digital signature quickly expired, but other examples of the StuxNet malware that were discovered were found to use other valid signatures. As with other techniques, scanning for valid digital signatures should not be considered as "silver bullet" solution, but should instead be considered as part of an overall detection process.

Windows File Protection

WFP is a process that runs in the background on Windows XP and 2003 (WFP was not something that was carried over to Vista systems and beyond) systems and monitors for file change events that occur on the system. When such an event is detected, WFP determines if the event is related to one of the files it monitors, and if so, WFP will replace the modified file from a "known good" version in its cache, which in many instances is the C:\Windows\system32\dllcache directory. A more comprehensive description of WFP can be found online at http://support.microsoft.com/kb/222193.

Many times, an attacker will get malware on a system that temporarily disables WFP and replaces or infects a "protected" file, after which WFP is re-enabled. WFP does not poll or scan files, but instead "listens" and waits for file change events, so once it has been re-enabled, the modified file goes undetected. Sometimes, only the file that does not reside in the cache is modified, and other times, analysts have found that both the file in the cache as well as the one in "runtime" portion of the file system (i.e., the system32 directory) were modified.

One means for detecting attacks where only the noncached copy of a "protected" file was modified is to compute cryptographic one-way MD5 hashes of all of the files in the cache directory, and then locate the noncached copies of those files, hash them, and compare the hashes. I wrote an application called "WFP Checker" several years ago (2008) that does exactly that, and writes its output to a comma-separated value (.csv) formatted file so that it can be easily viewed in a spreadsheet program or easily parsed via a scripting language. The UI for WFP Checker (following a scan of a mounted volume) is illustrated in Figure 6.8.

WFP Checker is a pretty straightforward tool for scanning live systems for indications of "protected" files that have been modified in the manner described earlier in this section. Keep in mind, however, that following hashing the files in the dllcache directory, only those corresponding files in the system32 directory are hashed and compared (it should be noted that depending on the source of the files, cached copies may be maintained in other directories). Some application installers may place files in other directories, and in order to maintain a relatively low "noise" level (I didn't want to introduce more data to be analyzed) and reduce false positives, the rest of the volume is not searched. As you can see in Figure 6.6.wfp1, a log file of the application's activity is maintained along with the output file.

Alternate data streams

Alternate data streams (ADSs) are an artifact associated with the NTFS file system that have been around since the implementation of NTFS itself. ADSs were originally meant to provide compatibility with the Macintosh Hierarchal File System (HFS),

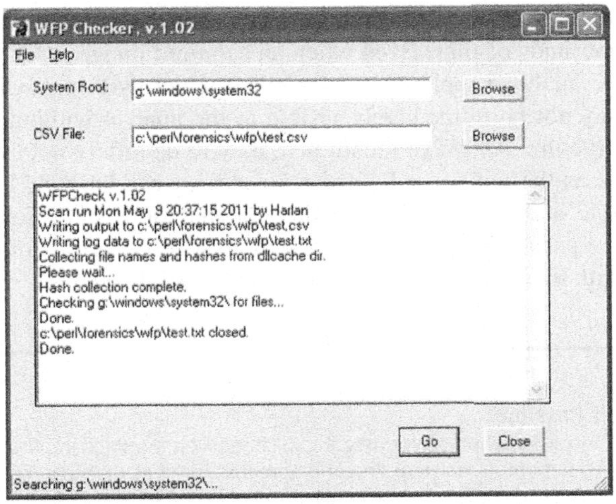

FIGURE 6.8

Description.

providing the ability to store resource forks for files shared between Windows NT and Mac systems. ADSs have been covered in great detail in other resources [2], but suffice to say, ADSs can be particularly insidious based on how they can be created and used, and the fact that an analyst may be unaware of or unfamiliar with them. Windows systems contain all of the necessary native tools to create and manipulate ADSs, as well as launch executables and scripts "hidden" in ADSs; however, until recently, Windows systems did not contain any native tools for locating arbitrary ADSs created within the file system. By "until recently," I mean to say that it wasn't until Vista was released that the "dir" command, used with "/r" switch, could be used to view arbitrary ADSs. There are also a number of third party tools that you can add to your system or toolkit that will allow you to view ADSs, including Frank Heyne's command line lads.exe (available from heysoft.de), streams.exe (available from Mark Russinovich's site at Microsoft), and the GUI-based alternatestreamview.exe, available from nirsoft.net. Any of these tools can be run against a mounted image file, but keep in mind these artifacts are specific to NTFS. If the file system of the imaged system is FAT based, there's really no point in checking for ADSs.

NOTE

Poison Ivy RAT

Poison Ivy is a GUI-based client server "remote administration tool" (RAT) that is freely available on the Internet. The Poison Ivy GUI provides a point-and-click interface for configuring and creating a custom version of the "tool." One of the configuration options allows the tool to be installed within an ADS. An intruder with no programming skills simply has to select a checkbox to use this mechanism to hide their malware on the computer of an unsuspecting victim.

So why are ADSs an issue? Well, there are a number of files on systems; in many cases, thousands of files. Even when an acquired image is loaded into a commercial forensic analysis application (several of which will highlight ADSs in red font), ADSs may not be immediately visible to the analyst without digging within the directory structure. As we've mentioned, they're definitely not easy to detect on the live system, as the native tools for doing so are very limited. Therefore, while ADSs are simple and were never intended for malicious purposes, like anything else, they can be particularly insidious if an analyst or system administrator simply isn't familiar with them, and doesn't even know to look for them.

WARNING

Knowing What's Possible

Knowing what to look for when performing digital forensic analysis is important, and this is where having a documented malware detection process (or checklist) can be so valuable. I've been to a number of conferences and given many seminars and presentations where I will ask the attendees (analyst, administrators, etc.) about things like ADSs, and will not be surprised at all when no one indicates that they're aware of them. That's why we have professional education and development, and that's also why it's so important for analysts to share information with each other.

The trap you want to avoid is basing your findings or conclusions on assumptions and speculation. We've all seen where something "new" has been discussed and this suddenly becomes the *cause célèbre*, as incidents are attributed to this "new" artifact or finding. Be sure to follow your documented analysis process, and if you rule out four items based on your analysis, don't simply assume that the issue is the fifth item. Run that scan or perform that analysis. What you want to avoid is stating that the issue has to do with ADSs, only to have someone come back later after having run the appropriate scan and determined that there were no ADSs within the acquired image. Don't assume that just because something is possible, that's what happened—check it.

On September 20, 2011, an interesting post regarding the creation of "stealth ADSs" appeared on the Exploit-Monday.com web site (the post can be found online at http://www.exploit-monday.com/2011/09/stealth-alternate-data-streams-and.html). The post outlines, in part, how to add an ADS to a file, which was first created using specific names (i.e., NUL, CON; part of the device namespace in Windows). These files can be created by appending "\\?\" to the file path. The author of the post found that neither streams.exe (available from Microsoft at http://technet.microsoft.com/en-us/sysinternals/bb897440) nor the use of "dir/r" (command line switch available on Windows starting with Vista) included the capability of detecting ADSs "attached" to these files, unless the file path was specifically prepended with "\\?\." The blog post also illustrated how Windows Management Instrumentation could be used to launch executables from within these "stealth ADSs," illustrating the risk associated with this capability. Michael Hale Ligh (also known as "MHL," one of the coauthors of *The Malware Analyst's Cookbook*) quickly followed with a blog post of his own (found online at http://mnin.blogspot.

com/2011/09/detecting-stealth-ads-with-sleuth-kit.html) which illustrated the use of tsk_view.exe (see his blog post for a link to the tool) to detect these stealth ADSs.

PE file compile times

Another check that we can run against individual files (this may take a little bit of programming to automate) is take advantage of metadata embedded within PE files in order to attempt to detect suspicious files. The compile date is a 32-bit value (the number of seconds since December 31, 1969, at 4:00 pm) which is a time date stamp that the linker (or compiler for an object file) adds to the header of a PE file, as illustrated in Figure 6.9.

As illustrated in Figure 6.9, the compile date appears as "2006/08/01 Tue 21:10:42 UTC." The created and modified time stamps within the file's metadata are often modified (referred to as "timestomped") in order to disguise the malicious file and make it blend in with legitimate operating system and application files. While the compile time stored in the PE header could be similarly modified (using a hex editor, for example), it is not often seen in practice. Therefore, comparing the compile time from the PE header with the created and modified times from the file metadata and looking for anomalies may allow you to identify malware.

On "normal," uninfected systems, the PE files provided by Microsoft will generally be from the installation medium and have the dates of when the original operating system (OS) binaries were compiled. There are a number of PE files, of course, that may be updated by patches and Service Packs, and will subsequently have compile dates associated with when the patches were built. However, consider this example—in November 2009, a malware author creates a PE (.exe or.dll) file, and shortly thereafter, deploys it to compromised systems. As part of the infection mechanism, the file metadata times are "stomped"—in this case, the file times are copied from a file known to be on all Windows systems. This is usually done to hide the existence of the file from responders who only look at those times. One file from which malware authors seem to prefer to copy file times, noted by malware analysis conducted by AV vendors and reverse engineers, is kernel32.dll, found in

pFile	Data	Description	Value
00000064	014C	Machine	IMAGE_FILE_MACHINE_I386
00000066	0005	Number of Sections	
00000068	44CFC352	Time Date Stamp	2006/08/01 Tue 21:10:42 UTC
0000006C	00000000	Pointer to Symbol Table	
00000070	00000000	Number of Symbols	
00000074	00E0	Size of Optional Header	
00000076	010F	Characteristics	
	0001		IMAGE_FILE_RELOCS_STRIPPED
	0002		IMAGE_FILE_EXECUTABLE_IMAGE
	0004		IMAGE_FILE_LINE_NUMS_STRIPPED
	0008		IMAGE_FILE_LOCAL_SYMS_STRIPPED
	0100		IMAGE_FILE_32BIT_MACHINE

FIGURE 6.9

Compile time in PE file header seen in PEView.

the system32 directory. So, if the compile time of the suspicious PE file is relatively "recent" (with respect to your incident window), but the creation time of the file is before the compile time, you may have found a suspicious file.

You might also find suspicious files by considering the executable file's compile time in isolation. For example, if the values were all zeros, this might indicate that the malware author directly edited the values. Another example of a suspicious compile time might be one that predates modern versions of Windows, such as anything before 1993.

As with other techniques, you may find that you'll have a number of possible false positives. For example, legitimate system files on Windows systems get updated through the Windows Update mechanism, but may have creation dates from the original installation media (consider the discussion of file system tunneling from Chapter 4). Consider that these may be false positives and not explicit indicators of malware infections. As such, be sure to correlate your findings from other techniques.

Master boot record infectors

A great deal of malware runs from within the file system of the infected system itself, that is, the malware or a bootstrap mechanism for the malware exists some place within the file system. The malware may be an executable PE file on the system (it may be encrypted), or instead of the malware itself, a downloader may exist on the system that, when activated, downloads the latest and greatest malware and launches it. However, malware has been seen to exist on the disk, albeit originate from outside the active volumes; these are often master boot record (MBR) infector malware.

Perhaps the first known MBR infector was known as "Mebroot." According to the Symantec write up (found online at http://www.symantec.com/security_response/writeup.jsp?docid=2008-010718-3448-99) this MBR infector was first written in November 2007 and later modified in February 2008. Once this malware was discovered, analysts determined just how insidious it was, in that an MBR infector allows the malware author to infect a system very early during the boot process, before most protection mechanisms have been initiated. In particular, artifacts of a Mebroot infection included the finding that sectors 60 and 61 of the disk (on many, albeit not all systems, the MBR is found at sector 0 and the first partition begins at sector 63) contained kernel and payload patcher code, respectively, and that sector 62 contained a preinfection copy of the MBR. Now, this may not be the case for all variants of Mebroot, but it is important to note that on a normal Windows system these sectors are usually full of zeros (and more importantly do not contain copies of the original MBR!).

About two months after the Symantec description of Mebroot was published, an article titled "MBR Rootkit, A New Breed of Malware" appeared on the F-Secure blog (found online at http://www.f-secure.com/weblog/archives/00001393.html) and provided some additional information about Mebroot. Then, in mid-February 2011, another article titled "Analysis of MBR File System Infector" was posted to the F-Secure blog (the article can be found online at http://www.f-secure.com/

	Slot	Start	End	Length	Description
00:	Meta	0000000000	0000000000	0000000001	Primary Table (#0)
01:	-----	0000000000	0000000062	0000000063	Unallocated
02:	00:00	0000000063	0097482419	0097482357	NTFS (0x07)
03:	00:01	0097482420	0488263544	0390781125	NTFS (0x07)
04:	-----	0488263545	0488281249	0000017705	Unallocated

FIGURE 6.10

Output of mmls.exe.

weblog/archives/00002101.html), which described yet another bit of malware named "Trojan:W32/Smitnyl.A," that modifies or infects the MBR. The description of Smitnyl.A includes such artifacts as a copy of the original MBR copied to sector 5, and the infector payload starts at sector 39. According to the description, there is also apparently an encoded executable located in sector 45.

So how does this help us, as forensic analysts, in detecting the presence of MBR infectors in an acquired image? Well, one check that we can run programmatically (which is a fancy way of saying "we can write code to do this for us") is to determine where the first partition starts (we can confirm this by running *mmls.exe* from the TSK tools against the image), and then to run from sector 0 to that sector (usually—though not always—63) and locate any sectors that do not contain all zeros.

Let's take a look at an example; Figure 6.10 illustrates the output of *mmls.exe* (one of the Sleuthkit tools) run against an acquired image of a Windows system.

As we can see in Figure 6.10, the first 63 sectors are "Unallocated," and the first NTFS partition for this system (in this case, the C:\volume) starts at sector 63. Sample Perl code to check the sectors with a raw/dd format image for any content other than zeros might look like the following:

```
my $file = shift;
my $data;
open(FH," < ",$file) || die "Could not open $file: $!\n";
binmode(FH);
for each my $s (0..63) {
    seek(FH,0,$s * 512);
    read(FH,$data,512);
    my $str = unpack("B*",$data);
    if ($str! = 0) {
        print " Sector ".$s."\n";
    }
}
close(FH);
```

When I ran the above code against an image that I had already checked manually (by opening the image in FTK Imager and tabbing through sectors 0 through 63 in the hex view pane), I found that as expected, sectors 0, 10, and 63 contained something more than zeros. At this point, I've reduced the amount of data I need to look at (data reduction through coding is a wonderful thing) from a total of

64 sectors to just one, as sector 0 contains the MBR and sector 63 contains the beginning of the C:\volume. Running this same code against a system infected with either of the discussed MBR infectors would produce markedly different results, but still only have to dig into about half a dozen (as opposed to 64) sectors.

However, our coding doesn't need to stop there … and because this really rocks, I didn't stop with just the above sample code. I ended up writing *mbr.pl*, a Perl script that provides much more functionality than the above sample code (the code for *mbr.pl* is a bit too lengthy to list here) which not only tells the analyst which 512 byte sectors are nonzero, but will also provide other capabilities. For example, we can see just the sectors that contain something other than zeros using the following command line:

```
C:\Perl > mbr.pl -f f:\case\disk0.001 -s
Sector 0
Sector 10
Sector 63
```

If we want to see more, we can remove the "-s" switch (stands for "summary") and have the script print out the nonzero sectors in a hex editor-like format, as illustrated in Figure 6.11.

Finally, the script also allows us (via the "-d" switch, for "dump") to dump the raw contents of the 512 byte sectors to files on the disk. This allows us to run *diff* commands on the sectors, or generate MD5 or ssdeep hashes for the sectors; the raw sectors or the hashes can be uploaded to sites like VirusTotal for a modicum of analysis. Further, file hashes generated using Jesse Kornblum's ssdeep.exe (freely available online from http://ssdeep.sourceforge.net/) can be compared to determine if any of the hashes are similar, as some MBR infectors (albeit not all) will copy the original MBR to another sector.

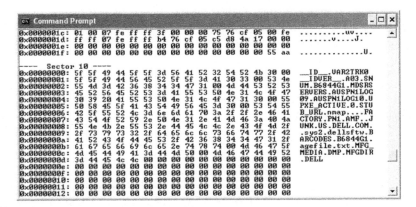

FIGURE 6.11

Sample mbr.pl output.

Other checks can be added to this code; for example, we could check the first two bytes of the sector for "MZ," which is just a quick and dirty check for the *possibility* that the sector is the beginning of a PE file. The mbr.pl script is provided as part of the materials associated with this book.

TIP

Coding Skillz

Having some ability to program, whether it's writing batch files or via a scripting language like Python or Perl, can prove to be an extremely valuable skill. Programming requires the ability to compartmentalize a task into smaller subtasks, to think methodically, and to spell; if you misspell your variable names in Perl (and don't use the "use strict" pragma) you're going to get unexpected results. All of these skills are valuable to an analyst, as is the ability to have the computer system do the bulk of the "heavy lifting" for you, allowing you to automate repetitive tasks.

Registry analysis

Earlier in this chapter, we discussed persistence mechanisms and malware artifacts, and how both can be found in the Registry. In Chapter 5, we discussed various tools and techniques for parsing data from the Registry, and we can use those to detect the presence of malware on systems. Registry analysis can be an extremely important and revealing technique when looking for the presence of malware in an image. For example, as new variants of Conficker were released, they weren't immediately detected by installed AV products on a good number of systems, but one thing did remain constant across the variants; the malware used a random service name, running as part of the svchost.exe process, as its persistence mechanism. In many instances, within malware families that use the Registry for persistence, there is some consistency across the family.

In addition to persistence mechanisms, malware will many times also have other artifacts that you can look for, that will indicate the presence of malware when AV scanner applications do not do so. Consider some of the artifacts discussed earlier in this chapter as well as Chapter 5, such as values beneath the MUICache key, Prefetch files, processes listed in the Dr Watson log file, etc.; these (and others) can provide indications of malware on a system that may be missed by AV products.

Additionally, you may want to check locations within the Registry that provide indications that programs have executed. For example, consider the AppCompatCache value within the System Registry hive, first discussed publicly by Andrew Davis (of the consulting firm Mandiant) on April 17, 2012 (the blog post can be found online at https://www.mandiant.com/blog/leveraging-application-compatibility-cache-forensic-investigations/). Be sure to read the white paper linked to in the article, as it describes how this value is implemented on various versions of Windows, as well as how analysts can use this information during an investigation. Corey Harrell has also posted several articles to his blog (http://journeyintoir.blogspot.com) in which he describes how he has used the data from this value to further his own examinations. The RegRipper *appcompatcache.pl* plugin can parse data extracted from this value for Windows systems from XP through Windows 8, although the compatibility with Windows 8 systems is still somewhat in beta (due to a limited amount of test data being available). Another Registry location to check for indications of program execution is the AppCompatFlags subkey values from the Software and user NTUSER.DAT hives. If the subkeys contain values, they can provide information about programs that have executed on the system, as described in the Microsoft Developer Network (MSDN) article posted online at http://msdn.microsoft.com/en-us/library/bb756937.aspx.

Internet activity

Many analysts look to a user's Internet activity in order to determine web sites that they've visited, often as part of a wider examination. However, the same technique can be used in order to check for the presence of malware, as well as potentially identify the source of the malware (from whence it came). Many times, when an intruder gets malware onto a system, they do so with elevated privileges; for example, if the intruder gains Administrator-level access to a system, they can use those privileges to create a Scheduled Task or a Windows service, both of which will run with elevated, System-level privileges. If the malware running with elevated privileges uses the WinInet API (also used by Internet Explorer) in order to communicate off of the system, there will be artifacts of this communications, including entries in the Temporary Internet Files (TIF) index.dat file for the "Default User" user.

On November 15, 2006, Robert Hensing (a Microsoft employee who used to lead their incident response team) posted to his TechNet blog (found online at http://blogs.technet.com/b/robert_hensing) about malware "hiding" in the "Default User" user profile. Robert had seen some of the same odd entries in a user profile's web history that I'd seen during examinations, and had gone so far as to test his theories by launching Internet Explorer as a Scheduled Task (so that it would run with System-level privileges). After surfing to several sites using this "super IE," Robert then found web history in the "Default User" profile. It's also important to note that Robert had actually posted to his blog much earlier (January 27, 2005, with a post titled "Anatomy of a WINS server hack") with respect to finding the artifact of content in the TIF directory in the "Default User" profile.

An analyst has a number of means available to parse the Internet history from within an image. I have found that ProDiscover (both the IR and Basic editions; I mention these two specifically as they are the ones to which I have access) is very good at parsing this data; simply open the project file and navigate to your image via the Content View. Navigate through the tree to the user profile directory and then right click to reveal the drop-down menu illustrated in Figure 6.12.

Select "Find Internet Activity..." and allow the application to populate the Internet History Viewer, as illustrated in Figure 6.13.

Christopher Brown released ProDiscover (Incident Response Edition) 6.10.0.1 on May 5, 2011, and one of the updates that he included in this version is the ability for ProDiscover to also parse Internet history from the Chrome and Firefox browsers. (*Note*: ProDiscover version 8.2 was available at the time of this writing.)

FIGURE 6.12

ProDiscover drop-down menu.

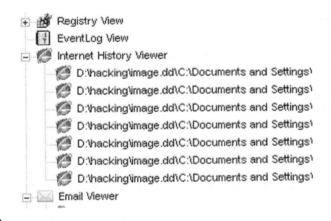

FIGURE 6.13

Populated ProDiscover Internet History Viewer.

I have also seen Internet history for the LocalService account during analysis, and in a manner similar to what Robert was able to demonstrate, have been able to trace these artifacts back to malware that was making use of the WinInet API and was installed as a Windows service, running under the LocalService account. Examination of the malware indicated that it did, in fact, use the WinInet APIs, and testing of the malware in a lab environment illustrated that the malware did communicate off of the infected system through the use of HTTP requests.

Another way to quickly check for the potential presence of this type of malware artifact is to navigate to the TIF directories for the profiles in question and quickly check to see if the index.dat files contain any entries. You can do this by checking the size of the file and seeing if it contains all zeros (I've seen this before), or extract strings from the files. As we will discuss in more detail in Chapter 7, you can also use a Perl script that uses the Win32::UrlCache module to parse the contents of the index.dat file. The method or tool you use to perform a check like this is really up to you, as the examiner, but the important point of this section is to understand that Internet history is not something that we normally expect to see in association with the "Default User" or "LocalService" user profiles on a Windows system, and as such, this is something worth checking for, and something I do for most cases that are suspected to involve some type of malware.

Additional detection mechanisms

In addition to the various detection techniques we've discussed so far, there are a number of other locations within an image that you can look for indications of a malware infection, for example, looking for unusual Scheduled Tasks, either the actual.job files in the Tasks directory or listed in the Scheduled Tasks log file (SchedLgU.txt) for Windows XP and 2003, and the Microsoft-Windows-TaskScheduler/Operational Event Log on Windows Vista systems and beyond (discussed in Chapter 4).

TIP

AT Jobs

Scheduled tasks created using the native at.exe utility are often used by intruders to install malware on or execute other processes on a system. While Administrator privileges are required to create these scheduled tasks, the tasks themselves run with elevated privileges. Within most infrastructures, at.exe is not commonly used for routine system administration, and as such, the existence of scheduled tasks named "at1.job," "at2.job," etc. would merit a closer look.

We've discussed malware that uses a Windows service as a persistence mechanism and other artifacts associated with services. Another place you might want to look is to examine the System Event Log (discussed in detail in Chapter 4) for indications of services being started (event ID 7035) with a user security identifier (SID), rather than a system SID. Services are usually started by LocalService (SID: S-1-5-19) or NetworkService (SID: S-1-5-20) or similar accounts (depending upon their configuration), so services (particularly the PSExecSvc service) started by a user account are definitely worth a closer look. Also, services usually start when the system is booted; services that are started hours or days after a system start may also indicate something suspicious.

Another location within the file system that you may find indications of malware includes Temp directories, either the Windows Temp directory (C:\Windows\Temp) or the Temp directory within the user profile. Further, the Tasks folder (C:\Windows\Tasks) is often used to store malware or a location from which to conduct operations, as this is one of the "special" Windows folders in which the true contents are not visible when viewed via Windows Explorer. The same is true for the

Fonts (C:\Windows\Fonts) folder, as well as the Recycle Bin. With these folders, the true contents can be seen via the command line, using the "dir" command.

As with many of the techniques that we've described so far in this chapter, none of them provides us with 100% guaranteed detection of malware. However, we can correlate the output from multiple techniques and use these techniques to perform data reduction and address the potential for malware being on the system you're analyzing. Remember that there are no silver bullets in information security and digital forensics, but by automating the use of multiple techniques to look for different artifacts of malware, from different perspectives, the goal is to provide enough coverage to minimize the chance of the malware avoiding detection. We should never expect to completely eliminate the possibility of a system being infected, but what we can do is continually improve our process and checklist, and perform as complete and thorough of an assessment as we can.

Seeded sites

Not long ago, an excellent question was posed in an online forum as a hypothetical event. Essentially, someone is found to have contraband images and videos on their system, potentially as a result of using a P2P sharing network. During the examination of the system, several instances of malware are found, and the claim is made that the purveyor of the contraband materials purposely "seeded" his site with malware in order to provide his customers with a plausible excuse, and that this was actually part of the "contract" for accessing the site.

Given something like this (and you'd think that this will be something that we'd need to address), what could an analyst do to address the issue? As we've discussed in this chapter, running an AV scan on a system and locating files identified as malware is simply one step of several in the process of addressing the "Trojan Defense." Once the malware files have been identified, the game isn't over. Just because malware files were found on a system, it doesn't immediately follow that those files were responsible for downloading the contraband. The first thing that an analyst would want to do is determine and document where the malware files are located within the file system, particularly with respect to the contraband files. Were the files identified as malware found in the P2P download directory, or were they located in the web browser cache directory? This can be a very important factor, as the presence of malware on a system does not immediately lead to that malware being responsible for populating the system with contraband images.

A next step would be to determine if the malware had ever actually executed. After all, just because the malware files were located on the system doesn't mean that the "Trojan Defense" can effectively be employed (the operative word being "effectively"). If the malware files were written to the file system, but the malware was never executed (and this fact can be proven), then the defense is nullified. What are the file times for the malware files? What are other artifacts of the identified malware? Does the malware modify Registry keys or values when run? Are other files created as a result of the malware executing? What is the malware's persistence mechanism (i.e., "Run" key, Windows service), and does that mechanism exist on the system? Remember, *the absence of an artifact where one is expected is itself an artifact.* As such, the analyst may be able to build a thorough case demonstrating that while the malware files were found on the system, there were no indications that the malware had actually been executed, and completely obviate the "Trojan Defense."

TIP

Did Malware Run?

An excellent example of determining whether malware had run occurred during an exam that involved the Coreflood bot. When this malware actually executes and infects a system, there are several Registry keys and values created, and files containing configuration information and collected data are also created. Finding the Registry artifacts allowed me to identify unique instances of the infection, and differentiate those from detection events, where the installed AV product detected the file and deleted it before the system could be infected. This not only allowed me to identify how many times (and when) systems had been infected but also see where the malware had been modified to avoid detection, only to be detected and deleted later following a subsequent AV update.

Finally, did the identified malware have the capability to download contraband, as well as the functionality to place the contraband within the file system where they were found? This may require a modicum of reverse engineering skill to determine, but sometimes it's as simple as opening the malware.exe or.dll file in a tool such as PEView (found on the web at http://www.magma.ca/~wjr/) and looking at the Import Address Table in order to see if it imports any DLL functions that allow for network or off-system communications (remember our discussion in this chapter regarding the WinInet APIs). Determining whether the identified malware could have downloaded contraband files may simply be an additional step to further address the "Trojan Defense." In one malware examination, I was able to locate actual indications of off-system communications after our malware reverse engineer succeeded in running the malware and providing me with unique strings that were specific to the malware. I ended up locating several instances of the keywords within the pagefile extracted from the system, and examining the surrounding bytes, was able to see HTTP GET request headers and responses, which included time stamps.

NOTE

Digging Deeper

Once you've located the malware, and used the four characteristics discussed earlier in this chapter to gather further information about the malware, there may be a need to find out just a little bit more about it. At this point, you've very likely documented the malware, including where within the file system you found it, how you found it (i.e., suspicious Registry value, AV scan), any other associated artifacts, etc. There may be additional work you can do, and do quickly, to add a bit more information about the malware to your documentation. This section is not intended to teach malware reverse engineering, as this topic would (and has) filled a book of its own; however, there are other excellent books already available that provide comprehensive coverage of this topic, in particular, the *Malware Analyst's Cookbook* [1].

SUMMARY

Detecting malware on a system can be difficult, and detecting potential malware within an acquired image even more so. However, this is something analysts in law enforcement, as well as in the public and private sectors have to deal with, and as such, need the knowledge, skills, and process in order to accomplish this task. AV scanning applications may prove insufficient for this task, and analysts may have to look for artifacts of a malware infection, rather than the malware itself, in order to locate the malware. As such, it is important for analysts to understand the characteristics of malware in order to understand the types of malware artifacts that may be present on a system, as well as where and how to locate those potential. Analysts should always document their activities, and developing a checklist of malware detection techniques can be very valuable, particularly when the analyst fills that checklist in with the results of each technique, or a statement or justification for not using the technique.

In the next chapter, we will walk through the process of creating a timeline of system activity for analysis; this is a technique that can be used in order to determine a great deal of additional information about not just the infection vector used to get the malware on the system but also actions that occurred in association with the malware following the infection. This analysis technique has a number of other uses, and as such deserves a chapter of its own.

References

[1] Ligh MH, Adair S, Hartstein B, Richard M. Malware analyst's cookbook and DVD. Wiley Publishing, Inc., <http://www.amazon.com/Malware-Analysts-Cookbook-Techniques-Malicious-ebook/dp/B0047DWCMA/ref=sr_1_1?s=books&ie=UTF8&qid=1390439970&sr=1-1&keywords=malware+analyst%27s+cookbook>; 2011. 978-0-470-61303-0.

[2] Carvey HA. Windows forensic analysis, 2nd ed. Syngress Publishing, Inc., <http://www.amazon.com/Windows-Forensic-Analysis-DVD-Toolkit-ebook/dp/B002ZFXTXI/ref=sr_1_2?s=books&ie=UTF8&qid=1390440014&sr=1-2&keywords=windows+forensic+analysis>; 2009. 978-1597494229.

Timeline Analysis

CHAPTER OUTLINE

INFORMATION IN THIS CHAPTER

- Timelines
- Creating Timelines
- Case Study

INTRODUCTION

I've mentioned several times throughout the book thus far that there are times when commercial forensic analysis applications simply do not provide the capabilities that an analyst may need to fully investigate a particular incident. Despite all of the capabilities of some of the commercial applications, there's one thing I still cannot do at this point; that is, load an image and push a button (or run a command) that will create a timeline of system activity. Yet the ability to create and analyze timelines has really taken the depth and breadth of my analysis forward by leaps and bounds.

Throughout the day, even with no user sitting at a computer, events occur on Windows systems. Events are simply things that happen on a system, and even a Windows system that appears to be idle is, in fact, very active. Consider Windows XP systems; every 24 hours, a System Restore Point is created, and others may be deleted, as necessary. Further, every three calendar days a limited defragmentation of the hard drive is performed; as you would expect, sectors from deleted files are overwritten. Now, consider a Windows 7 system; Volume Shadow Copies (VSCs) are created (and as necessary, deleted), and every 10 days (by default) the primary Registry hives are backed up. All of these events (and others) occur automatically, with no user interaction whatsoever. So even as a Windows system sits idle, we can expect to see a considerable amount of file system activity over time. When a user does interact with the system, we would expect to see quite a bit of activity: files are accessed, Registry keys and values are created, modified, or deleted, etc. When malware executes, when there is an intrusion, or when other events occur, an analyst can correlate time-stamped data extracted from the computer to build a fairly detailed picture of activity on a system.

Finally, throughout this chapter, we'll be using tools that I've written, and for anyone who knows me, most of my programming over the years has been done in Perl. All of the tools that I wrote and that are listed in this chapter will be available in the online resource, and most of them will be Perl scripts. I've also provided them as standalone Windows executable files, or ".exe" files ("compiled" using Perl2Exe); I've done this for your convenience. The focus of this chapter is the *process* of creating timelines; however, if at any point you have a question about a command or what the options are for the command, simply type the command at the command prompt by itself, or follow it with "-h" (for help) or "/?" (also, for help). For most tools, you'll see the syntax listed with the various options and switches listed; in a few cases, you'll simply be presented with "you must enter a filename," which means that the only thing you need to pass to the command is the filename. If, after doing all of this, you still have questions, simply email me.

Timelines

Creating timelines of system activity for forensic analysis is nothing new, and dates back to around 2000, when Rob Lee (of SANS and Mandiant fame) wrote the *mac-daddy* script to create ASCII timelines of file system activity based on metadata extracted from acquired images using The Sleuth Kit (TSK) tools. However, as time has passed, the power of timeline analysis has been recognized and much better understood. As such, the creation of timelines has been extended to include other data sources besides just file system metadata; in fact, the power of timelines as an analytic resource, using multiple data sources, potentially from multiple systems, is quickly being recognized and timeline analysis is being employed by more and more analysts.

Throughout this chapter, we will discuss the value of creating timelines as an analysis technique and demonstrate a means for creating timelines from an acquired image. The method we will walk through is not the only means for creating a timeline; for example, Kristinn Gudjonsson created log2timeline (found online at http://log2timeline.net/), described as "a framework for [the] automatic creation of a super timeline." This framework utilizes a number of built-in tools to automatically populate timelines with data extracted from a number of sources found within an acquired image.

NOTE

log2timeline and Plaso

Kristinn's log2timeline framework is a valuable resource for analysts and is comprised of various Perl modules that can be used to parse different data sources for time-stamped data. Currently, log2timeline supports modules to parse various structures discussed in this chapter, as well as history files from common web browsers, metadata from some common document types, and log data from widely used applications such as Apache, IIS, or Squid. As of this writing, Kristinn is replacing log2timeline with a new Python-based framework called "plaso," which can be found online at https://code.google.com/p/plaso/.

This framework can be extremely useful to an analyst. While the approach and tools that I use (which will be described throughout the rest of this chapter) and Kristinn's log2timeline may be viewed by some as competing approaches, they are really just two different ways to reach the same goal. log2timeline allows for a more automated approach to collecting and presenting a great deal of the available time-stamped data, whereas the tools I use entail a much more command-line-intensive process; however, at the same time, this process provides me with a good deal more flexibility to address the issues that I have encountered.

NOTE

Approaches to Timelines

From my perspective, there are two schools of thought at opposite ends of the spectrum when it comes to creating timelines. This is not to say that one is any better or any more correct than another, as it's simply a matter of the goals of your analysis and of your preference. I refer to one school of thought as the "kitchen sink" approach, where everything possible is included in a timeline and the analyst begins to sort things out from there. Personally, I find this cumbersome, but I do understand why some analysts might prefer this approach. I tend to take a minimalist approach, building my timeline a layer at a time, based on the goals of my analysis and adding specific data sources in order to bring the available context into focus. For example, when addressing an issue of contraband images on a system, the question was posed as to whether or not someone logged into the system remotely and somehow added the images. I saw from the Security hive data that auditing of both successful and failed logins was enabled, so as part of my analysis, I created a timeline of just the remote login events available in the Security Event Log (for Windows XP, event ID 528, and 540 events). This way, I had something concise that I could create and refer to quickly, rather than having to open a much larger timeline file composed of a bunch of data sources that had little if anything to do with the question I was trying to answer. During another examination, I was confronted with a Windows system that had been compromised through SQL injection; as the web server and database server (both components are required for SQL injection) had both been installed on the same platform, I was only analyzing a single system. I started by taking an iterative approach to locating the SQL injection statements in the web server logs. I located what appeared to be indicators of SQL injection in the logs and sorted those by source IP address. I then removed those attempts that, based on the source IP address, appeared to originate from a legitimate scanning service that had been engaged by the customer and performed searches for all requests originating from the remaining IP addresses. I was able to "see" (using a mini-timeline of just the pertinent web server log entries) clusters of activity on specific dates; when I added these events to the file system metadata, I was able to see not just the commands sent to the system via the SQL injection statements, but also the effect they had on the file system. In the end, I was able to build a complete picture of what happened on the system, and when it happened, using only two data sources.

Personally, I will use a completely automated approach only if I understand exactly what data is being collected and added to the timeline. If some data sources that might be valuable to my analysis, such as the fact that the NetworkService profile on a Windows 2008 R2 system has a populated Internet Explorer browser history (index.dat) file, are not included in the timeline, I would either seek another means for adding those data sources or move to another methodology.

Again, the approach that any particular analyst uses should be based primarily on the goals of their examination, but will likely also include their preference, how comfortable they are with their knowledge of the data and tools, and any documented processes and procedures they employ.

Data sources

The early days of digital forensic analysis included reviewing file system metadata: metadata which is associated with the time stamps from the $STANDARD_ INFORMATION attributes within the master file table (MFT). As we know from Chapter 4, the time stamps within this attribute are easily modified via publicly accessible application programming interfaces (APIs); if you have the necessary permissions to write to a file (and most intruders either get in with or elevate to System-level privileges), you can modify these file times to arbitrary values (this is sometimes referred to as "time stomping," from the name of a tool used to do this).

However, in many cases, rather than "stomping" the file times, the intruder or malware installation process will simply copy the file times from a legitimate system file, such as kernel32.dll, as this is simply much easier to do, requires only a few API function calls, and leaves fewer traces than "stomping" times.

TIP

Time Stamp Manipulation

Timestomp.exe (a description of the tool can be found online at http://www.forensicswiki. org/wiki/Timestomp), developed by James C. Foster and Vincent Lui (at the time of this writing, I could not locate a reliable site from which to download a copy of timestomp. exe), reportedly has a 32-bit granularity with respect to its ability to modify file times (as opposed to the 64-bit granularity used in the common Windows FILETIME structure), and it modifies only the time stamps found in the $STANDARD_INFORMATION attribute within the MFT. As such, the use of a tool such as this would be easy to detect, by first checking the granularity of the time stamp within the MFT to see if the lower 32 bits are all zeros, and then comparing the creation dates in the two attributes ($STANDARD_INFORMATION and $FILE_NAME). Subsequent methods for modifying file time stamps have relied on the GetFileTime() and SetFileTime() API functions to copy the time stamps from one file (such as kernel32.dll) to a target file. This method preserves the granularity of the time stamps. However, additional measures are required to modify the $FILE_NAME attribute time stamps, such as moving the file to a different folder and then back again.

At the time of this writing, a tool for modifying Registry key LastWrite times called "setregtime" could be found online at https://code.google.com/p/mft2csv/wiki/SetRegTime.

As the Windows operating systems developed and increased in complexity, various services and technologies were added and modified over time. This made the systems more usable and versatile, not only to users (desktops, laptops) but also to system administrators (servers). Many of these services and technologies (i.e., the Registry, application prefetching, scheduled tasks, Event Logs) not only maintain data, but also time stamps which are used to track specific events. Additional services and applications, such as the Internet Information Server (IIS) web server, can provide additional time-stamped events in the form of logs.

As you can see and imagine, Windows systems are rife with timeline data sources, many of which we've discussed throughout the book (particularly in Chapter 4). Also, in Chapter 3, we discussed how to get even more time-stamped data and fill in some analytic gaps by accessing VSCs. Overall, Windows systems do a pretty decent job of maintaining time-stamped information regarding both system and user activity. Therefore, it's critical that analysts understand what data sources may be available, as well as how to access that time-stamped information and use it to further their analysis.

Time formats

Along with the variety of data sources, Windows systems maintain time-stamped information in a variety of formats. The most frequently found format on modern

Windows systems is the 64-bit FILETIME format (the structure definition is available online at http://msdn.microsoft.com/en-us/library/ms724284(v=vs.85).aspx) which maintains the number of 100-nanosecond intervals since midnight, January 1, 1601, in accordance with Universal Coordinated Time (UTC—analogous to Greenwich Mean Time (GMT)). As we saw in Chapter 4, this time format is used throughout Windows systems, from file times to Registry key LastWrite times to the *ShutdownTime* value within the Registry System hive.

Every now and again, you will see the popular 32-bit Unix time format on Windows systems, as well. This time records the number of seconds since midnight on January 1, 1970, relative to the UTC time zone. This time format is used to record the TimeGenerated and TimeWritten values within Windows 2000, XP, and 2003 Event Log records (a description of the structure is found online at http://msdn.microsoft.com/en-us/library/aa363646(VS.85).aspx).

A time format maintained in a great number of locations on Windows systems is the DOSDate format. This is a 32-bit time format, in which 16 bits hold the date and the other 16 bits hold the time. Information regarding the format structure, as well as the process for converting from a FILETIME time stamp to a DOSDate time stamp, can be found at the Microsoft web site (http://msdn.microsoft.com/en-us/library/windows/desktop/ms724274(v=vs.85).aspx). It is important to understand how the time stamps are converted, as this time format can be found in shell items, which themselves are found in Windows shortcut files, Jump Lists (Windows 7 and 8), as well as wide range of Registry data.

Other time-based information is maintained in a string format, similar to what users usually see when they interact with the system or open Windows Explorer, such as "01/02/2010 2:42 PM." These time stamps can be recorded in local system time after taking the UTC time stamp and performing the appropriate conversion to local time using the time zone and daylight savings settings (maintained in the Registry) for that system. IIS web server logs are also maintained in a similar format (albeit with a comma between the date and time values), although the time stamps are recorded in UTC format.

Yet another time format found on Windows systems is the SYSTEMTIME format (the structure definition is available online at http://msdn.microsoft.com/en-us/library/ms724950(v=vs.85).aspx). The individual elements within the structure of this time format record the year, month, day of week, day, hour, minute, second, and millisecond (in that order). These times are recorded in local system time after the conversion from UTC using the time zone and daylight savings settings maintained by the system. This time format is found within the metadata on Windows XP and 2003 Scheduled Tasks (.job files), as well as within some Registry values, particularly on Vista and Windows 7 (refer to Chapter 5).

Finally, various applications often maintain time stamps in their own time format, particularly in log files. For example, Symantec AntiVirus logs use a comma-separated, text-based format in six hexadecimal octets (defined online at http://www.symantec.com/business/support/index?page=content&id=TECH100099).

So, it's important to realize that time stamps can be recorded in a variety of formats (to include UTC or local system time), and we will discuss later in this chapter tools and code for translating these time stamps into a common format in order to facilitate analysis.

Concepts

When we create a timeline of system activity from multiple data sources (i.e., more than simply file system metadata), we achieve two basic concepts (credit goes to Cory Altheide for succinctly describing these to me a while back); we add *context* and *granularity* to the data that we're looking at, and we *increase our relative level of confidence* in that data.

Okay, so what does this mean? Well, by saying that we add context to the data that we're looking at, I mean that by bringing in multiple data sources, we begin to see more details added to the activity surrounding a specific event. For example, consider a file being modified on the system, and the fact that we might be interested in what may have caused the modification; that is, was it part of normal system activity? Was the file modification part of an operating system or application update (such as with log files)? Or was that file modification the direct result of some specific action performed by a user? By using time-stamped information derived from multiple data sources, normalizing the data (i.e., reducing the time stamps to a common format), and incorporating it into an overall view, we can "see" what additional activity was occurring on the system during or "near" that time. I've used timelines to locate file modifications that were the result of a malware infection (see Chapter 6) and could "see" when a file was loaded on a system, and then a short while later the file (i.e., with a "suspicious" name or in a suspicious location) of interest was modified.

How does the term "granularity" fit into a discussion of timelines? When we add metadata from certain data source to our timeline, we can add a considerable amount of details to the timeline. For example, let's say we start with a timeline that includes file system and Windows Event Log metadata. If we then find a particular event of interest while a user is logged into the system, we can then begin to add metadata specific to that user's activities to the timeline, including metadata available from historical sources, such as what might be found in any available VSCs. If necessary (depending upon the goals of our analysis) we can then add even more detail, such as the user's web browsing history, thereby achieving even more granularity. So, separate from context, we can also increase the detail or granularity of the timeline based on the data sources that we include in the timeline, or add to it.

When we say that timelines can increase our relative level of confidence in the data that we're analyzing, what this means is that some data sources are more easily mutable than others, and we have greater confidence in those that are less easily mutable (or modified). For example, we know that the file time stamps in the $STANDARD_INFORMATION attribute of the MFT can be easily modified through the use of open, accessible APIs; however, those in the $FILE_NAME attribute are not as easily accessible. Also, to this date, I have yet to find any indication of a publicly available API for modifying the LastWrite times associated with Registry keys (remember Chapter 5?) to arbitrary values. These values can be updated to more recent times by creating and then deleting a value within the key, but we may find indications of this activity using tools and techniques described in Chapter 5. The point is that all data sources for our timeline have a relative level of confidence that the times associated with those sources are "correct," and that relative level of confidence is higher for some data sources (Registry key LastWrite times) than for others (file times in the $STANDARD_INFORMATION attributes of the MFT, log file entries, etc.). Therefore, if we were to see within our timeline a Registry key associated with a specific malware variant being modified on the system and saw that a file also associated with the malware was created "nearby," then our confidence that the file system metadata regarding the file creation was accurate would be a bit higher.

We also have to keep in mind that the amount of relevant detail available from time-stamped information is often subject to *temporal proximity*. This is a Star Trek-y sounding term that I first heard used by Aaron Walters (of the Volatility project) that refers to being close to an event in time. This is an important concept to keep in mind when viewing time-stamped data; as we saw in Chapter 4, some time-stamped data is available as metadata contained within files, or as values within Registry keys or values, etc. However, historical information is not often maintained within these sources. What I mean by this is that a Registry key LastWrite time is exactly that; the value refers to the last time that the key contents were modified in some way. What is not maintained is a list of all of the previous times that the key was modified. The same holds true with other time-stamped information, such as metadata maintained within Prefetch files; the time stamp that refers to the last time that particular application was launched is just that—the last time this event occurred. The file metadata does not contain a list of the previous times that the application was launched since the Prefetch file itself was created. As such, it's nothing unusual to see a Prefetch file (for MSWord, Excel, the Solitaire game, etc.) with a specific creation date, a modification date that is "close" to the embedded time stamp, and a relatively high run count, but what we won't have available is a list of times and dates for when the application had been previously launched. What this means is that if your timeline isn't created within relative *temporal proximity* to the incident, some time-stamped data may be overwritten or modified by activities that occurred following the incident but prior to response activities, and you may lose some of the context that is achieved through the use of timeline analysis. This is an important consideration to keep in mind when performing timeline analysis, as it can explain an apparent lack of indicators of specific activity. I've seen this several times, particularly following malware infections; while there are indicators of an infection (Registry artifacts, etc.), the actual malware executable (and often, any data files) may have been deleted and the MFT entry and file system sectors overwritten by the time I was able to obtain any data.

Benefits

In addition to providing context, granularity, and an increased relative confidence in the data that we're looking at, timelines provide other benefits when it comes to analysis. I think that many of us can agree that a great deal of the analysis we do (whether we're talking about intrusions, malware infections, contraband images, etc.) comes down to definable events occurring at certain times, respective to and correlated with each other or to some external source. When we're looking at intrusions, we often want to know when the intruder initially gained access to a system. The same is often true with malware infections; when the system was first infected determines the window of compromise or infection and directly impacts how long sensitive data may have been exposed. With respect to payment card industry (PCI) forensic assessments, one of the critical data points of the analysis is the "window of exposure"; that is, answering the question of when the system was compromised or infected and how long credit card data was at risk of exposure. When addressing issues of contraband images, we may want to know when the images were created on the system in order to determine how long the user may have possessed them, what actions the user may have performed in relation to those images (i.e., launched a viewing application), and when those actions occurred.

These examples show how analysis of timeline data can, by itself, provide a great deal of information about what happened and when for a variety of incidents. Given that fact, one can see how creating a timeline has additional benefits, particularly when it comes to triage of an incident, or the exposure of sensitive data is in question. One challenge that has been faced by forensic analysts consistently over the years has been the ever-increasing size of storage media. I can remember the days when a 20-megabyte (MB) hard drive was a big deal; in fact, I can remember when a hard drive itself was a big deal! Over time, we've seen hard drive sizes go from MB to gigabytes (GB) to hundreds of GB, even into terabytes (TB). I recently received a 4-TB hard drive as a reward for winning an online challenge. But storage capacity has not only going up for hard drives, it's increased for all storage media. External storage media (thumb drives, external hard drives) have at the same time increased in capacity and decreased in price. The same is also true for digital cameras, smart phones, etc.

Where creating timelines can be extremely beneficial when dealing with ever-increasing storage capacity is that they are created from metadata, rather than file contents. Consider a 500-GB hard drive; file system metadata (discussed later in this chapter) extracted from the active file system on that hard drive will only comprise maybe a dozen or so kilobytes (KB). Even as we add additional data sources to our timeline information (such as data from Registry hives, or even the hive files themselves), and the data itself approaches hundreds of KB, it's all text-based and can be compressed, occupying even less space. In short, the relevant timeline data can be extracted, compressed, and provided or transmitted to other analysts far more easily than transmitting entire copies of imaged media.

> **NOTE**
>
> **Timeline Sizes**
>
> I went back and looked at a couple of timelines I've created for various test cases. In all cases, the timelines were less than 60 KB in size. One timeline for a Windows XP test image is less than 5 KB in size; the original image is 20 GB. The largest timeline is just under 60 KB, and the image file from which the timeline data originated is 500 GB. As the timeline is comprised of nothing but text, it compresses to a file of less than 4 KB. If an on-site analyst requires support from off-site resources, it's clear that it would be much easier to send a 4-KB zipped archive than a 500-GB image file.

In order to demonstrate how this is important, consider a data breach investigation where sensitive data (such as PCI) was possibly exposed. These investigations can involve multiple systems, which require time to image, and then time to analyze, as well as time to search for credit card numbers. However, if the on-site responder were to acquire images, and then extract a specific subset of data sources (either the files themselves or the metadata that we will discuss in this chapter), this data could be compressed, encrypted, and provided to an off-site analyst to conduct an initial analysis or triage examination, all without additional exposure of PCI data, as file contents are not being provided.

The same can be said of contraband image investigations. Timeline data can be extracted from an acquired image and provided to an off-site analyst, without any additional exposure of the images themselves; only the file names and paths are provided. The images themselves do not need to be shared (nor should they) in order to address such questions as how or when the images were created on the system, or whether the presence of the images is likely the result of specific user actions (as opposed to malware). While I am not a sworn law enforcement officer, I have assisted in investigations involving contraband images; however, the assistance I provided did not require me (thankfully) to view any of the files. Instead, I used time-stamped data to develop a timeline, and in several instances was able to demonstrate that a user account had been accessed from the console (i.e., logging in from the keyboard) and used to view several of the images.

In short, it is often not feasible to ship several TB of acquired images to a remote location; this would be obviated by the time it would take to encrypt the data, as well as by the risks associated with the data being lost or damaged during shipment. However, timeline data extracted from an acquired image (or even from a live running system) can be archived and secured, and then provided to an off-site analyst. As an example, I had an image of a 250-GB hard drive, and the resulting timeline file created using the method outlined in this chapter was about 88 KB, which then compressed to about 8 KB. In addition, no sensitive data was exposed in the timeline itself, whereas analysis of the timeline provided answers to the customer's questions regarding malware infections.

Another aspect of timeline analysis that I have found to be extremely valuable is that whether we're talking about malware infections or intrusions or another type of incident, in the years that I've been performing incident response and digital forensic analysis as a consultant, it isn't often that I'm able to get access to an image of a system that was acquired almost immediately following the actual incident. In most cases, a considerable amount of time (often weeks or months) has passed before I get access to the necessary data. However, very often, creating a timeline using multiple data sources will allow me to see the artifacts of an intrusion or other incident that still remain on the system. Remember in Chapter 1 when we discussed primary and secondary artifacts? Well, many times I've been able to locate secondary artifacts of an intrusion or malware/bot infection, even after the primary artifacts were deleted (possibly by an AV scan, or the result of first responder actions). For example, during one particular engagement, I found through timeline analysis that specific malware files had been created on a system, but an AV scan two days later detected and deleted the malware. Several weeks later, new malware files were created on the system, but due to the nature of the malware, it was several more weeks before the portion of the malware that collected sensitive data was executed (this finding was based on our analysis of the malware, as well the artifacts within the timeline). By locating the secondary artifacts associated with the actual execution of the malware, this allowed us to specify the window of exposure for this particular system to a more accurate and narrow time frame, for which the customer was grateful.

Finally, viewing data from multiple sources allows an analyst to build a picture of activity on a system, particularly in the absence of direct, primary artifacts. For example, when a user logs into a system, a logon event is generated but it is only recorded in the Security Event Log if the system is configured to audit those events. If an intruder gains access to or is able to create a domain administrator account and begin accessing systems (via the Remote Desktop Protocol), and that account has not been used to log into the systems previously, then the user profile for the account will be created on each system, regardless of the auditing configuration. The profile creation, and in particular the creation of the NTUSER.DAT hive file, will appear as part of the file system data, and the contents of the hive file will also provide the analyst with some insight as to the intruder's activities while they were accessing the system. I've had several examinations where I was able to use this information to "fill in the gaps" when some primary artifacts were simply not available.

Format

With all of the time-stamped information available on Windows systems, in the various time stamp structures, I realized that I needed to create a means by which I could correlate all of it together in a common, "normalized" format. To this end, I came up with a five-field "TLN" (which is short for "timeline") format to serve as the basis for timelines. This format would allow me to provide a thorough description of each individual event, and then correlate, sort, and view them together. Those five fields and their descriptions are discussed below.

Time

With all of the various time structures that appear on Windows systems, I opted to use the 32-bit Unix time stamp, based on UTC as a common format. All of the time stamp structures are easily reduced or normalized to this common format, and the values themselves are easy to sort on and to translate into a human-readable format using the Perl *gmtime()* function. Also, while Windows systems do contain a few time values in this 32-bit format, I did not want to restrict my timelines to Windows systems only, as in many incidents valuable time-stamped data could be derived from other sources as well, such as firewall logs, network device logs (in syslog format), and even logs from Linux systems. As I did not have access to all possible log or data sources that I could expect to encounter when I was creating this format, I wanted to use a time stamp format that was common to a wide range of sources, and to which other time stamp structures could be easily reduced.

Tools and functions available as part of programming languages make it easy to translate the various time structures to a normalized Unix epoch time UTC format. Most time stamps are stored in UTC format, requiring nothing more than some math to translate the format. Remember, however, that the SYSTEMTIME structure can be based on the local system time for the system being examined, taking the time zone and daylight savings settings into account. As such, you would first need to reduce the 128-bit value to the 32-bit time format, and then make the appropriate adjustments to convert local time to UTC (86,400 seconds/hour times the ActiveTimeBias value from the Registry, for that system, and for that time of year).

TIP

Registry Analysis

As we will discuss later in this chapter, there may be some modicum of Registry analysis that needs to occur prior to creating a timeline. For example, if we know that we're going to be working with a number of time stamps in the SYSTEMTIME object format, we'll want to examine the system's time zone settings (found beneath the Control\TimeZoneInformation key within the appropriate ControlSet) so that we can properly translate these to UTC format.

Source

The source value within the TLN format is a short, easy-to-read identifier that refers to the data source within the system from which the time-stamped data was derived. For example, as we'll see later in this chapter, one of the first places we often go to begin collecting data is the file system, so the source would be "FILE." For time-stamped data derived from Event Log records on Windows 2000, XP, and 2003 systems I use the "EVT" (based on the file extension) identifier in the source field, whereas for Vista, Windows 7, and Windows 8 systems, I use the "EVTX" identifier for events retrieved from the Windows Event Logs on these systems. I use "REG" to identify data retrieved from the Registry, and "SEP" or "MCAFEE" to identify data retrieved from Symantec EndPoint Protection Client and McAfee AV log files, respectively.

You might be thinking, what is the relevance of identifying different sources? Think back to earlier in this chapter when we discussed the *relative level of confidence* we might have in various data sources. By using a source identifier in our timeline data, we can quickly see and visualize time-based data that would provide us with a greater level of relative confidence in the overall data that we're looking at, regardless of our output format. For example, let's say that we have a file with a specific last modified time (source FILE). We know that these values can be modified to arbitrary times, so our confidence in this data, in isolation, would be low. However, if we have a Registry key LastWrite time (source REG) derived from one of the most recently used (MRU) lists within the Registry (such as the *RecentDocs* subkeys, or those associated with a specific application used to view that particular file type) that occurs prior to that file's last modified time, we've increased our confidence in that data.

I do not have a comprehensive list or table of all possible timeline source identifiers, although I have described a number of the more frequently used identifiers. I try to keep them to eight characters or less, and try to make them as descriptive as possible, so as to provide context to the data within the timeline. A table listing many of the source identifiers that I have used is included along with the materials associated with this book.

System

This field refers to the system, host, or device from which the data was obtained. In most cases within a timeline, this field will contain the system or host name, or perhaps some other identifier (based on the data source), such as an IP address or even a media access control address. This can be very helpful when you have data from multiple sources that describe or can be associated with a single event. For example, if you're looking at a user's web browsing activity, you may have access to the user's workstation, firewall logs, perhaps web server proxy logs, and in some cases, maybe even logs from the remote web server. In other instances, it may be beneficial to combine timelines from multiple systems in order to demonstrate the progression of malware propagating between those systems, or an adversary moving laterally within an infrastructure, from one system to another. Finally, it may be critical to an investigation to combine wireless access point log files into a timeline developed using data from a suspect's laptop. In all of these instances, you would want to have a clear, understandable means for identifying the system from which the event data originated.

User

The user field is used to identify the user associated with a specific event, if one is available. There are various sources within Windows systems that maintain not just time-stamped data, but also information tying a particular user to that event. For example, Event Log records contain a field for the security identifier (SID) of the user associated with that particular record. In many cases, the user is simply blank, "System," or one of the SIDs associated with a System-level account (LocalService, NetworkService) on that system. However, there are a number of event records that are associated with a specific user SID; these SIDs can be mapped to a specific user name via the SAM Registry hive, or the ProfileList subkeys from the Software hive.

Another reason to include a user field is that a great deal of time-based information is available from the NTUSER.DAT Registry hive found in each user profile. For example, not only do the Registry keys have LastWrite times that could prove to be valuable (again, think of the MRU keys), but various Registry values (think UserAssist subkey values) also contain time-based data. So, while many data sources (e.g., file system and Prefetch file metadata) will provide data that is not associated with a specific user, adding information derived from user profiles (specifically the NTUSER.DAT hive) can add that context that we discussed earlier in this chapter, allowing us to associate a series of events with a specific user. Populating this field also allows us to distinguish the actions of different users.

Description

This field provides a brief description of the event that occurred. I've found that in populating this particular field, brief and concise descriptions are paramount, as verbose descriptions not only quickly get out of hand, but with many similar events analysts will have a lot to read and keep track of when conducting analysis.

So what do I mean by "brief and concise"? A good example of this comes in representing the times associated with files within the file system. We know from Chapter 4 that files have four times (last modified, last accessed, when the file metadata was modified, and the file creation or "born" date) associated with each file, usually derived from the $STANDARD_INFORMATION attribute within the MFT. These attributes are often abbreviated as "MACB." As such, a concise description of the file being modified at a specific time would be "M... <filename>." It's that simple. The "M" stands for "modified," the dots represent the other time stamps (together they provide the "MACB" description), and the filename provides the full path to the file. This is straightforward and easy to understand at a glance.

I have found that doing much the same thing with Registry LastWrite times is very useful. Listing the key name preceded by "M...," much like last modified times for files, is a brief and easy-to-understand means for presenting this information in a timeline. Registry key LastWrite times mark when a key was last modified, and by itself, does not contain any specific information about when the key was created. While it's possible that the LastWrite time also represents when the key was created, without further contextual information, it is best not to speculate and to only consider this value "as is"—that is, simply as the LastWrite time.

When populating at timeline with Event Log records, I've found that a concise description can be derived from elements of the event itself. Using the event source from the Event Log record, along with the event identifier (ID), the type (warning, info, or error), and the strings extracted from the event (if there are any), I've been able to create a brief description of the event. For example, on Windows XP and

2003 systems, event ID 520 (source is "Security") indicates that the system time had been successfully changed; from such an event record, the Description field would appear as follows:

```
Security/520;Success;3368,C:\WINDOWS\system32\rundll32.exe,vmware,
REG-OIPK81M2WC8,(0×0,0×91AD),vmware,REG-OIPK81M2WC8,(0×0,0×91AD),
1/17/2008,4:52:28 PM,1/17/2008,4:52:27 PM
```

To understand what each of the fields following "Security/520;Success;" refers to, see the event description found online at http://www.ultimatewindowssecurity.com/securitylog/encyclopedia/event.aspx?eventid=520. A Description field such as the above example might seem a bit cryptic at first to some analysts, but over time and looking at many timelines, I've developed something of an eye for which events to look for when conducting analysis. In addition, I've relied heavily on the EventId.net web site, purchasing a new subscription every year so that when the next exam comes up I can search for and review the details of the various event sources and IDs.

TLN format

Now that we've discussed the five basic fields that can comprise a timeline, you're probably asking yourself, "Okay, in what format are these events stored?" I have found that storing all of these events in an intermediate "events" file (usually named "events.txt") in a pipe ("|") delimited format makes them very easy to parse (we will discuss parsing the events file later in the chapter). As such, each individual event appears as follows in the events file:

```
Time|Source|System|User|Description
```

The use of a pipe as a separator was a pretty arbitrary choice, but I needed to use something that wasn't likely to show up in the Description field (like a comma or semicolon) and play havoc with my parsing utility. The pipe seemed like a pretty good choice.

Creating Timelines

With all this talk about timelines, it's about time we created one. What we'll do is walk through a demonstration of creating a timeline from a Windows XP image, start to finish, pointing out along the way different techniques for getting similar information from Vista and Windows 7 systems, as well as some alternative techniques for obtaining the same information.

This process is going to be modular in nature, allowing us a great deal of flexibility in creating timelines. As we walk through the process, you'll notice that we're creating the timeline in stages. In some of the steps, the data that we extract will be stored in an intermediate file. We will first extract the data into an intermediate file in one format (generally whatever format is used by the tool capable of extracting our data of interest). We'll then use another tool to manipulate that data into a normalized format (TLN format) in an intermediate "events" file. Since our events file will contain multiple sets of unsorted data appended to the file, our last step will be to parse the events file and sort it into a final timeline. This can be very beneficial, particularly if an application uses a new format to store its data, or something happened with the application that corrupted the data that we're parsing—think of this as something of a debugging step, as checking the contents of the intermediate file can help you figure out whether something wrong, and how to fix it. Remember, *there are no commercial forensic analysis applications that allow us to press a button and create timelines from all available data*; rather, we often have to rely on multiple open-source and freely available tools to extract the necessary data. As these tools are often created by various authors with completely disparate goals in mind, we often have to extract the data into the format provided by the tool, and then manipulate or restructure the data so that we can add it more easily to our timeline format.

So, starting with an acquired image, we will extract the data we want or need in whatever format is provided by the available tools, and then use or create the necessary tools to put that data into our common timeline format in an "events" file, which we will then parse into a timeline. I know that this process does seem terribly manual and perhaps cumbersome at first, but to be honest, over time I've found that having this sort of granular level of control over the information that is added to a timeline can be advantageous. However, once you've walked through this process once or twice and seen the value of creating a timeline, seeing the perspective that you can get on a case by viewing different and apparently disparate system events correlated together, you'll recognize the power that a timeline can bring to the analyst. Hopefully, through the course of our discussion, you will see just how powerful an analysis technique creating a timeline can be and take the opportunity to use it.

NOTE

Modular Approach

You will notice throughout the process that we're about to walk through that it's modular. That is, the process is not about pushing a button and having everything done for you, but about determining what data you need and using the appropriate tools to extract that data. Each tool used is separate and distinct, and in some cases, the tool provides additional capabilities beyond simply spitting out data for a timeline. Creating full timelines can generate a considerable amount of data, and I've found over time that creating mini-, micro-, or even what I refer to as nano-timelines (i.e., creating separate timelines from very limited data sources) has been an extremely valuable tool. Using the tools along with the *find* command has allowed me to create distinct timelines of just remote login or AV detection events. In many cases, this has provided me with an initial event that I could then take to the full timeline and view other surrounding events and context. For example, if I'm interested in off-system communications by malware, and I found during the course of my initial analysis that the malware was running in the user context (i.e., the persistence mechanism was the user's Run key), I might find it useful to parse the user's Internet Explorer history (index.dat) file, but separate out those URL records that include the malicious domains, rather than add them all to the timeline. This is a great way to perform data reduction and to limit the data that's included in the timeline.

Before we get started, we need to make sure that we have the necessary tools available. The process that we will be discussing makes use of Perl scripts that I have written; those scripts are available in the materials associated with this book, and include executable files "compiled" using Perl2Exe, so that a Perl distribution does not need to be installed in order to use the tools. In addition to these tools, you will need TSK tools, which can be found online at http://www.sleuthkit.org/sleuthkit/download.php. Once you've assembled this collection of tools, you will be ready to start creating timelines.

Do not feel that you are necessarily limited by the process that we're about to discuss; rather, look at it as an introduction. If you have a favorite tool that provides data that you'd like to add to your timeline, feel free to use it. The process that we're going to discuss should simply be considered a foundation, in order to provide an understanding of where the data comes from, and how it can be used to build a timeline.

As we're going to be creating a timeline from an acquired image, you will need to have an image available so that you can follow along with and use the commands that comprise the process that we will walk through in the rest of this chapter. There are a couple of ways to obtain an image of a Windows system if you don't already have one—one is to simply use FTK Imager to acquire an image of one of your own systems. There are also a number of images available online; for example, there is the Hacking Case image available from the National Institute of Standards and Technology (NIST) web site (the image can be found online at http://www. cfreds.nist.gov/Hacking_Case.html). Lance Mueller has posted several practical exercises to his ForensicKB.com web site, which include images that can be downloaded. For example, the scenario and link to the image for his first practical can be found online at http://www.forensickb.com/2008/01/forensic-practical.html. In fact, an acquired image from any Windows system (Windows 2000 through Windows 7) would serve as a good learning tool as we understand how to create timelines. The steps that we're going to walk through in this chapter to create a timeline are listed in the timeline cheat sheet, a PDF format document available in the materials associated with this book. That being said, let's get started.

File system metadata

One of the first sources of timeline data that I generally start with is the file system metadata. This data is most often referred to as "MACB" times, where the "M" stands for last modification date, "A" stands for last accessed date, "C" stands for the date that the file metadata was modified, and "B" refers to the "born" or creation date of the file. Another way of referring to these times is "MACE," where "C" refers to the creation date and "E" refers to when the file metadata was modified (or "entry modified"). For consistency, we'll use the MACB nomenclature. Regardless of the designation used, this data is derived from the $STANDARD_INFORMATION attribute within the MFT (discussed in detail in Chapter 4).

> **TIP**
>
> **NTFS File Times**
> MS KnowledgeBase article 299648 (found online at http://support.microsoft.com/?kbid=299648) provides descriptions of the effects that various operations (copy, move) have on the file system metadata associated with files and folders within the NTFS file system. This KnowledgeBase article should be used as a reference and support (rather than replace) analyst testing of various events and conditions.

We can use TSK tools (specifically mmls.exe and fls.exe) to easily extract this data from an acquired image into what is referred to as a "bodyfile." When an image is acquired of a physical hard drive, it will often contain a partition table. Using mmls.exe (man page found online at http://www.sleuthkit.org/sleuthkit/man/mmls.html), we can parse and view that partition table. The command used to view the partition table of an image acquired from a Windows system appears as follows:

```
C:\tools> mmls -t dos -i raw <image>
```

Optionally, you can save the output of the command by using the redirection operator (i.e., ">") and adding "> mmls_output.txt" (or whatever name you prefer) to the end of the command. An example of the output that you might see from this command is illustrated in Figure 7.1.

From the sample output that appears in Figure 7.1, we can see the partition table and that the NTFS partition that we would be interested in is the one marked 02, which starts at sector 63 within the image. If you downloaded the "hacking case" image from the NIST site mentioned earlier in this chapter, the output of the *mmls* command run against the image would look very similar to what is illustrated in Figure 7.1. However, if you get an error that begins with "Invalid sector address," the image you're looking at may not have a partition table (such as when an image is acquired of a logical volume rather than the entire physical disk), and you can proceed directly to the part of this chapter where we discuss the use of fls.exe.

You may also find that the partition table isn't quite as "clean" and simple with some acquired images. Figure 7.2 illustrates the output of mmls.exe run against a physical image acquired from a laptop purchased from Dell, Inc.

```
DOS Partition Table
Offset Sector: 0
Units are in 512-byte sectors

     Slot    Start         End           Length        Description
00:  Meta    0000000000    0000000000    0000000001    Primary Table (#0)
01:  -----   0000000000    0000000062    0000000063    Unallocated
02:  00:00   0000000063    0312576704    0312576642    NTFS (0x07)
03:  -----   0312576705    0312581807    0000005103    Unallocated
```

FIGURE 7.1

Sample mmls.exe output.

In Figure 7.2, the partition we'd most likely be interested in (at least initially) is the one marked 04, which starts at sector 178176. We will need to have this information (i.e., the sector offset to the partition of interest) available to use with fls. exe (man page found online at http://www.sleuthkit.org/sleuthkit/man/fls.html), in order to extract the file system metadata from within the particular volume in which we're interested.

Using the offset information, we can collect file system metadata from the partition of interest. Returning to our first example (Figure 7.1, with the NTFS partition at offset 63), the fls.exe command that we would use appears as follows:

```
C:\tools > fls -i raw [-o 63] -f ntfs -r -p -m C:/ < image> >
bodyfile.txt
```

In this command, the various switches used all help us get the data that we're looking for. The "-m" switch allows us to prepend the path with the appropriate drive letter. The "-o" switch allows us to select the appropriate volume. (I've included the "-o" switch information in square brackets as it can be optional; if you get an error message that begins with "Invalid sector address" when using mmls. exe, it's likely that you won't have to use the "-o" switch at all. Alternately, the value used with the "–o" switch may change, depending on the image you're using (volume or physical image) or the offset of the volume in which you're interested. For example, offset 63 would be used for the volume listed in Figure 7.1, but offset 21149696 would be used to extract information from the partition marked 05 in Figure 7.2 (and you'd likely want to use "-m D:/," as well).) The "-p" switch tells fls.exe to use full paths for the files and directories listed, and the "-r" switch tells fls.exe to recurse through all subdirectories. Explanations for the other switches, as well as additional switches available, can be found on the fls man page at the linked site listed above.

You should also notice that the listed *fls* command includes a redirection operator, sending the output of the command to a file named "bodyfile.txt." The bodyfile (described online at http://wiki.sleuthkit.org/index.php?title=Body_file) is an intermediate format used to store the file system metadata information before translating it into the TLN event file format that we discussed earlier.

```
        Slot    Start        End          Length       Description
00:     Meta    0000000000   0000000000   0000000001   Primary Table (#0)
01:     -----   0000000000   0000000062   0000000063   Unallocated
02:     00:00   0000000063   0000176714   0000176652   Dell Utilities FAT (0xde)
03:     -----   0000176715   0000178175   0000001461   Unallocated
04:     00:01   0000178176   0021149695   0020971520   NTFS (0x07)
05:     00:02   0021149696   0307335167   0286185472   NTFS (0x07)
06:     Meta    0307335168   0312578047   0005242880   Win95 Extended (0x0F)
07:     Meta    0307335168   0307335168   0000000001   Extended Table (#1)
08:     -----   0307335168   0307337215   0000002048   Unallocated
09:     01:00   0307337216   0312578047   0005240832   Hidden CTOS Memdump?   (0xdd)
10:     -----   0312578048   0312581807   0000003760   Unallocated
```

FIGURE 7.2

Sample mmls.exe output from a Dell system.

> **NOTE**
> **Events File**
> We discussed the use of intermediate formats earlier in this chapter; timeline data stored in the five-field, pipe-delimited TLN format is referred to as an "events file," simply because it contains the events that will comprise the timeline in their raw, unsorted form. The actual creation of the timeline originates with this file.

Using this approach allows us to not just keep track of the information output from our various tools, but to also keep that data available for use with other tools and processes that may be part of our analytic approach. In order to translate the bodyfile (output of the fls.exe command) information to a TLN events file format (the five fields described earlier in this chapter), we want to use the bodyfile.pl script, which is available as part of the additional materials available with this book, in the following command:

```
C:\tools > bodyfile.pl -f bodyfile.txt -s Server > events.txt
```

The above bodyfile.pl command is pretty simple and straightforward. To see the syntax options available for bodyfile.pl, simply type the command "bodyfile.pl" or "bodyfile.pl –h" at the command prompt. The "-f" switch tells the script which bodyfile to open, and the "-s" switch fills in the name of the server (you can get this from your case documentation, or by running the compname.pl RegRipper plugin against the System hive, as described in Chapter 5). Also, notice that we redirect the output of the command to the events.txt file; as with many of the tools we will discuss, the output of the tool is sent to the console, so we need to redirect it to a file so that we can add to it and parse the events later. Again, the bodyfile.pl script does nothing more than convert the output of the *fls* command to the necessary format for inclusion in the events file. Once the events file has been populated with all of the events we want to include in our timeline, we will convert the events file to a timeline.

At this point in our timeline creation process, we should have a bodyfile (bodyfile.txt) and an events file (events.txt), both containing file system metadata that was extracted from our acquired image. However, there may be times when we may not have access to an acquired image, or access to the necessary tools, and as such cannot use fls.exe to extract the file system metadata and create the bodyfile. One such example would be accessing a system remotely via F-Response; once you've mounted the physical drive on your analysis system, you can then add that drive to FTK Imager as an evidence item just as you would an acquired image. You might do this in order to extract specific files (Registry hives, Event Log files, Prefetch files) from the remote system for analysis. FTK Imager also provides an alternative means for extracting file system metadata, which we can use in situations where we may choose not to use fls.exe.

One of the simplest ways to do this is to open the newly acquired image (or the physical disk for a remote system accessed via F-Response) in FTK Imager, adding

FIGURE 7.3

Image partition listing visible in FTK Imager.

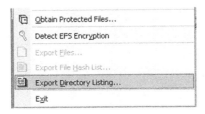

FIGURE 7.4

FTK Imager "Export Directory Listing..." option.

it as an evidence item. Figure 7.3 illustrates the image examined in Figure 7.2 loaded into FTK Imager version 3.0.0.1442.

Now, an option available to us once the image is loaded and visible in the Evidence Tree is to select the partition that we're interested in (say, partition 2 listed in Figure 7.3) and then select the "Export Directory Listing..." option from the File menu, as illustrated in Figure 7.4.

When you select this option, you will then be offered a chance to select the name and location of the comma-separated value (CSV) output file for the command (as part of my case management, I tend to keep these files in the same location as the image itself if I receive the image on writeable media, such as a USB-connected external hard drive). Once you've made these selections and started the directory listing process, you will see a dialog such as is illustrated in Figure 7.5.

At this point, we should have a complete directory listing for all of the files visible to FTK Imager in the volume or partition of interest within our image. However, the contents of the file will require some manipulation in order to get the data into a format suitable for our timeline. I wrote the script ftkparse.pl specifically to translate the information collected via this method into the bodyfile format discussed earlier in this chapter. The ftkparse.pl script takes only one argument, which is the path to the appropriate CSV file, and translates the contents of the file to bodyfile format, sending output to the console. An example of how to use the ftkparse.pl script appears as follows:

```
C:\tools > ftkparse.pl c_drive.csv > bodyfile.txt
```

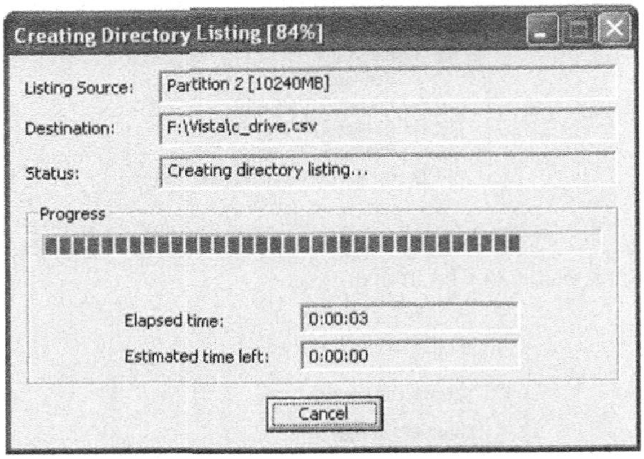

FIGURE 7.5

FTK Imager creating a directory listing.

If you use the above command, be sure to use correct file paths for your situation.

> **WARNING**
>
> **Installing Perl Modules**
>
> When running Perl scripts discussed in this chapter, you may see error messages that indicate that a particular module could not be located. If you're using the ActiveState ActivePerl distribution, you can use the Perl Package Manager (PPM) to install the appropriate modules and supporting documentation. For example, the ftkparse.pl script uses the DateTime module; if you need to install this module, simple open a command prompt, change to your Perl directory and type "ppm install datetime"; PPM will take care of installing the module for you.
>
> If you installed Strawberry Perl instead of ActiveState's distribution (TechPathway's ProDiscover ships with Strawberry Perl, and the distribution is available online at http://strawberryperl.com/), you can install modules launching the "CPAN Client" via the Start menu and then typing "install <Module::Name>."

After running the command, if you open the resulting bodyfile in a text editor, you will notice that the file and directory paths appear with some extra information. For example, when I ran through this process on the Vista image described in Figure 7.2, the bodyfile contained paths that looked like "RECOVERY [NTFS]\ [root]\Windows\," where "RECOVERY" is the name of the particular volume from which the directory listing was exported. To get this information into a more usable format, use your text editor (Notepad++ works really well for this) to perform a search-and-replace operation, replacing "RECOVERY [NTFS]\[root]\" with "C:\" (or whichever volume or drive letter is appropriate). Once you've completed this process with the appropriate volume information, you can then proceed with creating your timeline. The biggest difference between using the FTK Imager directory listing, as opposed to the output of fls.exe, is that the file/directory metadata change date (the "C" in "MACB") would not be available (FTK Imager does not extract the "C" time) and would be represented as a dot (i.e., ".") in the bodyfile.

Once you've completed this search-and-replace operation, you can run the bodyfile.pl Perl script against the bodyfile.txt file that resulted from running ftk-parse.pl, translating it into an events file.

In summary, the commands that you would run to create your events file for file time stamp data from an acquired image using fls.exe would include:

- mmls -t dos -i raw < image >
- fls -i raw [-o 63] -f ntfs -r -p -m C:/ < image> > bodyfile.txt
- bodyfile.pl –f bodyfile.txt –s Server > events.txt

If you opted to use FTK Imager to export a directory listing, the steps you would follow to create an events file for file time-stamped data are:

- Export directory listing via FTK Imager (dir_listing.csv)
- ftkparse.pl dir_listing.csv > bodyfile.txt
- Search-and-replace file and directory paths with appropriate drive letter
- bodyfile.pl –f bodyfile.txt –s Server > events.txt

Now, if you've created separate events files for different volumes (C:\, D:\, etc.) or even from different systems, you can use the native Windows *type* command to combine the events files into a single, comprehensive events file, using commands similar to the following:

```
C:\tools > type events1.txt » events_all.txt
C:\tools > type events2.txt » events_all.txt
```

Notice in the previous command that the redirection operator used is "»," which allows us to append additional data to a file, rather than creating a new file (or over-writing our existing file by mistake; I've done this more than once … a lot more).

Event logs

As discussed in Chapter 4, Event Logs from all versions of Windows can provide a great deal of very valuable information for our timeline; however, how we extract timeline information and create events files for inclusion in our timeline depends heavily on the version of Windows that we're working with. As we saw in Chapter 4, Event Logs on Windows 2000, XP, and 2003 are very different from the Windows Event Logs available on Vista, Windows 2008, and Windows 7 systems. As such, we will address each of these separately; but ultimately, we will end up with information that we can add to an events file.

Windows XP

Event Log files are found, by default, on Windows 2000, XP, and 2003 systems in the C:\Windows\system32\config directory, and have a.evt file extension. You can normally expect to find the Application (appevent.evt), System (sysevent.evt), and Security (secevent.evt) Event Log files in this directory, but you may also find other files with .evt extensions based on the applications that you have installed. For example, if you have MS Office 2007 (or above) installed, you should expect to find ODiag.evt and OSession.evt files. You can access these files in an acquired image by either adding the image to FTK Imager as an evidence item, navigating to the appropriate directory, and extracting the files, or by mounting the image as a volume via FTK Imager version 3 (or via ImDisk) and navigating to the appropriate directory. Once you have access to these files, you should use the evtparse.pl Perl script to extract the necessary event information using the following command:

```
C:\tools > evtparse.pl -d < directory> -t > evt_events.txt
```

This command tells the evtparse.pl script to go to a specific directory, extract all event records from every file in that directory with a.evt extension, and put that information into the evt_events.txt file in TLN format, adding "EVT" as the data source. So, if you've mounted an acquired image as the G:\ volume, the argument for the "-d" switch might look like "G:\Windows\system32\config." Many times, I will extract the Event Log files from the drive or the image using FTK Imager, placing them in a "files" directory, so the path information might then look like "F:\ < case > \files."

If you do not want to run this script against all of the .evt files in a directory, you can select specific files using the "-e" switch. For example, if you want to create an events file using only the event records in the Application Event Log, you might use a command similar to what follows:

```
C:\tools > evtparse.pl -e G:\windows\system32\config\appevent.evt
-t > app_events.txt
```

I actually use this technique quite often. As I mentioned earlier in this chapter, there are times when I do not want to create a full timeline, but would rather create a mini- or micro-timeline, based on specific data, so that I can get a clear view of specific data without having to sift through an ocean of irrelevant events. For example, I once worked an examination where the customer knew that they were suffering from an infection from specific malware, and informed me that they had installed the Symantec AntiVirus product. After running the evtrpt.pl Perl script (described in Chapter 4) against the Application Event Log, I noticed that there were, in fact, Symantec AntiVirus events listed in the event log (according to information available on the Symantec web site, events with ID 51 indicate a malware detection; evtrpt.pl indicated that there were 82 such events). As such, I used the following command to parse just the specific events of interest out of the Application Event Log:

```
C:\tools > evtparse.pl -e appevent.evt -t | find "Symantec
AntiVirus/51" > sav_51_events.txt
```

The resulting events file provided me with the ability to create a timeline of just the detection events generated by the Symantec product, so that I could quickly address the customer's questions about the malware without having to sift through hundreds or thousands of other irrelevant events.

TIP

Find

The "find" command is native to Windows systems and is used to search for a string in a file or within several files; you can see the command syntax by typing "find/?" at a command prompt. As noted in the syntax information, "find" can search information piped from another command, as illustrated in the previous example. I tend to use variations of this command as a means of data reduction.

You'll notice that unlike the bodyfile.pl script, the evtparse.pl script doesn't require that you add a server (or user) name to the command line; this is due to the fact that this information is already provided within the event records themselves.

TIP

Additional Event Record Sources

There may be times when you can find additional Event Log files on a system. For example, I've examined systems where an administrator had logged in and backed up the Event Logs as part of her troubleshooting procedures and copied those files off of the system without deleting them. As such, I was able to extract the event records from those files, adding a significant amount of historical data to my timeline.

Also, as discussed in Chapter 4, it's possible that you might be able to find a number of event records in the unallocated space of an image, particularly when someone recently cleared the Event Logs.

Windows 7

The Windows Event Logs on Vista, Windows 2008, Windows 7 and 8 systems are located (by default) in the C:\Windows\system32\winevt\logs directory and end in the ".evtx" file extension. As discussed in Chapter 4, these files are of a different binary format from their counterparts found on Windows XP and 2003 systems, and as such, we will need to use a different method to parse them and create our events file. Another difference is the names; for example, the primary files of interest are System.evtx, Security.evtx, and Application.evtx. As with Windows XP, additional files may be present depending on the system in question; for example, I have also found the file "Cisco AnyConnect VPN Client.evtx" on a Windows 7 system that had the Cisco client application installed. However, once you get to Vista systems, there are many more Event Log files available; on the system on which I'm currently writing this chapter, I opened a command prompt, changed to the logs directory, and typed "dir"—the result was that a total of 142 files flew by! This does not mean that all of these files are populated with event records; not all of them are actually used by the system. In fact, as you're conducting your analysis, you'll find that there are some Windows Event Logs that are populated on some systems and not on others; on my Windows 7 laptop, the Windows Event Logs that include records for remote connections to Terminal Services are not populated because I don't have Terminal Services enabled; however, on a Windows 2008 R2 system with Terminal Services enabled, I have found those logs to be well populated and extremely valuable. On a side note, I typed the same *dir* command, this time filtering the output through the *find* command in order to look for only those Windows Event Logs that included "Terminal" in their name, and the result was nine files. Again, not all of these log files is populated or even used, but they're there.

As you would expect, parsing these files into the necessary format is a bit different than with Event Log (.evt) files. One method would be to use Andreas Schuster's Perl-based framework for parsing these files; the framework is available via his blog (found online at http://computer.forensikblog.de/en). Using this framework, you can parse the .evtx files and then write the necessary tool or utility to translate that information to the TLN format. Willi Ballenthin developed his own Python-based solution for parsing .evtx files, which can be found online at http://www.williballenthin.com/evtx/index.html. He also wrote a tool for parsing .evtx records from unstructured or unallocated space called EVTXtract, which can be found online at https://github.com/williballenthin/EVTXtract.

The method that I've found to be very useful is to install Microsoft's Log Parser tool on a Windows 7 system, and then either extract the .evtx files I'm interested in to a specific directory, or mount the image as a volume on my analysis system. From there, I can then run the following command against an extracted System Event Log using the following command:

```
Logparser -i:evt -o:csv "SELECT RecordNumber,TO_UTCTIME(TimeGenerat
ed),EventID,SourceName,ComputerName,SID,Strings FROM D:\Case\File\
System.evtx" > system.csv
```

This command uses the Log Parser tool to access the necessary Windows API to parse the event records from the System.evtx file. The "-i:evt" argument tells Log Parser to use the Windows Event Log API, and the "-o:csv" argument tells the tool to format the output in CSV format. Everything between the "SELECT" and "FROM" tells LogParser which elements of each event record to retrieve and display. Not only can you open this output file in Excel, but you can use the evtxparse. pl Perl script to parse out the necessary event data into TLN format, using the following command:

```
C:\tools > evtxparse.pl system.csv > sys_events.txt
```

Again, this process requires an extra, intermediate step when compared to parsing Event Logs from Windows XP systems, but we get to the same place, and we have the parsed data available to use for further analysis. One difference from evtparse.pl is that evtxparse.pl adds the source "EVTX" to the TLN-format events instead of "EVT"; another difference is that the evtxparse.pl script only takes one argument (the file to parse), where evtparse.pl has a number of switches available.

> **WARNING**
> **Parsing Windows Event Logs**
> Remember when parsing Windows Event Logs using Log Parser, you must run Log Parser on a Windows 2008 or Windows 7, due to the fact that Log Parser relies on the native API for accessing data within the .evtx files. Attempting to run Log Parser on a Windows XP system to parse an Application.evtx file extracted from a Vista or Windows 7 system will result in unusable data, as the APIs are not compatible. The opposite is also true; you cannot run Log Parser on Vista or Windows 7 to parse Event Log (.evt) files obtained from a 2000, XP, or 2003 system.

As with the other timeline events files that we've discussed thus far, you will ultimately want to consolidate all of the available events into a single events file prior to parsing it into a timeline. You can use a batch file to automate a great deal of this work for you. For example, let's say that you have an image of a Vista system available on an external hard drive, and the path to the image file is F:\vista\disk0.001. You can mount the image as a volume on your Windows 7 analysis system (i.e., G:\) and create a batch file that contains commands similar to the following to parse the System Event Log (repeat the command as necessary for other Windows Event Log files):

```
Logparser -i:evt -o:csv "SELECT RecordNumber,TO_UTCTIME(TimeGenera
ted),EventID,SourceName,ComputerName,SID,Strings FROM %1\Windows\
system32\winevt\logs\System.evtx" > %2\system.csv
```

If you name this batch file "parseevtx.bat," you would launch the batch file by passing the appropriate arguments, such as follows:

```
C:\tools > parseevtx.bat G: F:\vista
```

Running the previous command populates the %1 variable in the batch file with your first command line parameter (in this case "G:," representing your mounted volume) and the %2 variable with your second command line parameter (in this case "F:\vista," representing the path to where your output should be stored), and executes the command. You would then use (and repeat as necessary) a command similar to the following to parse the output .csv files into event files:

```
evtxparse.pl %1\system.csv > %1\sys_events.txt
```

Again, you will need to repeat the above command in the appropriate manner for each of the Windows Event Logs parsed. Another available option, if you want to parse several Windows Event Log files in succession, is to use the "*" wildcard with the *Logparser* command, as follows:

```
Logparser -i:evt -o:csv "SELECT RecordNumber,TO_UTCTIME(TimeGenera
ted),EventID,SourceName,ComputerName,SID,Strings FROM %1\Windows\
system32\winevt\logs\* evtx" > %2\system.csv
```

This command will parse through all of the .evtx files in the given folder (entered into the batch file as the first argument, or %1). With all of these different records, there are going to be a wide range of SourceName and EventID values to deal with, and it's likely going to be impossible to memorize all of them, let alone just the ones of interest. In order to make this a bit easier, I added something to the evtxparse.pl Perl script—actually, I embedded it. One of the first things that the script (or executable, if you're using the "compiled" version of the tool) will do is look for a file named "eventmap.txt" in the same directory as the tool. Don't worry, if the file isn't there, the tool won't stop working—but it works better with the file. In short, what this file provides is event mappings, matching event source, and IDs to a short descriptor of the event. For example, if the event source is "Microsoft-Windows-TerminalServices-LocalSessionManager" and the event ID is 21, this information is mapped to "[Session Logon]," which is much easier to understand than "Microsoft-Windows-TerminalServices-LocalSessionManager/21."

The eventmap.txt file is a simple text file, so feel free to open it in an editor. Any line in the file that starts with "#" is treated as a comment line and is skipped; some of these lines point to references for the various information that I've accumulated in the file thus far, so that it can be verified. All of the event mapping lines are very straightforward and easy to understand; in fact, the structure is simple so that you can add your own entries as necessary. I would suggest that if you do intend to add your own mapping lines, just copy the format of the other lines and be sure to include references to that you can remember where you found the information. In this way, this tool becomes self-documenting; once you've added any entries and references, they're in the file until they're removed, so all you would need to do is copy the eventmap.txt file into your case folder.

Prefetch files

As discussed in Chapter 4, not all Windows systems perform application prefetching by default; in fact, Prefetch files are only usually found on Windows XP, Vista, and Windows 7 and 8 systems (application prefetching is disabled by default on Windows 2003 and 2008 systems, but can be enabled via a Registry modification). Also, Prefetch files can contain some pretty valuable information; for the purpose of this chapter, we're interested primarily in the time stamp embedded within the file. We can use the pref.pl Perl script to extract the time value for the last time the application was run (which should correspond closely to the last modification time of the Prefetch file itself) and the count of times the application has been run into TLN format, using the following command:

```
C:\tools > pref.pl -d G:\Windows\Prefetch -t -s Server > pref_
events.txt
```

Now, we have a couple of options available to us with regard to the previous command. For example, as the command is listed, the "-d" switch tells the tool to parse through all of the files ending with the ".pf" (the restriction to files ending in ".pf" is included in the code itself) extension in the Prefetch directory (of an acquired image mounted as the G:\ volume); if you would prefer to parse the information from a single Prefetch file, simply use the "-f" switch along with the full path and filename for the file of interest. By default, the pref.pl script will detect which version of Windows from which the Prefetch files originated and automatically seek out the correct offsets for the metadata embedded within the file. The "-t" switch tells the Perl script to structure the output in TLN format and adds "PREF" as the source. Also, you'll notice that as with some other scripts that we've discussed thus far, pref.pl has a "-s" switch with which you can add the server name to the TLN format; Prefetch files are not directly associated with a particular user on the system, so the user name field is left blank.

Finally, at the end of the command, we redirected the output of the script to the file named "pref_events.txt." Instead of taking this approach, we could have easily added the output to an existing events file using "» events.txt."

TIP

Windows 8 Prefetch Files

As discussed in Chapter 4, Windows 8 Prefetch files can contain up to eight times, indicating when the program pointed to by the .pf file was previously run prior to the last run time. When generating timeline output, the pref.pl tool will display all of the available times embedded within the Windows 8 .pf files.

Registry data

As we've discussed several times throughout this book, the Windows Registry can hold a great deal of information that can be extremely valuable to an analyst. Further, that information may not solely be available as Registry key LastWrite times. There are a number of Registry values that contain time stamps, available as binary data at specific offsets depending on the value, as strings that we need to parse, etc. As such, it may be useful to have a number of different tools available to us to extract this information and include it in our timelines.

Perhaps one of the easiest ways to incorporate Registry key LastWrite time listings within a timeline is to use the regtime.pl Perl script (part of the additional materials available for this book). I was originally asked some time ago to create regtime.pl in order to parse through a Registry hive file and list all of the keys and their LastWrite times in bodyfile format; that is, to have the script output the data in a format similar what fls.exe produces. I wrote this script and provided it to Rob, and it has been included in the SANS Investigative Forensic Toolkit (SIFT) workstation (found online at http://computer-forensics.sans.org/community/downloads/), as well as Kristinn's log2timeline framework. A bit ago, I modified this script to bypass the bodyfile format and output its information directly to TLN format. An example of how to use this updated version of regtime.pl appears as follows:

```
C:\tools > regtime.pl -m HKEY_USER -r NTUSER.DAT -s System -u User>
reg_event.txt
```

Similar to the fls.exe tool discussed earlier in this chapter, regtime.pl includes a "-m" switch to indicate the "mount point" of the Registry hive being parsed, which is prepended to the key path. In the above example, I used "HKEY_USER" when accessing a user's Registry hive; had the target been a Software or System hive, I would have need to use "HKLM/Software" or "HKLM/System," respectively. The "-r" switch allows you to specify the path to the hive of interest (again, either extracted from an acquired image or accessible by mounting the image as a volume on your analysis system). As you would expect, the "-s" and "-u" switches allow you to designate the system and user fields within the TLN format, as appropriate; the script will automatically populate the source field with the "REG" identifier.

With respect to parsing time-stamped information from within Registry values, there are two options that I like to use: one involves RegRipper, described in Chapter 5. By making slight modifications to rip.pl (new version number is 20110516) and adding the ability to add a system and user name to the TLN output, I can then also modify existing RegRipper plugins to output their data in TLN format. For example, I modified the userassist.pl RegRipper plugin to modify its output format into the five-field TLN format and renamed the plugin "userassist_tln. pl." I could then run the plugin using the following command line:

```
C:\tools> rip.pl -r D:\cases\test\ntuser.dat -p userassist_tln -s
SERVER -u USER
```

An excerpt of the output of this command appears as follows in TLN format:

```
1163016851|REG|SERVER|USER|UserAssist - UEME_RUNCPL:SYSDM.CPL (4)
1163015716|REG|SERVER|USER|UserAssist - UEME_RUNCPL:NCPA.CPL (3)
1163015694|REG|SERVER|USER|UserAssist - UEME_RUNPATH:C:\Putty\
putty.exe (1)
```

Clearly we'd want to redirect this output to the appropriate events file (i.e., "» events.txt") for inclusion in our timeline.

There are a number of RegRipper plugins that provide timeline-format output, many of which can provide valuable insight and granularity to your timeline. It's very easy to determine which plugins provide this information by typing the following command:

```
Rip.pl -l -c | find "_tln"
```

What this command does is list all of the available RegRipper plugins in .csv format, so that each entry is on a single line, and it then runs the output through the *find* command, looking for any plugins that include "_tln" in the name. The output of the above command will appear in the console, so feel free to redirect the output to a file for keeping and review. If you send the output to a .csv file, you can open it in Excel and sort on the hive to which the plugin applies (System, Software, NTUSER.DAT, USRCLASS.DAT, etc.), making it easier to pick which ones may be applicable to your analysis and you'd like to run.

Another means for adding any time-stamped information (other than just from the Registry) to a timeline events file is to use the graphical user interface (GUI) tln. pl Perl script, as illustrated in Figure 7.6.

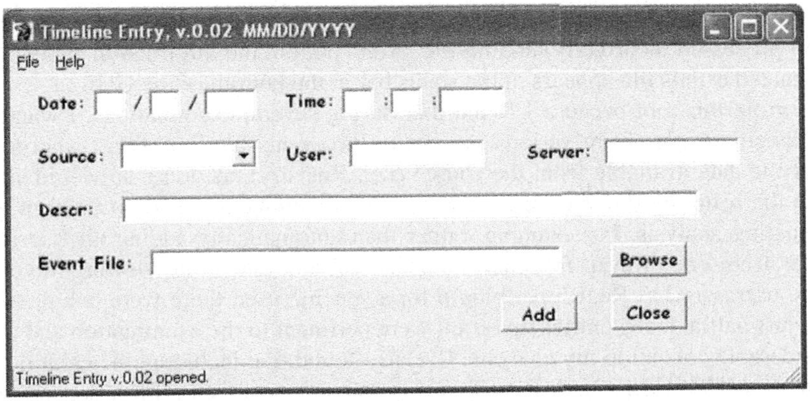

FIGURE 7.6

Tln.pl GUI.

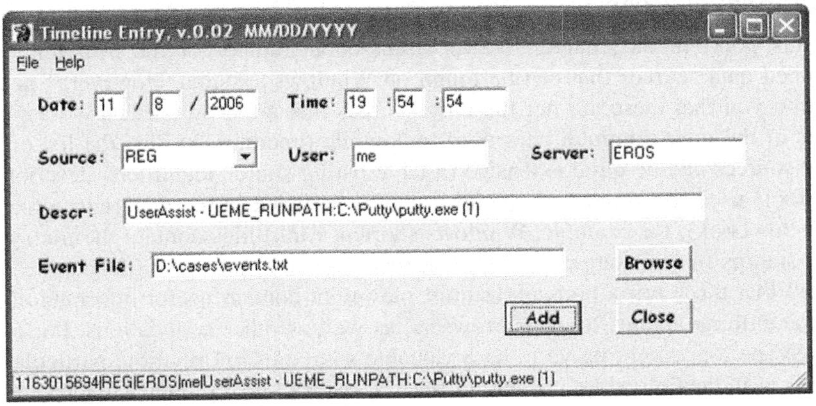

FIGURE 7.7

Tln.pl GUI populated with data.

Okay, how would you use the GUI? Let's say that rather than running the userassist_tln.pl plugin mentioned above, we instead ran the userassist2.pl plugin against the same hive file, and based on the nature of our investigation we were only in the entry that appears as follows:

```
Wed Nov 8 19:54:54 2006 Z
UEME_RUNPATH:C:\Putty\putty.exe (1)
```

Opening the tln.pl GUI, we can then manually enter the appropriate information into the interface, as illustrated in Figure 7.7.

Once you've added the information in the appropriate format (notice that the date format is "MM/DD/YYYY," and a reminder even appears in the window title bar; entering the first two values out of order will result in the date information being processed incorrectly) and hit the "Add" button, the information added to the designated events file appears in the status bar at the bottom of the GUI.

I wrote this tool because I found that during several examinations, I wanted to add specific events from various sources to the events file, but didn't want to add all of the data available from the source (i.e., Registry), as doing so would simply make the resulting timeline larger and a bit more cumbersome to go through when conducting analysis. For example, rather than automatically adding all UserAssist entries from one or even from several users, I found that while viewing the output of the userassist2.pl RegRipper plugin for a specific user, there were one or two or even just half a dozen entries that I felt were pertinent to the examination and added considerable context to my analysis. I've also found that including the creation date from the MFT $FILE_NAME attribute for one or two specific files, depending on the goals of my exam, proved to be much more useful than simply dumping all of the available MFT data into the timeline.

Additional sources

To this point in the chapter, we've discussed a number of the available time-stamped data sources that can be found on Windows systems. However, I need to caution you that these are not the only sources that are available; they are simply some of the most common ones used to compile timelines. In fact, the list of possible sources can be quite extensive (a table listing source identifiers, descriptions, and tools used to extract time-stamped data is included in the materials associated with this book); for example, Windows shortcut (.lnk) files contain the file system time stamps of their target files embedded within their structure. Earlier we mentioned that the Firefox bookmarks.html file might contain useful information, and the same thing applies to other browsers, as well as other applications. For example, Skype logs might prove to be a valuable source of information, particularly if there are indications that a user (via the UserAssist subkey data) launched Skype prior to or during the time frame of interest.

Speaking of UserAssist data from user Registry hive files, another data source worth mentioning is VSCs. As illustrated and discussed in Chapter 3, a great deal of time-stamped data can be retrieved from previous copies of files maintained by the Volume Shadow Copy Service (VSS), particularly on Vista and Windows 7 systems. One of the examples we saw in Chapter 3 involved retrieving UserAssist data from the hive file within a user's profile. Consider an examination where you found that the user ran an image viewer application, and that application maintains an MRU list of accessed files. We know that the copy of the user's NTUSER.DAT hive file would contain information in the UserAssist key regarding how many times that viewer application was launched, as well as the last date that it was launched. We also know that the MRU list for the viewer application would indicate the date and time that the most recently viewed image was opened in the application. As we saw in Chapter 3, data available in previous versions of the user's NTUSER.DAT hive file would provide not just indications of previous dates that the viewer application was run, but also the dates and times that other images were viewed. Depending upon the goals of your examination, it may be a valuable exercise to mount available VSCs and extract data for inclusion in your timeline.

So, this chapter should not be considered an exhaustive list of data sources, but should instead illustrate how to easily extract the necessary time-stamped data from a number of perhaps the most critical sources. Once you have that data, all that remains is to convert it into a normalized format for inclusion in your timeline.

TIP

Data Volume

The only drawback to using multiple data sources (and the benefits far outweigh any drawbacks) is the potential volume of timeline data. While a timeline of less than 100 KB is much less data to go through than a 250-GB hard drive, it can still be a great deal of data. For example, I've seen a number of Windows XP systems where there was simply a lot of file system activity when System Restore Points were created and deleted. One way to address this is to parse the resulting events file with tools such as *grep -v*, which specifies inverse matches or selects nonmatching lines. Writing a regular expression that parses through the events file, looking for, and removing all of the file system activity for the Restore Points directory can reduce the volume of data that you then need to analyze. I would suggest, however, that techniques such as this are used wisely; depending on the nature of your investigation and the syntax of your grep command, you could inadvertently exclude pertinent data from your timeline.

Parsing events into a timeline

Once we've created our events file, we're ready to sort through and parse those events into a timeline, which we can then use to further our analysis. So, at this point, we've accessed some of the various data sources available on a Windows system and created a text-based, pipe-delimited, TLN-format events file. The contents of this file might appear as follows:

```
1087549224|FILE|SERVER||MACB [0] C:/$Volume
1087578198|FILE|SERVER||MACB [0] C:/AUTOEXEC.BAT
1087578213|FILE|SERVER||..C. [194] C:/boot.ini
1087576049|FILE|SERVER||MA.. [194] C:/boot.ini
1087549489|FILE|SERVER||...B [194] C:/boot.ini
1087578198|FILE|SERVER||MACB [0] C:/CONFIG.SYS
1200617554|FILE|SERVER||.A.. [56] C:/Documents and Settings
1087586327|FILE|SERVER||M.C. [56] C:/Documents and Settings
1200617616|EVT|SERVER|S-1-5-18|Service Control
Manager/7035;Info;IMAPI CD-Burning COM Service,start
1200617616|EVT|SERVER|N/A|Service Control Manager/7036;Info;IMAPI
CD-Burning COM Service,running
1200617616|EVT|SERVER|N/A|Service Control Manager/7036;Info;IMAPI
CD-Burning COM Service,stopped
```

```
1200617621|EVT|SERVER|N/A|EventLog/6006;Info;
1087585113|PREF|SERVER||AGENTSVR.EXE-002E45AB.pf last run (1)
1087602543|PREF|SERVER||CACLS.EXE-25504E4A.pf last run (2)
1200617562|PREF|SERVER||CMD.EXE-087B4001.pf last run (3)
```

TIP

Creating Events Files

Just a reminder, albeit an important one—we don't always have to throw everything and the kitchen sink into a timeline. Sometimes, particularly based on the goals of our analysis, we may not want to start with everything and instead start with specific items. For example, if information about logins to a Windows system is important to my examination, I will start by using RegRipper to parse the Security Registry hive in order to determine the audit policy; if logon/account logon events are not being audited, then it doesn't necessarily make sense to attempt to parse the Security Event Log for those events. Even so, I will also use the evtrpt.pl Perl script to parse the Security Event Log and see if there are any events related to logons available, just to be sure.

We should be ready to parse the events file into a timeline, the purpose of which is to sort through the events within the events file, grouping those that occur within the same time together, and then sorting them and presenting them in an understandable format. I've written a script for this purpose, aptly named parse.pl, and the simplest, most basic way to use this script is to run it against your events file using a command line similar to the following:

```
C:\tools > parse.pl -f D:\case\events.txt > D:\case\tln.txt
```

This command produces an ASCII-based timeline file with all of the times sorted with the most recent time first, and with all events within the same time grouped together. The output looks like:

```
Time
Src System User Description
Src System User Description
Time
Src System User Description
```

An example of what this might look like in a "real" timeline file appears as follows:

```
Fri Jun 18 19:16:02 2004 Z
FILE SERVER - MACB [12864] C:/WINDOWS/Prefetch/DFRGNTFS.EXE-
269967DF.pf
Fri Jun 18 19:16:01 2004 Z
FILE SERVER - MACB [8622] C:/WINDOWS/Prefetch/DEFRAG.EXE-273F131E.pf
Fri Jun 18 19:15:52 2004 Z
FILE SERVER -.A.. [99328] C:/WINDOWS/system32/dfrgntfs.exe
FILE SERVER -.A.. [51200] C:/WINDOWS/system32/dfrgres.dll
PREF SERVER - DFRGNTFS.EXE-269967DF.pf last run (1)
```

It should be easy to see from this timeline format how the five-field TLN format plays right into not just collecting and correlating the events, but also displaying them for analysis. Again, the times are formatted in a human-readable format, based on UTC. Normalizing the times to this format allows us to incorporate data from multiple sources independent of time zone or location and present the information in a uniform manner. All of the events that occurred within that second are then listed below the time value, slightly indented. This text-based format allows you to browse through the timeline using any text editor (as opposed to requiring a specific editor or viewer). I use UltraEdit, as it's very good at handling large files, and if I find some text of interest that I want to search on, I can highlight the text and hit the F3 key to automatically jump to the next instance of that text.

The parse.pl Perl script also provides some additional capabilities that can be very useful to you. For example, if you know that you're looking for all events that occurred within a particular time window, you can use the "-r" switch to specify a time window for the events that will be displayed within the timeline. For example:

```
C:\tools > parse.pl -f events.txt -r 02/12/2008-03/16/2008 > tln_
short.txt
```

The above command line will parse the events file, but only place events that occurred between 00:00:00 February 12, 2008, and 23:59:59 March 16, 2008, into the timeline file.

Another option that I recently added to parse.pl is the ability to output the timeline information to CSV or .csv format, which would allow you to open the output file in a spreadsheet application such as MS Office Excel or OpenOffice Calc. When the information is written to the timeline file, all five fields are included on each line, separated by commas, so each row in the spreadsheet application begins with a time value in the "YYYYMMDDhhmmss" format. Spreadsheets have long been used to view and analyze this sort of time-stamped information, although in the past the information was populated manually. One of the aspects of this approach that I really think is useful to a lot of analysts is that the analyst can highlight specific events with color coding and can even add notes into a sixth column (e.g., adding MS KnowledgeBase articles as references, notes to clarify the information that is available in the timeline).

The parse.pl script has two additional capabilities. First, the "-o" switch will list the timeline with the oldest events; by default, the most recent events will appear first. Second, by default, the script will automatically remove duplicate entries; this comes in handy when you've added data from VSCs and not all of it has changed. You may parse some data sources from within a VSC, such as the UserAssist information for a user (as discussed previously in this chapter), and some entries have the exact same values in all five fields of the TLN output. You likely don't want this duplicate data populating your timeline, so the parse.pl script will automatically remove these duplicate entries.

So now that we have a timeline, how do we go about analyzing it? I think that the best way to do this is with an example. An excerpt from a timeline created from a system that had experienced a malware infection (trimmed to make it easier to view and with slight modifications) appears as follows (times removed to make the information easier to view):

```
FILE SYSTEM -...B [720] C:/WINDOWS/system32/irrngife.dat
FILE SYSTEM -...B [506] C:/WINDOWS/system32/msgsvuc.dat
FILE SYSTEM -...B [2700] C:/WINDOWS/system32/kbdrxyl.dat
FILE SYSTEM -...B [0] C:/Documents and Settings/user/Local Settings/
Temp/~~x103D.tmp
REG SYSTEM - - M... HKLM/Software/Classes/CLSID/{GUID}
REG SYSTEM - - M... HKLM/Software/Classes/CLSID/{GUID}/
InprocServer32
REG SYSTEM - - M... HKLM/Software/Microsoft/Windows/.../
ShellIconOverlayIdentifiers/msgsvuc
```

Other portions of the timeline appeared similar to what you see above, with specific Registry keys being created and grouped along with specific .dat files being created (remember, "B" refers to the "born" date) within the system32 directory. By looking for groupings similar to this throughout the timeline, you can distinguish between infections and other events where the installed AV product detected a malicious file and deleted it before any further actions could occur.

Thoughts on visualization

I've talked to a number of analysts and read questions posted to online forums regarding the use of visualization tools and techniques with timeline analysis. Most of these questions seem to center around entering all of the available event data into some sort of visualization model or tool, so that the analyst can then perform analysis. This isn't something that, at this point, I can see being entirely feasible or useful toward furthering analysis.

Yes, I know that having some sort of visualization tool seems as if it would make things much easier for the analyst, but we have to keep in mind that Windows systems are extremely verbose, even when they're just sitting there, apparently idle. By themselves, Windows systems will perform housekeeping functions, creating and deleting System Restore Points and VSCs, installing updates, performing limited defrags of the hard drive, etc. Once you include some of the applications and their automated functions (Java and Apple products, among others, automatically look for updates), it becomes clear that there's a lot that goes on on Windows systems when no one's around. So if you think back to Chapter 1 where we discussed Least Frequency of Occurrence, it quickly becomes clear that any sort of visualization mechanism for representing the abundance of time-stamped data available on a Windows system will quickly not simply overwhelm the analyst, but also completely mask the critical events of interest.

What this really comes down to is how an analyst uses timelines for analysis; even so, once analysis has been performed, the analyst's job isn't complete—her findings still need to be reported and presented to the "customer." Most often pertinent excerpts of timelines are included in the report as a narrative or encapsulated in a table, although there are templates for spreadsheet applications that will allow you to create visual timelines; these should only be used after the pertinent events have been clearly identified; otherwise, everyone (the analyst, the customer, etc.) will be overwhelmed by the sheer volume of available data.

Case Study

After all of this discussion, it would be a good idea to do a complete walk-through of the process for creating a timeline from an acquired image. As such, this will require an image to use and a great place to go online to get one is Lance Mueller's first forensic practical posted via his blog (found online at http://www.forensickb. com/2008/01/forensic-practical.html). The first thing you will need to do is to download the 400-MB expert witness format (EWF, also known as "Encase" format) image, and then open it in FTK Imager (get version 3 from the AccessData downloads page if you don't already have it) and reacquire the image into a 1.5-GB raw/dd format image file named "xpimg.001." We'll be using this name throughout the rest of this case study; if you use a different name, use that name. Also, from the scenario that Lance provided on his web site, this appears to be a malware-related issue, so this would likely be a good opportunity to develop a timeline.

Once you have the raw/dd format image available, you'll see when you run the *mmls* command described earlier in this chapter that you get the "Invalid sector address" error message, which is an indication that a partition table wasn't found. As such, you can proceed directly to using the *fls* command without the need for an offset to a specific partition. You can use the following command to create the bodyfile from the file system metadata within the image:

```
D:\tools\tsk > fls -i raw -f ntfs -r -p -m C:/ d:\case\xpimg.001 >
d:\case\bodyfile.txt
```

We can then use FTK Imager version 3 to mount the image on our analysis system (as the F:\ volume) and use rip.pl to obtain the system name, using the following command:

```
C:\tools > rip.pl -r f:\[root]\windows\system32\config\system -p
compname
```

From this command, you will see that the system name is "REG-OIPK81M2WC8." You can then use the following command to parse the bodyfile into the events file:

```
C:\tools > bodyfile.pl -f d:\case\bodyfile.txt -s REG-OIPK81M2WC8 >
d:\case\events.txt
```

At this point, you've created your initial events file, and you can then go about adding Event Logs records and Prefetch file metadata as additional data sources using the following commands:

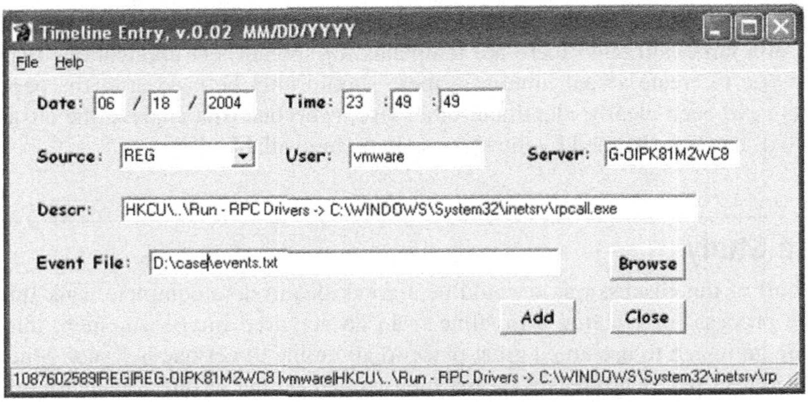

FIGURE 7.8

Adding an event to the events file with tln.pl.

```
C:\tools > evtparse.pl -d f:\[root]\Windows\system32\config -t »
D:\case\events.txt
C:\tools > pref.pl -d f:\[root]\Windows\Prefetch -s REG-OIPK81M2WC8
-t » D:\case\events.txt
```

As part of your process for detecting malware, you run RegRipper against various hive files available within the image, including the NTUSER.DAT hive for the "vmware" user. When examining the RegRipper output file from this hive for malware autostart locations (something you remembered from Chapter 6), you notice an unusual value in the CurrentVersion\Run key and enter that single entry into your events file using tln.pl, as illustrated in Figure 7.8.

Based on this, you then decided to add the UserAssist subkey information for that user to your events file using the following command:

```
C:\tools > rip.pl -r "f:\[root]\Documents and Settings\vmware\
ntuser.dat" -u vmware -s REG-OIPK81M2WC8 -p userassist_tln » D:\
case\events.txt
```

You then run regtime.pl against the System and Software hives from within the image in order to add the time-stamped data from these Registry hives to your events file using the following commands:

```
C:\tools > regtime.pl -r f:\[root]\Windows\system32\config\software
-m HKLM/Software -s REG-OIPK81M2WC8 » D:\case\events.txt
C:\tools > regtime.pl -r f:\[root]\Windows\system32\config\system
-m HKLM/System -s REG-OIPK81M2WC8 » D:\case\events.txt
```

At this point, you have a pretty comprehensive events file compiled, and you decide to parse it into a timeline. Using this technique, you can take an iterative approach, by adding additional events as necessary to the events file and regenerating the timeline file, as necessary. To create your timeline file, you can use the following command:

```
C:\tools > parse.pl -f D:\case\events.txt > D:\case\tln.txt
```

You then open your newly created timeline file in a text editor and search for inetsrv\rpcall.exe within the timeline and find the following entries:

```
Fri Jun 18 23:49:49 2004 Z
 FILE REG-OIPK81M2WC8-..C. [524288] C:/Documents and Settings/
vmware/NTUSER.DAT
 FILE REG-OIPK81M2WC8- MACB [21396] C:/WINDOWS/Prefetch/SMS.EXE-
01DC4541.pf
 FILE REG-OIPK81M2WC8-...B [15870] C:/WINDOWS/Prefetch/RPCALL.EXE-
394030D7.pf
 FILE REG-OIPK81M2WC8- M.C. [152] C:/WINDOWS/system32/inetsrv
 FILE REG-OIPK81M2WC8-.A.. [16384] C:/WINDOWS/system32/ping.exe
 PREF REG-OIPK81M2WC8- PING.EXE-31216D26.pf last run (1)
 PREF REG-OIPK81M2WC8- RPCALL.EXE-394030D7.pf last run (2)
 PREF REG-OIPK81M2WC8- SMS.EXE-01DC4541.pf last run (2)
 REG REG-OIPK81M2WC8 vmware - UserAssist - UEME_RUNPATH:C:\System
Volume Information\...\RP2\snapshot\Repository\FS\sms.exe (1)
 REG REG-OIPK81M2WC8 vmware - HKCU\..\Run - RPC Drivers - >
C:\WINDOWS\System32\inetsrv\rpcall.exe
 REG REG-OIPK81M2WC8- M... HKLM/Software/Microsoft/Windows/
CurrentVersion/Run
 REG REG-OIPK81M2WC8- M... HKLM/Software/Microsoft/Windows/
CurrentVersion/RunServices
 REG REG-OIPK81M2WC8- M... HKLM/System/ControlSet001/Services/
SharedAccess/Parameters
 REG REG-OIPK81M2WC8- M... HKLM/System/ControlSet001/Services/
SharedAccess/Parameters/FirewallPolicy
 REG REG-OIPK81M2WC8- M... HKLM/System/ControlSet001/Services/
SharedAccess/Parameters/FirewallPolicy/StandardProfile
 REG REG-OIPK81M2WC8- M... HKLM/System/ControlSet001/Services/
SharedAccess/Parameters/FirewallPolicy/StandardProfile/
AuthorizedApplications
 REG REG- OIPK81M2WC8- M... HKLM/System/ControlSet001/Services/
SharedAccess/Parameters/FirewallPolicy/StandardProfile/
AuthorizedApplications/List
```

Noticing the entries at the end of the listing that point to the firewall settings on the system (from the System hive), you then run RegRipper against the System hive and looking at the firewall settings output for the report file, find the following:

```
C:\WINDOWS\System32\inetsrv\rpcall.exe - > C:\WINDOWS\System32\
inetsrv\rpcall.exe::Enabled:RPC Drivers
```

So at this point in your analysis, you have likely found a good candidate for the malware thought to be on the system; in this case, the rpcall.exe file. Not only that, you have additional context available regarding how the malware was activated on the system; specifically, from the above timeline listing, you see the following:

```
vmware - UserAssist - UEME_RUNPATH:C:\System Volume
Information\...\RP2\snapshot\Repository\FS\sms.exe (1)
```

This indicates that sms.exe was run from the "vmware" user context, but the path indicates that the executable file itself was found within a System Restore Point (RP2). You know that users should not normally be able to access this directory path, let alone launch executable files. An additional search of the timeline indicates that the tool cacls.exe, which can be used to modify permissions of various objects (files, directories, Registry keys) on Windows systems, was run shortly before the timeline listing we see above.

While this is a brief case study, my hope is that it serves to demonstrate how powerful and beneficial timeline analysis can be, and that it encourages analysts to explore the use of this as viable analysis technique. Not only does it demonstrate how timelines can be used to detect the presence of malware within an image (often much faster than or even in lieu of AV), but it also illustrates the concept of context that we discussed earlier in this chapter, as well as how timelines can provide an increased level of relative confidence with respect to the various data sources used to populate the timeline. Finally, while the original image file was 1.5 GB in size, the resulting timeline file is just under 6 MB and compresses down to 511 KB.

SUMMARY

Properly employed, timelines can be an extremely valuable analysis tool. The nature of our complex operating systems, applications, and various other data sources almost necessitates an open-source approach to creating tools for parsing time-stamped data and converting it into a normalized format. Timelines can provide and facilitate a level of visibility into examinations that analysts have not seen using commercial forensic analysis applications, in cases ranging from malware infections, to suspected intrusions, to violations of acceptable use policies and contraband image cases, as well as the more "advanced" incidents that have been discussed in the media.

The open-source approach also means that an analyst isn't restricted to a specific analysis platform; many of the available tools and scripts, including those discussed in this chapter, can be run on Linux and MacOS X platforms, often without any modification.

However, analysts should keep in mind that as versatile and powerful a technique as this is, it's still just a tool and isn't necessarily something that would or should be employed in every situation. Be sure that you fully understand the goals of your analysis before you decide to employ any particular tool, including timeline analysis.

Finally, in this chapter, we've discussed a number of tools that can be used for creating timelines. These tools simply make up and implement the approach that I've used to create timelines, and this chapter has been about the *process* of creating a timeline, not about tools themselves. That being said, all of the tools discussed are command line tools, and I'm aware that there are a good number of analysts who aren't entirely familiar with how to use or run command line tools; that's okay. Most of the tools we've discussed are Perl scripts, and the source code for these tools is provided online with the materials for this book. If at any point you have questions about what the tool is capable of doing, or what options are available within the tool, you can open the Perl scripts in an editor (Notepad++ is a great option). Another option is that for your convenience, I've provided standalone Windows executables for each tool ("compiled" using Perl2Exe), and you can type the command by itself, or followed by "-h" or "/?," to see what options are available.

Correlating Artifacts

8

INFORMATION IN THIS CHAPTER

- How-Tos

INTRODUCTION

So far in this book, we've discussed a number of artifacts and data sources that analysts can look to within a Windows system in order to help address the goals of their analysis. However, all we've really done so far is point to various individual artifacts; what we haven't really addressed to a great extent is how these artifacts can be correlated and combined during analysis, allowing the examiner to "paint a picture" and address the goals of their exam.

In order to help analysts, particularly those new to the industry, see how various artifacts can be correlated and used in combination, I thought that it might be useful to present analysis examples in the format of "How-Tos," brief descriptions of various, apparently disparate artifacts that can be brought together like links in a chain. While working on writing this book, I started posting "HowTo" articles to my blog (found online at http://windowsir.blogspot.com), and these articles started to receive some attention from within the digital forensics and incident response community. For a while, I've been aware (through writing blog articles and books, as well as presenting and teaching courses) that folks just like to see and hear things like this, in order to get insight into how other examiners are going about analyzing various artifacts and types of cases. As such, I thought I'd extend some of them here in my book, and add a couple of others, in hopes of providing a view into how these types of examinations might be pursued, as well as generating discussion along these lines. I think it's important that analysts share what they do (their processes), and engage in exchanging this sort of information with others, because that's really the only way we'll improve our ability to conduct analysis (be it digital forensics or incident response) in a timely and more thorough, comprehensive manner.

NOTE

Sharing Processes

There's a big difference between sharing processes and sharing data, and I'm not sure that most analysts make that distinction. In my experience, most analysts seem reticent to "share," because they feel that they can't disclose specific details and information from or about their cases; this seems to be particularly true with respect to law enforcement analysts, and those working for the government. I can tell you that I, for one, do not want to know the graphic details of a law enforcement case, such as names and case-specific information; I think that most analysts would agree with me. However, I don't see what the issue is with sharing information about analysis processes, particularly when doing so benefits so many others.

Think about it—if you're always doing the same thing, the same sort of analysis, how do you get better? Let's say that you work for a company in an internal position, and you perform investigations mandated by the human resources director, with respect to violations of acceptable use policies (AUPs). If you engage with other analysts and exchange findings with them, you may find new artifacts to look for or a new perspective on the type of analysis that you do. What happens if your company gets hit with an intrusion? If all you've done is AUP investigations, responding to an intrusion is going to be a new experience, but it can be easier if you've seen different perspectives from other analysts.

Again, I hope these "How-Tos" are useful, provide insight as to how different examinations might be conducted, and ultimately serve to generate discussion amongst analysts within the community.

How-Tos

With the "How-Tos," my hope is to provide a starting point, not just for examiners to begin their analysis, but also for discussion, and the exchange of ideas regarding analysis processes. My thoughts are that the way that we all improve our abilities as analysts—to become capable of conducting more thorough and comprehensive analysis, in a timelier manner—is for analysts to engage, and to discuss this topic, and any issues that they may have.

Many times, when I've attended a conference, I think I will have an opportunity for my mind to be focused on something else other than the analysis that I've been working on; this is often far from the case. Rather, what tends to happen is that the analysis I've been working on—either a current exam, or one that was finished six or eight months prior—is still quietly simmering on the backburner of my mind. I will go to a conference and listen to a presentation, a question asked, or a snippet of conversation, and suddenly something will click. When this happens, I want to discuss it with other analysts, to see if they're seeing the same thing, to see how they might use or take advantage of the information during an exam, etc. I honestly believe that it's this type of engagement that allows everyone involved to become a better examiner. It's not solely about hearing how other examiners go about their analysis; rather, we need to become engaged. When we hear a "war story" or a "case study" about how someone discovered something new, or how they analyzed a fairly prevalent malware infection, the best way to take advantage of that information is to process it in the context of what we do, and from our own perspective, and then start asking questions. What if you don't have or use the same commercial application that the speaker was using? How would you go about retrieving or analyzing the same data? Is there a freeware alternative? It's only through this sort of engagement amongst analysts that we can all become better and more thorough at our jobs.

Correlating Windows shortcuts to USB devices

Perhaps one of the least understood and most difficult aspects of analysis is correlating apparently disparate artifacts in order to "paint a picture" or "complete a story" for your examination. For example, identifying USB devices that had been connected to a system, and to which users they were available has been published and understood (for the most part) for some time, but this isn't where analysis of these artifacts stops. When analyzing the device artifacts, we may need to know more about the usage of those devices, such as the drive letter to which the device was mapped. We may not be able to easily obtain this information simply from a cursory review of the *MountedDevices* key within the System Registry hive, as the drive letter may have been reused for multiple devices (it turns out that this is often the case; the drive letter "E:\," for example, has been assigned to more than half a dozen different devices at different times on my own system). As such, in order to really understand the full breadth of USB device detection within an image acquired from a Windows system, it's very important to understand the full breadth of artifacts, and how they can all be used together during an exam.

We know from analysis of USB devices on Windows 7 and 8 systems that there is a valuable key within the Software hive named *EMDMgmt*; the full path is *Microsoft\Windows NT\CurrentVersion\EMDMgmt*. According to information available from the Microsoft web site, this key is associated with ReadyBoost, a capability of more modern Microsoft systems (Vista and beyond) to examine USB devices for suitability for use as external random access memory. The subkeys beneath this key include information about various USB thumb drives, as well as drive enclosures, that had been connected to the system. Specifically, keys associated with USB thumb drives have names that start with _??_USBSTOR#, and drive enclosures have names that start with either an underscore or several letters. The names can be split into individual elements separated by underscores, and the last two elements of the name are the volume name, if available, and the volume serial number, in decimal format. For USB thumb drives, the subkey names contain the device ID, as well as the device serial number, just as we usually find beneath the *Enum\USBStor*, also within the System hive.

NOTE

Signatures and Serial Numbers

There are important distinctions that must be made and understood between the various signatures and serial numbers that are available, specifically with respect to USB devices. A big issue faced by the digital forensics community at large is the lack of specificity of language, which leads to significant misunderstanding and confusion.

A USB device will have a device serial number, which is embedded within the firmware of the device itself, and is not accessible in the memory storage area of the device. It can, however, be modified through the use of the appropriate application programming interfaces (APIs) or firmware updates, usually available from the manufacturer. The point, however, is that this information—the device serial number found in *Enum\USBStor* subkeys within the System hive file—is read from the device firmware. The volume serial number is a value that is assigned to a volume (C:\, D:\, E:\, etc.) when the volume is formatted, and can easily be changed by reformatting the volume. Volume serial numbers can be found embedded in application Prefetch files, Windows shortcuts/LNK files, as well as within *EMDMgmt* subkey names. A disk signature is part of a physical disk, and is a 4-byte value found at offset $0 \times 1b8$ (440 in decimal format) within the master boot record of the disk. Disk signatures can be found in some value data beneath the *MountedDevices* key in the System hive.

When a user accesses a volume or a file on a USB device, a Windows shortcut (LNK file) is created in either the *AppData\Roaming\Microsoft\Windows\Recent* or..*Office\Recent* folder within the user's profile folder, depending upon the type of file that was accessed. The format of these files includes, in most cases, the volume name (if one is available) and volume serial number of the volume where the file was located. By correlating the volume serial numbers from the *EMDMgmt* Registry subkeys to those found in the LNK files, we're able to not only determine the drive letters assigned to the USB device volumes, but we're also able to get insight into the directory structure within that volume. As noted in Chapter 4, Windows 7 and 8 systems also include *.automaticDestinations-ms Jump Lists (within the *AppData\ Roaming\Microsoft\Windows\Recent\AutomaticDestinations* folder in the user profile), which are compound documents that incorporate streams that follow the LNK file format, and therefore also contain volume name (if available), volume serial number, and drive type (in this case, we're interested in removable drives) information, as well. An example of this information extracted from a Jump List LNK stream is illustrated in Figure 8.1.

Drive Type	DRIVE_REMOVABLE
Serial No.	E6BE863F
Volume Name	USB20FD

FIGURE 8.1

Drive type, volume serial number, and volume name extracted from a Windows 7 Jump List LNK stream.

Correlating the volume serial numbers from the *EMDMgmt* subkeys to those found within the user's LNK files or Jump List streams can serve a number of purposes for the analyst. For one, this can provide information regarding the drive letter assigned to the device, which may not be available through analysis of the "current" System hive (via the *MountedDevices* key values), nor those hives within available volume shadow copies (VSCs). Second, this information allows the analyst to determine the use of a specific device, particularly if that device was collected and was not reformatted by the user. Finally, this allows the analyst to determine specific folder structures found within the volume, which can then be correlated with other artifacts, such as shellbags or *UserAssist* entries, to develop a more detailed understanding of what existed within the volume.

TIP

Shellbags Artifacts

Yet another indicator as to why understanding the differences between various versions of Windows is so vitally important is illustrated in the shellbags artifacts. For one, on Windows XP, the shellbags artifacts are maintained in the NTUSER.DAT hive file, while on Windows 7 and 8, they're found in the user's USRCLASS.DAT hive file. On Windows XP systems, the data beneath the *Software\Microsoft\Windows\ShellNoRoam\BagMRU* subkeys can be correlated, via the *NodeSlot* value, to the values beneath the *Software\Microsoft\Windows\ShellNoRoam\Bags\{NodeSlot}\Shell* keys whose names start with "ItemPos." These values have been found to contain what amounts to a directory listing of the accessed folder, stored in shell item format within the binary value data. For example, in practical exercise available online, the user on Windows XP system accessed a System Restore Point and launched a malware sample; the shellbags artifacts from the system not only illustrated that user accessed the Restore Point folder (as did other artifacts on the system), but they also contained a listing of the files located in that folder. I've been told by several investigators that they've been able to use this same information, when correlated with other artifacts, to illustrate a user's access to TrueCrypt encrypted volumes, as well as the contents of those volumes. Again, this particular type of artifact appears to be available on Windows XP systems, and not on Vista, Windows 7, or Windows 8 systems.

Demonstrate user access to files

There are a great number of artifacts that allow an analyst to see the names, and in some cases the paths, of files that a user accessed. This information can be extremely useful in a variety of situations, ranging from a quick triage (did a user access a file in particular) to a full investigation in which the use of anti-forensics techniques (deletion of content, use of encrypted volumes, etc.) may be suspected. I am not a sworn, badged police officer, but I have assisted officers in cases involving illicit images by reviewing various data sources and providing the names (and paths) of files the user accessed, and in some cases, when the files were accessed. In such cases, I leave the actual file content up to those better suited to address and assess that—I simply provide file name and path information using the various data sources to which I can get access.

Beyond that, however, demonstrating user access to files can be addressed through examining a number of artifacts, and this can be useful to an analyst in a number of ways. First, most analysts are familiar with the fact that beginning with Vista, updating of the last accessed times on files, through normal user access to the files, was disabled by default. Given this, it can be valuable to determine other means by which to determine when a user accessed a file. Second, there are tools available for "cleaning up" information about files that a user accessed; these may be referred to as "anti-forensics" tools. Having additional artifacts to examine that may not be addressed by these tools can be very valuable to an analyst. Finally, many of the artifacts that are available persist well beyond when the files themselves are no longer available (deleted, external drive is reformatted, network drive no longer available, etc.).

When a user accesses a file, such as a document, image, video, and just about anything other than launching an executable file, a great deal actually goes on "under the hood." For example, if a user double-clicks a file to open it, most analysts are familiar with the fact that a Windows shortcut/LNK file is created. On Windows 7 and 8 systems, an *.automaticDestinations-ms Jump List is created; the application ID portion of the Jump List name identifies the application that launched to open the file, and when the file was accessed can be found in the DestList stream embedded in the compound document format of the Jump List file.

There are a number of Registry locations where information is maintained about files that the user accessed, and many of these are "most recently used" (MRU) lists, which means that under normal conditions, with no fiddling or modification by the user, the LastWrite time of the Registry key refers to when the file listed first in the MRU list was accessed. This also means that when other files were accessed may be determined by viewing the key contents found in VSCs.

Applications can maintain their own MRU listings, and are most often associated with a specific user. For example, MS Paint maintains an MRU list of files within the user's NTUSER.DAT Registry hive, beneath the *Applets* key (use the RegRipper *applets.pl* plugin to extract and view this information). Adobe Reader maintains its own MRU listing, as does the MS Office suite of applications. I have MS Office 2010 installed on my authoring system, and the path to the MS Office applications key within my NTUSER.DAT hive is *Software\Microsoft\Office\14.0*. Beneath this key, each of the individual Office applications that I have installed (Excel, PowerPoint, Word, etc.) has a *File MRU* key, and the values are listed by

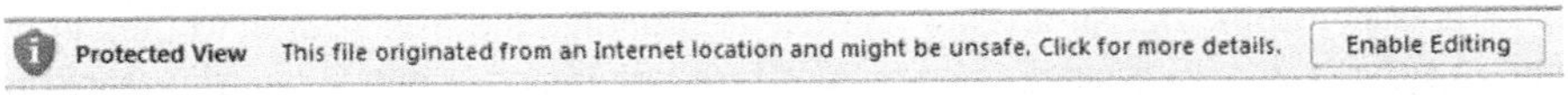

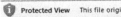

ⓘ Protected View This file originated from an Internet location and might be unsafe. Click for more details. [Enable Editing]

FIGURE 8.2

MS office protected view.

item number (i.e., Item 1, Item 2). The string data for each of the values appears as follows:

```
[F00000000][T01CE1E8BD536AA20][000000000]*C:\Course\rr\plugin.csv
```

The portion of the string data that starts with "T" is the text representation of a 64-bit FILETIME time stamp, and can be retrieved and parsed by the RegRipper *officedocs2010.pl* plugin (originally written by Cameron Howell). More testing is required, but at the moment, the time stamp appears to indicate when each document was last closed. However, regardless of the exact action represented by the time stamp, the contents of these keys clearly indicate that a user accessed a file with an explicit path at some particular point in time, and can provide significant context to our examination.

When a user accesses an MS Office document from a network resource (Internet, or file share in a corporate environment) using one of the Office 2007 and 2010 applications, there's yellow "Protected View" bar (illustrated in Figure 8.2) that appears, telling the user that the file may be unsafe.

As illustrated in Figure 8.2, the user must explicitly click the "Enable Editing" button in order to be able modify the document. When the user clicks this button, a value is created beneath the following key within the user's NTUSER.DAT hive:

Software\Microsoft\Office\n\app\Security\Trusted Documents\TrustRecords

In this key path, "n" is the version of MS Office ("12.0" for MS Office 2007, "14.0" for MS Office 2010), and "app" is the application used to open the file (Word, Excel, Access, etc.). The values created beneath this key are named with the path to the file opened, and the first 8 bytes of the binary data are the FILETIME time stamps which indicate when the user clicked the "Enable Editing" button. The RegRipper *trustrecords.pl* plugin can be used to extract this information (if available) from a user's NTUSER.DAT hive.

In March 2013, Jason Hale published a blog post (found online at http://dfstream.blogspot.com/2013/03/windows-8-tracking-opened-photos.html) in which he discussed a new Registry artifact that he'd found related to a user's access to images via the Windows 8 Photos tile. On Windows 8, tiles on the desktop represent applications, and users viewing images via the Photos tile result in a great deal of information being added to their USRCLASS.DAT hive. This information includes not only the path to the file, but also a value whose data is a stream that follows the Windows shortcut/LNK file format. The full path to the Registry key in question is quite long, and can be found in Jason's blog post, as well as in the RegRipper *photos.pl* plugin.

Another means that an analyst can use to demonstrate user access to files is by parsing the user's Internet Explorer (IE) browser history (index.dat file), looking specifically for entries that begin with "file:///."

The list of artifacts that demonstrate user access to files can be expected to grow, as new applications and versions of Windows become available. The list in this section is not intended to be all inclusive, but is instead intended to provide insight into some artifacts with which analysts may not be familiar.

IE browser analysis

There's been a great deal of information published, largely via the Internet, regarding artifacts pertaining to the use of web browsers, in particular Internet Explorer (MSIE), Mozilla Firefox, and Google's Chrome browser. There's also been considerable research conducted and everything from white papers to theses for graduate degrees to blog posts published regarding the use of these browsers in what's often referred to as "private" mode, which is essentially a mode of using the web browser that is meant to minimize the artifacts left on the system. It is also widely known within the digital forensics community that perhaps one of the best tools available for collecting artifacts pertaining to the use of web browsers, in general, and social media, in particular, is Magnet Software's Internet Evidence Finder (IEF) tool, in version 6.1 at the time of this writing. I should note that IEF garnered the award from computer forensic software product of the year at the 2013 SANS Forensic Summit, based on a Forensic 4Cast poll.

What I'd like to do in this "HowTo" section is take a look at some of the artifacts related to Microsoft IE with which analysts should become familiar, in hopes that by providing this information, it might also provide a greater understanding of, and provide additional context for, a user's activities. This section is not intended to be a comprehensive treatment of web browser forensics, as numerous other resources have been dedicated to the subject, and an entire book could be devoted just to it; rather, what I'd like to do is present some artifacts that may be of interest to the analyst, and means for accessing those artifacts. My goal is not to completely address the topic of web browser forensic analysis, but to instead present some artifacts specific to IE with which the analyst may not be familiar.

For versions of IE up to and including version 9, the "database" of web sites that a user visited is maintained in a file named "index.dat." Now, IE actually has several files of the same name that it uses to maintain information (i.e., cookies, daily and weekly histories) but the one we're interested in is the index.dat file located in the path "C:\Documents and Settings*user*\Local Settings\Temporary Internet Files\Content.IE5" on Windows XP, and "C: \Users*user*\AppData\Local\Microsoft\Windows\Temporary Internet Files\Content.IE5" on Windows 7. This is the file that maintains the current history of web sites that the user has accessed. Joachim Metz has put a good deal of work into documenting the structure of this file, which he maintains at the ForensicsWiki web site (found online at http://www.forensicswiki.org/wiki/Internet_Explorer_History_File_Format). This resource documents not only the format of the file header, but also the format of the individual records (i.e., URL, REDR, HASH, LEAK) that are maintained within the file. I have found this information to be extremely valuable for two reasons: the first being that it allows me to see exactly what information is maintained in the records, most particularly the URL records. For example, from the ForensicsWiki page, we can see that the URL record header not only includes a last accessed time (i.e., the last time the user accessed the particular site), but it also contains a last modification time of the file (when it was modified on the web server), as well as a time stamp that, according to Mr. Metz, indicates when the page expires. Further, by having a detailed view of the contents of the index.dat headers and individual records, we can write parsers to print out valid records based on the directory table within the file, as well as all records, valid and deleted, by parsing the file on a binary basis.

> **NOTE**
>
> **Date Interpretation**
>
> As mentioned in this section, there are a number of index.dat files that IE uses to maintain records of user access to web sites. This is important to keep in mind, as the interpretation of the dates stored in the individual records within those files varies depending upon in which folder an index.dat file is located. For example, within the weekly history index.dat file, the time stamp that Joachim Metz identified as the last modification time (starts at offset 0×08 within the record header) within the URL record header is interpreted in local time format, whereas the time stamp identified as the last accessed time (starts at offset 0×10 within the record header) is interpreted in Universal Coordinated Time format. This difference is important to keep in mind, particularly as you use various tools to parse the data, so that the data is correctly interpreted.

The second reason I find the format specification information to be useful is due to the fact that it allows me to see what the various fields are for the index.dat file header, and to what those fields refer. This has made it relatively straightforward to write a parser that looks solely at the identified fields, and can present information to the analyst quickly, without parsing the entire file. I have found this to be extremely useful as a malware detection technique; I can mount an acquired image (from an XP or Windows 7 system), and point a script at the folder where user profiles are located ("C:\Documents and Settings" or "C:\Users," respectively). The script will then access each subfolder and attempt to locate the index.dat file; if it finds it, it parses the header in order to determine if the index.dat file is the default, unpopulated file, or if the file illustrates indications of web activity via the WinInet API. This check usually only takes a second or two, and provides me with indications of which user may have used the IE browser, or, if the Network Service or Local Service accounts provide indications of activity, if the system has potentially been infected with some sort of malware.

TIP

Local Service Account Activity

As discussed in Chapter 6, the IE web browser does not populate the index.dat (for IE versions up to and including version 9); rather, it is the WinInet API that does so. What this means is that if malware utilizes this API for any sort of off-system communication, that activity will be seen in the index.dat file.

Not long ago, I was examining a system for indications of a malware infection; in this case, the customer had specifically identified ZeroAccess as the culprit. Once I received and verified the image that they sent, I then mounted it read-only, and ran an index. dat parsing script across all of the user profiles, and found out that the Local Service account had a considerable number of records within the index.dat file for that profile. This indicated that something on the system was running with System-level privileges and communicating off of the system by way of the WinInet API. Analysis of the extracted records confirmed findings from antivirus (AV) vendor write-ups for the malware that it is used for click-fraud.

When analyzing user web browser activity, specifically as it relates to IE, there are several Registry keys that may provide a good bit of useful information. For example, within the user's NTUSER.DAT hive file, the *Software\Microsoft\Internet Explorer* key contains a subkey named *TypedURLs*, which contains an MRU listing of addresses that the user has typed into the IE address bar. Windows 8 introduced an additional key of interest, named *TypedURLsTime*, which maintains an MRU list of the times (in 64-bit FILETIME format) that the URL was typed into the IE address bar, and the values beneath this key can provide two valuable bits of information. First, in the absence of any modifications to the Registry, the values beneath the *TypedURLsTime* key should follow a one-to-one correlation to the URLs beneath the *TypedURLs* key, providing time-based information for when the user performed the corresponding action. Second, if the times do not correlate to the URLs (i.e., there are a different number of entries beneath both keys), or if they do not correlate to other available artifacts (records within the user's index.dat file, etc.), then this may be an indication of the use of anti-forensics techniques. Both findings can be extremely useful to the analyst.

One of the aspects of IE browser analysis that analysts need to keep in mind is that web browsing history is not kept forever; it simply would not be feasible to do so. While users can manually clear their browsing history, most browsers (IE included) will clear their own history at a set interval. For IE, the default interval is 20 days; I have seen systems in a corporate domain all set to 14 days, and when I used IE more regularly, I set my system to keep web history for 0 days. IE also includes a setting that will tell the browser to clear the history when the application exits. In the case of IE, this value is named "ClearBrowserHistoryOnExit," and is found in the *Software\Microsoft\Internet Explorer\Privacy* key in the user's NTUSER.DAT Registry hive file. Individually, these settings may not make much difference, but when attempting to determine the user's web browsing activity, they can significantly impact the analyst's findings. For example, if the user has entries beneath the *TypedURLs* key, including one or more that are of interest to the analyst, but the IE index.dat history file is empty, the analyst needs to take the necessary steps to determine if the user intentionally deleted the history, or if the history was deleted due to IE application settings. Fortunately, with Windows 7, there was a new addition to the Registry regarding the user's use of IE. Beneath the *Software\ Microsoft\Internet Explorer\Main\WindowsSearch* key, there may be a value named "Cleared_TIMESTAMP," which is a 64-bit FILETIME object that refers to when the user last cleared their IE history.

The RegRipper *ie_settings.pl* plugin will determine if these values are present within the user's NTUSER.DAT hive, and if so, parse and display them.

On most Windows systems, a user can manually organize the applications and groups that appear in their Start Menu, as well as their IE Favorites (analogous to bookmarks in other browsers). For example, a user may opt to have some applications listed first in their Start Menu, or they may choose to create specific subfolders for grouping and ordering their IE Favorites. If the user opts to do either of these, the ordering is maintained in the Registry in the corresponding key beneath the *MenuOrder* key. This key is found in the user's NTUSER.DAT hive file, and the path to that key is *Software\Microsoft\Windows\CurrentVersion\Explorer\ MenuOrder*. The RegRipper *menuorder.pl* plugin will extract, parse, and display this information, if it is available.

Web browsers have long had the capability for users to bookmark web sites of interest; with IE, these are referred to as Favorites, and are text-based.url files located by default in the user's Favorites (i.e., *C:\Users\username\Favorites*) folder. The contents of an example IE Favorites.url file is illustrated in Figure 8.3.

Per MS KnowledgeBase (KB) article 191656 (found online at http://support. microsoft.com/kb/191656), the globally unique identifier (GUID) listed in the .url file illustrated in Figure 8.3 is the class identifier for the "My Computer" system folder. As the IE Favorites are each maintained in a separate file (as opposed to all bookmarks in an XML format in a single file), the time and date of when a user created or modified the bookmark will appear in a timeline as a result of adding file system metadata to the timeline. On Vista and above systems, the last accessed times on files are not updated by default, so we're not likely to see when the user accessed a location stored in a Favorites.url file within a timeline.

```
[DEFAULT]
BASEURL=http://www.yahoo.com/
[{000214A0-0000-0000-C000-000000000046}]
Prop3=19,2
[InternetShortcut]
URL=http://www.yahoo.com/
IDList=
IconFile=http://www.yahoo.com/favicon.ico
IconIndex=1
```

FIGURE 8.3

IE Favorite.url file content, via FTK Imager.

TIP

File Last Accessed Times and Timelines

It's commonly known within the digital forensics community that as of Windows Vista, Microsoft opted to disable with updating of file last accessed times when files are accessed via normal user activity. As such, in many (albeit not all) cases within a timeline, a file's last accessed time may be the same as the date and time that it was created. Before assuming that something suspicious or even malicious occurred when a file's last accessed time comes into question, analysts should check the appropriate Registry value to determine the setting for the system, and consider other possibilities, such as the file having been extracted from a zipped archive, or copied from another volume.

Finally, most browsers have a means for saving the current session so that it can easily be restored if, for some reason, the browser crashes. I'm sure most users have experienced this capability; they may have several tabs open in the browser, and then they visit a site that may cause their browser to crash. When they reopen the browser, each of the tabs themselves are opened, and the browser attempts to load the pages that were visible in each tab when the browser crashed. For IE versions 8 and 9, the file in question is named "RecoveryStore.{*GUID*}.dat," and on Windows 7 is located in the user's *AppData\Local\Microsoft\Internet Explorer\ Recovery\Last Active* folder (the final elements of the path are *High\Last Active* if the user account has elevate Administrator privileges). There may also be other files present in the folder, with names similar to "{*GUID*}.dat." Even though the file extensions are ".dat," the files actually follow the compound file or structured storage format, similar to Jump Lists and older versions of MS Office file formats. As such, the structure, embedded streams and their contents can be viewed using the appropriate tool (see Chapter 4). There isn't a great deal of information available regarding the format of the various streams found within the files, but Yogesh Khatri has conducted some research and posted his findings on his blog, found online at http://www.swiftforensics.com/2011/09/internet-explorer-recoverystore-aka.html.

More information about web browser session restore forensics can be found in Harry Parsonage's paper of the same name (found online at http://computerforensics.parsonage.co.uk/downloads/WebBrowserSessionRestoreForensics.pdf), which provides some valuable information on the topic, including session restore forensics for web browsers other than IE.

Detecting system time change

Modifying the system time is one of those activities usually identified as an "anti-forensic" technique, as many analysts may feel that the only reason for doing something like this is to hide activity on the system. I have seen, however, less nefarious uses for this sort of activity, such as to run (or continue running) sample versions of programs that are designed to stop functioning after a certain date.

> **NOTE**
> **Program Testing**
> Analysts may need to set their system time back to a certain date, particularly if they're
> testing an application that someone may have downloaded and run. If the program is
> designed to stop functioning after a certain date, setting the system clock back in time
> prior to the shut-off date will allow the analyst to test the application and determine the
> artifacts that remain following different usage scenarios.

In many cases, detecting the change of the system time can be relatively straightforward. Most often, a user will modify the system time by accessing the Date and Time applet in the Control Panel, and accessing this applet seen within the UserAssist subkey data in the user's Registry hive file (via the output of the RegRipper *userassist.pl* plugin). However, this data does not tell us definitively that the user changed the system time, only that the user accessed the Date and Time Control Panel applet—but that may be just the first bit of information that we need.

Steve Bunting, an independent forensic consultant, pointed out at his web site (found online at http://www.stevebunting.org/udpd4n6/forensics/timechange.htm) that with the proper auditing enabled on Windows XP and 2003 systems, the Event Logs may contain events with ID 520 (system time change) and/or 577 (privilege use). On more recent versions of Windows (i.e., Vista and above) the event ID 520 appears as event ID 4616.

Another means for detecting significant system time changes that I have found to be fairly fruitful is to parse the Event Log records, but not for their full data; instead, event records contain a sequence number and a time stamp which signifies when the event was generated. Listing all of the events in order, sorted by sequence number, with their corresponding time stamps makes it relatively easy to detect significant time changes. For Windows XP and 2003 systems, the *evtparse.pl* script discussed in Chapter 4 allows me to conduct this analysis easily, by supplying the "-s" switch. For Vista and above systems, a bit more work is required (*evtparse.pl* was not designed to be used with Windows Event Logs from these systems), but using LogParser.exe (available from Microsoft for free) and Excel, it is relatively easy to employ this analysis technique.

> **TIP**
> **System Time Change Example**
> A great example of how evtparse.pl can be used to detect a system time change can be
> seen in Lance Mueller's first practical exercise example, available online from http://
> www.forensickb.com/2008/01/forensic-practical.html. Download the 400-megabyte (MB)
> EnCase-format image file, open it as an evidence item in FTK Imager, and extract the
> Event Logs from the *C:\Windows\system32\config* folder. Then run *evtparse.pl* with the
> "-s" switch against the files, and you'll see a great example of how the technique can

illustrate a system time change. In the case of this practical exercise, the time change is significant, to the point of being glaringly obvious, but it does illustrate what to look for with this technique. For example, running the command against the appevent.evt Event Log file, we see in the output of the tool that there a number of events that were apparently generated in June 2004, and then we see that the event record with the sequence number 27 has a time generated date in January 2008, and then event record 38 switches back to June 2004.

Who ran defrag?

I've seen this question asked a number of times in public forums, and I've been asked the same question by customers, as well. This question usually comes up in spoliation cases, particularly after there's been a legal hold of some kind (many times based on current or anticipated litigation), and individuals have been instructed to not delete any documents or data from their systems.

The fact of the matter is that modern computer systems, particularly Windows systems, are very active even when there is no user sitting at the keyboard. With Windows XP, a System Restore Point was created under a variety of conditions, one of them being that 24 hours had passed since the last one had been created. Many of us install third-party software that adds some capability to our systems to look for updates, such Apple's QuickTime and iTunes, and Adobe Reader, to name a few.

With Vista systems and beyond, many automated functions exist on systems a Scheduled Task. One such task backs up copies of the four main Registry hive files (Software, Security, System, and SAM) to the *Windows\system32\config\RegBack* folder every 10 days. On Windows 7 and 8 systems, the Scheduled Tasks that ship with the systems are found in the *C:\Windows\system32\Tasks\Microsoft* folder. The task that handles running defrag for the system is the XML-formatted file named "ScheduledDefrag" (no file extension), located in the *C:\Windows\system32\Tasks\Microsoft\Windows\Defrag* folder. You can open this file in an editor such as Notepad++, and easily view the XML contents. On my Windows 7 system, I can see that the scheduled task is set to run the command "%windir%\system32\defrag.exe –c" every Wednesday while the system is idle. While the file is located in the same location on Windows 8, the contents of the XML file are slightly different, and it's worth taking a look at the file contents to understand a bit more about what's going on.

If you want to see when scheduled tasks have actually been run, you can find this information in the Microsoft-Windows-TaskScheduler/Operational Windows Event Log. With this log open in the Event Viewer on my own Windows 7 system on Friday, July 26, 2013, I searched for the word "defrag," and quickly found hits for Wednesday, July 24, 2013. The event IDs, as they appear in order, are 100 (task started), 200 (action started), 201 (action completed), and 102 (task completed).

As you might suspect, there's an application Prefetch file in the *C:\Windows\ Prefetch* folder on my Windows 7 system, as well. However, when I viewed the embedded metadata, and in particular the time that the application was last executed, the time stamp was for Friday, July 26, 2013—because I had opened the command prompt, navigated to the system32 folder, and typed the command "defrag /?" to see the meaning of the "-c" switch. If the user never launched defrag. exe, then the last run time from the application Prefetch file for defrag.exe should correlate pretty closely to the most recent "action completed" event within the TaskScheduler/Operational Windows Event Log.

Now, something we have to consider is how a user might go about launching the disk defragmenter, and what that might "look like" on the system. One way to do this is the same way that I did; run defrag.exe via the command prompt. As discussed previously in this book, we might find indications of this in the user's *MUICache* entries, or perhaps the *RunMRU* entries. Unfortunately, running programs via the command prompt doesn't leave as many artifacts as launching them via the Windows Explorer shell.

Another way to do this is to open the volume properties, choose the Tools tab, and click the "Defragment now..." button. This in turn opens the Disk Defragmenter dialog box. From here, the user can highlight any available volume and then simply click the "Defragment Disk" button.

These are by no means the only ways a user might defragment the hard drive. For example, rather than creating a new Schedule Task via the Task Scheduler wizard (accessible via the Administrative Tools in the Control Panel), the user may download a third-party application or simply go to the command prompt and use the *at* command to create a Scheduled Task. I did this at 4:11 pm, by typing the command "at 4:15 pm 'defrag –c'." This created a task named "At1" in the *C:\ Windows\system32\Tasks* folder. When I checked the TaskScheduler/Operational Windows Event Log at 4:19 pm, I saw event IDs 100 and 200, but they were followed by two error messages, one with event ID 203 (action failed to start), and the other with event ID 103 (action start failed).

Determine data exfiltration

Data exfiltration is a significant problem for organizations. There are a vast number of ways to sneak data out of an infrastructure, and attempting to determine data exfiltration (customers most often ask, "What data was taken?") from a single system can be a daunting task. Was the data sent out as an attachment to an email (web-based or otherwise), was it typed into a chat window, or was it uploaded to "the cloud"? The possibilities are staggering. When it comes right down to it, unless you're monitoring the system and the network (and by "monitoring," I mean full packet captures) at the time that the data was exfiltrated, it can be very difficult to determine what data was actually taken.

> **NOTE**
>
> **Illustrating Exfiltration**
>
> Some bad actors are known to stage the data that they're planning to exfiltrate off of a system by first archiving the data. So let's say that you're analyzing a system and you find that what appears to be a staged archive file—does that mean that the data was actually exfiltrated? Just because the data archive is in the directory, does that mean it was exfiltrated from the system? I would suggest that the answer is a resounding "No"; if you cannot clearly demonstrate that the data was in fact exfiltrated, the best you can report to the customer is that it "may have been" exfiltrated. What if the bad actor had archived the data, but had been distracted, or the connection to the system was terminated, before they were able to exfiltrate the archive? What if they'd failed to make a connection to the system meant to receive the data archive?
>
> Assumption should not be used in place for facts derived from data correlation and analysis when conducting an examination. Sometimes, these are simply questions that cannot be emphatically answered through analysis of the available data.

This section will not address all possible means by which data exfiltration can be determined, as that would lead to a chapter so massive that it would be unlikely that it, or this book, would ever be published. There has been quite a bit of information published with respect to searching for Internet-based artifacts, including access to web-based email (such as those from Yahoo or Google) and chat services. Information regarding analysis of the user of peer-to-peer (P2P) applications has similarly been published. There is also ongoing research being conducted with respect to a user's access to cloud-based services, and this information changes quite often. For example, not long after tips regarding the analysis of user access to Dropbox, the service and application were apparently changed, such that an important file on the user's system was encrypted. What I hope to do with this section is present some examples of artifacts that an analyst can look for on a system with respect to data exfiltration, specifically artifacts that the analyst may not have considered. This section is not intended to be a comprehensive treatment of all possible artifacts, but instead is intended to present some novel artifacts that analysts should include in their analysis process.

One means of data exfiltration that might be considered "old school" is the use of the file transfer protocol (FTP). Most users may not be aware, but Microsoft systems ship with a native, command line FTP utility, ftp.exe. This utility is found in the *Windows\system32* folder, and is actually very easy to use, so much so that I've seen a number of SQL injection cases where the bad guy issued commands to the target system to create and run an FTP script, and then launched the FTP utility with that script in order to download tools and applications to the system. A simple example of how to run the utility with a script of commands can be found in MS KB article 96269, found online at http://support.microsoft.com/kb/96269.

When a user launches the FTP utility, an application Prefetch file will be created, but as the utility is run from the command line, there will be few artifacts indicating what commands the user issued and what files may have been transferred off of the system. A number of third-party, graphical user interface (GUI) file transfer protocol (FTP) utilities exist which make it easier for a user to transfer files; the use of these utilities will result in the expected artifacts, but again, without monitoring the system at the time that a file transfer occurred, it is very difficult to determine which files may actually have been transferred. I am not aware of any FTP utility or application that maintains a log file on the user's system of what files were transferred off of the system.

When I first started working with a publisher, the process for transferring and exchanging files required me to access an FTP site via Windows Explorer. This amounted to me opening Windows Explorer and typing the appropriate URL (i.e., "ftp:\\www.site.com" or something similar) into the address bar. A dialog box would prompt me to authenticate to the FTP server, and once I had done so, I could navigate the site just as if I were navigating my local hard drive, and file transfers would occur via drag-and-drop. Once I had authenticated, the FTP server I had connected to and the account that I had used to authenticate (but not the password) could be seen beneath the *Software\Microsoft\FTP\Accounts* key in my Registry hive file. Further, as I was using Windows Explorer, the server to which I connected appeared in a uniform resource item shell item within my shellbags artifacts. Interestingly enough, when I was later performing timeline analysis of a system that had been compromised via Terminal Services (the admin password had been easy to guess), I could see right there in the timeline that the intruder had used this method for accessing an FTP site, in this case to download files. However, the same method could easily be used to transfer files off of the system, just as I did when transferring chapters of a manuscript to the publisher.

There's another means of data exfiltration that I don't believe is considered by many analysts: Bluetooth. A number of systems, particularly laptops, come with Bluetooth radios, and anecdotal information suggests that the necessary drivers and a native Windows application named "fsquirt.exe" may be installed during the operating system installation process if a Bluetooth radio is found. Fsquirt.exe is the Bluetooth file transfer wizard, and is described online at the Microsoft web site, at http://msdn.microsoft.com/en-us/library/windows/hardware/dn133848(v=vs.85). aspx. This wizard is a GUI application, and when launched, the user can select Bluetooth devices to pair with, as illustrated in Figures 8.4 and 8.5, respectively.

Once the user pairs their system with an appropriate device, they then launch a common dialog in order to select files to transfer to the device. As such, Registry data regarding discovered (not necessarily paired with) devices will appear in a timeline, followed by an application Prefetch file illustrating that fsquirt.exe had been launched (or, the file may be modified if it has been launched several times), and an entry in the user's *ComDlg32* Registry key, when correlated together, may provide indications of the user selecting a folder from which to send selected files to the device.

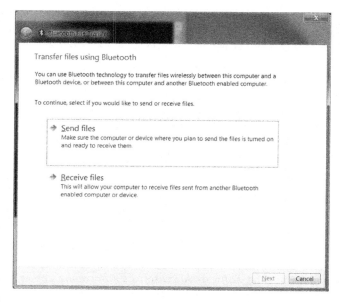

FIGURE 8.4

Bluetooth file transfer wizard (fsquirt.exe) GUI.

FIGURE 8.5

Locating a device for pairing.

NOTE

Fsquirt Artifacts

When testing pairing a Bluetooth device to a Windows 7 system for use in file transfers, I found some initial artifacts within the value data beneath the *ComDlg32\FirstFolder* subkey; however, the really valuable artifacts were found in the value data beneath the *ComDlg32\LastVisitedPidlMRU* key. One of the values had data that included a reference to fsquirt.exe, followed by a shell item ID list that pointed to the folder from which I had selected a file to transfer. The file that I had selected to transfer ended with the ".txt" extension, and was found in the shell item ID list within a value found beneath the *ComDlg32\OpenSavePidlMRU\txt* key. This information can be extracted from a user's NTUSER.DAT hive file using the *comdlg32.pl* RegRipper plugin.

The actual Registry keys that list devices discovered via Bluetooth may vary, depending upon which drivers are installed for the radio. For example, the *bthport.pl* RegRipper plugin parses data from the Registry keys used by the Microsoft drivers, whereas Broadcomm drivers or those from other manufacturers may use other keys.

Finding something "new"

One of perhaps the most fascinating things about digital forensic analysis is that there's so much out there yet to learn. I don't profess to know everything about anything; all I can say is that I'm curious. I'm not an expert on anything; rather, I'm curious and always willing to learn or discover something new.

But how do we do that? How do we learn about or find something new, particularly when we always seem to be on the verge of being overwhelmed, with too much work to get done in too little time? After all, it isn't bad enough that we've got the Leaning Tower of Forensic Casework threatening to come crashing down on our desks, but then a new device or operating system becomes widely available and we need to figure out how to acquire and analyze data from it, without ever actually having access to or having used it. Sometimes it just seems as if the horizon is moving away faster than we can approach it.

What I've found over time is that the best way to find something new depends upon the process that I'm using. For example, when I'm creating a timeline of system activity for analysis, I will be sure to incorporate Registry key LastWrite times (per Chapter 7, this would be done via *regtime.exe*) from the available hive files. This approach adds "general" data to the timeline, as opposed to several of the RegRipper plugins (specifically, those that end in *_tln.pl*) which add extremely targeted information, such as a user's UserAssist data, or the first item of an MRU list, to the timeline. In several instances, this step in my timeline creation process has shown me potential artifacts that I might otherwise have missed. During one particular exam, I was examining a system that had been infected with a variant of a fairly prevalent bit of malware. By incorporating all of the Registry key LastWrite times from the various hive files into the timeline, there was one particular key that had been modified at a specific time, which was right in the middle of the time window during which the system had been infected. Because of the granularity provided by the timeline, I could see the entire infection process, and this one Registry key stood out to me as somewhat odd. So the first thing I did was to open the hive in question in a viewer, and navigate to the key, and found that it had a single value. At this point, I was left wondering, was the value data modified, or was something (a subkey or value) deleted, causing the LastWrite time to be updated? I had the key LastWrite time, so I mounted the image of the system using the virtual hard drive (VHD) method (as outlined in Chapter 3), determined the available VSCs, and then extracted the hive file from the VSC that has been created immediately prior to the key LastWrite time. I attempted to locate the key in question, but could not find it. I checked the hive files available in other VSCs (there were only two more) and even ran *regslack.exe* against the hive file, just to verify that the key hadn't existed, been deleted, and then recreated. All of these attempts yielded negative results, which let me to conclude that the key and value had actually been created during the infection process; online research determined that the key/value pair, along with the associated data, essentially "disconnected" the IE web browser from Java. In short, the system had been infected by a browser drive-by that compromised Java, and the infection process disconnected IE from Java, basically "shutting the door" so that the system could not be infected via the same means any longer. What I found fascinating about this was that it was not only very simple and very clever, but it was not directly associated with the malware binary itself; rather, it was associated with the infection process. Therefore, this Registry key being created would not become part of a malware analyst's write-up if a customer located the malware binary and sent it (just the binary) to the analyst. This method of analysis means that important information about the infection process, which can be used to address protection and detection mechanisms within the organization (often referred to as "threat intelligence"), is then missed, as the focus is solely on a single binary. Adding the Registry key LastWrite times to the timeline essentially amounts to "casting a wide net," providing a high-level view of activity on the system right alongside the more tactical data extracted from specific Registry value data, which allowed me to find something new in my analysis. Adding this data is simply part of my process, and that step served me well in this instance.

NOTE

Threat Intelligence

Very often when AV vendors write up their analysis of malware, we have to keep in mind that the analysis itself is most often based on submitted samples, not full analysis of infected systems. As such, we will see self-inflicted artifacts (associated with how the malware is launched for analysis), as well as artifacts directly associated with the malware itself, mutexes, persistence mechanisms, files created, etc., but what won't be available are artifacts associated with the particular method by which the malware ended up on the system in the first place; from Chapter 6, we know that this is referred to as the "initial infection vector." So we don't see the delivery mechanism, be it a browser drive-by, infected document, etc. As such, there is a loss of significant intelligence that can be used by breached organizations to determine how best to allocate resources to defend against further compromises, as well as how to determine the scope of the compromise itself. Malware that may have been seen previously to be delivered via a Java exploit from compromised web sites may later be updated (producing a new variant) that is instead embedded within a malicious document. Without this information, resources may be allocated incorrectly in an effort to prevent future compromises, and the organization may again be compromised while they remain unprotected.

Having an analysis process provides additional advantages, as well. In particular, one of the things that will very often jump out at me during analysis is gaps in data. For example, if my analysis goal is to determine the files that a user accessed on a Windows 7 system, there are a number of locations I'll check, including the user's Jump Lists. If during analysis, I find that the user had been logged into the system at a particular time, but there were no Jump Lists; not just those associated with applications such as MS Office or Adobe (applications used for accessing and viewing files) but for all applications, this might be suspicious, and I would want to look for indications of the use of anti-forensic tools, such as CCleaner, Evidence Eliminator, etc. An analysis process not only helps me document what I did (what data was looked at or added to my timeline), but it also tells me what I should be seeing in the data. If I had parsed the DestList streams in a user's Jump Lists, and via an automatic, scripted process, also parsed those streams available in Jump Lists found in VSCs, and found no indication of access to files during a specific time frame, when I knew that the user was logged into the system (via interviews, data analysis, etc.), then this gap might be explained by the use of tools that would remove the data.

My point is that knowing about different artifacts will only get an analyst so far in their analysis. The key is to have a process for incorporating and correlating various artifacts based on the goals of the exam, in order to not only determine "new" findings (and potentially very significant threat intelligence), but to also assist in locating gaps in the data that is being analyzed.

SUMMARY

No two examiners will perform the exact same analysis; given the same data or image to analyze, it is unlikely that you'll find any two analysts who will pursue identical goals by following identical steps. This is largely due to training and experience. Many times, it can be useful to see how other examiners go about their analysis process, how they pursue the goals of their examinations, and how they address and overcome problems that they face during an exam (i.e., absence of information). Sharing this information about analysis processes (not the actual case data itself, or case specifics) not only gives other examiners ideas on how to approach their own analysis, but also allows them to ask questions so that in the end, everyone benefits from improved processes and views into the examinations. The best way to achieve this is open up what we do to review by peers, and people we can trust and rely on to be supportive.

Reporting

9

CHAPTER OUTLINE

INFORMATION IN THIS CHAPTER

- Goals
- Case Notes
- Reporting

INTRODUCTION

Perhaps one of the most difficult aspects of digital analysis work is communicating results and findings. However, this is also perhaps the most important aspect of our jobs, as well. We write reports because we have to communicate our findings to someone else, be they a customer or an attorney, or another analyst, in such a manner that they can use that information to make critical business or legal decisions. As such, we need to clearly and concisely address the issues at hand and provide information on which the reader can base their decisions.

In this chapter, I will be sharing a method of reporting that has worked for me, as a consultant. This means that I'm usually hired by a company or organization to perform some sort of examination or assessment, and provide information describing my findings, usually in a written report (I have done work for customers who wanted verbal responses before they decided if they wanted something written). Most often, those reading my reports have been nontechnical executive or senior level management, and in some cases, attorneys. As such, I need to ensure that the information in my report can be understood and used by whoever is reading it to make the critical business or legal decisions with which they are faced.

While I have seen reports written by law enforcement analysts, I have not yet been in a position to do so myself. As such, I do not have a great deal of insight to offer for writing reports and communicating findings specifically for this segment of the digital forensics community. I have, however, used the approach discussed in this chapter from reporting findings of internal investigations, such as human resources (HR) and internal security incident investigations that remain within the organization and do not employ external third party or law enforcement assistance. The reporting methodology I have used as a consultant works equally well for these investigations. Hopefully some, if not most, of what I discuss in this chapter will be applicable to your needs.

Goals

Every examination or engagement starts with goals; after all, without some sort of goals, there would be no reason for the analysis, right? Someone wouldn't want you to perform a considerable amount of analysis work and reporting unless they had a question that needed to be answered, right? Now, they may not have what you consider the "right" question, or they may have additional questions that only come about after you provide your findings, but my point is that every examination begins with a goal, or goals, of some sort.

While I was on active duty in the military, I heard a statement that stuck with me; "If you can't communicate an issue on a 3 × 5 index card, you don't know enough about it." This is very true when it comes to defining the goals of an examination. Very often, I will hear analysts say that the customer could not define their goals, or the customer's goals were very vague, such as "...find all bad stuff." Most often, this is the result of minimal interaction with the customer. I once worked with an analyst who had returned from a customer's site with the goals of "find all bad stuff." They worked diligently on the case and sent in a report stating that they'd located not just a directory full of "hacking" tools, but also indications that the user in question had actually run these tools. The customer response was that the use of the "hacking" tools was part of that employee's job—their job function was explicitly to test the security of the company systems and web sites, so the tools that were discovered were not "bad."

Goals focus our attention and work. This is not to say that we focus so narrowly on the goals that we provide nothing more than a "yes" or "no" answer. However, goals do help us identify the analysis process and techniques that we would want to employ, what artifacts we need to be looking for or at, as well as what other information may be of use in order to help us answer the questions we have before us. For example, if a goal of an examination is to determine what information, if any, left the system then I would want to seek additional information regarding what led the customer to believe that information had left the system, what type of information (Office documents, etc.) might have left the system, and when they believe this might have happened. I might also want to know what other logs might be available from within the infrastructure, such as web proxy logs, email server logs. The point is that there are a *lot* of ways that information can make its way off of a system, and not all of them require the use of technological means to achieve this, so without narrowing down the goals of the examination, as well as the customer's expectations, considerable time and money could be spent on an examination that would, in the end, have very little return on that investment.

TIP

Defining Goals

Defining goals for an examination can be difficult, particularly if the analyst does not normally think in those terms. I was perusing a forum not long ago when I ran across an interesting post; an analyst was looking for assistance with respect to what to look for in a "counterfeiting case." The analyst stated that they most often conducted examinations involving illicit images, and this case was a little beyond their reach. It seemed that the analyst had some difficulty defining the goals of the case; going back and forth in the forum, and then directly via email, they eventually got to the point of stating that they'd found images on the system that were of interest, but they had no idea if the images had been printed. To me, it sounded as if those were the goals of the examination, right there.

"It's a counterfeit case" is not a goal—where does one go from there? "Determine if applications or materials used in counterfeiting US currency or passports exist on the system, and if so, were those materials printed" are goals for an examination. Using those goals, an analyst can begin building a checklist of discrete tasks that need to be performed in order to meet the goals.

Goals should be discrete, achievable, and manageable. We should be able to tell when we've met a goal, or if we don't have enough information to adequately address a goal, and in such cases, we should be able to identify what else it is that we need to accomplish the goal. For example, I have done a good bit of dead box analysis; that is, analyzing images acquired from hard drives removed from systems after they've been shut down. In such cases, I have not had access to the system when it was in a live, running state; I have no information about processes that were running on the system, network connections initiated from the system, etc. So when a customer asks me to determine what information was exfiltrated off of the system several weeks (or even months) prior to when they contacted me, I know that this will be a difficult goal to achieve. After all, the only definitive way to determine what data was exfiltrated from a system is to capture and analyze traffic emanating from the system at that time; anything else might amount to varying degrees of speculation. Yes, it may be possible to locate a .rar archive of files in a staging folder, and the usual actions associated with the threat actor may be that they export these archives off of the system in some manner, but the fact is that unless you have a network traffic capture what you can parse and from which you can retrieve that archive, the exfiltration of the archive is speculation, at best.

Often, through the experience of multiple and repeated examinations, we may know what the customer is going to ask before they do. Companies that haven't experienced a breach or intrusion, and don't have experience with dealing with such incidents, will often start by asking if a system is infected with malware. This may seem to be a simple "yes" or "no" goal, but it's really just the first in a series of questions that they're going to be asking. "Was the system infected?" will usually lead to, "what were the capabilities of the malware?", which will then lead to, "what data was exposed by the malware?" There is an inevitable refinement in the goals over time, as the analysis provides answers and those answers are processed. As such, it is a good idea to work with the customer up-front, and present these questions as possibilities, and let them know that you understand where they will be going with their questions. For consultants, this can have an impact on the work that you do, as if the customer keeps coming back with another question, you will have to go back and request additional hours in order to complete the work. Sitting with the customer ahead of time and working through the questions that they have, as well as those that they are likely to have, will allow you to provide a much more realistic estimate of how long they can expect the work to take. This has much more of an impact on the customer than just their wallet; many organizations are subject to some sort of compliance regulations, which in some cases will specify a time frame within which the customer needs to respond.

Incident triage

The goals of your examination will most likely originate through your initial contact with your "customer." I use this term, because as analysts, we are not performing analysis for ourselves—we're most usually performing analysis for someone else. We may do this while acting as a consultant, and the term "customer" is used in the classic sense, and synonymous with "client." For a law enforcement analyst, the "customer" may be the prosecution team, or the courts. For an analyst working in a full-time employment position within an organization (i.e., part of the internal security team), the "customer" may be the HR director, the CIO, or someone to whom they are providing support and analysis. Regardless of the position in which you're functioning, your analysis goals are going to come from that first contact with your "customer," during those initial information gathering steps.

As such, it is very often helpful (and in some cases, critical) to have a checklist of questions handy for when you're engaged with someone regarding an incident of any kind. As a consultant, I've used what can be referred to as a *triage checklist* of questions that will be asked of a customer, either when they first call, or when I get to meet with them. Often, it is also helpful to have the answers to these questions from the initial call in front of you when meeting with the customer, and then asking the questions again. In many cases, the customer may not have thought of the questions you asked, or when you're sitting with them, there may be someone with more knowledge of the incident available. The questions asked will vary depending upon your experience, type of work that you do, who you work with, etc. For example, as a consultant who dealt with different customers from different verticals all the time—I might talk to a restaurant owner one week, and the next week meet with the CIO of a hospital—the questions I ask will likely be different from those asked by a law enforcement examiner.

One of the first things I ask a customer to do is provide a concise description of their understanding of the incident. This will often lead to either additional questions depending upon the nature or the description of the incident, and in many cases, has led to the customer agreeing with me that we need to have someone a bit more familiar with the incident on the call to answer questions. For example, I've been on the phone with someone who knew that there were 3000 server systems in the data center, but had no idea if any of them were involved in the incident. Keep in mind that when someone is calling for your assistance, it is likely that incident response or digital analysis is not what they do on a daily basis; if they're calling about an incident that they'd like you to respond to, this may be the first time that they've encountered something like this. Ever. As such, having them describe the incident is a great way to get an understanding of what's going on; for example, if they call and say, "we have a malware infection," one of the first things I would like to know is, how do they know that? Getting them to describe the incident or issue is a great way to open up the conversation a bit and start getting not just a view into the issue, but what their concerns are, as well.

Another question I will ask is if there are any network diagrams and device logs available. It can be very helpful to understand which devices network traffic will have to traverse in order to make it from point A to point B, as well as which of those devices might be capable of logging. I've worked with organizations that have employed an automated process for archiving their firewall logs on a regular basis. Most web servers will maintain logs by default, but I have worked with organizations that had disabled logging on several of their web servers. If an incident was detected due to lateral movement within an organization (i.e., traffic did not leave the internal infrastructure and make it out on to the Internet), it can be very helpful to understand the devices the traffic would have traversed.

Case Notes

Maintaining case notes is extremely important to a case, especially when it comes to reporting. There is a well-known euphemism in the community about an analyst "getting hit by a bus," which could refer to a wide range of events, such as that the analyst was transferred, on vacation, sick, that their computer ceased to function, or that the data somehow became corrupted. Without case notes, no one knows what that analyst was working on, what they had done, or what they had found. Often we look at the euphemism as just that—something that might happen, but to someone else. The need for case notes becomes very real when the euphemism becomes manifest, and we learn our lessons about keeping case notes the hard way, most often after the fact.

Another question to ask yourself when writing your case notes is, what happens when the customer comes back and asks questions six months or a year after you completed the original work and submitted your report? What's funny—well, not really—about this is that it actually happens. I know many analysts have heard their manager say those words, and thought nothing of it. And then a year after they did the work, the customer did, in fact, come back and ask questions—questions that the analyst couldn't answer because they didn't keep case notes. And it doesn't have to be a full year. Often, analysts may work several cases at the same time, as well as in rapid succession. Maintaining case notes allows you to differentiate your analysis, and even answer questions just a few weeks after you completed the work. As such, when discussing the need for case notes with another analyst, I will ask them, how will you be able to answer questions about a case six months or a year after you completed it? This may sound notional and far-fetched, but I'm sure that we can all recall having been on a conference call when we were asked questions about an examination had done, a full year after we had completed the work and sent the report to the customer. This sort of scenario can happen in a number of cases, such as with legal cases that don't go to trial right away, as well as when an organization is fined or somehow penalized by a regulatory body and appeals that finding. Often, the reasons we give for keeping case notes seem contrived and unlikely to occur, but then we learn the value of having kept case notes when those reasons come true and actually do happen.

Another important benefit of maintaining case notes is that doing so reduces the risk of commingling case work in the analyst's mind and memory. Even if you're working just a few, or even two, cases without notes, you may often find yourself remembering details from one case while discussing another. I've seen this a number of times; I once spent a considerable amount of time discussing a case with another analyst, who would say things such as, "the time zone for the system was set for Egypt"; when I asked for clarification that the acquired system had been physically located in Baltimore, MD, the analyst corrected herself. She hadn't been keeping case notes; as she was handling multiple cases, she was commingling the details from various cases. Doing this on the report, or in court, can have some significant repercussions.

Something else that analysts will often say about case notes is that they don't keep everything; in particular, they don't keep what they tried, but didn't work. For example, some analysts will say that if they have a theory about something and they check a Registry value or perform a keyword search and they don't find what they might have expected, they won't document that aspect of their analysis. I say, why not? This can be very valuable information, supporting other findings, and helping you complete your analysis goals. Often, the absence of an artifact where you would expect to find one is itself an artifact. Not finding something can be as valuable as locating the data that you're actually looking for. For example, during one particular case, I found that the user's NTUSER.DAT Registry hive did not have a RecentDocs key; experience and testing showed me that when a new user profile is created on a system, the NTUSER.DAT hive has a RecentDocs key, albeit an empty one. I then used a tool to examine the hive file for deleted keys and values, and found the date and time of when the key had been deleted, and using that information was able to determine that the user had used a tool to purposely delete the key and its contents. Having this information documented in my case notes was invaluable in supporting my later findings.

So, how do you keep case notes? We've already talked about the need to keep case notes, but what application or tool should you use? Again, this is another question that I hear quite often. One of the tools I have used to great success is Forensic Case Notes from QCC Information Security (available online from http://qccis. com/resources/forensic-tools/casenotes-lite/). This tool was specifically designed to allow an analyst to keep case notes, and has a good deal of built-in functionality that can be extremely useful, such a hashing of entered data, the ability to add additional tabs, encryption, and language support. When I used this application, I found the rich text format of the text fields to be very useful for entering data, particularly if I wanted to include a picture in my notes.

If your analysts use multiple platforms, however, a Windows-only tool may not be the best choice. A number of applications support the document format used by MS Word (MS Office for Mac, OpenOffice for Linux, etc.), so this may be a more suitable choice of application platform for maintaining and sharing case notes. Documents in MS Word format can be created and accessed on a variety of platforms, including (but not limited to) an iPad. Case notes files can also be converted to PDF format for archival purposes, or for sharing with other analysts.

Documenting your analysis

I'm often asked, to what standard should case notes be kept? My response is simply this—if you "get hit by a bus," someone should be able to take your case notes and replicate what you did, not just the steps you took, but your findings, as well. They should be able to follow your case notes like a recipe, and using the same data, same tools (and versions of the tools), and the same commands to launch those tools, be able to reproduce your findings. Based on your own training and experiences, as well as how well you document your case notes, the conclusions may be different, but another analyst should be able to run same version of the same tool against the same data and get the same results.

When keeping case notes and documenting your analysis, you should keep detailed information regarding the tools you use to parse and interact with the data, including the name and version of the tool. This can be very important, as the capabilities of tools tend to evolve over time. For example, when I started with the ISS Emergency Response Services (ERS) team, each analyst was provided a dongle and a copy of Guidance Software's EnCase version 4.22. By the time I moved on from the team 3½ years later, EnCase was at version 6.17 or 6.19, and the capabilities of the tool had greatly expanded.

If you're using free and/or open source tools, you should also document the location from where you retrieved a copy of the tool, in addition to the other information discussed thus far. Many times you may find a number of tools for parsing various types of data (files, data structures, etc.), all with the same name, but with vastly different capabilities and output formats. As such, knowing from where the tool was retrieved can be extremely important when it comes to answering questions at some point in the future. Also, documenting this information allows another analyst to review your work and easily understand what you had done to that point (remember the "hit by a bus" euphemism?).

Why does any of this matter? Remember that as stated in Chapter 1, tools provide a layer of abstraction over the data that analysts interface and interact with, often translating a binary stream or flag value into something readable by humans. An example of this is can be found in parsing the security accounts manager (SAM) Registry hive file—there is no actual string that says that an account is disabled; rather, it is a flag value, and when found, most tools will display some variation of "account disabled," while the value itself is a single bit within a 32-bit section of a binary stream. Different tools written by different authors with different perspectives may parse or display things differently, and, as stated, tools will evolve over time. This is particularly true with open source tools. In 2012, I had found that the Windows Registry Recovery tool from MiTeC (found online at http://mitec.cz/wrr. html) did not correctly parse "big data," or value data larger than about 3 kilobytes or so (a different structure is used to store this "big data"). As of this writing (in the summer of 2013), this issue does not appear to have been corrected; however, other tools, including RegRipper and the underlying Parse::Win32Registry Perl module have long since been updated to be able to correctly access these "big data" entries. This should clearly illustrate the fact that there's a big difference between stating in your case notes that you "parsed/analyzed the Registry," and specifically stating what tools you used to do so, and why doing so is important.

Over the past year or so, one data structure in particular has garnered a great deal of attention from a very small segment of the forensic analysis community; shell items. While Microsoft provides a good deal of documentation regarding structures that make use of the shell items, these structures are not themselves clearly defined, and as such, have only been identified by the tireless efforts of a few researchers within the community. These data structures are very important because they have actually existed on Windows systems for quite some time. For example, Microsoft's shell link binary file format specification (found online at http://msdn.microsoft.com/en-us/library/dd871305.aspx) identifies the section of the Windows shortcut files that is comprised of shell items (more specifically, of a shell item ID list). Up until about two years ago, very few, if any, of the commonly used tools for parsing Windows shortcut/shell link (LNK) files parsed this shell item ID list, and instead went straight to the LinkInfo block. I have seen examples of legitimate Windows shortcut files during analysis that were comprised of just the shell item ID list and did not have a LinkInfo block, meaning that the commonly used tools would simply not show any output. This could be a critical piece of evidence—the shortcut was for a digital camera that had been connected to the system, and could lead to identifying a source of images. There have been examples of malware that have created Windows shortcut files consisting solely of shell item ID lists (no LinkInfo block), and there have been examples of how the shell item ID list can be manipulated (without modifying the LinkInfo block) to force the shortcut to execute something other than the intended target file. More recently, tools have been created to parse the shell item ID lists found in LNK files, as well as to parse other artifacts that include shell items. The point is that tools develop and evolve over time as new information becomes available, so identifying the name and version of the tool, as well as from where the tool was obtained, can be a very critical part of your case notes.

When I start my case notes, the first item I include, at the top of the page, are the goals of the analysis. This way, I have them right in front of me so that I can continually review them and keep focused. Too many times when conducting analysis, I've found interesting artifacts—Registry keys, log files, or entries in log files—that, while interesting, have not been pertinent to the goals of the examination. Spending too much time conducting research into these artifacts can significantly hamper my ability to complete the analysis in a thorough and timely manner. Putting the goals at the beginning of my case notes also allows me to review those goals each time that I open the case notes, such as beginning work again on subsequent days.

The next item I tend to incorporate into my case notes is a listing of the exhibits or items that I am analyzing. I identify from where I received the items, in what condition I received them, and any identifying marks or tags. For example, if I receive an image or log files on an external drive, I include the serial number of the drive. If I receive a laptop system and have to remove the hard drive in order to acquire an image, I will include identifying information about the laptop (serial number, asset tag number, etc.), a link to instructions that I use to remove the hard drive (many manufacturers make this information available online), and identifying information about the hard drive itself. I then include specific information regarding how the image was acquired, stating such things as whether I used a Tableau bridge and AccessData's Forensic Toolkit (FTK) Imager, or if I employed a hardware write-blocker.

I generally keep my case notes on a daily basis, detailing what actions I took in my analysis, as well as the results. In some cases, I will even include specific excerpts from the output of tools that may direct or affect future analysis. While the goals of the exam will direct my analysis, a lot of the analysis work that I actually do is predicated in large part based on my experience, as is knowing what data may impact future analysis. As a consultant, I will also keep track of the number of hours that I work right there in my case notes. This can be very important if I'm working on several cases at once, as it is easier to keep track of this information for billing purposes.

Other information that may be critical to your case notes, particularly if it's not maintained somewhere else, is point of contact information for your customer. Many times, it is important to maintain their full name, mailing and email address, phone number, etc.

Reporting

Reporting is often the most difficult aspect of digital analysis work. This is largely due to the fact that for many of us, communicating our findings in written form is not something that is necessarily included in our experiences, nor in our training. Personally, I do not have a great deal of formal training in digital analysis; with the exception of one vendor course in 1999, I have not attended any formal training, nor completed any coursework that is specific to this field. However, I have spoken to and worked with a number of analysts, and two of the common factors across all experience that they have shared with me has been that there are few courses that teach reporting, and that how reports are written and what they contain will vary not only between positions but also between managers. All of these factors combine to make report writing one of the most arduous and least "sexy" aspects of digital analysis.

NOTE
Writing
I happen to have a great deal of writing experience in my academic and professional background, and it may be a positive factor that much of that experience is varied. I had writing classes in college, and opportunities for writing reports based on assignments. In the military, I wrote personnel evaluations, reports, etc. In graduate school, I had an opportunity to write to a completely different audience while completing my master's thesis. After I entered the civilian community, I had opportunities to write reports based on vulnerability assessments, penetration tests, as well as incident response. I also had an opportunity to work with both managers and peers who brought different, and valuable, perspectives to the work, as well as the reporting process. What I am sharing in this chapter is the culmination of all of those combined experiences, but that is not to say that the method I'm presenting is necessarily the only way to complete a report.

So far in this chapter, we've addressed the role of goals in analysis, as well as how to document our analysis work in the form of case notes. By this point, the report should almost write itself. I mean, after all, we've got all of the components necessary for the actual report, and all we need to do is assemble them.

Format

The format you use for your reports can vary depending upon your audience. You may be in a portion of the industry with a law enforcement focus, and as such, the format you use for reporting may be different from what is used by a consultant communicating findings to a customer, or an analyst working for a company reporting their findings to the company's HR director. My hope is that there are elements of and information shared in this chapter that are useful to you, regardless of the portion of the industry in which you operate.

When I was part of an emergency incident response team, we used one report format for our consulting work, and another for our Payment Card Industry (PCI) forensic assessment reports. While these formats were vastly different, there were both good and bad aspects of each. In particular, there were some aspects of the PCI report format that were very useful, and those are aspects that I'll mention. These aspects of the format were useful enough that I've used them again and again in the various positions I've held in my career.

Executive summary

The executive summary of the report should be just that—a summary, for executives. Executives are generally not interested in the minutiae and details of an examination; more often than not, their concerns and interest are more closely aligned with the business itself. The executive summary should be no more than two pages, max, and be able to stand completely on its own. It's useful, when writing the executive summary, to imagine that someone is going to tear it off of the report, and hand it to someone else. This is what I mean when I say that the executive summary should be able to stand on its own—it should be able to provide enough information to senior management to be able to address their concerns when separated from the body of the report.

I generally begin the executive summary with a brief description of the background of the incident, providing enough detail to make it clear as to why I or my employer was contacted by the customer in the first place. An example of a background statement might appear as follows:

> *On 21 July 2011, ACME Corporation (ACME) contacted the Example Consulting Team (ECT) regarding a potential computer security incident, thought to include compromise of and intrusion into the ACME computing infrastructure. ACME had reportedly been contacted by a federal law enforcement agency regarding information specifically associated with ACME being found on a web site external to ACME.*

TIP

Terminology

When provided a piece of information by a customer that I am not able to confirm through the review or analysis of actual data, I will refer to that information using terms such as "reportedly," or "as provided or reported by." This differentiates those pieces of information shared in the report that were found as a result of data analysis, and those that were provided perhaps anecdotally during conversations with the customer.

Following the background statement, I then clearly list the goals of the examination. If the goals are concise and limited, this section might simply be a sentence. For example, consider a case involving a corporate HR complaint, the goal statement in the executive summary may appear as follows:

The goal of this exam was to determine if a specific user had violated corporate acceptable use policies by accessing unauthorized web sites.

For multiple goals, this statement may appear as "The goals of the examination were as follows:", followed by a numbered bullet list of the goals. As described previously in this chapter, it is important that the goals be clear and concise, and broken down into achievable tasks. This way, each individual goal can be addressed as a specific task to be accomplished through analysis of the available data.

The conclusions listed in the executive summary should directly follow the goals; that is to say that for each goal, you should have an associated conclusion. Generally speaking, your conclusions will likely be one of three different responses; yes, no, or there wasn't enough information available to determine an accurate response. For example, your conclusion for the HR goal listed previously might be (analysis performed by Acme Consulting):

Acme Consulting was able to determine that the user did, in fact, violate corporate acceptable use policies by visiting unauthorized web sites.

What web sites are determined to be "unauthorized" may be detailed in the HR policy handbook, the acceptable use policies signed by the user, or they may have been provided by the HR director during the course of the analysis. A similar approach would apply for other analysis goals, such as whether a user accessed resources (file shares) or documents for which they were not authorized. The conclusions statement above can further include the dates of the activity, or those dates can be included in an attachment or appendix to the report.

Next, let's consider a malware incident, which may be a bit more expansive and include additional goals. The goals of such an exam may be listed in the executive summary as follows:

The goals of this examination were as follows:

1. *Determine if the system in question was infected with malware.*
2. *If the system was found to have been infected with malware, determine if that malware was capable of collecting and exfiltrating information from the system.*
3. *Determine what data, if any, was exfiltrated from the system by or through the use of the malware.*

Following the goals, the conclusions (again, the analysis was performed by the ECT) may appear as follows:

Through detailed and thorough analysis, Acme Consulting was able to determine the following:

1. *The system was in fact infected with malware; the malware was identified as \<insert name\>.*
2. *The identified malware was found to be written specifically to collect authentication information from the infected system, and then exfiltrate that information to a compromised system.*
3. *The ECT was unable to definitely determine data that may have been exfiltrated from the system by or through the use of the malware, as neither full network traffic captures nor detailed network session logs were available for analysis.*

Again, these goals and conclusions are notional, and the point has been to illustrate how the conclusions should be as concise and clear as the goals, and directly associated with each of the goals. For each analysis goal, there is an associated conclusion, so that anyone reading the report, even weeks or months after the fact, can clearly see what was asked, and then see what was found or determined. This means of reporting is clear, concise, and simple.

Body

The body of the report goes well beyond the executive summary, and contains the details of the analysis conducted and the associated findings. Some aspects of the report may require, due to size, that they be incorporated into an appendix or attachment to the report.

Background

At the beginning of the body of the report, I have found it valuable to also include a description of the background of the incident, or the reason for the analysis, similar to what was included in the executive summary. What I tend to do is copy the background from the executive summary, paste it into the body of the report, and then add additional detail for clarity, as necessary. Again, I tend to assume that the executive summary will be removed from the actual report, and this methodology ensures consistency in the overall report.

TIP

Consistency

One of the things I've found in writing numerous reports, under a variety of circumstances, is that when communicating technical information to a nontechnical audience, maintaining consistency in reporting goes a long way toward reducing confusion, and ensuring that the reader walks away with the understanding that you're hoping to communicate. It simply appears to be human nature that when confronted with a good deal of technical information, presented in an inconsistent manner, people tend to walk away with the inconsistencies in the forefront of their minds.

Throughout the entire report, and particularly in the background informa-tion found in the body of the report, I tend to not refer to specific individuals by name, unless specifically asked to do so. I refer to customers by their organiza-tional name, and depending upon the circumstances, I may refer to individuals by title. I have found that this tends to avoid confusion, particularly when engaging with a large organization. If every name of every individual with whom I had com-municated and received information or exhibits were listed, the point of the report would be lost. Further, confusion can result from simple disparities in commu-nications, such as when stating that "...the laptop was shipped by John Doe, the ACME Corporation Director of IT...," and Mr. Doe had, in fact, tasked someone from the shipping department ensure that the item in question was safely packed and shipped. It is much simpler to state, "ACME Corporation provided the identi-fied laptop computer system for analysis...."

In addition to the background information, I will also include a clear description of the provided items or exhibits, taken directly from my case notes. For a relatively small number of exhibits, a short paragraph or bullet list will suffice; for a larger number of exhibits, a table or even an appendix to the report might be more appro-priate. Regardless, keeping a detailed list of exhibits or items provided for analysis lends a modicum of context to the report, by clearly identifying what data sources were available. This way, there's little confusion as to what was available for analy-sis, and ultimately from where the conclusions originated.

Analysis

The analysis section of the report easily contains the most technical detail in the report; after all, this section of the report essentially embodies the customer con-tacted and engaged you in the first place.

I find it beneficial to start the analysis findings section of the report by clearly stating the goals of the analysis. This information is duplicated directly from (or, depending upon the order in which you write the report, to...) the executive sum-mary, in order to maintain consistency in the report. This also makes it much easier to write the report overall, as copy and paste is far simpler than having to think up another way of saying the same thing. Further, this helps keep me focused when it comes to writing the report, in the same manner as including the analysis goals at the beginning of my case notes keeps my analysis focused. By including the goals at the beginning of the analysis section, I not only keep my own analysis focused as I write this section of the report, but it also serves to help focus the attention of the reader, as well.

After adding the goals to the report, I then detail my analysis and findings. Most of this is taken directly from my case notes, albeit in perhaps a more organized and consistent manner. What I mean by this is that regardless of the sequence in which I conducted my analysis process (as detailed in my case notes), I want to ensure that this section flows smoothly to my conclusions. As such, I may need to present some of my findings out of order, with respect to when I actually conducted the analysis. For example, if, as detailed in my cases notes, I began my analysis on day

1 and then opted (or was required) to perform a scan or keyword search, and on the second day of analysis, made another finding, in my report I would not necessarily make the distinction as to when the actual analysis had been conducted. It may be far more beneficial to list the findings in succession, so that they crafted a better understanding and flowed into the conclusion in a manner that makes better sense. The order of how you arrived at your findings is not as important as communicating those findings in a manner that leads logically to your conclusions.

An example of an analysis findings statement from a malware examination might appear as follows:

> *The Example Consulting Team (ECT) mounted the acquired image as a read-only volume (via AccessData's FTK Imager version 3.1.3), and scanned the volume using < name and version of AV product > , which had been updated immediately prior to the conducting the scan. < AV product name> identified several cookies associated with a previously-used user profile on the system, but no malware was identified.*

Had the antivirus product used to scan the mounted volume identified malware within the volume, this fact would be reflected in the statement along with the name of the malware provided by the product. This can be very important, as various vendors often refer to the same malware with different names.

TIP

Identify Product Versions
It is very important in your report that you identify the version of the tool that you use. When using antivirus products, you should be sure to identify the version not only of the product itself, but the scanning engine (if available) and the virus definition file, as well. The reason for this is that tools and products tend to evolve and often take on new capabilities over time. Any version of a particular tool may have new capabilities or functionality three or six months later. If the report is reviewed at a later date and the tool's new capabilities are known, the some data or finding not identified in the analysis within the report may be called into question. Capabilities can be directly tied to the version of a tool or application, and as such, the tool or product version numbers should be included in your case notes, as well as the report.

Another example of an analysis statement included in this section of the report might appear as follows:

> *The Security hive file found in the Windows\system32\config folder within the acquired image was parsed using the auditpol.pl plugin (plugin version 20121128) included in the 18 April 2013 plugin archive, for RegRipper version 2.8. The output of the plugin indicated that auditing was not enabled, and the LastWrite time for the PolAdtEv Registry key indicated that it had last been modified more than three years before the date of the incident. This finding indicates*

that the audit configuration on the date of the incident was not the result of actions taken by the intruder, but instead part of configuration policies associated with provisioning the system for use by the employee. Parsing the Security hive files located in the available System Restore Points via the use of ripxp.exe (uploaded to the RegRipper Google Code site on 29 June 2013) produced consistent findings of the same PolAdtEv key LastWrite time.

Notice that the elements of this analysis statement is consistent with the one listed previously in this chapter; the data being analyzed and the tool used to access or parse the data, as well as the version of the tool, is clearly identified, as are the results, and the analyst's findings based on those results. This information can be taken directly from the analyst's case notes. The analyst might follow the above statement with one regarding analysis of the Event Logs available on the system, which might appear as follows:

The Security, System, and Application Event Logs (secevent.evt, sysevent.evt, and appevent.evt, respectively) were exported from the Windows\system32\config folder within the acquired image, and each file was parsed using evtparse. exe (no version information was provided by the tool). The Security Event Log was found to not include any event records, which is consistent with the previous finding regarding the audit configuration of the system. This was verified manually by opening the Event Log file in a hex editor and after skipping over the 48-byte header of the file, observing that the remainder of the 512 kilobyte file did not contain any valid event records.

Notice the flow of how the analysis is presented in these two statements. It demonstrates a logical flow of analysis from one artifact to another, and assists in building the foundation for your conclusions. Further, these statements provide enough detail that another analyst, perhaps one of your customer's employees, can validate your findings should any questions arise.

I firmly believe that is important to provide not just the portions of your analysis where you actually find something, but you should also include those analysis actions that you take that do not produce any (or, the expected) results. The reason is that this illustrates a thorough approach to your analysis, and tells the reader that, yes, you not only considered a particular avenue of analysis, but you pursued it and the result was that nothing was found. Including this information in your report helps you to answer the overall question, "how did you arrive at your conclusions?"

Conclusions

You should complete the body of your report with a reiteration of the conclusions listed in the executive summary; I tend to do this by duplicating these directly from the executive summary, or vice versa (you may opt to write the body of the report first, and then duplicate the conclusions in the executive summary). Again, each of the listed goals of the analysis should have a corresponding conclusion; if, as one of the goals of your analysis, you were asked to determine if the system had been infected with malware, you should have an associated conclusion that flows directly from your analysis findings that addresses this goal directly.

NOTE

Recommendations

In some cases, you may be asked to include recommendations in your report, particularly if you're an analyst with a consulting company. When I was conducting large-scale vulnerability assessments, providing recommendations as to how a customer might improve their overall security posture was simply part of the job. Often with digital analysis, the scope of the data analyzed may be much smaller and not consist of a representative sample from the infrastructure. For example, you may find during your analysis that the audit capabilities of the system were not enabled, which in turn led to minimal findings in your analysis of the Windows Event Logs. In the case where only one system, or a relatively small number of systems is being examined, I would be extremely hesitant to make any recommendations with respect to the overall infrastructure. I tend not to incorporate a recommendations section in my analysis reports unless asked to address specific questions, and those questions are specific to the system being analyzed.

Writing tips

I have found over time that it can be very useful to keep a few simple tips in mind when writing a report. One of perhaps the most useful aspects of the PCI report format specified by Visa (during the time that I was conducting this type of examination) was consistency. Information and analysis regarding how someone went about stealing credit card numbers can be extremely technical, but the audience to whom the report is intended—the affected merchant, the bank, and the staff at Visa—are more adept in business areas than the world of bits and bytes. As such, maintain a consistent writing style in the report was invaluable in communicating technical finding and conclusions to those readers.

Throughout my (at this writing) over fourteen years working in incident response and digital analysis, one thing that I see again and again is that no matter how efficient and thorough an analyst may be, they are most often hung up on the report writing aspect of the job. This is very often true even when there is a very clear format, or even a detailed template, available. This can be due to the fact that as the analyst is writing the findings section of their report, they are looking for new and different ways to describe or explain their analysis steps, and what they did. Noodling over the prose of a report is not productive. For one, it wastes time. How many different ways are there to say, "…I took this data, ran this tool to parse and display information derived from that data, and based on the output displayed by the tool, here are my findings"? Remaining consistent in writing your findings, as well as how the goals and conclusions are presented in different part of the report, help to clearly communicate your findings, as well as minimize confusion on the part of the reader.

Not long after I got out of the military, I was working for a company where the predominance of my job was to conduct vulnerability assessments. We did a lot of vulnerability assessments, in part, because we were good at them, but our volume of work had in large part to do with the fact that our team salesman could sell ice cubes to someone living in northern Alaska, and leave them feeling like they'd gotten a deal. As we did more and more work, we started to see that we were seeing a lot of the same sorts of vulnerabilities and issues within the various organizations that we visited, and it often turned out that we'd reuse paragraphs from previous reports, often tweaking them slightly to meet the needs of the particular customer or assessment. This was especially true if someone on our team had come up with a truly magical combination of words that ideally suited that particular finding or aspect of the report. Honestly, if the findings were the same or similar enough to require minimal changes, then why rewrite the entire section of the report when copy and paste, perhaps with a little bit of tweaking, will do just fine? We instead opted to save time by not trying to come up with new ways to say the same things.

Okay, so what does this have to do with the PCI reports? The format was specified and provided to us, and applied to all of the forensic assessments that we did; the format was to be used in each and every engagement, which meant that reports between customers would be pretty consistent. That made it easy, as there was little guess work; we knew exactly which tool to use for various sections of the report, the reporting format provided to us specified that certain actions (searches for magnetic stripe or "track" data, keyword, as well as file name and file hash searches, etc.) were to be performed during every engagement. In the section of the report that addressed the analysis work that was actually performed, each subsection was similarly consistent. We would describe the tool and version that we used, what we did, and provide a description of our findings. Over and over. This may sound monotonous, but rather than being boring, it did two things for us. First, it made the report easier and quicker to write, because all you had to do was go to your case notes, and transpose the information over to the report. Include the tool name, version, what was done, what you found—all of this was taken directly from the analyst's case notes, and the Findings section of the report pretty much wrote itself.

Second, being consistent simply made it easier to communicate technical information to less- or nontechnical people—such as our customers. A reader from say, the merchant organization or the bank, is adept at what they do, and we were hired for our expertise at performing these examinations. That isn't to say that our customers weren't smart, but we were dealing with extremely technical information which our customers needed to understand in order to make critical business decisions. What I saw was that if we weren't consistent, then our customers didn't so much have questions regarding the technical information that we included in the report; rather, the questions most often pertained to why things were different. What I saw over time was that when trying to communicate technical and potentially unfamiliar information, it's best to be consistent in your formatting and phrasing; otherwise, the reader picks up on the differences, rather than the technical content, or what you're really trying to communicate to them.

I also found it useful, even valuable, to stick with plain, simple language. Don't try to embellish things, as this can lead to confusion. I'm as guilty as anyone else (perhaps even more so) of at times trying to use flowery language to express myself, in the hopes that it conveys professionalism and credibility. I've found more often than not that this can also lead to confusion, particularly if the person reading the report (in hopes of gleaning the necessary understanding to make a business or legal decision) either doesn't understand the terminology being used, or has a different understanding of it all together. If you parsed data from a Registry hive file using a particular RegRipper plugin, or by opening the hive file in a viewer and simply navigating to the key or value in question, just say that. If you did the same thing for other Registry keys or values, simply say so. This approach to writing your report reduces ambiguity and confusion.

NOTE

Ordering and Consistency

A number of years ago, I was involved in an incident response engagement with another analyst. We arrived on-site mid-evening, and worked nonstop through the night. The following day, after 22 hours of continuous work (also, keep in mind that we'd already been up as part of our normal day prior to getting the initial call for assistance), we were preparing to provide a status report for the organization's leader, the top guy. We knew that we had a great deal of highly technical information, and we were still somewhat in the process of wrapping our heads around what we had. As such, we decided to show some representative data, remove all other data and equipment from view, and we worked out a quick description of what we had and where we were.

Finally, after more than an hour of preparation and waiting, it was time for our briefing. The boss walked into the room, looked at one of the two laptops we had set up, asked, "Why isn't this data in alphabetical order?", and then turned around and left the room. He had uttered the only seven words in the entire briefing—we hadn't had a chance to respond before he left, and he left with the understanding that the data was not in alphabetical order.

While this may be something of an extreme example, it does illustrate how a reader's first impressions of your findings can be the beginning and the end of their understanding.

Peer review

One aspect of reporting of which I have seen very little in the 25 or so years that I have been involved in information security, and the 14+ years that I have been specifically involved in digital forensics and incident response, is peer review of what's being written, in particular case notes and reports. Now, I know that not everyone has the luxury of time for conducting peer review, as time is often not on our side. As a consultant, it's always important to deliver your findings to your customer in a timely manner; however, this does obviate the opportunity for and value of peer review at a later date. Most often, the review and scrutiny to which my case notes and reports have been subject has been conducted by my manager, before the final report was sent to the customer. Having those same items reviewed by my peers, who are doing the same sort of work that I'm doing every day, can lead to all of us learning new things and improving our analysis processes.

Peer review, while a critical component to establish the credibility of an author in other fields (particularly academia), seems to only be conducted within the digital analysis field by those analysts who actively seek self-improvement. Don't get me wrong—I know that reports cannot be shared outside of organizations, and that this is especially true for law enforcement. But what about within an organization? If you're a member of team of analysts, have you asked another analyst to review your case notes, to see if you've missed anything? Have you asked another team member to review a report before you sent it to your manager?

I've been told that within law enforcement, at all levels, reports are reviewed by a supervisor before being accepted as a final report. Often, this review will reveal that additional information or analysis is required, and the report will be updated. At a minimum, the supervisor ensures that that elements of the crime are articulated in the report.

TIP

Report Review Process
It should go without saying that before sending a report draft to anyone (peer, manager, etc.) for review, you should review the report for spelling and grammar errors, ensure that the report table of contents have been updated, etc. A report rife with spelling and grammar errors appears unprofessional, and can be difficult to read. On more than one occasion, I've sent reports back to analysts, asking them to check the spelling and grammar prior to providing the report for review.

SUMMARY

Analysts will very often tell you what that what they enjoy most about their chosen profession is the analysis, and that what they enjoy the least is report writing. I can honestly say that until I "cracked the code" and understood what this one particular manager expected to see in reports that he approved for final delivery to customers, I felt the same way. Like many analysts, at first, I struggled with report writing; however, once I began to see patterns in what this manager was looking for, it got easier. Eventually, I got to the point where I would send a report draft to this manager, and within a couple of hours (or by the following morning) receive approval to "go final" and follow our process for final report delivery. I hope that in this chapter, I've been able to convey the accumulated knowledge of what I learned, not only from working with that manager but also as a result of the breadth of various writing assignments I've had throughout my career, and that this information is helpful to you in some way. After all, the smartest, most capable analyst is ineffective if they are unable to communicate their findings.

Index

Note: Page numbers followed by *"f" and "b"* refer to figures and boxes, respectively.

CPSIA information can be obtained
at www.ICGtesting.com
Printed in the USA
BVOW09s0550240717

489973BV00004B/7/P